The William Van Horne Collection

The William Van Horne Collection

A Dutch Treat

Mary Eggermont-Molenaar

The William Van Horne Collection:
A Dutch Treat

Design & layout: Colin McDonald

Eggermont-Molenaar, Mary, 1945-
The William Van Horne Collection: A Dutch Treat
ISBN: 978-0-9812819-4-0

On the cover:
- Sir William Van Horne adapted from the City of Vancouver Archives
- Author photo by Hannie de Ruiter-Peltzer

To:
Jos Eggermont

ALSO BY
MARY EGGERMONT-MOLENAAR

Montana 1911: A Professor and his Wife among the Blackfeet.
University of Calgary Press, 2005 | University of Nebraska
Press, 2005

Missionaries among Miners, Migrants and Blackfoot: The
Van Tighem Brothers' Diaries, Alberta 1875-1917. University
of Calgary Press, 2007

Gustave Aimard: Feiten, Fictie, Frictie. Calgary: Special
Snowflake, 2009

Hannah, Anna, Michael & Mary: Mennonite, Hutterite &
Sons of Freedom Narratives. Calgary: Memo Books, 2013

Een beschaafde en godsdienstige opleiding: In en om de
MMS te Huize Bijdorp, Voorschoten. Leiden: Ginkgo, 2014

CONTENTS

PREFACE

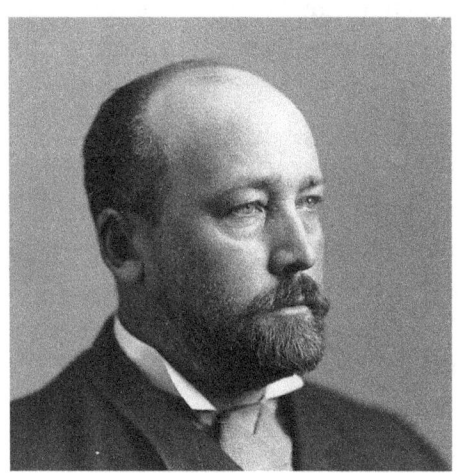

WILLIAM VAN HORNE (1843-1915) was appointed general manager of the Canadian Pacific Railway (CPR) in 1882. Two years later, he became the company's vice president, and in 1885 he saw Canada's countrywide railway completed. He became the CPR's president in 1888 and in 1894 was knighted by Queen Victoria.

Pierre Berton (1971: 47) describes Van Horne shortly after his arrival in Canada from the US in 1881. "Van Horne indulged his varied fancies for the sheer love of it. He was a first-rate gardener (roses were his specialty); he was a caricaturist; he was a conjuror; he was a mind reader; he was a violinist; he was a practical joker; he was a gourmet; he was a marathon poker player." Such character and career commands biographies.

After his death in 1915, Van Horne became the subject of several biographies: Walter Vaughan's *Life and Work of William Van Horne* (1920); Stephen Mayles' *William Van Horne* (1976); Valerie Knowles' *The Life of William C. Van Horne: From Telegrapher to Titan* (2004) and *William Van Horne, Railway Titan* (2010).

These biographies not only elaborate on Van Horne's magnificent railway career but also describe his deep interest in the fine arts. During his lifetime, Van Horne was known as an accomplished painter and as a collector of a wide range of paintings and other works of art. Most of his biographers pay scant attention to his collection, but a hitherto unknown biography by J. L. Pierson (1854-1944), one of the earliest investors in the Canadian railway, included in its second (1929) printing a comprehensive description. The book is titled *Sir William Van Horne en de Canadian Pacific Spoorweg: Met een brief van Mevrouw C. Pierson over haar bezoek aan het huis van Van Horne in Montreal.* (*Sir William Van Horne and the Canadian Pacific Railway: With Mrs. C. Pierson's letter about her visit to the Van Horne mansion in Montreal.*)

I came across this book while researching Dr. C. C. Uhlenbeck (1866-1951), a Dutch linguist who studied the Blackfoot language in 1911 on the Blackfeet Reservation in Montana. After having crossed the Atlantic, the Uhlenbecks had taken a train from New York to Browning, Montana. As the Van Horne bibliography by Pierson was published by Mrs. Uhlenbeck's cousin, I thought that perhaps Pierson might have been in touch with Van Horne on the subject of trains on the American continent. It was a long shot, and I missed. However, the letter of Pierson's daughter led me to writing this book: not about trains, but about Van Horne's fine art collection.

In the preface to his book, Pierson writes, in Dutch:[1] "When in 1882 two Amsterdam bankers increased the stocks of the Canadian Pacific Railway to 60%, the railway was not yet built and the entire Canadian West was essentially not yet developed, so the share certainly was of a speculative nature."[2] After elaborating on the business aspects of the CPR, Pierson continues:

> The pioneers of the Canadian Pacific: William Van Horne, George Stephen, Donald Smith, Angus, Shaughnessy, are no longer among us [...] The following pages are dedicated to, in my opinion, the most brilliant and remarkable among them, William Van Horne.
>
> At the end I have included a letter from my youngest daughter, Mrs. C. Pierson, about her visit to his mansion in Montreal.[3] She used the opportunity of her stay in New York to make a side trip to Montreal, inspired as she was by her reading of my study about Van Horne. Her account, which I have left in letter form, sketches a lively image of the interior of the mansion with its unbelievable art treasures that his wife and daughter left, with utmost devotion, in the same place where they were at the time of his death, eleven years ago. It shows Van Horne and his environment from its most attractive side.

Van Horne's name, suggesting that he was a descendant of someone from Hoorn, interested me. He was indeed from

---

1   Translations in this book are mine, unless otherwise indicated.
2   [Footnote in Pierson 1929: v] "My company then: Adolph Boissevain & Co and H. Oyens & Zonen." In 1917, the Boissevan/Oyens company name was changed to Pierson & Mees.
3   At the time Caroline wrote her letter she was not yet married again, so her father refers to her as "Mevrouw," which translates into "Mrs."

Hoorn, a small city north of Amsterdam where I attended elementary school. One of his ancestors arrived in New Amsterdam in 1635 and helped establish the Dutch colonial settlement on Manhattan Island.

Reading Caroline Pierson's 1926 letter made me feel as if I was walking through the Van Horne mansion, seeing the collection for myself, eighty years after she did. Wondering what had happened to this collection, I saw that it had been scattered from the 1940s on and that its home, the Van Horne mansion in Montreal, had been demolished in 1973.

But, before all that happened, in April 1933 a fire had raged through the mansion. According to newspaper reports, many of the paintings were damaged or destroyed. But, the newspapers had exaggerated. The paintings had survived the fire. After cleaning they were exhibited among the 194-piece selection of the Van Horne collection in October 1933.

Penciled scribbles though, such as "Can be a Rdt.," "not a Maes" on the 1933 exhibition catalogue – by Frits Lugt (1884-1974), a Dutch connoisseur – question the authenticity of some of the paintings. It made me look into the coming-about of the Van Horne collection, which in turn revealed the identity of Van Horne's Dutch bona and not so bona fide dealers – hence the subtitle of this book, *A Dutch Treat*.

Van Horne's dealers had also become his friends and investors in his side businesses. Records of their dealings with other collectors showed that this had lead to 'affairs' and 'matters' and had changed the way art dealing was conducted on the American continent.

The last chapter deals with the impact of the Great War on Van Horne's collection, on the art business and the description of the Van Horne household during the last days of his life, as witnessed by Willem Witsen, a Dutch painter.

Appendix 1 gives a room-to-room list of paintings in the Van Horne collection in his mansion in Montreal and at his Covenhoven Estate in St. Andrews, New Brunswick. Appendix 2 provides a view of the disposition of Van Horne's collection.

�

THE VAN HORNE FAMILY

**Sir William Cornelius
Van Horne**
Montreal, QC, 1886
Photograph – Wm. Notman
& Son
© McCord Museum
II-81628.1

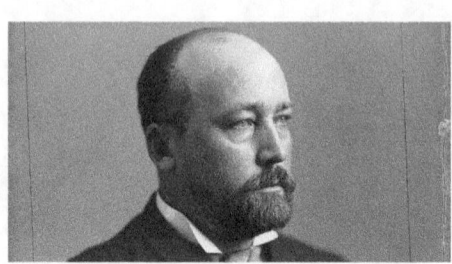

Mrs. Lucy Adaline Van Horne
(nee. Hurd)
Painting (detail)
Lady Van Horne, reading
Richard Matthews
© McCord Museum
M991.14.78

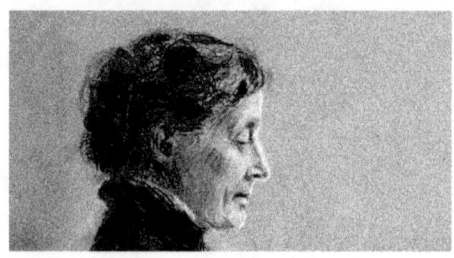

Adaline Van Horne
LAC e007914036

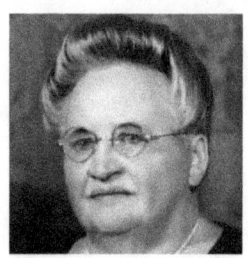

Richard Benedict Van Horne
(Bennie)
LAC e007914029

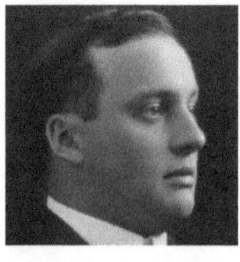

William Cornelius
Covenhoven Van Horne
(Billy)
Montreal QC, 1910
Photograph – Wm. Notman
& Son
© McCord Museum
II-180314
❯

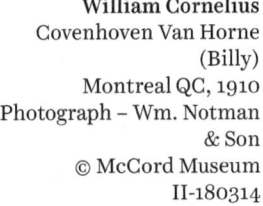
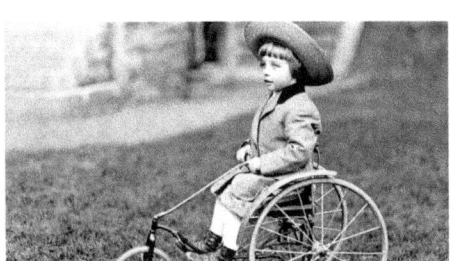

The Van Horne Mansion
rue Sherbrooke, Montreal,
1900,
Photograph – Wallis &
Shepherd
© Musée McCord
MP-0000.27.38
❯

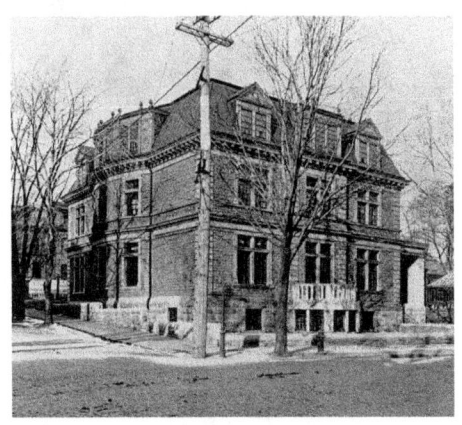

Covenhoven
St. Andrews-by-the-Sea, NB
[copied] 1926-27
Photograph – Anonymous
© McCord Museum
VIEW-23944.0
❯

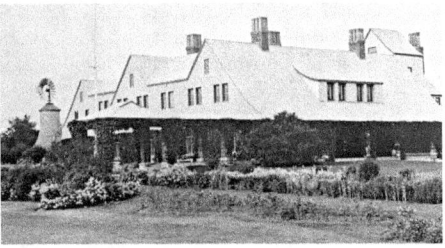

PEOPLE & PAINTINGS

Caroline Jaffé-Pierson
Courtesy Wilco Jiskoot
Grijpma 1999: 121
➜

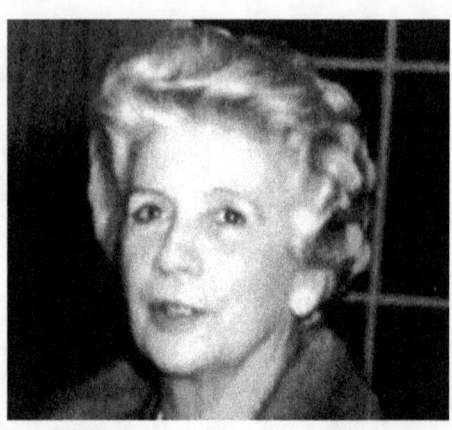

Sorensen, Lee. "Frits Lugt."
dictionaryofarthistorians.org/
wittkowerr.htm
➜

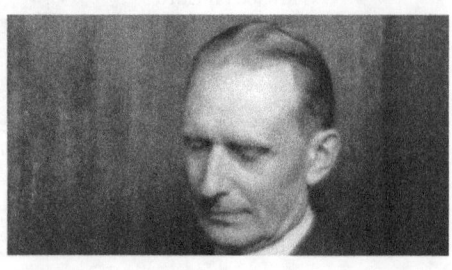

Old Man with Black Cap
Not by Rembrandt.
Courtesy Rembrandt Research
Project.
(detail)
➜

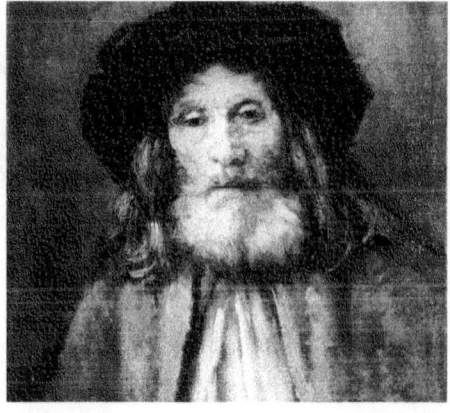

Head of Old Man
Not by Rembrandt.
Courtesy Rembrandt Research
Project.
(detail)
➔

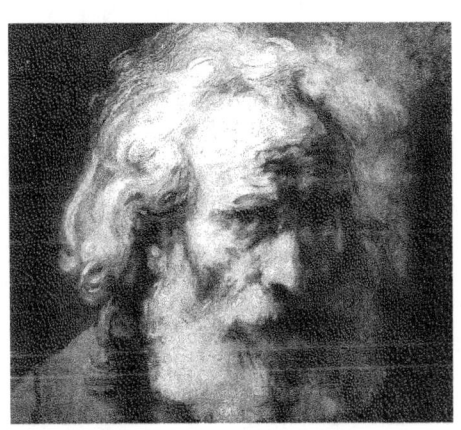

Young Rabbi
Rembrandt, 1668.
Courtesy Rembrandt Research
Project.
(detail)
➔

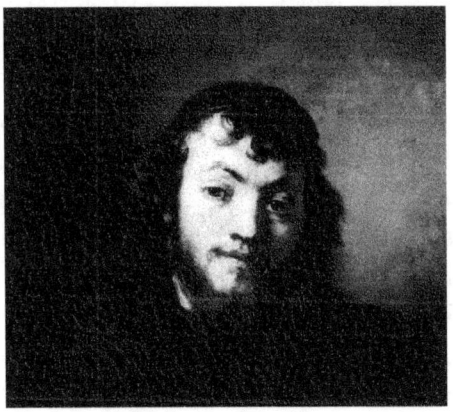

Landscape with Cottages
Rembrandt, 1654.
Courtesy Montreal Museum of
Fine Arts.
(detail)
➔

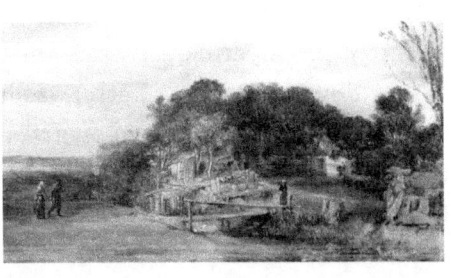

CHAPTER 1

THE WILLIAM VAN HORNE COLLECTION

Caroline Jaffé-Pierson

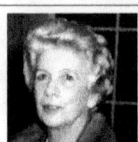

IN 1926 CAROLINE Elisabeth Pierson (1898-1994) visited the Van Horne mansion in Montreal. That was eleven years after Van Horne's death. In a letter to her father, she described the Van Horne collection room by room. Pierson's letter is probably the only description of the intact Van Horne collection.

Caroline was a granddaughter of Allard Pierson (1831-1896), the first professor of classical archaeology at the University of Amsterdam. Her father, J. L. Pierson (1854-1944), kept himself occupied with translating studies and publishing several books, the Van Horne biography among them, after distancing himself somewhat from his banking firm Pierson & Co. in 1921. In 1932, he established the Allard Pierson Association, which lives on as the Allard Pierson Museum at the Turfmarkt in Amsterdam.

Caroline was married to Willam Herman van Rees from 1917 to 1923. After her divorce, she went on to marry Dr. Paul Jaffé (1889-1978) in 1935, who was first part of Pierson & Co. but later on mostly focused on arts and spirituality. After her marriage with Jaffé, Carrie, as Caroline was called by her family, no longer bought her clothes at the Paris couturiers Lanvin, Rouff or Dessés, but had them made at Heymans and Dolder. These Dutch couturiers allowed her husband to have their designs for his wife's dresses altered; he even drew patterns for her himself (Grijpma 1999: 119). Pauline Kruseman, a former director of the Amsterdam Museum, described Caroline's home after her second marriage: "[The Jaffé-Pierson family] lived in a splendid house in Naarden/Bussum, which I once visited with my father. They were of his age." [4] The couple had no children and left most of their estate to the Jaffé-Pierson Foundation, which sponsored the purchase of expensive works of art. In October 1994, Mrs. Caroline Jaffé-Pierson died in Huizen, North Holland at her estate "The Island" at the age of ninety-six years.[5] The foundation expired in 2013.

Caroline mentions three people in her letter: Van Horn's daughter Adaline Van Horne; his daughter-in-law Edith Bagley Van Horne-Molson; and grandson Billy, who was also known as William Jr. or William Cornelius Covenhoven Van Horne.

Adaline (1868-1941), Van Horne's only daughter, never married and was "the trusted one," caring for her father's estate as he would have trusted her to do. Her life with her partying brother Benny and nephew Billy must not have been an easy one.

Edith (1877-1960) was the daughter of William Alexander Molson (1852-1920) and Esther Shepherd (1854-1912). She married Van Horne's only son, Benedict Richard (1873-1931) and was the mother of Van Horne's only grandson, Billy.

Billy (1907-46) was passionate about cars. He established the Auburn Motor Sales Company and served for some time as its president. In 1934, he lost his first wife, Audrey Van Horne-Fraser, in a car accident, leaving him with their daughter, Beverley Ann. Billy's second wife was Mrs. Margaret Van

---

4   E-mail of March 17, 2009.
5   E-mail of March 19, 2009.

Horne-Hannon (†1987). Like his father, Billy died young from liver disease.

1926: CAROLINE PIERSON'S LETTER[6]

On December 15, 1926, I left New York for Montreal via Albany, where, invited by Miss Van Horne, I would spend a few days in the famous mansion of her brilliant father.

In Albany I spent the night with our friends Mr. and Mrs. William Gorham Rice. He played a political role, is currently only interested in old and new Carillon music in Belgium and Holland and attends regularly the carilloneurs' meetings.

Mrs. Rice established an information bureau in Geneva in order to inform the Americans who want to attend the League of Nations' meetings.

That evening we had a grand dinner in honour of Sir Herbert Ames, treasurer-general of Canada. In the evening he gave a lecture about his experiences in Geneva, where he had represented Canada the first seven years.[7]

The reporters and photographers were of course very keen and also interviewed me, the result being that I was sent a rather stupid article *"head line . . . . Long tresses at court of Queen Wilhelmina."*

Really fun for the Albanese to know about just that!

The eight-hour trip from Albany to Montreal through lonely endless snow plains is monotonous but magnificent

---

6   Mary E. M. translated this letter from Dutch to English. (Italics denote Caroline's use of English.)

7   From 1919 to 1926 Sir Herbert Ames (1863-1954) was financial director for the secretariat for the League of Nations (Regehr 1988: 70).

the St. Lawrence River was full of ice floes and there was no boat to be seen. At the few small places where we stopped, it was a sensation to see that the only human beings I saw after many hours [of traveling] were on fantastically lit rinks, very busy moving their legs on a surface of about 20 m^2.

The train had barely halted in Montreal or officials of the Canadian Pacific Company jumped into the cars, calling *"Mrs. Pierson."* When they had finally found me, one said, quite reproachful, *"Lady Van Horne is waiting for you, you are an hour late and on the wrong track,"* as if *I* had made the train run late!

At the end of the long quay stood *Miss Van Horne*, as heavily built as her father with his characteristic slightly arched nose and full lips. Of course I said that I regretted to had made her wait, to which she answered: *"oh that is nothing at all. I had a grand time watching the people in the waiting room." We proceeded after that royally out of the station*, passing *red caps*[8], who were in a row, bowing, while higher officials, giant gents with fur hats, stood at attention and saluted.

So we arrived at a big, black Rolls-Royce with driver and groom dressed completely in black astrakhan. We drove through the streets of the half-French Montreal, which were thickly covered with snow, and stopped 10 minutes later in front of the grandiose mansion.

Here I soon stood in an enormous corridor; welcomed as it were by a big painting of Zurbaran, Elizabeth of Hungary[9] with roses on her lap. It was already late, so after having something to eat we went to bed.

---

8   [Footnote in Pierson 1929: 126]: "Canadian negro-porters."
9   Exhibition: *A Selection from the Collection of Paintings of the Late Sir William van Horne, K.C.M.G. 1843-1915* (hereafter indicated as Cat. 1933), the catalogue for the exhibition held from October 16 to November 5, 1933, in the Galleries of

The next morning breakfast was supposed to be at nine-thirty; the maid let me into a room, where I waited until ten for my hostess to arrive. She could surely have had me wait a bit longer, because there was a beautiful collection of paintings from the Barbison school; a small Corot, two Daubigny's, a Rousseau, a threatening Courbet, a portrait of George Sand by Troyon, and further, a Monet, Delacroix, Géricault, Ribot, Daumier, Diaz, Salvator Rose, and Cézanne.[10]

At a more advanced age, Van Horne became a great admirer of the modern French school and wanted his housemates to share in it; actually they did not share his admiration but did not dare to admit it!

I was finally invited to the breakfast table and started a scary meal served by two servants, scary because of the quantity. Fruit, *porridge*, fried fish, bacon and eggs, *sausages, hot buns, toast* and jam, coffee and cream.

---

the Art Association of Montreal, lists this painting under no. 23: *St. Elizabeth of Hungary*: Francisco de Zurbaran 1598-1662.

Each title in Cat. 1933 is preceded by its number. Notes in Cat. 1933 that accompanied the name of a painting were, and are here, italicized.

Inserted notes by Frits Lugt are translated from Dutch to English and are hereafter preceded by Note by Frits Lugt (NFL).

10 A number of the painters mentioned in Caroline's list appeared in Cat. 1933 as follows:

• J. B. C. Corot (1796-1876) 125 Les Gaulois; 126 Landscape – Sand Dunes; 127 Peasant Girl by a Wall; 128 Mother and Child.
• Charles Daubigny (1817-1878) 131 Sketch in Brittany; 132 Building the Stack; 132a Landscape.
• Gustave Courbet (1819-1877) 137 Still-life.
• Constant Troyon (1810-1865) 136a La Guitariste, A portrait of George Sand.
• Claude Monet (1840-1926) 151 Bougival; 152 Normandy Coast.
• Eugene Delacroix (1799-1865) 113 Lion and Lioness; 114 Christ on the Lake of Gennesaret – one of seven renderings of this subject painted in 1853. Another is in the Metropolitan Museum – Havemeyer bequest.
• Theodore Gericault (1791-1824) 123a Horses in their Stable.
• Théodule Ribot (1823-1891) 159 Two Girls reading; 160 The Artist's Daughters; 161 Balzac in his Study.
• Honoré Daumier (1808-1879) 139 Nymphs pursued by Satyrs. Exhibited at the Paris Salon, 1850.

When we had finally finished, Mrs. Van Horne showed me around the house a bit. We started in the small dining room adjacent to the big one where we had breakfast. Only paintings done by Sir William himself were hung here, the two from your book and another twelve with river views, snowy landscapes and splendid trees with fall colours at his retreat Covenhoven.[11] He tried using different techniques such as pointilled or painted with broad strokes using lots of paint, or painting mostly with only a tiny bit of paint, smooth and therefore quite flat, but everything was done quite cleverly and really with love.

Then we went back to the dining room, where I could quietly admire the splendidly represented English school.

There were a big Raeburn, Reynolds and Romney, all portraits of *society ladies*, as well as a Lawrence, Turner, three Constables, one of the few English landscape painters, Crome, a beautiful warm piece, and an old mill, with Rembrandt-like colours.[12]

At the end of the room, facing the light, was a five-piece screen with female dancers by Thys Maris.[13]

---

11   In 1891, Van Horne bought part of Minister's Island in New Brunswick, on which he had built a residence that he called Covenhoven after his father Cornelius Covenhoven Van Horne (Sullivan 2007: 18). After 1892, he had it extended with a barn and a carriage house.

12   The artists in this list appeared in Cat. 1933 as follows:
- Sir Henry Raeburn (1756-1823) 96 Mrs. Glengowen and Daughter.
- Sir Joshua Reynolds (1723-1792) 89 Countess of Carnarvon; 90 Lady Talbot. From the collection of Stanford White.
- George Romney (1734-1802) 104 Miss Morland. 105 Jane, Duchess of Gordon and her Son.
- Sir Thomas Lawrence (1769-1830) 106 Georgiana, Lady Dover.
- Joseph M. W. Turner (1775-1851) 93 Shakespeare's Cliff, Dover.
- John Constable (1776-1837) 97 The Vale of Dedham; 98 The Villa; 99 Hampstead Heath; 100 The Glebe Farm; 102 On the Stour; 103 Landscape with Cottages.
- John Crome, Old Crome, (1768-1821) 95 The Lock-gate.

13   In The New York Times Magazine (September 23, 1917), this four- (not five-) panelled screen was titled A Service to Isis. It is now part of the Rijksmuseum collection under the name Dancing Figures (BK-2000-9) (Heijbroek 2008: 105).

"Pappa," as his daughter always refers to him with special warmth in her voice, *"was a personal friend of Maris on whom he always called when in London."*

Beside the dining room was the pool room/library where, through small painted windows, a nice northern light shone on the many, many pieces of art by our old masters. What treasures! There was a big portrait of Tromp by Van der Helst, a Bol, four Cuyps, one of which was a small jewel of a painting showing a river view, a Van Goyen, two Jacobs and a Salomon Ruysdael, a Terborgh, a Van Ostade, a De Witte, two Bosbooms, two Jaap Maris, a praying woman by Maes, and surely i have forgotten a few.[14]

In this room was also a big Japanese horse from the 13th century, *plus rare que beau!*

Under the paintings were 30 cupboards containing three shelves, each for about twelve books, all about art history.

Then we went back to the hallway, splendidly wide with big windows at both ends. Only Spanish masters hung in the hallway, which gave the entire house an extraordinary stateliness and great cachet.

---

14   The artists listed here appeared in Cat. 1933 as follows:
- Bartholomeus van der Helst (1613-1670) 34 Admiraal Cornelius Tromp. NFL: "no, not Tromp, but excellent, here en fond, painted in yellow jerkin."
- Ferdinand Bol (1616-1680) 48 Young Man holding a Medallion. NFL: "(front), false signature Rembrandt."
- Aelbert Cuyp (1620-1691) 36 Woman with Ruff; 37 River with Cattle. NFL: no. 36 "?"; no. 37: "insignificant, and there is also a Cabreal-like piece: 2 horses."
- Jan van Goyen (1596-1656) 43 Wintersports. NFL: "good, there is also a small oval one, not important and poor."
- Salomon van Ruysdael (1600-1670) 47 The Marien Kirche at Utrecht. NFL: 47 "very free. Building looks a bit like it, but borders to water! Curious, but not beautiful. There is also a small marine."
- Emanuel de Witte (1617-1692) 29 Interior of a Church. NFL: "under pulpit with green curtain."
- Johannes Bosboom (1817-1891) 58 Chamber of the Council.
- Nicholas Maes (1632-1693) 54 Old Woman with Bible. NFL: "no, not Maes."

Apart from Rembrandt and Hals, how fine and precious our Holland school is, but it still comes across as lesser art when right after having viewed them, one comes across Velasquez, Greco and Goya.

There is a big portrait of Philip IV and another Velasquez, five Goya's, among which was a bust of a lady with a black lace veil, mentioned by Veth and Bode as being the most beautiful that Goya had ever painted.[15]

Then there were several El-Greco's.[16] Miss Van Horne told me that her father became furious when someone insisted that El Greco suffered from eye problems. He was certain that the long drawn out figures simply conveyed his chosen view, merely a stylization of the saints, which he did not consider to be ordinary humans. I loved it! It also bothered me greatly, since I sense that the insistence on the eye problems tends to diminish that great unique artist.

---

15   These artists appear in Cat. 1933 as follows:
- Don Diego de Silva Y Velasques (1599-1660) 14 Portrait of Young Nobleman Described by Dr. August Mayer. Formerly attributed to Murillo; 15 Philip IV of Spain (full length), 16 Christ on the Cross, 17 Philip IV (small). NFL: 15, 16, 17 "not very convincing."
- Francisco José de Goya y Lucientes (1746-1828) 1 Peasants fighting Soldiers; 2 The Horrors of War; 3 The Actress Rita Molinos; 4 The Marques de Castrofuerte; 5 The Marquesa de Castrofuerte; 6 A Corner in Madrid; 7 A Slave Market; 8 The Sculptor Cameron.

16   Cat. 1933: Dominico Theotocopuli, called El Greco, about 1547-1614; 11 Portrait of La Casa. Mentioned in "El Greco" by M. Soccio, "Die Kunst des Greco" by Hugo Kehrer and "Dominico Theotocopuli" by Mayer; 12 The Holy Family with a Dish of Fruit. NFL: "as in Cleveland , but less;"13 Head of St. Maurice. Mentioned in "El Greco" by M. Soccio, "Die Kunst des Greco" by Hugo Kehrer and "Dominico Theotocopuli" by Mayer. NFL: "small, beautiful head; clear."

There were also two Murillo's,[17] among which the Cavalier from your book, two big Ribera's,[18] one of which I remember was a beautiful monk, and then a Zurbaran at the entrance, depicting Elizabeth of Hungary. There was also a Julian del Merzo, showing a young woman with children, who was said to be Velasquez' daughter-in-law.

Meanwhile two bronze statues were pointed out to me as well as Chinese plates, gifts from the Emperor of Japan,[19] altar tables, costly Persian rugs and many old ships.

The room I was shown later was a small office with a big table in the middle with many, many books scattered on it. There were also some unbelievable treasures there; a drawing by Da Vinci, a Titian, (a small landscape with a single figure in it), a Tintoretto, Bellini, Moroni, Holbein, and a miniature of Washington painted by Goya during the latter's visit to Spain.[20] Van Horne had been offered great sums for this gem, but he did not want to part with it.

---

17   Cat. 1933: Bartolome-Esteban Murillo (1617-1682) 21 A Spanish Gentleman. NFL: "in oval, good."

       Pierson (1929: 81) refers to this painting as "Portrait of a Nobleman around 1670 by Murillo." He also describes Van Horne's acquisition of the painting: "In April 1909 Van Horne undertook a journey to Europe with his wife and daughter. He used this opportunity to enrich his collection of paintings with two master works of art, a rabby by Rembrandt from the R. Kann collection and the famous Cavalier by Murillo."

18   Cat. 1933: Jusepe Riberta (1589-1652) 19 Diogenes.

19   [Original footnote Pierson 1929: 129]: "As proof of his appreciation for opening a line to Japan and giving Japanese names to several of the ships from this line."

20   Some of the artists listed here appeared in Cat. 1933 as follows:

    • Leonardo da Vinci (1452-1519) 82 Study of a Woman's Head (Florentine School).

    • Jacopo Robusti, called Tintoretto (1518-1594) (Venetian School). 84 A Venetian Councillor.

    • Giambattista Moroni (1520-1578) (School of Brescia) 78 Portrait of a Young Italian Nobleman. From the collection of Count de Montbrison. Mentioned by Dr. Bode.

    • Hans Holbein the Younger (1497-1543) 72 Portrait of Philip Melanchthon. From the collection of Horace Walpole. NFL: "?."

Then I could no longer handle more and took a rest, *although you need not pretend to be interested because you are very much interested, but of everything one can get too much!*

After lunch we drove outside of Montreal along the St. Lawrence River to the *Forest and Stream Club*, it was splendid in the freezing weather and much snow, although very cold. I really loved this trip.

The next morning I was shown the other rooms and I could barely believe my eyes when we entered the so-called red saloon: four, I repeat, four Rembrandts, four Frans Hals's, one Bol and one Fabricius.[21] It was a perfectly square room with a high ceiling, wallpapered in red velour, and there was no furniture other than a few chairs near the tall, narrow window. To be allowed to quietly look, with the light from behind, at these revelations from this good judge of human nature, the greatest among the most great, was intensely enjoyable. Because these portraits are revelations, they (a small portrait of an old man, a soldier, and a portrait of a young man) and one landscape – a dark foreground, one single tree, very sober, very simple and then a lightning-filled sky which confesses of a deep faith in things Better, in Godliness, a hallowed room.

---

21   In Cat. 1933 as follows:
• Rembrandt van Ryn (1606-1669) 39 The Landscape; 40 Head of an Old Man; 41 Portrait of a Young Rabbi; 42 The Prophet or Old Man with Slashed Black Cap. NFL: 39 "can be Rdt [Rembrandt];" 40 "as Erickson, NY, but smaller, looks quite good;" 41 "very good;" 42 "not finished."
• Frans Hals (1584-1666) 30 Portrait of a Dutch Gentleman. Mentioned by Sir Martin Conway in "The Connoisseur" July, 1905. Also mentioned by Bode, [Hofstede] de Groot and Mayer; 31 Portrait of a Dutch Lady. Mentioned by Bode, [Hofstede] de Groot and Valentiner; 33, Samuel Ampsing. Mentioned by Bode, de Groot and Valentiner. NFL: 30 and 31: "good pair, quite sober;" 33 'small, lively and good."
• Karel Fabritius (1620-1654) 35 Young Man in a Fur Cap. NFL: "rather Bernard."

On the opposite wall was a laughing guy by Frans Hals,[22] a world of its own, done so lucidly and flowing, worthy to hang opposite the great master. Also a fine self-portrait of Bol, and an old man by Fabricius went well there.

It was difficult to become interested in anything else after this, but Miss Van Horne first wanted to show me the big reception room, which was also full of treasures. Little by little nothing astonished me anymore, but then I was no less impressed by the all-encompassing Van Horne collection. In general it takes generations to assemble such a collection, but Van Horne managed it as a hobby in about 30 years, in addition to his enormous job!

In this reception room, the least suitable room, all kinds of stuff was hung up. I counted 12 Monticelli's, of which he was fond; he purchased them, traded them, and sold them in order to keep the most beautiful.

From all corners and ends of the world, traders and art connoisseurs kept him posted of what was offered on the world market because he wanted this information before they were sent to the auctions. Once he was offered a fine Greuze, but right then he also thought that moment that he could not *"leisten"* (afford) the Greuze.[23] So he found a way around it; Lady Van Horne would soon celebrate her birthday and, though she would have liked something else and thought that there were enough paintings in her house, the Greuze was offered to her, *"of course Mamma said that she was delighted because Pappa loved the picture so and was as happy as a schoolboy to possess it."* From this telling tale and many others the daughter told me, I understood why this great man could keep up such invin-

---

22   Cat. 1933: Frans Hals. The Jolly Trooper. *Mentioned by Bode and Valentiner.* NFL: "red cap. Good."

23   Cat. 1933: Jean Baptiste Greuze (1725-1805) 115 Portrait of Madame Mercier.

cible good spirits and achieve so much. There was peace in his house, peace achieved through great love and respect. Later on I looked with affection at an intimate painting, a youthful portrait of his wife, a beautiful, fine and intelligent face. She was one of the first women in the United States who had been educated.

At the end of that room was another big Rubens, most interesting. The feast of Herodes and Salome, with Rubens himself as Herodes and Hélène Fourment, his second wife, as Herodias.[24]

A Bosboom painting, one of a farm girl by Thijs Maris, and a small boy by Reynolds looked odd beside it.[25]

It was nearly three o'clock and I had to wrap up as warm as possible for a sleigh ride.

Full [of] expectation I went to the front door and certainly was not disappointed. There stood a splendid sleigh with the inside completely covered in *skunks'* pelts, a typical tall English coachman on the box and the same kind of groom at the door and two high-spirited horses that could hardly stand still. We sleighed to the *Mont Reale*, saw skis and sledges, and there was a beautiful view overlooking Montreal, both rivers and one of the great Canadian Pacific bridges about which Miss Van Horne told me a funny story.

---

24   One must have been Cat. 1933: Peter Paul Rubens (1577-1640) 66 Adoration of the Shepherds. NFL: "sketch, good contemporary." The other one Cat. 1933: Peter Paul Rubens, 67 The Feast of Herod. Mentioned in Max Rooses' "L'Oeuvre de Rubens." *It has been suggested that the characters in Rubens' painting are portraits of the following personages, the artist's contemporaries, to whom they bear a striking resemblance: Vasari, Palma the Elder, Raphael, Tintoretto, Paul Veronese, Titian, the mother of Rubens, Rubens's son Nicholas, Isabella Brant, Helen Fourment and Rubens.* NFL: "unimpressive schoolwork."

25   Cat. 1933: Sir Joshua Reynolds (1723-1792) 89 Countess of Carnarvon; 90 Lady Talbot. *From the collection of Stanford White;* 91 Cherubs. *After Rubens;* 92 On reverse, Boar Hunt. *After Snyders;* Master Gawler.

The land at one end of the bridge had belonged to a monastery, but the monks had refused to part with it as the peace and quiet of the place was not to be desecrated by the noise of a train.

Sir William had no great faith in these monks and their anxiety about disturbing the peace, and one evening he went there for a visit.

As he approached the gate he heard lots of lively noises and upon coming nearer he could distinguish the noises to be all kinds of non-religious songs with music, laughter and much talking. He waited one minute with his hand on the doorbell and then suddenly rang very loudly. Everything became silent, the door was prudently opened and a moment later he stood among the frightened monks. Not much was said, but when Van Horne left the monastery, he had the contract for the sale of the land in his pocket!

In the evening Mrs. Van Horne showed me Sir William's office. I entered with devotion and respect into a high, big space with an entire collection of Japanese porcelain. The shelves were full of books and there was a big *bureau-ministre* in the middle with a well-worn chair in front of it and a number of ashtrays: *"they were always put round him, hoping that one day he would drop some of the ash of his eternal cigars not on the floor"!* It seemed as if he had just left his office, even though he died 11 years ago.

It was shown to me by Sir William's daughter-in-law. Her son, Van Horne's only grandson, his darling and pride, is now 19 years old. He lives in the house, but I only saw him momentarily when he ran through a hallway with a pair of skates, much barking of a dog, a boom from the pontifical front door being slammed and [I thought]: *"youth had passed through this now very quiet and dignified house."* Once in a while I saw a big pair of muddy boots, a jacket and leather gloves lying around, and suddenly I got the feeling that they were part of the house as well. When Billy's grandfather came home from his long tiring inspection trips and *"tramps,"* there must have been much ado with boots and big overcoats, walking up and down, slamming of doors, cigar smoke, life and bustle in the big house then, also.

Many more paintings hung in the hallway upstairs. I remember 3 Cézannes, female figures, Pissaro, fine Sisley's, strange Manets, stark, circumscribed figures without shading, beautiful Monets, Lenoir, Morland, and suddenly I discovered a Neuhuys, a Kamerlingh Onnes and a Blommers![26]

The next day there was a big lunch with prominent Montreal people. I was introduced to everyone *"as the daughter of one of the few, who in the dark, dark days of the CPR believed in it and worked for it. These foreign friends were always highly appreciated and warmly spoken of by my father. Now the CPR has millions of friends, but then every single-one was worth a million to it!"*

After they had all left, I visited the office again with Mrs. Van Horne. There were cupboards and cupboards filled with Japanese earthenware and porcelain, the shelves were full, the walls were covered with it, and much more was still on the floor. Van Horne made a small sketch of each piece as soon as it came into the house so that later, when he had more time, he could make an aquarelle of the actual size. There were folders full of them, which on their own were very worthwhile. The daily sketchbook looks well taken care of, and behind each artifact was the

---

26 Some of the artists listed here appear in Cat. 1933 as follows:
- Paul Cézanne (1839-1906) 146a Portrait of the Artist's Wife. The other Cézanne at the exhibition was: 147 Roadway in the Province.
- Camille Pissaro (1830-1903) 153 Old Chelsea Bridge, London.
- Alfred Sisley (1839-1899) 150 On the Oise.
- Claude Monet (1840-1926) 151 Bougival; 152 Normandy Coast.
- George Morland (1763-1804) 110 The Fisherman's Dog.

description, name, period and year and, if possible, the maker and ... the price. Mrs. Van Horne pointed out that it was only the quasi price, a joke to fool curious people, with the actual wording ... $ ... ½! Exactly like this!

Kipling often stayed with them. Van Horne sketched him while he [Kipling] was writing the story of locomotive No. 007 in *"The Day's Work."*[27] Later Van Horne, inspired by the story, made a painting of a locomotive appearing out of the night with the one bright light, and he called it No. 007, a fascinating piece.

On December 22 I packed my suitcases again and was walked out by many bowing staff and the eternally barking dog.

To my astonishment I found this time the boy William at the steering wheel of the big black car. Mrs. Van Horne brought me to the station, from where I returned to New York feeling most satisfied.

---

27 Could Van Horne have sketched Kipling while the latter was writing the short story "Locomotive No. 007," which appeared in *The Day's Work*, first published in 1898?

Kipling (1937: 213) wrote about his encounters with Van Horne: "At Quebec [1907] we met Sir William van Horne, head of the whole CPR system, but, on our wedding trip fifteen years before [1892], a mere Divisional Superintendent who had lost a trunk of my wife's and had stood his Division on its head to find it. His [Van Horne's] deferred, but ample revenge was to give us one whole Pullman car with coloured porter complete, to take and use and hitch on to and declutch from any train we chose." In 1907 Kipling was again in Canada, this time to "give rousing speeches on imperial unity to Canadian Clubs. Repeating a gesture that he had made fifteen years earlier, Van Horne arranged for the couple to have the use of a special green velvet and mahogany 'private car'" (Knowles 2004: 315).

Cat. 1933 lists R. G. Mathews 169a Rudyard Kipling writing in Sir William Van Horne's Library.

1933: APRIL, THE VAN HORNE MANSION ON FIRE

During the search for the whereabouts of the Van Horne collection, I discovered not only that it had been dispersed during
the 1940s, but also that the collection had almost been lost in a
bad fire in 1933, seven years after Caroline Pierson's visit. The
Montreal newspaper *La Patrie* printed a screaming headline
about the fire on page three: Des Rubens, Rembrandt, Velasquez,
etc. sont détruits par les flames. [Rubens, Rembrandt, Velasquez,
etc., destroyed by flames.] The elaborate subtitle, translated
from French, reads: "One of the most beautiful private collections in the universe, estimated at more than $2 000 000,
is threatened with complete destruction. Two firefighters are
injured. Nine water hoses operated for four hours."

La Patrie printed the names of all the paintings. Hereunder
are listed only those pieces mentioned in Caroline's letter.

- Ferdinand Victor Eugène Delacroix: *Le Christ sur le lac de
  Génézareth (1854)*
- Diego Velasquez: *Philippe IV*
- Frans Hals: *L'homme en noir [Portrait of Young Man in
  Black Coat]*
- John Constable: *Bergholt*
- Rembrandt van Rijn: *Paysage, Un rabbin, Un jeune homme,
  signé et date de Rembrandt, mais attributed à Ferdinand
  Bol. On dit que Rembrandt signait lui-meme les oeuvres de
  ses protégés qu'il jugeait les plus remarquables.*
- Monticelli: *La conversion de Saul*
- Peter Paul Rubens: *Salomé et Hérode*
- Goyer: *La Miniature de Washington*
- Hans Holbein: *Portrait de Philip Melanchton*
- El Greco: *La Sainte Famille*

As well as the masterpieces, some pictures Van Horne had
painted were also listed as being *"détruits par les flames."*

The same newspaper article elaborates on the start of the fire. That evening there had been *"une fête intime,"* also attended by Mrs. Adaline Van Horne and two friends of the family, M. Bradley and Dr. George W. Sugden, D.D.S. Although the police officers still did not know the cause of the fire, they believed it started in Billy's [young William's] bedroom on the fourth floor. One officer, however, believed that it had started in a lounge on that same floor. Regardless of where it began, according to the *La Patrie* article, 40 percent of the main, authentic paintings were completely destroyed or beyond repair.

On April 4, 1933, the *Globe and Mail* reported that:

> The world of art will learn with dismay of the near-destruction by fire of many magnificent paintings in the home of the late Sir William Van Horne, in Montreal, and will be thankful the loss was not heavier. The former CPR president had in his palatial residence an art collection valued at $2 000 000, and it is estimated that the damage will amount to about $1 000 000.

In several regards, the fire proved to be less dramatic than the newspaper articles had suggested. First, some of the scenes painted by the Old Masters, mentioned in the newspaper article, were painted more than once. El Greco painted *Holy Family* five times, twice with Joseph holding up a bowl of fruit. Delacroix painted *Le Christ sur le lac de Génézareth* (1854) seven times: in some versions, the boat had a mast and in others it did not, and in some versions the background differed.[28] Even though some paintings had one or more twin

---

28 Shiff (2007: 136) refers to Delacroix as someone who would have claimed "that he had achieved independent mastery [...] that others would copy him as their

brothers, the loss caused by this fire was incalculable. Or was it? Were all the paintings what they were reputed to be?

1933: OCTOBER, THE VAN HORNE COLLECTION EXHIBITION

In October/November an exhibition of a selection (194 pieces) of the Van Horne collection was held at the galleries of the Art Association of Montreal. All paintings mentioned in Caroline's 1926 letter, which were also mentioned in a 1933 *Montreal Gazette* article, were exhibited. The exhibition caused quite a stir. Many newspaper articles expressed the pride that people took in having such a splendid collection in Montreal. The *Montreal Gazette* of October 17, 1933, reported:

The Van Horne Exhibition

Montreal has been singularly fortunate in the past in having numbered among its citizens several men whose love of art and understanding of painting, combined with the requisite wealth, enabled them to assemble collections of pictures that compared favourably with the greatest private galleries in the world. Among them no name stands out more clearly than that of Sir William Van Horne. He was the perfect example of the great executive seeking relief from business worries in the world of culture. He loved art in its manifold forms, but most of all he loved good pictures. And during his long life he brought together

---

classic model, but he would have no need to imitate anything outside himself." That Rembrandt painted Jesus on the same Lake Genesareth (the painting was stolen in 1990 from the Isabella Stewart Gartner Museum in Boston) must have escaped Delacroix, or perhaps he was too proud to acknowledge that he had used someone else's example. Connoisseur Abraham Bredius dismissed this Rembrandt and the two others in the Gardner collection as "not of the first rank" (Scallen 2004: 201).

a collection that is amazingly diversified and contains notable examples of both classic and modern schools. These pictures are now on view at the galleries of the Art Association of Montreal, through the courtesy of the Van Horne family.

Another article in the same *Gazette* on the same day elaborates on the "Treasures of the Van Horne Collection" that drew a crowd to the art gallery. Under the headline "Many Famous Works: Spanish, Dutch, Flemish, Italian, British, French, American and Canadian Artists Represented," it gives an in-depth overview of the works and ends with a note about the paintings by Van Horne himself:

All the paintings by Sir William Van Horne, done, according to the foreword to the catalogue, "from memory and by artificial light in the small hours of the night – the hours of relaxation of an exceedingly busy man," show that no problem was too big to tackle. Here are "Japanese Fete." A nocturne; landscapes at different seasons of the year, so uncompromising a subject as "Steel Mills at Sydney, CB," "Moonlight at St. Andrews" and "Railroad Station at Night," where the glare of a locomotive headlight flushes a string of cars and the depot building. This was inspired by Kipling's story "007." These performances are of ample size and show that a love of painting was a very real force.

One day later, the *Montreal Daily Herald* ran a similar article, providing a short description of most of the exhibited paintings. It concluded: "The present exhibition is a tribute to a man who was obviously sensitive and a lover of the fine arts, and for Montrealers should constitute an all-too-rare artistic adventure. There will be some who will haunt the galleries during the coming three weeks."

On October 18, 1933, a "Children's Friend" wrote the following letter to the *Montreal Daily Star*:

A unique opportunity for education and culture is offered, these coming weeks, to the young people of Montreal, through the display in the Art Gallery of the Van Horne Art Collection. Every schoolboy and girl over twelve years of age ought to be given the opportunity to see this unique display of paintings by the world's greatest artists [...]

The collection is so amazingly rich that a child could take in no more than a small choice of pictures, but if he has been told something about Rembrandt and Frans Hals, about Holbein and Rubens, about Goya, and El Greco [...] he will enjoy the fun of trying to recognize the work of these, the greatest amongst the great masters, and will never forget the experience.

In 1936, Toronto art critic Graham C. McInnes rated Van Horne's collection as "the finest" in Canada (Knowles 2010: 149). As pleasing as these evaluations were, back in The Netherlands, Frits Lugt, a Rembrandt connoisseur and collector of catalogues, had obtained the 1933 exhibition catalogue. [29] Although he had not seen the exhibition himself, he had perused the titles of the exhibited paintings and inserted some critical notes beside them.[30]

---

29   Frits Lugt (1884-1970) began his career as an employee at the art auction house Frederik Muller in Amsterdam in 1901 and was a partner in the firm from 1911 to 1915. One of his tasks, compiling the auctioneers' sales catalogues, spawned an intense interest in catalogues, which eventually led to his *Répertoire des catalogues de ventes publiques intéressant l'art et la curiosité* (*"Repertory of catalogues of public sale concerned with art or objets d'art"*), published in 1938, 1953, 1964, and (posthumously) in 1987. This four-volume work details sales catalogues published from 1600 to 1925, now found in public collections in Europe and North America. While working on this project, he donated his huge collection of sales catalogues and other documents, as well as his personal library, to the Rijksbureau voor Kunsthistorische Documentatie (RKD; Netherlands Institute for Art History) in The Hague. Lugt's art and catalogue collection is in Fondation Custodia, which was created in 1947 in Paris (Heijbroek 2010).

30   "According to Freek Heijbroek, Curator of the Rijksmuseum in Amsterdam, Frits Lugt did not visit the Van Horne exhibition in 1933." E-mail of July 15, 2009 from

LUGT'S SCRIBBLES

Frits Lugt	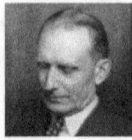

Catalogue 1933 verifies Caroline Pierson's account: for example, the catalogue lists by name the four Rembrandts that she saw in the Van Horne mansion. But Lugt's penciled scribbles behind the titles of the paintings cast doubt on whether Caroline saw four authentic Rembrandts, and questioned whether the collection was really that "fine."

The footnotes I made to Pierson's letter are transcriptions of the 1933 catalogue, followed by Frits Lugt's scribbles behind the titles of the paintings. Lugt scribbled behind three Velasquez paintings: *Philip IV of Spain* (full length); *Christ on the Cross* and *Philip IV* (small) "None of these very convincing;" behind Bartholomeus van der Helst's *Admiraal Cornelius Tromp* Lugt scribbled: "No, also not Tromp, but painted here excellently *en fond*, in yellow yerkin." Behind Rembrandt's *A Landscape Study* he scribbled: "Might be a Rdt." And, behind Maes' *Old Woman with Bible*: "No, not Maes."

The preface to the Montreal exhibition's catalogue raves about Van Horne's extraordinary achievement in the history of collection, claiming that it represents a "splendid breadth of taste."

Was Rembrandt's *Landscape* a "Rdt [Rembrandt]" or wasn't it? What about the other Rembrandts in Van Horne's collection?

Rhea Sylvia Blok, Curator of the Fondation Custodia / Collection Frits Lugt in Paris.

As mentioned, Lugt's notes are included in the footnotes to Caroline Pierson's letter preceded by NFL.

1972: THE REMBRANDT RESEARCH PROJECT

Old Man with Black Cap 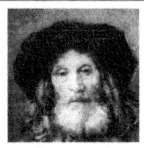   Head of Old Man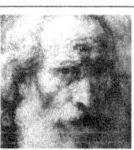

Young Rabbi 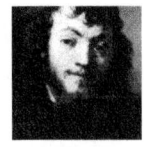   Landscape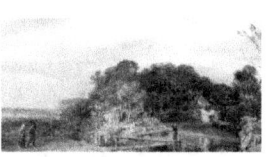

Finding more information about the authenticity of Rembrandt's *Landscape with cottages* and the three other Rembrandts in the Van Horne collection proved to be possible. In the 1950s, art historians in Amsterdam and experts from other fields set out to reassess the authenticity of works attributed to Rembrandt and to compile a complete new catalogue of his paintings. (In 2010 the fifth volume of *A Corpus of Rembrandt Paintings* was presented at the Frankfurt Book Fair.)

The Rembrandt Research Project (RRP), led by Dr. S. H. Levie, began in 1968 and ended in 2011. On January 17, 2008, Prof. Dr. Ernst van de Wetering, who began as a young staff member and eventually became its director, was interviewed on a Dutch radio station. At the beginning, he said, he was charged with organizing the committee members' travels. Although he knew little about Rembrandt in 1972, he always critically and eagerly listened to the establishment of consensus among the group of Rembrandt scholars. "Each painting was considered to be a fake," he said, "which was caused by the aftermath of the Van Meegeren affair. [...] At the start, people believed in a scientific investigation such as into the age of the panels, the paint and the canvas – in x-rays and so on. Now the role of the connoisseurs' consensus is alarmingly big."

The Rembrandts in the Van Horne collection had not escaped the RRP's attention. On June 20, 1972, Dr. Levie asked

Mrs. William van Horne, the widow of grandson Billy, whether she would allow him and Mr. Van de Wetering to see, under adequate light and without glass, *Portrait of a Young Jew* (known under Bredius 1969: 300) on September 3 or 4.[31] On July 9, 1972, Mrs. van Horne replied that she would do whatever she could to assist Dr. Levie but that the suggested dates coincided with "our North-American Labour-Day-holiday. Please let me know if you plan to be in New York following the Labour-Day-holiday. It may be possible for me to take the three Rembrandts to you in New York in September."[32] She further informed Levie that her late husband's grandfather had had four Rembrandts in his possession. She enclosed photographs of *The Prophet* or *Old Man with Slashed Black Cap* and *Head of Old Man* and assumed that Levie had a photograph of *A Young Rabbi,* "inaccurately referred to in your letter as *Portrait of a Young Jew.*" She added that *Landscape* had been given to the Montreal Museum of Fine Arts.[33]

Margaret Van Horne, as she signed this letter, concluded: "We have never had X-Ray or infra-red photographs made of any of our paintings. The latter have been quietly kept in our family residence since Sir William's death in 1915." Perhaps Mrs. Van Horne had forgotten about the 1933 events. (When I later told Van de Wetering about the fire, the story was new to him.) On July 25, 1972, Levie wrote to Mrs. Van Horne, thanking her for her permission to study the three Rembrandts. He also said he regretted that she would not be in Montreal on

---

31   Letter from Dr. Levie to Mrs. van Horne, June 20, 1972, Van Horne Family Fonds, Art Gallery of Ontario, E. P. Taylor Research Library and Archives, box 43, file 9. From now on letters from the Van Horne Family Fonds will be indicted in footnotes as (VHFF 43/9).

32   VHFF 43/9

33   As we will see later, in 1941 Adaline van Horne had bequeathed her share, about sixty paintings by both old and new masters (El Greco, Ruysdael, Canaletto, Francesco Guardi, Tiepolo, Daumier, Renoir, Cézanne and others) to the Art Association of Montreal, which this association obtained in 1945. Rembrandt's *Landscape* was no. 75 at the 1960 exhibition in Montreal.

September 4, and proposed September 9 or 20, the latter date "not being very convenient to us." [34] After a flurry of cablegrams between Levie and Mrs. van Horne, the meeting was set for September 20.

Dr. Levie and his young assistant, Van de Wetering, set out for Montreal to research Rembrandt's *Landscape*, which had resided in the Montreal Museum of Fine Arts since 1945. According to Van de Wetering, upon arriving in Montreal they went to a big house to conduct research on a Rembrandt. At the gate of this house, they were stopped by a tough-looking, sun-glassed detective, who thought that they had come to steal the Rembrandt painting. "It was then and there," said Van de Wetering, "that we heard of the theft [of the *Landscape*] from the museum." [35]

$1 million Rembrandt stolen

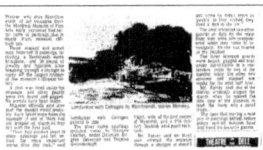

Interpol called in

Like the 1933 fire, the news of the theft of Rembrandt's *Landscape* did not make it to the front page; it appeared in the *Globe and Mail*'s entertainment pages on September 5 and 6, 1972.

Thirty-five years later the theft remained unsolved, as stated in this feature article:

34   Letter from Dr. Levie to Mrs. van Horne, July 25, 1972, VHFF 43/9.
35   Telephone communication with Van de Wetering, June 17, 2009.

Stolen paintings mystery lingers, 35 years later
Bill Bantey, CanWest News Service
Published: Saturday, September 1, 2007

MONTREAL — Were the paintings destroyed? Is the new "owner" sitting on them, afraid to show them off? Could they be in South America?

Thirty-five years ago Monday, three armed and hooded bandits broke into the Montreal Museum of Fine Arts through a skylight under repair and made off with 18 paintings and 37 objects of decorative arts and jewelry.

It was the biggest theft in the museum's 112-year history. The loot, valued at $2 million by the museum, included a Rembrandt oil, Landscape with Cottages, valued at $1 million in 1972.

All but one of the stolen paintings — a small Jan Breughel The Elder — remains missing today.[36]

David Giles Carter, director of the museum at the time of the robbery, today says the "worst possible scenario" is that the paintings have been destroyed, perhaps because the pictures were too "hot" to be disposed of on the art market.

Much later, Julian Radcliffe, chair of the Art Loss Register, described the theft (quoted in Houpt 2009: 12): "At the Montreal Museum of Fine Arts, it is always September 4, 1972, when armed thieves descended from a skylight and, after tying up the lone guard on duty in the middle of the night, grabbed eighteen painting and other objects, including a Rembrandt Harmensz. Van Rijn, two Corots, a Pieter Brueghel (the Elder), a Thomas Gainsborough, a Ferdinand Delacroix

---

36   Four decades later the painting is still missing. See http://unsolved-1972-theft-montreal.blogspot.ca/ (last accessed in April 2014).

[Radcliffe probably meant Eugène Delacroix], and a Peter Paul Rubens." [37]

The meeting between Levie, Van de Wetering, and Mrs. van Horne had still not taken place and was set for September 20, 1972, at the Catskill Motor Lodge at exit 21 of the New York Thruway. After travelling from Montreal to New York, Levie and Van de Wetering were driven "in a limousine with dark tinted glasses to a place hours from New York (i.e., to Catskill). There we stepped into the small car of a shaky old lady. She drove us to a Little Red Riding Hood wood, where we stopped at an atom bomb–proof bunker. That is where she had the three Rembrandts stored because of the many break-ins at her house in Montreal. We put the paintings against a tree and saw that the two old men, the one with a black cap and the one with the fuzzy beard, were not Rembrandts. She was quite devastated." [38]

Of the three presumed Rembrandts in Van Horne's collection, then, only *The Young Rabbi* was deemed to be a genuine Rembrandt.[39] The meeting of Levie and Van de Wetering with Mrs. van Horne still had a cordial ending. On September 29, 1972, Levie thanked Mrs. Van Horne for showing them the paintings and for the additional travel money she had provided, and advised her: "As we already told you, the *Portrait of a Rabbi* or *Jewish Scholar* will certainly improve, when you

---

37   Houpt (2009: 174-76) provides particulars on the stolen paintings, include the following: Rembrandt, *Landscape with Cottages*; Corot, *La rêveuse à la fontaine and Jeune fille accoudée sur le bras gauche;* Gainsborough, *Portrait of Brigadier General Sir Robert Fletcher*; Millet, *Portrait de Madame Millet and La batteuse*; and Delacroix, *Lionne et lion dans une caverne.* All have been missing since September 4, 1972, and their estimated current value is "priceless."

38   Telephone conversation with Van de Wetering on June 17, 2009.

39   On May 12, 2009, Margaret Oomen of the Rembrandt Research Project confirmed in an e-mail that the three paintings shown to Levie and Van de Wetering were *Portrait of a Young Jew*, 1663 (Bredius 300), now in the Kimbell Art Museum in Fort Worth; *A Prophet*, or *Old Man with Slashed Black Cap*, later attributed by Prof. Bruyn to Titus van Rijn; and one of the versions of *Head of an Old Man* (Bredius 295A).

have it cleaned and restored." [40] A few days later, on October 2, 1972, he wrote to her again, in English:

> First of all I would like to say how sorry I am that I did not inform you in a more cautious way about the two imitations after Rembrandt in your collection. I can imagine that it was a great shock to you hearing it. Afterwards I am fully aware of that. I did not know though, that you were not acquainted with the fact that both the artworks do not figure in the Rembrandt literature. On its own that is no proof those two paintings are not by Rembrandt. [...] I realize too, that you on one hand are disappointed about the many connoisseurs, who never told you anything negative about the paintings and on the other hand that perhaps your image of Sir William as a collector has got a little tiny dent.
>
> But it could not hardly be else for a man, who had such a busy and important business-life, that he was more or less doomed to make a mistake in a field that is not his. And probably the art-dealer concerned, or the advisor of that moment, are more to blame for such an error than he.

Due to theft, *Landscape* escaped the RRP's authentication efforts.[41] As noted earlier, Lugt had expressed his doubts on the 1933 catalogue; as it turned out, he was not alone. Van de Wetering and Albert Blankert, both Dutch Rembrandt

---

40   (VHFF 43/9). In an e-mail on May 7, 2009, Dr. Albert Blankert, a Rembrandt and Vermeer connoisseur, wrote about the *Portrait of a Young Rabbi*, certified by the RRP: "It was one of the top pieces on my exhibition 'Rembrandt: a Genius and his Impact' in Melbourne and Canberra in 1997, when I extensively discussed and analyzed it on page 173 etc. no. 25 of the exhibition catalogue."

41   Whether the thieves, or the staff of the museum, may have doubted the authenticity of *Landscape* and whether one thought the theft could have been triggered by the upcoming visit of the RRP staff are at this point unanswered questions.

connoisseurs, advised me to read the revised version of
Bredius's *Rembrandt: The Complete Edition of His Paintings*
(Bredius 1969: 453), which states (590):

> *Evening landscape with cottages.* Signed: Rembrandt f.
> 1654. HdG 950. Bach 555. The same spot appears repeat-
> edly in drawings and etchings both by Rembrandt and by
> his pupils. See: F. Lugt (*Mit Rembrandt in Amsterdam,*
> 1920, p. 120 and *Jahrbuch der Preussischen Kunstsamm-
> lungen* 52, 1931, p. 60). Bredius wrote (in a PS note to the
> compiler of the first edition of this book): "Probably right,
> but it has something which alarms me"; I [Gerson] have
> the same feeling of uneasiness about the attribution.

After the theft in Montreal, twenty-five insurance companies forked over a total of $1 million to the museum for a
somewhat alarming Rembrandt that causes feelings of uneasi-
ness. As noted earlier, Lugt's scribbles raised the question of
whether Caroline Pierson saw four authentic Rembrandts
in Van Horne's mansion in 1926. Preliminary investigation
shows that only one of the four, *The Young Rabbi,* was without
doubt a Rembrandt, and the stolen *Landscape* perhaps as well.

Did Van Horne have any notion that his Maes may not have
been a Maes, or that the authenticity of his Rembrandts could
be doubted? According to an article published in the *New York
American* on November 16, 1908, this is what he knew.

> **Millionaires paid fortunes for bogus "Old Masters."**
> **P. J. Carter, Expert Restorer Bares Widespread Frauds for the**
> **American.**[42]
> **Swears to his charges.**

---

42   The full title of this journal is *The New York American Journal.*

Corroborated by dr. De groot, assistant director of the Hague gallery.

10 000 Percent profit.

Real old masters sometimes cut in pieces, which are sold separately

[...] Mr. Carter spent more than two months in the big collection of Sir William Van Horne at Montreal. Of the three hundred pictures, about one hundred are from Sir William's own brush, and the expert pays high tribute to the railroad builder's personal skill as an artist. Much to his sorrow, however, he found that some cleverly "faked" pictures had crept into that collection. He said: "I was asked to clean and reline a portrait which bore the name of Nicholas Maas [sic], the celebrated contemporary of Rembrand [sic]. It was of an old lady, but I had not been at work on it long before I discovered the old lady's old gentleman had been painted out. I called Sir William and told him the circumstances.

But the "old Gentleman" was kept in hiding.

"Will you have the old gentleman, too?" I [Carter] asked.

"Leave him under cover," returned Sir William, who evidently feared to lose an "old Master" if the truth showed fort [sic].

That in the end the truth had "showed forth" for Van Horne is also evident in Vaughan's biography, who quotes Van Horne as saying: "It doesn't matter a damn whether a great man painted the poor one or an unknown man painted the fine one" (1920: 268-69). Van Horne, then, appeared to have had notions about the authenticity of certain pieces in his collection, which raises certain questions: Who were his dealers, especially the dealers that "were to blame" for his Rembrandt purchases, and how did his acquisitions come about in general? Looking for answers rendered a multi-faceted impression of Van Horne's art of collecting and his collection *an sich* confined to his Dutch acquaintances in the art world.　　　✕

PEOPLE & PLACES

Leonardus Salomon /
Leo Nardus
@Wikipedia/PublicDomain
➡

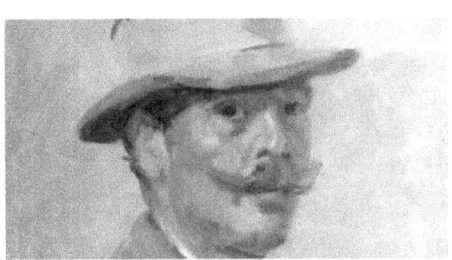

Château d'Arnouville-lès-
Gonesses
Courtesy Clicsouris
➡

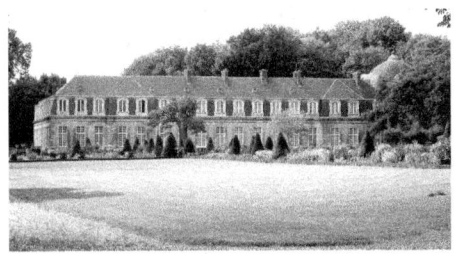

Michel Van Gelder
Courtesy
Barbara van der Veen
➡

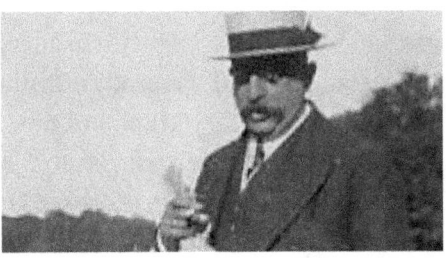

Chateau Zeecrabbe
University of Gent library/
PublicDomain
➡

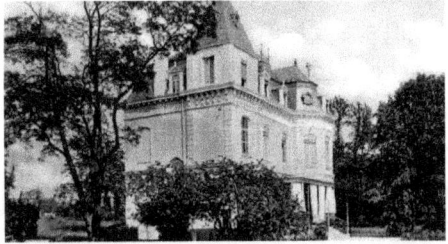

CHAPTER 2

COLLECTOR WILLIAM VAN HORNE

REASONS FOR AND Requirements of a Fine Art Collection. Simon Houpt (2006: 16) writes about the genesis of collecting: "In the beginning collectors were as satisfied to possess objects of natural history – shells, minerals, animals and other curios – as they were to gather works of art." Later on, objects from the fields of art or natural science were desirable if they were considered to be rare, and "the European bourgeoisie could therefore use the objects to set themselves above and apart from the common man." English journalist Robert Lacey, in fact, labels collecting fine art as "bidding for class" in his 1998 book *Sotheby's* subtitled as *Bidding for class.*

On November 8, 1913, a writer for *American Art News* related an anecdote about the three types of collectors: those who know, those who frankly admit that they don't know, and those who think they know, but don't. One priceless example concerned a collector "who knew:" he had bought a Steen during the World's Fair in St. Louis. Clinging to his claim of its authenticity, he had said: "I bought it direct from Mr. Steen's representative."

In the case of private collector William Van Horne, one could say that his achievements in this field read as a blueprint for the traditional stages of collecting. Knowles (2004: 26) writes that Van Horne, when still a young boy, found a chunk of rock in which, "after some chipping, he had found a "worm-in-the-rock." This rock became Van Horne's first treasure. The cherished possession had invested him with "a sense of increased importance both in his own mind and in the minds of those schoolmates to whom he showed it." After this find,

Knowles writes, he kept looking for specimens. According to a second-hand account of the evening prior to the 1973 Van Horne mansion demolition, "Another huge item of furniture [that had to be removed] was his rock collection in an appropriate cabinet." [43] Obviously, Van Horne's rock collection was dear to him, despite most of it being presented to an American university, according to English art critic and mountaineer, Martin Conway (1905: 135).

Of course, many collectors have an active interest in the arts. Van Horne can certainly be said to have been among them. His interest began when his mother showed him that he could make scratches on a slate or stone with a pebble. He soon discovered that he could make rude drawings on it as well. Encouraged by his mother and given chalks and pencils by his lawyer-father, "before long young William had covered every wall in the house, as high as his small arm could reach, with drawings" (Knowles 2004: 24-25; 2010: 145).

That Van Horne continued his active interest in fine art is apparent from Catalogue 1933, which lists the following works by his own hand: 176 *Japanese Fête*; 177 *Minister's Island*; 178 *Harvest Scene*; 179 *Canadian Village*; 180 *View from Minister's Island*; 181 *Autumn Woods*; 182 *A Lowering Sunset*; 183 *Woodland Sunshine*; 184 *Railroad Station at Night*, "inspired by Kipling's story '007'"; 185 *Woods and Fields*; 186 *Moonlight at St. Andrews*; 187 *Evening, Old Chester*; 188 *Steel Mills at Sydney, CB*; 189 *Rainy Day*; and 190 *Winter Sunshine*. London critic Roger Fry (1866-1934), curator of European paintings in the Metropolitan Museum of Art from 1904 to 1910, called Van Horne's work "marvelously effective and on the spot" (Knowles 2010: 147).

---

43   See http://www.trainorders.com/discussion/read.php?15,2088545 (last accessed in February 2014).

Collard (1991: 145) relates a story about Van Horne showing off his collections. A visitor being shown the collection by Van Horne lingered in front of one picture, "and wanted to know the artist's name. "Oh, that's by an artist of very little account," he was told. The visitor, insisting on the name because the work reminded him of the work of l'Hermitte, the French landscape painter, peered at the signature, which read "Enroh Nav," and suddenly realized that it was "Van Horne," spelled backwards." [44]

Van Horne apparently had aspirations in addition to those in the business world and was eager to hear an unbiased appraisal. That became more evident as time went on. While Caroline Pierson did not mention any photographs by Van Horne in the Van Horne mansion during her 1926 visit, on November 12, 1910, *American Art News* profiled him as a proficient photographer. Under the heading "Chicago" was noted: "Sir William Van Horne recently showed several artistic photographs taken by himself in the Selkirk Mountains. The points of view were well chosen and the photographs are considered remarkably good."

Another manifestation of his interest in art appeared with the completion of the Canadian Pacific Railway: Van Horne handed out free passes or reduced-fare tickets "to thirty-three prominent artists and commissioned and or purchased at least fifty-six landscape canvases on the behalf of the CPR" (Knowles 2004: 292). The artists' paintings were used for CPR pamphlets and a number of them ended up in the collections of CPR board members (Knowles 2010: 86). In 2009, the Glenbow Museum in Calgary hosted a splendid exhibition of the

---

44   The "Van Horne Collection" in the New Brunswick Museum contains among others twenty-one paintings by Van Horne: #1150/R, Mount Cheops, Canadian Rockies, #1154/R Summer Pastime and # 1158/R Autumn Woods and Meadow are listed as being done by Enroh Nav (Van Horne, W. C.). A fine example of a 'Enroh Nav' is on view in the Banff Springs Hotel in Banff.

work of these "prominent artists," including Frederic Marlett Bell-Smith (1846-1923), William Brymner (1855-1925), Oliver B. Buell (1844-1910), John Arthur Fraser (1838-1898), Roger Gagen (1847-1926), John Hammond (1843-1939), Thomas Mover Martin (1838-1934), William McFarlane Notman (1857-1913), and Lucius Richard O'Brien (1832-1899).[45] A few of Van Horne's own railway landscapes were included.

Housing, time, and money

Besides insurance, maintenance, and security, collections of old and young masters need a roof over their heads. Private fine art collections have been stored or exhibited for private or public viewing in a wide variety of venues, including bomb-proof bunkers, canal houses, castles, courts, estates, factories, galleries, halls, houses, institute mansions, museums, palaces, offices, storage rooms, salt mines, and vaults. With regard to Van Horne's collection, Knowles (2004: 299) notes that the Van Hornes moved in 1890 from Dorchester Street West in Montreal to a much larger home at 917, later renumbered 1139, Sherbrooke Street: "This was not made for career-related reasons. Van Horne simply wanted a larger house in which to display his burgeoning art and pottery collection." After moving in, he began the necessary alterations that provided generous walls for his paintings.

An early, somewhat exalted description of Van Horne's large house is found in Conway's account (1905: 137): "The house he built is a monument of his own design, and is admirably suited to set off the variety of precious things that it contains – furniture, bronzes, pottery, pictures, and what-not." Nine years later, connoisseur Bernard Berenson (1865-1959), who lived in Italy, was urged by his "practical minded wife Mary" to

---

45   Short biographies of these artists are in Boulet's *Vistas: Artists on the Canadian Pacific Railway*.

visit Sir William Van Horne in Montreal inasmuch as "he was the foremost Canadian collector of art" (Samuels 1987: 86). In a letter dated January 10, 1914, Mary Berenson (quoted in Hadley 1987: 504-5) assessed Van Horne's house in tones quite different from those of Conway: "But one might know that provincialism is provincialism everywhere, and that the one thing these provincial millionaires think of is to build ultra-hideous brown-stone houses (here the stone is a gloomy slate-colour) and hang in their multifarious and overheated rooms a vast collection of gilt-framed mediocre pictures often spurious and almost always, even if authentic, poor."

In the same letter, she describes her husband Bernard lying on the sofa "nursing a heavy cold," and Van Horne as "laid up with inflammatory rheumatism." Perhaps that explains the overheating, not only in the house, but also in her writing. The derogatory tone may also have been used to assure her addressee, Isabella Stewart Gardner (1840-1924), the Berensons' benefactor, that Gardner's mansion (since 1903 the Isabella Stewart Gardner Museum), modelled after Venetian palaces, was not provincial at all.[46]

When Caroline Pierson visited the Van Horne mansion in 1926, however, nobody was laid up with anything, and in her letter she uttered not a word about overheating. In contrast, she reported on the Van Horne collection's housing: "In the

---

46   Much earlier, in October 1903, after the Berensons had visited Isabella Stewart Gardner for the first time in her country house in Brooklyn, Massachusetts, Mary Berenson wrote to her family about their hostess: "In two days I have lost an inch round the waist, between a plain spare diet and freezing cold" (Strachey & Samuels 1983: 111). On December 24, 1920, six years after her visit to the Van Hornes, Mary wrote the following lines to her family (ibid.: 236): "We went out to see Mrs. Gardner today. She will soon die. [...] But the worst of all is that her great Palace, in spite of the marvellous pictures in it, looks to our now enlightened eyes like a junk shop. There is something horrible in these American collections, in snatching this and that away from its real home and hanging it on a wall of priceless damask made for somewhere else, about furniture higgledripiggled from other places."

library a nice northern light shone on the old masters. [...] Spanish masters gave the entire house an extraordinary stateliness and great cachet; [...] the red room was perfectly square with a high ceiling."

Knowles (2004: 287-88), dedicating a whole chapter, "Art for Art's Sake," to Van Horne's dalliance with fine art, writes that he started his collection in the mid-1880s, when "he was pulling a large CPR salary." When Van Horne became CPR president, his annual salary was raised from $30 000 to $50 000 (Knowles 2010: 109). According to Molson (2001: 326), "Van Horne's CPR was pulling in a hundred million dollars a year." That could be the case. In this regard Berton (1971: 275) writes:

Economic conditions were such that, in the summer of 1883, ordinary shovel men were being paid $1.50 for a ten-hour day along Lake Superior and in some instances as little as $1.00 a day which is the going rate in the eastern cities ("Mr. Ross is trying to reach the $1 without a strike," Van Horne informed John Egan in June. "It may take him some weeks to do it.") Any attempt at labour organization brought instant dismissal; Van Horne had a reputation as a union buster. In the rare instances when strikes did occur, they were quickly broken.

The money may have been earned on the backs of the shovel men and other labourers, but money it was. Although money and time for collecting were lacking from 1900 to 1904 because of Van Horne's involvement in the Cuban railway, he was again in the purchasing mood by the spring of 1905. Among the paintings he snapped up was a George Romney.[47]

With regard to Van Horne's pastime of collecting, Knowles argues that he "was typical of many late-nine-tenth-century North American gentlemen of wealth, some of whom sought to veneer their *arrivisme* with the cultural trappings of the Old World." Whether, or in what way, Van Horne was one who "sought to veneer" his arrival among the rich and famous by "bidding for class" will be revealed through his extensive correspondence with his fine, and less fine, art connections. Van Horne's interests were diverse, but – as his correspondence, quoted below, indicates – sometimes they had to become more diverse than he may have bargained for.

A CATALOGUE

In general, collectors catalogue their collections to keep track of the contents, to show off, or to have the catalogue published and/or use one's catalogue as a conversation topic. The Van Horne Family Fonds, series three and four, in the Art Gallery of Ontario (AGO) clearly shows that Van Horne was very aware of the intrinsic importance of cataloguing to keep track of one's treasures. Boxes 9 to 11 in these fonds contain his own

---

47   In the Van Horne Family Fonds, most of the entries for the Wickenden catalogue (also known as "Billy's binders") are filed in box 50, files 1 to 6. Paintings mentioned in the main text are listed in footnotes starting with VH and catalogue number, here followed by a selection of Wickenden's data about the painter and the painting (denoted by a "Ⓦ" hereafter), and Henschel's evaluations (denoted by a "Ⓗ" hereafter). Charles Henschel (1885-1956) was Knoedler's grandson and later became the director of that firm (Goldstein 2000: 168).

The Romney that Van Horne bought in 1905 is listed as VH 3 Romney, George. Beckside, Dalton-in Furness 1734-Kendal 1802. *Portrait of Miss Morland.* In the alphabetical "Catalogue Raissonne" of Romney's works, compiled by Humphrey Ward and W. Roberts, (London: Thomas Agnew & Son, and New York: Charles Scribner's Sons), vol. 2, page 108, we find this portrait recorded, with the dates January 17 and 20, 1782, as the time of its production. Ⓦ: "Canvas H. 24 in, W. 20½ in (61 cm × 52 cm). From the coll. of T. J. Blakeslee, New York." Ⓗ: "7 500."

numerous notes on his collection: Japanese and Chinese pottery, pictures, furniture, household effects, *objets d'art*, catalogues of paintings, and albums of Dutch, French, German, Flemish, English, and North American paintings.

Van Horne began to catalogue his collection as early as 1892. From his correspondence, we know that he commissioned Stephan Bourgeois, one of his dealer friends, to draw up a catalogue in 1913. The Great War largely halted Bourgeois' efforts to finish it. Only in 1926 did talk about the catalogue resume. On December 20, 1926, Bourgeois wrote to Adaline:[48]

> As you know I have started during the summer to compile the catalogue of your father's collection and have nearly all the biographical notes ready. As for the descriptions, and a great deal of information in your possession, I need to go for a few days to Montreal. I wonder if after the New Year if it would be possible to discuss the whole matter thoroughly, so that I can proceed? Will you be so good to let me know if this time will be convenient to you and Bennie?

On January 21, 1927, Bourgeois wrote another lengthy letter to Adaline, who was in charge of the estate after the death of her father. An excerpt of his letter reads as follows:[49]

> Regarding the catalogue, you probably know, that I started on this work already in 1913 on Sir William's initiative. Unfortunately, when the war broke out, all the descriptions and notes, which I had made, and which were, then near completion, were in my apartment in Paris, which, as you know, I never recovered. So all the work, as well as a

48   Letter in VHFF (33/4).
49   Letter in VHFF (33/4).

complete set of photos, was lost. One day last winter Bennie called me up to come and see him at his apartment. I went there, and he proposed to me to take the matter up again. I should do all the old paintings as well as the very modern ones; also write the introduction to the catalogue. Mr. Wickenden should do the more conservative artists of the 19th century, and I should discuss collaboration with him. I accepted his proposal in principal. [50]

A few weeks later Mr. Wickenden called at my office, but as I had a great number of visitors, I did not come to a discussion with him, and have not seen him since then.

In the meantime, Bennie went to Cuba; my letters remained unanswered, and as I have time only in the summer to devote to writing, I thought I would ask you what decision had been taken. On my visit in the spring to Montreal I understood from my conversation with you that you had not an opportunity to discuss with Bennie, and that you were negotiating with Mr. Wickenden. There I left the matter for the time being, but when I did not hear from Bennie for a few weeks and in the beginning of May had to decide if I should stay here and write the catalogue or go to Europe, I past by his apartment and found him by chance at home. He told me then and there to go ahead and fixed with me my fee for the work, which would be paid after discussion with you.

Having then received payment a few weeks later by check from Montreal, I understood, of course, that you had discussed the matter fully and that I start working.

---

50   In the VHFF (p. 12) Robert J. Wickenden (1861-1931) is profiled as an English painter, writer, and lithographer: "He was recognized in his day as an authority on the Barbizon School of painters. In 1896 he travelled to Canada and began to produce a series of portraits of prominent citizens, including Sir William van Horne [...]. In 1927 he completed a series of typescript catalogues of Van Horne's art coll. – all catalogues hand-annotated by Wickenden."

Consequently by the beginning of the summer I went to Montreal, made an inventory of all the pictures, of which I gave Bennie copies and made a special list of those pictures, numbering 125, which should be published and illustrated in the catalogue, followed by a list of the less important ones to be appended to the catalogue. Of the principal list the numbers 79 till 112 were reserved for Mr. Wickenden, that is pictures by the following artists:

Constable[51]
Turner[52]
Delacroix[53]
Daumier[54]
Monticelli[55]

---

51 The following list will only indicate number, title, dealer, and Henschel's valuation or comment in the Wickenden catalogue (if there is one). Whether the price was in dollars or pounds is not always indicated. Constables listed are the following: VH 10, *The Villa* (⊡: $6 000); VH 12, *The Vale of Dedham* (last owned by T. J. Blakeslee. ⊡: $85 000); VH 13, *View on the Stour* (Nardus and Van Gelder 1900. ⊡: 1 500); VH 17, *Niedpath Castle* (Blakeslee 1900; ⊡: $6 000); VH 20, *Three Riverside Sketches* (Colnaghi & Co, London 1910). Cat. 1933 also lists 99 *Hampstead Heath*, 100 *The Glebe Farm*, and 103 *Landscape with Cottages.*

52 J. M. W. Turner (1775-1851): VH 21, *Launch at Chatham.* Beside Wickenden's statement that this painting has not been recorded, recent publications on Turner say that: "One must always remember that the Van Hornes did not encourage publication of their paintings." Cat. 1933 only lists 99 *Shakespeare's Cliff, Dover.*

53 VH 200 Delacroix. *Samson and Delilah.* ⊡: from Messrs. Carfax & Co. London. ⊡: $3 000.

54 VH 228 Daumier. *A Musical Party.* Gimpel & Wildenstein, New York 1910. ⊡: $20 000).

55 Monticellis listed (VHFF 50/5) are the following: VH 239, *A Southern Garden* (⊡: $1 000); VH 240, *Fete Champetre* (⊡: J. S. Inglis, NY 1889. ⊡: $3 000); VH 241, *A Walled Lane* (⊡: Inglis, NY 1889. ⊡: $2 500); VH 242, *The Adoration of the Magi.* (⊡: In poss. of D. Cottier & Son, NY. From the Mary J. Morgan coll., sold by the American Art Association, NY 1886. ⊡: $3 500); VH 243, *The Conversion of St. Paul* (⊡: In poss. of Cottier & Co, NY 1891. ⊡: $1 200); VH 244, *The Kitchen* (⊡: From Wallis & Sons. The French Galleries, London); VH 245, *The Decameron* (⊡: From Inglis, NY 1889. ⊡: $2 500); VH 247, *Mountainous Landscape near Algiers* (⊡: From Wisselingh & Co, A'dam 1911. ⊡: $3 000); VH 248, *The Fountain*; VH 250, *Dancers in a Wood* (⊡: Gift from R. B. Angus Esq. Montreal. ⊡: Final $3 000); VH 251, *Returning from the Chase* (⊡: $2 000).

Corot[56]

Troyon[57]

Rousseau[58]

Daubigny[59]

Courbet[60]

M. Maris[61]

Ryder[62]

Mary Cassat[63]

Consequently I had a number of conferences with Bennie about the catalogue and also about reproductions. He wanted the best pictures re-photographed by the best photographer here. I discussed this with Mr. McKillop, who is the most experienced man in America to photograph pictures. He made a proposition to me with special conditions for so large an order in form of a letter, of which I sent to Bennie the original with my recommendations. He has not yet acted upon this matter.

---

56   Van Horne wrote on Nov. 4, 1914 that he would ship back the Corot. On the other hand, Cat. 1933 lists 4 Corots: 125 *Les Gaulois*; 126 *Landscape – Sand Dunes*; 127 *Peasant Girl by a Wall*; and 128 *Mother and Child*.

57   Constant Troyon (1810-1865): VH 215, *La Guitariste: A Portrait of Georges Sand* (W: Cottier & Co. NY 1889. H: $5 000, Not Troyon, maybe Couture).

58   The paintings by Theodore Rousseau (1812-1867) are the following: VH 211, *The Great Oaks of Bas-Breau, Forest of Fontainebleau* (W: Bought from Blakeslee & Co NY in 1889. H: $5 000, Cost more); VH 212, *The Brook: Autumnal Landscape* (W: From Frederick A. Chapman, NY 1905, formerly in coll. of Mr. Arthur Stevens, Brussels. H: $1 000); VH 213, *Thatched Cottages* (W: From Blakeslee & Co NY. H: $50, Not Rousseau).

59   Charles François Daubigny (1817-1878), listed in 50/5: VH 193, *Sunset on the Oise, near the Isle-des-Vaux* (W: Purchased from Inglis, Cottier & Co. NY. H: No value). Cat. 1933 lists the following Daubignys: 131 Sketch in Brittany; 132 Building the Stack; and 132a Landscape.

60   Gustave Courbet's (1819-1877) *Still-Life of Fruit* is described and listed simply as "From the coll. of Mrs. William Van Horne."

61   Maris VH 175, see footnote 487.

62   Cat. 1933 lists Alfred P. Ryder (1841-1917) as 162 Siegfried and the Rhine-maidens and 163 Constance.

63   The Wickenden catalogue does not list a Cassat. Cat. 1933 lists Mary Cassat (1845-1926) 149 Mother and Child.

In the meantime, I went ahead and compiled most of the biographies of those artists, which came in my category, but having reached a point, where I needed the photographic material and all the information contained in bills and letters pertaining to the pictures to compile actual research work, I came to a stand still. Bennie told me that I had to wait till you returned from the country in the fall, as you were in charge of the papers, and I decided then by the end of August to go for a short trip to Europe.

Before leaving I spoke to Valentiner about the publication, and he promised me some new information pertaining to some of the Dutch pictures I saw also in The Hague in the house of a Mr. Van Deventer; an old print of an admiral, which I believe is the same man as the Van der Helst.[64]

I am expecting a photo of this print to make comparisons with your picture. If I would have had the photos I would have received a great deal of new information, as I spoke in Munich with Mayer about the Spanish pictures and in Berlin with Bode, who both promised supplementary information when I shall send them photos.[65] There the matter stands at this moment.

....

64 Wilhem R. Valentiner (1880-1958) started his career as a connoisseur in 1905 under the guidance of Dutch connoisseur Cornelis Hofstede de Groot. In 1906, he was hired as personal assistant to Wilhelm Bode at the Kaiser-Friedrich Museum in Berlin. He joined the Metropolitan in 1908. In 1913, he founded the journal *Art in America* (Scallen 2010).

W. A. van Deventer (1824-1893) was a Dutch landscape painter, who was trained at the The Hague Academy, where Navy painters such as Sam Verveer and Antonie Waldorp were teaching. See http://nl.wikipedia.org/wiki/W.A._van_Deventer (last accessed in February 2014).

65 Wilhelm Von Bode (1845-1929) was a German art historian and curator. Born Arnold William Bode in Calvörde, he was ennobled in 1914, so his name changed to Von Bode. In 1910 he was the creator and first curator of the Kaiser Friedrich Museum, since 1956 called the Bode Museum (Scallen 2004).

BENNIE VAN HORNE

Richard Benedict Van Horne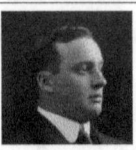

"Bennie," or Benedict Richard van Horne, was the father of William, the teenaged boy who Caroline saw running through the Van Horne mansion, skates dangling from his shoulders. Knowles (2004: 320) writes that Bennie, from a very young age, was smothered by fatherly love; became unmotivated, lazy, and spoiled; was fond of sailing; and was a hard drinker who would die in 1941 of liver disease at the age of fifty-four.

Despite this negative characterization, when a new sardine plant was about to be established in 1912, a local newspaper, the *New Brunswick Beacon*, duly keeping track of Bennie van Horne's socializing and sailing antics, reported on April 11, 1912, that R. B. Van Horne was one of the sardine plant's backers. Later, he became one of its directors. After Van Horne's death, "Bennie devoted himself to looking after Van Horne family railway and plantations interests," which "required that he spend a great deal of time on the island [where Covenhoven was] as well as in New York" (Knowles 2004: 430). Molson (2001: 324) sees Bennie as a victim of his parents' intense, ultimately destructive love and writes that he struggled with alcohol and gambling addictions: "Sir William made his son vice-president, then president, of the Cuba Company Railroad, which kept Bennie in New York for sixteen years."

In her vicious 1914 letter about the Van Horne collection's provincial housing, Mary Berenson wrote that Benny was "a powerful and intelligent man, but of course doubly busy with his father illness." Distracted by drinking, friends, sailing, sardines, railways, and plantations, Bennie may simply not have found time to assist Bourgeois with the catalogue. Instead, R. B. Wickenden (1861-1931), painter and family friend, finished the job. Wickenden's catalogue notes, perhaps leaning here and there on Bourgeois' notes, are used in this volume to describe the paintings mentioned in the correspondence and other publications.

DEALERS AND CONNOISSEURS

Time, money, housing, a catalogue. What else is required to host a number of paintings by young and old masters? Time is definitely an issue. Money takes care of housing, the cost of a catalogue, and import duties. As we will see, money can be saved through warm relationships with customs officers. However, the question is, collecting what and when? It should be possible for collectors to do all the purchasing themselves. But most of them are too busy making money, therefore they engage dealers to do the scouting, the bidding on auctions and sales, and the subsequent purchases. Dealers may bid or buy uncommissioned, always in the hope that they can sell their purchase, since these people do not only buy. Part of their job is selling, for which salesmanship is required; they have to be convincing about their expertise and taste. They have to guide their clients in terms of what, where, and how to buy. German connoisseur Wilhelm Bode even went so far as to credit the growth of private collections to the taste of their dealers (Scallen 2004: 399, footnote 34). Furthermore, art dealers may subsequently have their acquisitions cleaned, crated, shipped, stored, insured, and double billed as instructed to save some import duties. Sometimes, they even organize public relations, such as sending announcements to newspapers.

Van Horne began engaging dealers early in his collecting days. Knowles (2004: 287ff) mentions Joseph Duveen, R. F. Knoedler, Blakeslee Galleries, Daniel Cottier, and Stephan Bourgeois. But there were more. In this book the focus is mostly on Van Horne's Dutch dealers, initially: Leonardus Salomon, who called himself Leo Nardus, and Machiel van Gelder, who called himself Michel Van Gelder. They were the ones who sold Van Horne the paintings with questionable attributions. They also made a large contribution to Van Horne's social and business upheavals, one of which involved the so-called Widener scandal in 1908. More about this later on.

After 1908 other dealers come into focus because Nardus then became the "silent partner" of Dutch dealer Herman van Slochem and Stephan Bourgeois. Van Slochem had been dealing art around 1894 in New York, as Nardus and Van Gelder had, and he would marry Nardus sister, Esther Salomon. Both Nardus' wife Lany and Van Slochem's wife Esther, would have children in the same years, 1905 and 1908. Bourgeois was a German-born French dealer and cousin of Nardus' wife.

Van Horne had connections to more Dutch dealers; for example, E. J. van Wisselingh (1848-1912) from Amsterdam, his Scottish wife Isabella van Wisselingh-Angus (1858-1931), and the Van Wisselingh's business partner, P. C. Eilers (1864-1936). Then there were Ernst (1858-1907) and René Gimpel (1881-1945) and the Duveen Brothers, whose father originated from the Netherlands, and after a start there set up a business in England.[66] Florrie, the Duveen Brothers' youngest sister, was married to René Gimpel. While the "Dutchness" of the Duveens is somewhat tenuous, their contribution to the Van Horne collection is worth exploring, genuine dealers as they were.

After the 1908 scandal, important collectors, Van Horne among them, started to engage connoisseurs on a larger scale. According to Samuels (1987: 311), the roles of art critics and art historians at that time were intimately connected with art dealership. The story of the development of the Van Horne collection clearly demonstrates this. The Dutch connoisseurs who are part of this story are Cornelius Hofstede de Groot (1863-1930), Abraham Bredius (1855-1946), and Bredius' lover,

---

66   See Secrest (2004).

Joseph Otto Kronig (1887-1984). The Germans are Wilhelm
Von Bode (1845-1929), Max J. Friedländer (1867-1958), W. R.
Valentiner (1880-1958), and August Mayer (1885-1944). There
was also an Italy-based art connoisseur, Bernard Berenson
(1865-1959), whom we already saw lounging on the Van Horne
couch in 1914 nursing his cough.

VAN HORNE'S DUTCHNESS

Sir William Van Horne & Billy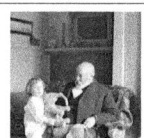

William Van Horne, born in 1864, descended from a family
that had left Holland in 1635. He could look back on a line
of successful ancestors. They had some "class," so to speak.
Knowles (2004: 17ff) notes that the first Van Horne to come to
the United States, Jan Cornelisse, a citizen from Amsterdam,
arrived in New Amsterdam in 1635 and helped establish the
Dutch colonial settlement on Manhattan Island. His grandson
Abram owned a residence on Wall Street and several mills. In
1752, his great-grandson also named Abram, "erected a large,
steep-gabled residence, known as the White House, from
which the present town of Whitehouse, New Jersey, takes its
name." This Abram, a minister, was our William's grandfather.

William's father was a lawyer, but he died when William was
ten, which meant that William came to understand the value
of money at a tender age.

William was so proud of his Dutch ancestry that he named
cities and towns after famous Dutch men. In 1886 he named
the city of Vancouver after the famous captain George Vancouver (1757-1798), whose family originated in the Dutch town
of Coevorden. Five years later, he named the town next to
the Samson 137 Reserve, one of the four Plains Cree Nations,

south of Edmonton, Hobbema after his beloved painter Meyndert Hobbema (1638-1709).[67] Van Horne's pride in his Dutchness took other forms as well. Knowles (2004: 311) notes that Van Horne gave much thought to Billy's nursery at the Covenhoven estate. The room featured at least "one mantel constructed of Dutch picture tiles," and he painted a "joyous mural" for young William. The photograph of Billy's nursery in Sullivan (2007: 56) shows that the mural depicts Dutch children with aprons and wooden shoes, as does the illustration on the chest behind Billy's bed.

According to Berton (1971: 45) Van Horne even looked Dutch. He describes his eyes as impassive and ice-blue, "the product of his Dutch-German ancestry." Since being of Dutch descent seemed to have been important for Van Horne, he must have enjoyed being in touch with Dutch fine arts dealers.

✕

---

67   Although some websites about the town of Hobbema state that Van Horne collected Hobbema paintings, the Van Horne inventory does not list one Hobbema. (By the way, the Hobbema Reserve was renamed the Maskewacis [Bear Hills] Nation in January 2014.)

DEALERS AT THEIR LEISURE

Michel Van Gelder
Courtesy
Barbara van der Veen
➔

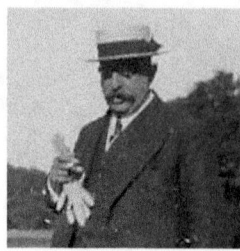

A Sea Sketch
Michel Van Gelder
Montreal Museum of Fine Arts
1945931
➔.

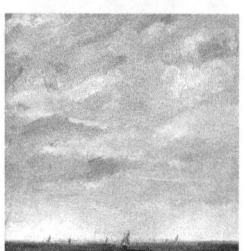

Booted Bantam
@Wikipedia / public domain
➔

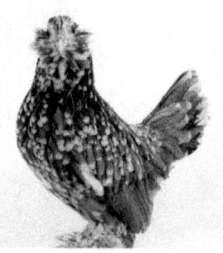

Self portrait
Leo Nardus
Courtesy Edward Winter
➔

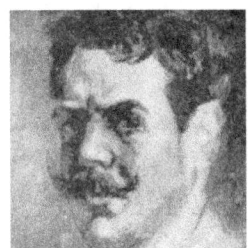

Nardus playing chess
public domain
➔

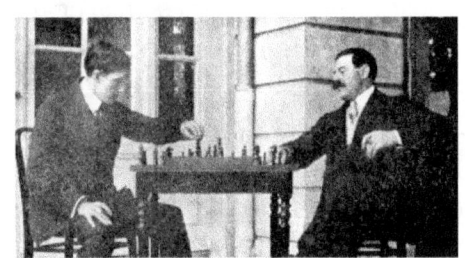

Nardus fencing
Courtesy
Edward Winter
➔

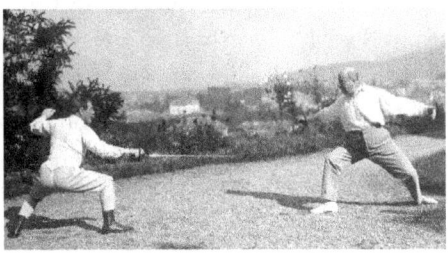

CHAPTER 3

DEALERS / THE JOHNSON BLUES

GROSS (2009: 101) notes that most American collectors started with Barbizon painters, with or without the help of dealers. According to Goldstein (2000: 87) it was Paul Durand-Ruel, whose father established an art gallery in Paris in the early 1830s, who admired, protected, and started to sell the works of Barbizon painters. Adding that Auguste Renoir once said, "Durand-Ruel [...] alone helped me to eat when I was hungry." Heijbroek and Wouthuysen (1999: 56) note that from 1875 on, Cottier introduced the Barbizon School (and the The Hague School) to North America. How and why the American taste developed is beyond the scope of this volume.

According to Saarinen (1958/68: 13), the Barbizon craze started with wealthy Bostonians such as Warren, Shaw, and Brimmer. Saltzman (2008: 145: 168) describes the Barbizon landscapes of Henry Clay Frick as "lush, melancholy images of the countryside outside of Paris, with its fields, gigantic trees and moody skies." [68] Quodbach (2005: 56) describes the Barbizons as wallpaper in the mansions of the American *nouveaux riche*.

By the turn of the century, Barbizons were still sold to Pennsylvania industrialists, but by then they were considered passé by Bostonian collectors. Dekker (1996: 73) argues that due to the great demand, "better works by the French school became

---

68   Henry Clay Frick (1849-1919) started as a partner in Carnegie Steel Company and later became chairman of United States Steel (Saltzman 2008: 145ff).

scarce, and substitutes, as *The Collector* wrote in 1892, therefore had to be found." According to a publication accompanying the 2007 exhibition, *The Hague School and the School of
Barbizon*, in the Municipal Museum in The Hague, The Hague
School painters were influenced by the Barbizon painters and
started to paint *en plein air* as well. In short, American collectors were first in thrall to the Barbizon School and later to the
The Hague School.

Like other American collectors, Van Horne started his
collection in the 1880s with the affordable and bountiful Barbizon School. In 1891, "Gad" described Van Horn's collection
in the *Toronto News* in terms of his elegant home, cabinets
of rare china (collections of Satsuma ware), a Rembrandt in
a deft mingling of light, a Gainsborough almost as desirable,
works of Dutch and French masters, books, maps, mathemat-
ical instruments, and a collection of swords (Sullivan 2007:
51-52). By 1892, Van Horne had catalogued his collection under
the endearing title "Catalogue of my Oil Paintings at 6th December 1892. (This book contains only those which I regard as
of superior class) WC Van Horne." [69] In it were indeed many
Monticellis, Ribots, Michels, and Bonvins. Van Horne's attrac-
tion to Barbizons might be explained by his close ties to James
J. Hill during the 1890s. [70] Hill's collection counted many
Barbizons.

By 1905, when time and money for the purchase of art
were loosening up again, Van Horn had bought a few more.
Caroline Pierson listed them all in her 1926 letter: "There was

---

69   This handwritten catalogue is in the Montreal Museum of Fine Arts. In addition
      to the name of the painter and the title, price and measurements of the paintings,
      Van Horne also provided rough sketches of them, in: https://www.gallery.ca/en/
      see/collections/artwork.php?mkey=14688 (last accessed March 2014).

70   James J. Hill (1838-1916), manager of the St. Paul and Pacific Railroad, later
      called the Great Northern, was the one who suggested, in 1881, to hire Van Horne,
      then head-inspector at the Chicago Milwaukee and St. Paul Railroad, as manager
      of Canadian Pacific Railroad (Pierson 1929:4-6).

a beautiful collection of paintings from the Barbizon school; a small Corot, two Daubigny's, a Rousseau, a threatening Courbet,[71] a portrait of George Sand by Troyon, further Monet, Delacroix, Géricault, Ribot, Daumier, Diaz, Salvator Rose, Cézanne." [72]

---

71   This is Courbet's 1871 *Still-Life*, listed as VH 206 and no. 137 in Cat. 1933. It was bought in 1913 from Alexander Reid (Glasgow). Later, the National Gallery of Art in Ottawa bought it and lists it as follows: "oil on canvas, 24 × 32 cm. Purchased 1978 with the assistance of a grant from the Government of Canada under the terms of the Cultural Property Export and Import Act National Gallery of Canada (no. 23004)."

   Sentenced to six months in the Sainte-Pélagie prison in Paris for his part in the 1871 populist uprising known as the Paris Commune, Courbet's only subjects during his incarceration were the flowers and fruit brought to him by his sister Zoé and his friends. These still-lifes, some of which were reworked after his release, mark the summit of his final stage of work." See https://www.gallery.ca/en/see/collections/artwork.php?mkey=14688 (last accessed March 2014).

72   The Wickenden catalogue records this list as follows:
   • VH 211 Rousseau, Theodore (1812-1867). *The Great Oaks of Bas-Breau, Forest of Fontainebleau*. Ⓦ: From Blakeslee & Co. NY. 1889. Ⓗ: 5 000, Cost more.
   • VH 212 Rouseau. *The Brook: Autumnal Landscape*. Ⓦ: From Frederick A. Chapman NY. 1905. Ⓗ: 1 000.
   • VH 213 Rousseau. *Thatched Cottages*. Ⓦ: From Blakeslee & Co, NY. Ⓗ: 50, Not Rousseau.
   • VH 215 Troyon, Constant (1810-1865). *La Guitariste, A Portrait of Georges Sand*. Ⓦ: From Cottier & Co. NY.
   • VH 203 Gericault, Theodore (1791-1824). *Study of a Negro's Head*. Ⓦ: Panel. Cardboard.
   • VH 200 Delacroix, Eugene (1799-1863). *Samson and Delilah*. Ⓦ: From Messrs. Carfax & Co. London. Ⓗ: 3 000.
   • VH 223 Ribot, Theodule-Auguste (1823-1891). *Children of the Artist*. Ⓦ: From the Edwin Davis Sale, NY. 1889. Ⓗ: 400.
   • VH 224 Ribot. *Balzac in his Study*. Ⓦ: Bought from Scott & Sons, Montreal. Ⓗ: 600.
   • VH 225 Ribot. *Still-Life: Apple and Pot*. Ⓦ: From Blakeslee's & Co. NY. Ⓗ: 400.
   • VH 226 Ribot. *A Little Girl Seated*. Ⓗ: 300.
   • VH 227 Ribot. *The Artist's Daughters Reading*. Ⓗ: 300.
   • VH 228 Daumier, Honore (1808-1879). *A Musical Party*. Ⓦ: Purchased from Gimpel & Wildenstein. NY. 1910. Ⓗ: 20 000.
   • VH 207 Diaz de la Pena, Narcisse-Virgile (1807-1876). *Venus Disarming Cupid*. Ⓦ: From the Tournier Collection, Paris. Ⓗ: 100.
   • VH 208 Diaz. *Forest Interior with Shepherdess and Sheep*. Ⓦ: From Hazeltine & Co. Philadelphia. 1886. Ⓗ: 150.
   • VH 209 Diaz. *The Tryst*. Ⓗ: 150.
   • VH 210 Diaz. *La Plaine de Barbizon*. Ⓦ: From Boussod, Valadon & Co. Paris. 1891. Ⓗ: 100.

As the Barbizon School ran out of fashion, or out of paintings, Dutch dealers who specialized in the Dutch School emerged. As early as 1893 at the Chicago World Exhibition, Leo Nardus came into Van Horne's sphere. German connoisseur William Von Bode, mentioned in Bourgeois' 1927 letter, was at the exhibition.[73] From his diary (Bode 1930: 99, 128), we know that both Van Horne and Leo Nardus were there as well: "In Chicago I met Sir William Van Horne, the well-known Director of the Canadian Pacific Railway. I accepted his invitation to Montreal and he brought me to the collectors there." Von Bode (1930: 128) also remarked in his diary that someone had unfortunately just exchanged a pendant of a woman's portrait with the "art dealer Leo Nardus (recte: Leonardus Salomon)." There is a fair chance that Van Horne also met with Nardus during the exhibition.

Since Van Horne's connections with dealers, connoisseurs, and so on can be best shown by quoting his elaborate correspondence, I must mention that most of these letters were written in English by people whose first language was Dutch, German, or French. The letters, therefore, contain many spelling errors such as "think" instead of "thing," "portret" instead of "portrait," or older English spellings such as "wonderfull." Often the syntax differs from standard English, but this is only changed here when the original was incomprehensible. Punctuation such as periods were often not followed by a capitalized word. The length and monetary units have been unified. Apart from the syntax, the main infelicities – especially spelling and punctuation – have been fixed in order to eliminate distractions from the letters' contents.[74]

• VH 166 Rosa, Savalator (1615-1673). *Mountainous Seashore with Soldiers.* ⬜: From Frederick A. Chapman, NY. 1905. ⬜: 1 000, Period Picture, but NOT Rosa.

73 Arnold William Bode (1845-1929) was ennobled Von Bode in 1913.

74 Both the AGO's Van Horne Family Fonds in Toronto and the Hofstede de Groot Fonds in the RKD in The Hague contains an extended correspondence between

The flattering endings of the letters – hopes that Van Horne would get better, reminders and kindest regards to his lovely family, and thanks for pleasant stays at Covenhoven, the New Brunswick estate, or the Montreal mansion – have been omitted. But it should be kept in mind that every dealer's letter ended in "Hoping that ..." followed by best wishes in a sea of politesses.

TWO DUTCH DEALERS: NARDUS AND VAN GELDER

The first invoice in the Van Horne Family Fonds, signed by Leo Salomon and dated 1894, reads: "Received from: Sir William C. van Horne, Montreal the sum of: Three Thousand Nine Hundred Dollars being the amount of two pictures sold to him according to the notes. Montreal, Nov. 29, 1894. Leonardus Salomon." [75] Under this note Van Horne scribbled what was purchased: "Cuyp – Marine + cattle 2 500[76] and Constable – Landscape with River 1 400 ($3 900)." [77]

The next invoice is signed by Leo Nardus (the name Salomon would only legally be changed to Nardus in 1911). It was "for the sum of Two Hundred fifty dollars One painting by Salomon

---

Van Horne, his dealers, and some of the connoisseurs. In addition, the John G. Johnson Fonds in the Philadelphia Museum of Art archives contains letters that bear witness to the mishaps of Van Horne's most trusted dealers, Nardus and Van Gelder. As far as is relevant, they are quoted from hereafter.

75   Letter in VHFF (5/11).

76   VH 43 Cuyp, Aelbert (Dordrecht 1620-1691). *Riverview with Cattle*. ▣: Near the foreground on the riverbank, seven cows are grazing, two lying down. Beyond the wide expanse of quiet water are several ships with raised sails flying the Dutch flag, and another at anchor [...]. Signed at the lower right, 'Cuyp.' Panel. H. 10½ in, W. 16⅜ in (26 × 41½ cm). Painted about 1650-60. In poss. of L. Salomon 1894. ▣: $3 000.

77   VH 13 Constable, John (East Bergholt 1776–Hampstead 1837). *View on the Stour*. ▣: The banks of this tidal river that separates Suffolk from Essex were Constable's favorite sketching grounds from boyhood and throughout life. Bedham, East Berghold, the mills and locks with their accompanying surroundings furnished subjects for many of his pictures [...]. Panel-board. H. 9½ in, W. 22 in (24 cm × 56 cm). From Nardus and Van Gelder. 1900. ▣: 1 500.

van Ruysdael,[78] representing: Dutch River from the collection: Swelheim, Holland, that I guarantee to be genuine. New York Dec. 27/1895 – signed Leo Nardus." [79] As will be discussed later, it is unlikely that at that time a Swelheim collection existed anywhere in the world.

The Wickenden catalogue states that the painting was bought in 1900, but the invoice is dated December 27, 1895. As for provenance, Wolfgang Stechow (1975: 133) refers only to the Van Horne collection, not to Nardus and Van Gelder, let alone to the Swelheim collection.

It is time to introduce Nardus and Van Gelder properly, especially since in art history circles, Van Gelder's name is said to be written with invisible ink.

Leonardus Salomon/Leo Nardus

Leonardus Salomon / LeoNardus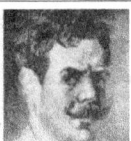

In the Van Horne Family Fonds (p. 12), Leonardus Salomon is referred to as "Leo Nardus, Dutch art dealer and reputed

---

78   VH 51 Ruysdael, Salomon van (Haarlem, 1600-1670). *Marine View.* ▣: On the greyish waters of a Dutch River is a fishing boat with sails raised, a flag flying at the mast-head and another at the peak, moving out of the left side of the picture, followed by a skiff [...]. Canvas. H. 7⅜ in. W. 9 in. (19 cm × 23 cm). In the Swelheim coll., Holland. From Nardus & Van Gelder, 1900. No. The attribution to Salomon Van Ruysdael, was confirmed by C. Hofstede de Groot, and by Dr. Friedländer in 1909. ▣: $3 000.

    Stechow (1975: 113) records this painting under no. 300 "Segelboot mit Beiboot. 1. Fährt nach l. (in volle Breite, das Beiboot reicht über die Bildmitte hinaus). Dahinter wird ein ferner Kirchturm sichtbar (r. von Hauptsegel). R. im Mittelgrund eine Landzunge mit zwei Häusern und einem Segelboot; l. davon fünf Stangen im wasser. –Skizzenhaft. Ca. 1660-62. L. 19 × 23. Sammlung Sir William van Horne (†) in Montreal."

79   Invoice, December 27, 1895, in VHFF (5/11).

swindler in old masters [sic] paintings." Other sources for information about Salomon, who called himself Nardus from 1895 on, include Winter (2013),[80] a fencing blog, newspaper articles, and a letter by his wife, Mrs. Lany Nardus-Bourgeois.

Citing Narriman El Kateb-Ben Romdhane's biographical sketch in the catalogue of the 1997 exhibition of Nardus's paintings in Carthage, Edward Winter (2012) reports that "Léonardus Nardus was born in Utrecht on 5 May 1868, the son of an antique dealer, Emanuel Salomon, and Alida Ballen. After training in art and antiques he undertook in 1889 a brief, unsuccessful gold-hunting expedition in Argentina." [81] From 1894 on, he worked as an art dealer, first in the United States and then in Paris.

Winter also cites a 1917 catalogue for a sale of Nardus' paintings and drawings, which states that Salomon *"fit ses études à l'Académie des Beaux Arts d'Amsterdam (Altmann)."* Lopez (2008: 36) expands on the compact overview in El Kateb-Ben Romdhane's 1997 catalogue:

> Nardus had apprenticed in the picture trade in Paris with the distinguished firm of Bourgeois Frères. His greatest commercial success, however, came not in Europe but in the United States, where he was a frequent visitor during the 1890s and early 1900s. Fluent in four languages, a champion swordsman, and an internationally known chess master, Nardus was a highly charismatic individual, and he used his charm to devastating effect in his business dealing, taking advantage of America's newly rich industrial millionaires, who had only just begun collecting art.

80   Winter's blog can be found at http://www.chesshistory.com/winter/extra/nardus. html (last accessed in October 2014).

81   Note that the civil registry of the municipality of the city of Utrecht gives the name of his mother as Catharina Alida Berlijn. See http://nl.wikipedia.org/wiki/ Leo_Nardus (last accessed in March 2014).

Lopez describes how Nardus made millions by selling newly manufactured fakes, old copies that would not sell in Europe "and, most astonishingly, an array of utterly undistinguished antique-shop pictures that he attributed, with a twirl of his handlebar moustache, to great artists such as Vermeer, Velásquez, Rembrandt, Turner, Botticelli, Raphael, and Leonardo da Vinci."

Quodbach (2005: 77) writes that Nardus, sometimes assisted by a Belgian companion, a Michel van Gelder, sometimes sold genuine paintings, "but alternated this with attributing famous names to insignificant works or doctoring them."

By now one will realize that collectors should have been wary of Nardus' merchandise. That Nardus was also a shrewd salesman is clear from Gaehtgens und Paul's (1997: 282) edited version of Wilhelm Von Bode's 1930 autobiography. In 1893, in Chicago, connoisseur Von Bode came across a man's portrait by Memling that was traded for DM4 500 to dealer Leo Nardus. "Bode complained that Nardus now wanted 120 000 francs for it." "The price seemed too high too me," wrote Von Bode, adding that he bought it anyway for his Kaiser-Friedrich-Museum.

Nardus' next communication with Van Horne, dated February 16, 1897, was about *Dutch River* by Ruysdael and featured a modest letterhead: 543 Fifth Avenue, New York.[82] The letter was accompanied by newspaper clippings about the enormously successful *Union League Exhibition*. Nardus wrote that Van Horne's "little Hals" had been greatly admired and that his Cuyp had made quite a sensation: "Mr. Johnson came over expressly and was tremendously taken with it, he left it with sorrow."[83] Here we see Nardus keeping his client informed

---

82 Letter in VHFF (5/1).
83 John G. Johnson (1841-1917), a fine art collector, was the son of a Philadelphia blacksmith and the greatest corporation lawyer in the English-speaking world (Saarinen 1958/1968: 92). Fine art collectors Pierpont J. Morgan and P. A. B. Widener and M. C. B. Borden were among his clients.

and, as he knew that collectors thrive on their peers' envy, reassuring him of his peers' fervour to own such a nice Cuyp.

As noted earlier, Caroline Pierson mentioned "4 Halses" in her 1926 letter, and four Halses were present at the 1933 exhibition. The "little Hals" referred to by Nardus was the portrait of Samuel Ampzing (1590-1632), a Dutch minister, poet, and language purist, which is now in a private collection.[84] In his February 16 letter, Nardus had also enclosed the catalogue in which he had put the "Rembrandt girl," although not under Sir William's name: "It has been very much loved and appreciated here," he wrote, "it was the star of the collection." It is unclear which "Rembrandt girl" this was, let alone whether it was, in fact, a Rembrandt. It was not among the four "Rembrandts" at the 1933 exhibition in Montreal, nor was it included in the Schedule of Pictures referring to no. 3 at the Benedict Richard Van Horne and Miss Lucy Adaline Van Horne estate (1940-1984) insurance form.

In this same letter, Nardus went on about the Holbein he did not like and mentioned the photographs of "our" studio and reception room, and "our" photograph "as remembrance of the charming week spent with you." The letter, signed by Nardus and Van Gelder, finished with "our warmest thanks for your cordial reception." Having enjoyed Van Horne's hospitality, Nardus requested that his former host "transfer please these feelings to the Ladies [Van Horne's wife, sister, mother, and daughter] and to Ben," showing his characteristic charisma and charm.

Conway (1905: 137), who illustrated his article with the portrait of Samuel Ampzing (the "little Hals"), wrote that Van Horne (who must have enjoyed reading this article):

---

84   This Ampzing was VH69 in the collection.

also possesses a fine half-length portrait of a man, by
Frans Hals, dated 1639, a characteristic example of the
free and powerful work of the painter's middle period. It
would scarcely be possible to see the man more vividly if
he stood alive before us than we can see him through the
medium of this picture. This, in fact, is how Frans Hals
saw him, with eyes that could see as few men's can see.

Winter (2013) writes that Nardus went back to Paris after
the turn of the century and started to develop his own painting
skills. He also married Hélène Jeanne Marie Bourgeois.

He subsequently lived in the outskirts of Paris: "first in
Château d'Arnouville-les-Gonesses and, subsequently, at the
Château de Suresnes, which he later named Léa-Flory after his
two daughters born in 1905 and 1908." [85]

Château d'Arnouville-les-Gonesses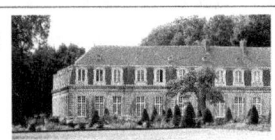

Lopez (2007) reports that Hélène Jeanne Marie's father, art
dealer Stephan Bourgeois, had died in 1899 and his brother
Gaspard died in 1904. By marrying the seventeen-year-old
Hélène (Lany) in 1904 after her uncle Gaspard died, Nardus,
then thirty-seven, gained a stake in the gallery that from then
on operated – on and off – under the name Nardus-Bourgeois.
The latter Bourgeois was Stephan Bourgeois (1881-1964),
Gaspard's son and Lany's cousin. [86] This Bourgeois is the one

---

85   For a nice family portrait, see: http://www.posamentir-stein.de/stephanbour-
geois1840.html (last accessed in October 2014).

86   Hubert Stephan Bourgeois was born in 1881 in Cologne, and died in 1964 in New
York. In 1921 Stephan Bourgeois would marry Marie-Thérèse Duncan, born

that will be often mentioned hereafter. He would turn out to become one of Van Horne's most faithful correspondents; he was also the one who did not manage – because of the war and Bennie's non-cooperation – to bring the catalogue to a good end.

Developing painting skills and establishing himself with a castle and a family was, of course, not all Nardus did. During the 1904-1910 exhibition in the Mauritshuis in The Hague he presented three pictures, in 1905, he presented *Still Life with Meat and Poultry in Arnouville* and in 1906 *A laughing man with a globe*, "attributed to Moreelse" at the same city.[87] Many more would follow, but listing them is beyond the scope of this book. Nardus died in 1955, in Tunisia.

The quotations in Pijl (2005) combined with the letterhead of Nardus' letter show that the latter shared space with Michel Van Gelder. That Nardus not only shared space, but also closely worked with Michel Van Gelder is apparent from a *New York Times* article of February 14, 1897, about the lost art of making vitreous, iridescent plaques "traced by some to the Egyptians, and taken to Spain by the Moors" had come up "on a question of customs dues presented by the artist Michael Van Gelder of 354 Fifth Avenue."

It is now time to investigate Nardus' long-time business partner, Michel van Gelder.

Therese Kruger, who was adopted by Isadora Duncan (hence her name). See http://articles.latimes.com/1987-12-17/news/mn-29286_1_isadora-duncan (last accessed in October 2014).

87   See: http://www.archive.org/stream/abridgedcataloguoomaurrich/abridgedcataloguoomaurrich_djvu.txt (last accessed in February 2014).

Michel van Gelder

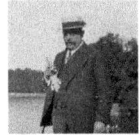

Van Gelder's Amsterdam birth certificate lists him as Machiel van Gelder, * Amsterdam, 10 December 1864, † unknown. Van Gelder's death certificate from the Belgian town of Uccle shows that he was born a son of Léon van Gelder and Henriette Swelheim. The *Nieuw Israelitisch Weekblad* of 23 November, 1877, announced Van Gelder's *bar mitswa* for Sunday November 24, 1877 in Amsterdam; same parents as already mentioned. In other words, Van Gelder was from the Netherlands, not from Belgium, but that would change.

According to the Amsterdam Civil Registry, Machiel Van Gelder left Amsterdam for South America on 21 January, 1889 – to go gold hunting with Nardus.[88] In the first part of this section about Nardus and Van Gelder, I mentioned the 1895 invoice about the sale of the Ruysdael. In the Wickenden catalogue, the names Nardus and Van Gelder are crossed out (but still very readable), the date of sale would have been in 1900 and the Ruysdael, representing *Dutch River* would be from the Swelheim collection. True? Van Gelder's mother, Henriette Swelheim (1843-1910) was the orphaned daughter of an Amsterdam diamante cutter.[89] It is unlikely that the painting came from a "collection" of her parents or grandparents. Later

---

88   See http://www.leonardus.fr (last accessed in October 2014).
89   E-mail of December 3, 2009 by Carla Swelheim. "Michel must have been a peculiar man. Streetwise. Also, there are two more painters/art dealers in the Swelheim family. They are Lion Schulman (member of the so-called Laren school) and his son David Schulman. David's brother, Louis was an art dealer. We talk now about the second half of the 19th and the first halve of the 20th century."

on, more about Van Gelder's career, which proved as colourful as his paintings and his bantams.

In 1896 the *New York Times* featured an article about custom duties, mentioning both Nardus and Van Gelder. One year later, in 1897, Michel Van Gelder (he changed the name Machiel to Michel) is profiled in the *New York Times* of February 16, 1897, as "a Dutch artist, residing at Fifth Avenue 354," an address he shared with Nardus. However, the 1895 Ruysdael sale – mentioning the fake Swelheim collection – and the *New York Times'* clippings provide a strong impression that Van Gelder was a dealer as well. This is confirmed in his letter of January 12, 1900, in which Van Gelder thanked Sir William for his kind letter.[90] He expressed the hope to see him the following week in New York, adding: "James has orders to serve us a little dinner for the occasion." Van Gelder then went on about "some objects sent from Paris, but not the vases, as they might break."

In another letter, March 7, 1900, Van Gelder reminisced about his visit to Van Horne: "with utmost pleasure the moments passed together, your chess playing was excellent, our games were unusually interesting."[91] In this same letter, Van Gelder came back to business: "Now Sir William, I am about to leave, I am anxious to know what you think of the 2 bronze statues; if you find time please write me at c/o North American Trust Co., Cuba." What was Van Gelder doing in Cuba?

Dutch biographer Pierson (1929: 63) writes that Van Horne went to Cuba in January 1900 to find out whether he would get a permit for building a railway, "within two months he was back in Montreal, as enthusiastic about the new Cuban Company as he had been eighteen years earlier about the Canadian Pacific." Pierson goes on: "At the start of the establishment of

---

90   Letter in VHFF (4/11).
91   Letter in VHFF (4/11).

the Cuba Company in April 1900 he [Van Horne] indicated its purpose as: to develop the natural resources of Cuba in every possible way. Capital was determined to be $8 000 000 – divided into 160 shares of $50 000. He placed them among friends who realized that this would not render any profit for the first years."

Van Gelder seems to have been one of those friends investing in the Cuban railway. He extended his relationship with Van Horne from dealer to friend and co-investor, and later he became involved in Van Horne's other businesses. While Van Horne busied himself in Cuba, Van Gelder and Nardus must have done such good business in New York that they could afford to settle down. As I mentioned, Nardus settled in Paris, where he became known *as l'homme aux cinquante millions*. Van Gelder lived in Paris too, at Avenue du Bois 72, but moved to the Belgian town of Uccle (now a suburb of Brussels), in 1903. According to Lowie (1997: 157) Van Gelder lived first in Villa Betsy, date and address not known, and subsequently took up residence at Zeecrabbe, sometimes referred to as Chateau Zeecrabbe, De Frélaan 66 in Ukkel (Flemish spelling) on July 8, 1903.

One year later Van Gelder's residence was said to be London, but perhaps he lived there only long enough to get married. The June 18, 1904 marriage certificate (entry 125) in the Register Office in the District of Kensington, County of London, reads that Michel van Gelder, age 39, bachelor, profession: artist painter, residence at time of marriage 11 Oxford Gardens, Notting Hill, married Irma Goretzky, age 23, condition spinster, no profession, residence at time of marriage Hyde Park Hotel, Knightsbridge.

In that same year, around the same time, Nardus married Lany Bourgeois in London.[92] There cannot have been much time for a honeymoon because Van Gelder established the *Club Avicole du Barbu nain* (Ukkel Booted Bantams Club) in Uccle the same year. Websites about "Ukkel booted bantams" [chickens] name Michel van Gelder, also known as "Dutch mecenas Van Gelder," as the man who, around 1905, succeeded in breeding about a thousand bantams a year.[93]

Van Gelder's breeding of bantams, travels, and fine house bear witness that his American business had been very successful. Soon, he deemed that being a merchant or dealer was beneath and beyond him. Lopez (2007) wrote about Van Gelder's newly acquired status and that Van Gelder, like Nardus, claimed to be a gentleman, not a merchant. "I am not dealing in pictures," he once told Johnson, "but simply ceding to you some works of art which I know you love and which help to enrich your collection."

However, in the same letter of March 7, 1900, about chess playing and a shipment of bronze statues, Van Gelder contradicts this self-label. In it he also thanks Sir William for his kind letter and mentions his new acquaintances, Mr. Hill,[94]

---

92   See: http://nl.wikipedia.org/wiki/Leo_Nardus (last accessed in February 2014). Witnesses to Van Gelder's marriage were a few Salomonson brothers.

93   The website http://www.ukkelsebaardkriel.be/ elaborates in Dutch, on Van Gelder's bantam breeding activities.

94   Mr. Hill was James Jerome Hill (1838-1916), who in 1881 recommended hiring Van Horne as manager of its construction (Knowles 2004). Comparing Mary Berenson's remark about Van Horne's "acres" of Barbizons, the *American Art News* of January 10, 1914 cited Bredius commenting on his recent visit to the collection of James Hill: "It is a magnificent collection, the best, perhaps in the world of the Barbizon school – Corot, Troyon, Millet, Daugbigny and Courbet. Of each master he has perfect specimens." A client-friendly remark? See: http://www.biographi.ca/en/bio/van_horne_william_cornelius_14E.html (last accessed March 2014).

Mr. Hopkins[95] and Mr. Berwind.[96] These were potential customers, which Van Horne must have directed to Van Gelder's
New York gallery. Merchant or not, the fact that Van Gelder
was known as a collector as well as a gentleman can be gleaned
in *Baedeker* (1910: 148). This travel guide warns people who
intend to travel from Brussels to Charleroi about the 'unimportant stations' of Forest, Uccle-Stalle, Uccle-Calevoet and
Linkebeek. However:

> At Uccle is the château of Zeecrabbe, belonging to M. van
> Gelder, who possesses a fine collection of 16th cent. wood-
> carvings and Italian and Delft fayence and a gallery of old
> Dekeyzer paintings (Rembrandt, Frans Hals, Alb. Cuyp,
> M. de Keyzer, S. van Ruysdael, A. Brouwer, Constable,
> Turner, Reynolds, early Flemish and Spanish masters,
> etc.). Visitors are admitted daily, except Sun., on applica-
> tion, 11-12 and 2-4.

Could it be that Van Gelder also attracted clients in this
way? Consider this report (originally in French) about members of the SOCIETÉ D' ARCHEOLOGIE DE BRUXELLES visiting the
Chateau Zeecrabbe[97] on Easter Monday 1912. It shows that
Van Gelder, artist, dealer, and breeder quite lived up to being
a "gentleman." In the report, Van Gelder, *Membre effectif de
notre société, le distingué collectionneur*, gladly guided his

---

95   Mr. Hopkins was George B. Hopkins, a New-York stockbroker, who supplied
     Virginia hams and stock tips to Van Horne (Knowles, 2004: 389). Mr. George B.
     Hopkins was a warm advocate of St. Andrews as a summer and yachting resort.
     Cf.: http://www.pendleburypress.ca/history/summerpeople/thompson_f_w.rtf,
     citing the *St. Andrews Beacon* of August 6, 1908.
96   J. E. Berwind was a founding member of the Cuba Company, which also had links
     to the house of Morgan and the coal business (Zanetti and Garcia, 2002: 294).
97   See page 10 of: http://scans.library.utoronto.ca/pdf/1/8/annuaire19123sociuoft/
     annuaire19123sociuoft.pdf (last accessed March 2014).

visitors through his gallery, which "invited them to live be-tween the splendors of the past harmonized with the comfort of the present." Paraphrased, the description of the entrance hall of the castle reads:

> Furnished with Italian Renaissance furniture; three paintings, Carel Fabritius' Good Samaritan, one Rem-brandt[98] and one Govert Flinck. The grand salon featured, apart from the tapestries, and panelling, some Italian primitives: Madonna and family (siennoies), a Filipino Lippi Nativity, a Neri di Bicci, and a Tintoretto. The small salon had gothic Flemish, Dutch, German paintings, a Thierri Bouts, the master of St. Ursule,[99] Gérard David and a Cranach, the Feast of Herodus (*si caractérestique*).

Chateau Zeecrabbe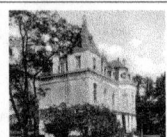

The description of the society's outing in Van Gelder's castle goes on about the pieces on the *rez-de-chaussée,* polychromes, marbles and bronzes of the Renaissance, wood sculptures, ancient fabrics and the Spanish/Moorish potteries that had figured at the 1910 Munich exhibition *Meisterwerke muhammedanischer Kunst*. On the first floor was the XVII Flemish century, which had been exhibited the previous year in Brussels, showing:

---

98   As we will see later on, this Rembrandt was Petronella Buys and Van Horne would
      not buy it.
99   See the letter of Jan. 29, 1909.

a portrait of a woman by Frans Hals. At the side an amaz-
ing landscape with a river and mills under a pale sky,
something by Rembrandt's palet (landscape in Kassel),
which is attributed to Carel Fabritius. We mention one
more Cuyp (horse riders by dusk); a small Brouwers, a
portrait of a woman by De Keyzer and View on Delft that
Gustave Van Zype recently described in his recent book
about the enigmatic Vermeer. Remarks about the en-
chanted visitors' being expressions of gratitude finished
this narrative.[100]

Lopez (2008: 43) is not impressed by Van Gelder: "one of
Leo Nardus' old business partners, a semi-legitimate dealer
and collector named Van Gelder, acquired a very dubious
Frans Hals *Boy with a Flute*. It answers to the description of
one of the rumored early Van Meegeren fakes, and today is not
considered genuine by the leading experts on Hals."
It is interesting to make a rough comparison between Nar-

---

100   Ukkel librarian Jan Vissers, who sent this report, and copies of Lowies' articles
e-mailed on July 13, 2009: "Van Gelder and his Hungarian [Ed. according to the
death certifcate, born in Podolin, Tchechoslovaquie] wife Irma Gorczky [Ed.:
Gorëtzky] resided in Chateau Zeecrabbe between 1910 [Ed.: 1903] and 1937 [Ed.
1935?]. In 1935 Goreczky had the castle demolished and in 1937 she sold the 5
hectares parc to the Sovjet Union. Currently it is the residence of the Russian
Embassy."
    Podolin was a Hungarian village until 1920. It then became a Tjechoslovakian
village. Since 1993 Podolin has been in Slovakia (E-mail from Piet van der Veen, a
relative of Van Gelder, Dec. 18, 2009).

dus and Van Gelder:

Leo Salomons/Nardus (1868-1951)	Machiel Van Gelder (1864-1929)
Son of a Utrecht antiquarian.	Son of an Amsterdam diamond cutter.
After a training in antiques, he went to Argentina to hunt for gold.	In 1889 went to Argentina to hunt for gold.
Both featured in 1896 art related articles in the *New York Times*. Both had the same address: 354, 5th Ave in New York. Both were known as amateur-painters. Both settled in Paris after 1900.	
Bought chateau d'Arnouville-les-Gonesses and around 1905 a chateau at Suresness, at the outskirts of Paris.	Bought a villa and then Chateau Zeecrabbe in Uccle in 1903.
Both married in June 1904 in London. Both were active art dealers and further trained in painting. After 1908 Nardus became Van Gelder's and Bourgeois' silent partner.	
Known for fencing: no. 3 at the 1912 Olympic Games, and he was a well-known as a chess player.	Known for breeding the Uccle Booted Bantam, and visiting many English and German Bantam exhibitions.

1905-1907: VAN HORNE'S TIME AND MONEY BECOME MORE PLENTIFUL

While Nardus and Van Gelder had left for Europe in 1900, Van Horne had left for Cuba in order to build a railway there. During the first years of that project he visited Cuba two to three times annually (Pierson 1929: 67-68) and Knowles (2004: 339-66 and 2010: 153-72).

Still, the railway in Cuba was not all that occupied Van Horne's time. The *Beacon* of April 23, 1903, mentions a seven thousand acre ranch that Sir William was establishing, "12 miles north of the city of Tumas, which is located on the Cuban railway about midway between Santiago and El Principe." Furthermore, energy, time, and money were spent on yachting and socializing. As Knowles phrases it: it was a time of daunting challenges, glaring shortage of funds and rising construction costs. However, Van Horne was incurring more expenses.

Sullivan (2007) mentions the development of the New Brunswick estate, Covenhoven: in 1900 peacocks, guinea hens, pea hens, ducks, African geese, Clydesdales, Tamworth pigs, horses and cows were brought in, in 1902 he had the residence there doubled in size and in 1905 a herd of the best Canadian French cattle was acquired.

As for activities, the *Biographical Sketch* in the Van Horne Family Fonds notes that Van Horne became executive director for more than forty companies and "was considered one of Canada's most successful businessmen." It lists Canadian Salt, Laurentide Paper, Dominion Iron and Steel, Dominion Steel, North West Land, Equitable Life Assurance, Royal Trust, and a number of western flour-milling and elevator companies that became quite profitable. Unfortunately, other ventures, such as a sardine-packing plant, a powder factory, and several gold-mining ventures failed.

Apart from his hectic schedule, he had political troubles to deal with too! The early years of the twentieth century saw troubles between America and Cuba, and in North America a fight erupted between Canadian Coal and the Dominion Iron and Steel Company on which boards he served. However, by 1905 things had calmed down and Van Horne took off on shopping sprees in New York, London, and Paris. A letter of March 29, 1905, shows that E. Gimpel, of the Amsterdam/New York Gimpel & Wildenstein Co. Inc., 250 Fifth Avenue, had met Van

Horne in New York. [101] Gimpel was now back in Paris (at 57 rue la Boétie) and wrote that he cherished the few hours he had spent in Van Horne's "charming company," that the little Goya was underway, that the Cesar Borgia would be put on a canvas, and that he would not forget the Velasquez. Gimpel would remain one of Van Horne's dealers. The "little Goya" mentioned had originally been in Van Gelder's possession. Van Gelder had sold it to Gimpel, and Gimpel sold it to Van Horne.[102]

Gimpel was also the one who had sold the Greuze to Van Horne at a time when there still seemed to be some financial restraint in the Van Horne household. Remember what Caroline Pierson wrote about the purchase of the Greuze, repeating what Van Horne's daughter had told her: "Once he was offered a fine Greuze, but right then he also thought that moment that he could not *'leisten' the Greuze*."[103] But, Adaline's mother got it for her birthday! (Even though she could not care less about

---

101   Letter in VHFF (2/18).
         "In the 1870's Nathan Wildenstein, began the business Wildenstein & Cie., selling 18th-century and old master paintings. In the early twentieth century, the business expanded to London and New York where their clients included Henry Clay Frick and J. P. Morgan. Georges Wildenstein (Paris 1892–Paris 1963) was art dealer, connoisseur, art historian and editor of the *Gazette des Beaux Arts*. He was the son of Nathan Wildenstein (1851-1934) who had founded the Paris based gallery that around the 20th century would expand to New York and London" (Secrest 2004: 82 ff).
         E. Gimpel (1858-1907) was married to Florence Duveen, the youngest sister of the Duveen Brothers" (Secrest 2004: 82 ff).
102   VH 106 Goya y Lucientes, Francisco Jose (Fuendetodos Aragon 1746 – Bordeaux 1828). *The Actress Rita Molines*. ▣: Leaning to the left, her head rests upon her right arm and hand [...]. In the Salomon coll, London; in poss. of Julius Bohler, Munich, in the coll. of Mr. Van Gelder, Uccle, Belgium. ▣: $25 000.
103   VH 164 Greuze (Jean Baptiste), (Tournus near Macon 1725 Paris 1805). *Portrait of Madame Mercier*. ▣: The title suggests the subject as being the wife of Greuze's intimate friend, L. S. Mercier, Author of *Entretiens du Palais Royal, 1786*, and *Tableau de Paris, 1781-1788*. Although the painter was a Royalist [...] 'Greuze never painted a more charming one.' Canvas H. 25¼ in. W. 21½ in (65.5 cm × 59.5 cm). From the coll. of the Baronne Auvray, Tours, France. In poss. of Messrs. Gimpel and Wildenstein, New York, 1905. ▣: $20 000.

it.) In a letter of April 14, 1905, Gimpel promised the arrival of the relined Greuze.[104]

Heijbroek and Wouthuysen (1999: 58) list the 1905 purchases from Van Wisselingh & Co.: two water colours with *Views in Spain*, a few etches by Bauer, a Breitner and M. Maris' picture *The Zaaier*. The fact that Van Horne was back in the collecting mood did not escape the attention of his former dealers.

Nardus' next letter of December 6, 1905, has a printed letterhead: Villa Léa, Suresnes, Seine.[105] During Van Horne's four financially lean years, he and Nardus must have stayed in touch and even have extended their relationship. It is remarkable that Conway (1905: 135) notes that "the Montreal collectors are by no means puppets in the hands of dealers; one and all of them choose for themselves. This is emphatically true of Sir Van Horne." Did Van Horne tell him that during Conway's visit to his Montreal mansion? Either way, Nardus wrote:

> I received your letter of November 22nd with certificates for 50 shares Laurentide preferred and cheque for £53.18.9 for dividend on this stock for which I am very obliged to you for this pleasant settlement, which finishes our account. I should like you to secure for me, if you advise 10 000 doll. capital of the Cuba Company Debenture stocks for which I will send you [a] cheque. I hope that you will come for sure in January next in London. I will come to meet you there at your arrival.

According to Knowles (2004: 373), both the Cuba and the Laurentide business adventures proved to be successful. She

---

104 Letter in VHFF (2/18).
105 Letter in VHFF (6/2). His first daughter, Lea, was born in 1905. His second daughter, Flory, was born in 1908 and caused the villa to be renamed Léa-Flory.

quotes from a 1910 letter by Van Horne to a friend: "The Laurentide Paper Company, of which I have been president for a good many years, is the most successful one in the country and its preferred and common stocks stand at something like 200." By 1910 this company paid an annual dividend of between six and eight percent. So, Nardus was now not only Van Horne's dealer and friend, but also a business partner.

A severe case of flu and the Johnson blues

From Nardus' letter of May 2, 1906, we learn that he sold Van Horne a little Gerard Dou, a little Greco, a Reynolds and *The Arab*, *Italian Woman*, and *Marine Heijst*; the last three by Nardus himself. [106] Furthermore, a Persian fort, and a Rhodes plate. And, that the Velasques and the Goya were being shipped, meaning, the Goya went from Van Gelder to Gimpel, and then Nardus shipped it. Nardus indicated that he would rather receive cash than Cuban debentures for it, as he had bought another picture and needed the money for it.

Nardus informed Van Horne in this letter that the Frans Halses were sold at the Hartz exposition and that J. P. Morgan had paid $200 000 for the two principal paintings and that four others had been sold "very dear." [107] Dealers keep

---

106   Letter in VHFF 6/2. The Dou is not listed in the Wickenden catalogue. The "little Greco" was VH 101 Theotocopuli, Domenico/ known as El Greco. Candia, Crete (about 1547–Toledo, Spain, 1614). *Head of St. Maurice*. ▣: Against a bluish background, his head turned and tilted slightly to the left, a young man with dark hair and eyes, slight moustache and beard, with a somewhat sad expression looks away in the direction from which the light falls [...]. Canvas H. 10 in, W. 8 in (25.5 cm × 21.5 cm). In the coll. of Don Antoni Vives, Madrid. [...] In *Art in America, 1916*: 31: Coll. of Sir William van Horne. ▣: $25 000.

     Three Reynolds are listed: VH 5, *Portrait of Master Gawler* from Wallis & Sons, the French Gallery in London. ▣: Not Reynolds, 250; VH 7, *The Countess of Carnarvon*. ▣: from T. H. Blakeslee, New York. ▣: 3 500; VH 24, *Two Studies after P. P. Rubens & Frans Snyders.*"

107   J. P. Morgan 1837-1913) was an American financier, banker and art collector. He merged the Carnegie Steel Company with other steel and iron business into the United States Steel Corporation in 1901 (Gross 2009: 65ff).

collectors posted on the acquisitions of other collectors, which makes sense and causes appetite, and perhaps Nardus also wanted to convey that his prices were not "very dear." In this same long letter Nardus also wrote that he would be pleased to let Sir William have the Goya and that he would charge $5 000 for it, adding: "about the Hals of Van G., I didn't hear anything and think I never shall." What Nardus is really saying is: better hurry up next time, these paintings go quickly.

For Van Horne the rest of the year was quiet with regard to his Dutch dealers and his family was happy: on June 12, 1906, his son Benedict married Edith Molson, daughter of Dr. William Alexander Molson, who was related to the Molsons of Molson Brewery.

On January 4, 1907, Van Horne got some news from art dealer René Gimpel (1881-1945).[108] His father, Ernest, married to Adele, Louis Vuitton's sister, had been forced to postpone his trip to Montreal because he was sick. René guessed that his father's sickness would keep him in bed for at least two more weeks. Three days later Ernest let Van Horne know that he "was taken sick yesterday with an attack of 'grippe' and hoped to visit within a few weeks." Only two days later the *New York Times* announced Ernest Gimpel's death.

A few days later René Gimpel was already thinking about business again. René was married to Florence, the youngest sister of Joseph Duveen, a British-born art dealer of Jewish Dutch decent who worked closely with Berenson. Van Horne replied to young Gimpel on May 3, 1907, saying that he would not bid for the picture by Raeburn: "I doubt if I could get the picture at the price, but, in any case, I do not wish to commit myself to any expenditure until after my return from Cuba. I should rather have a little extra money when I go to Paris."[109]

---

108   Letter in VHFF (7/19).
109   Letter in VHFF (7/20).

While Gimpel had been busy selling to Van Horne, two months earlier, on March 14, 1907, Philadelphia collector John Graver Johnson, (whom Van Gelder did not sell to, but just "ceded his works of art to") received a letter from Nardus that started with a soothing "My Dear Sir."[110] This letter reads like a lecture in the art of restoration, but that is not the reason it is quoted here. This letter indicates that the Widener affair, which would occur in 1908, was preceded by the "Johnson affair:" Nardus wrote:

> At last I have received the pictures and now after I had a fresh look at them I have to state loyally that all those pictures are correct.
>
> The Cuyp is in a very bad condition. Paint has peeled off and has been restored in an incompetent manner when they have cleaned this picture, with alcohol, they took off the cobalt varnish, which is very yellowish of color, and there you saw appear a grey bluish spot. This made you believe that the picture was modern. I took off myself all the cobalt varnish of the picture and here it appears in a coal tone, which resisted the alcohol of 900. This is chemical proof that the picture is ancient and I think I was right to insist that the picture is original [...].[111]
>
> For the Hobbema, this is most ridiculous. Here even it is unnecessary to go into many details, simply believe me that it is really a beautiful work of Hobbema, and that I guarantee it genuine and you can mention my name to the man, who said it to be a copy or something like it, that

---

110 JGJ is John G. Johnson Fonds. Letter in the Philadelphia Museum of Art, PMA (JGJ, 5/5,6). Letters in this Museum are further indicated as PMA (JGJ + number).

111 Nardus and Van Gelder employed Theo van Wijngaarden as their restorer. Later on Van Wijngaarden would become Han van Meegeren's infamous partner (Lopez 2008: 24).

he is an ignorant of pictures. The Turner made also a big impression on me; it is an audacious dramatic work. The Stable by Cuyp is a second rank work.

I see now very clear in this affair, and I frankly say that it is very bad that you listen to the arguments of men who state such aberrations. I repeat you can enjoy your collection and you can be proud of it. To you now to believe me, I feel that I am justified.

St. John (2007) argues that art curators, historians, and dealers "recognized John Graver Johnson's abilities" and increasingly sought his views on paintings. St. John also argues that Johnson thought that a significant collection could be assembled by exercising good judgment, and that he accumulated his collection without the advice of connoisseurs and dealers. Saarinen (1958/68: 93) writes that Johnson hobnobbed with scholars, studied books on painting, examined sales catalogues, traced the histories of painting, and so on. Perhaps his acquaintance with Nardus had caused Johnson's later single-handed approach to collecting.

Understandably Johnson decided to continue purchasing art himself. In 1909 he noted on that subject: "but I might have fared far worse in the hands of fools beside who base jackals are innocent – the Dealers in art" (cited in Saarinen (1958/68: 106). Lopes (2007–N. 28) shows another angle. Writing on the topic of collectors failing to pay due taxes, he wrote that "there is also evidence Johnson colluded to evade import duties in bringing some of his 'Nardus pictures' into the country." With regard to a supposed Ghirlandaio that Johnson bought for $16 000, Van Gelder wrote on 16 February, 1908, (in PMA. JGJ, 5/5): "I am sorry I cannot send it to you as before. I would suggest to ship it as "Italian School" and invoice it at $5 000." In other words, despite what Johnson wrote about the way he collected, he did engage dealers, and his imports seem to be undervalued to save on taxes, which was then a standard practice among fine art collectors – Van Horne among them – as I will show. Also, Nardus and Van Gelder's cooperation is apparent here.

Still, for the Van Horne family 1907 must have been an extremely joyous year, as on July 10, William Cornelius Covenhoven (Billy) Van Horne, was born. He was Van Horne's only grandson, the young man who would drive Caroline Pierson to the railway station in 1926. We move on to 1908.

Everything was going well for Van Horne when he got word from Nardus, letter of April 6, 1908, that he (Nardus) had received the $4,500 draft for the three pictures: Ruysdael, the Goya, and his own pictures.[112] However, he would keep the Tiepolo. In this letter Nardus also noted that he would ship the Greco and had secured "a splendid Frans Hals, a boy playing violin, most refined in colour." Nardus, now Van Horne's dealer, friend, business partner, and co-collector, expressed disappointment that Van Horne couldn't come in April, but May would be fine as well. This letter ends with: "My wife and Léa are well, Léa often asks *óu est Sir William, je l'aime de tout mon Coeur.*" Nardus' wife, Lany, added to this letter that she was very happy that Van Horne had enjoyed his few days in their home so much, "You know you and your family shall always be most welcome. We hope to see you all soon over here and send you my very best compliments."   ⌘

---

112   Letter in VHFF (6/2).

COLLECTORS & CONNOISSEURS

John G. Johnson
Catalogue of a Collection
of Paintings and Some Art
Objects (Philadelphia: 1913).
➔

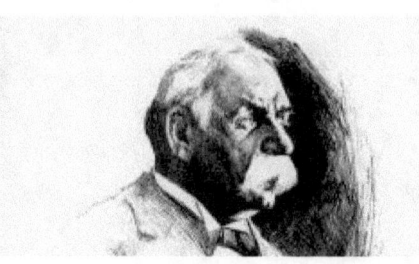

Hofstede de Groot (1863-1930)
Drawing Henk Meijer (1884-
1970) Courtesy RKD.
➔

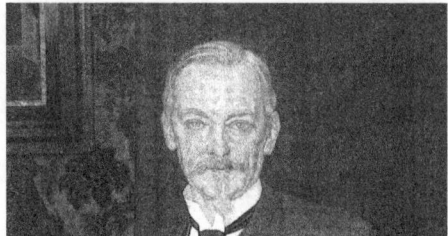

Abraham Bredius
Collectie Veenhuijzen,
Centraal Bureau voor
Genealogie, Den Haag
➔

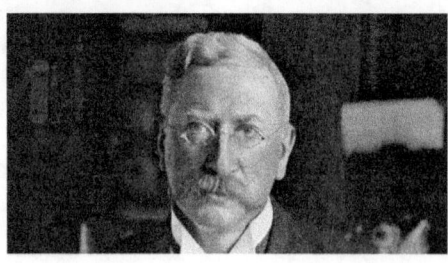

P.A.B. Widener
George Grantham
Bain collection. Lib. of
Congress. P.D

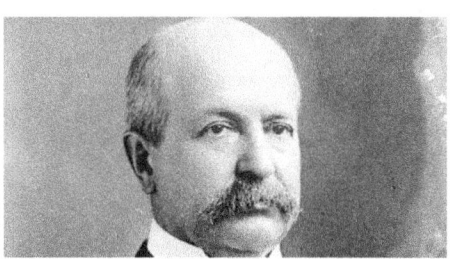

RKD archives
http://www.codart.nl

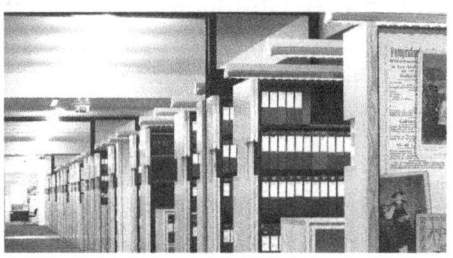

Museum Bredius
Lange Vijverberg 14 Den Haag
Courtesy Pauline van Till

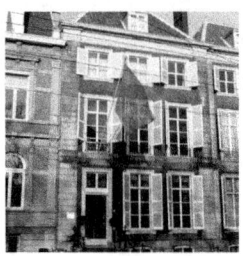

CHAPTER 4

CONNOISSEURS / THE WIDENER AFFAIR

ART HISTORIANS ARE knowledgeable about "connoisseurs" who came to America in the early 1900s to help culturally unsophisticated millionaires build their fine art collections. For starters, Scallen (2004: 2001) mentions Dutch connoisseur Hofstede de Groot culling "inferior or false works from the collection Widener (1834-1915) had already amassed."

Quodbach (2005: 65-79), describing Hofstede de Groot's first visit to American in 1908, writes that Widener's lavish spending on his palace-like estate might have been the reason he wanted to sell some of his art. One could certainly say that Widener had been spending lavishly, but, as I will show later, this was not the reason he wanted to sell some art.

The story behind Hofstede de Groot's visit to Widener's place in Philadelphia can also be found in the Nardus/Van Horne correspondence. As might become evident, the Widener story changed the way collectors, including Van Horne, purchased art.

In his letter of May 19, 1908, to Van Horne, Nardus dedicated only a few lines to a meeting in Paris with his client P. A. B. Widener.[113] Nardus obviously did not think it was very important; he would have been astonished had he known that,

---

113 VHFF (6/2). P. A. B. Widener (1834-1915) was the founding member of the Philadelphia Traction Company. Saarinen (1958/68: 80) refers to him as "a Philadelphia butcher boy who started his capital with selling mutton to the Union Army and then made millions out of trolley cars." Widener's son Georg and grandson

because of this meeting, the North American art world would never be the same again.

Under the impressive letterhead Bad-Hôtel, Prins Hendrik Park, Baarn, Nardus started his letter with letting Van Horne know that he was with his family in Baarn (Holland): "My wife needed a decided rest, and we are happy to say that we are here very comfortable."

Nardus went on about his wife expecting a baby in October of that year, so explained that was why he couldn't visit that summer. Nardus continued, a bit off-handedly:

I met Mr. Widener in Paris with his son. Yes; the poor man is very down and his son is entirely in the hands of the dealers. Our meeting was not an agreeable one, I am very sorry that Mr. Widener is in such a weak fortune. I hope Sir William to receive very soon *bon* news of you and also to hear that you are all in good health. My wife joins me in including our warmest regards, and believe us that we are very disappointed to be prevented to come over.

I have shipped to you the Tiepolo and the Goya. I acknowledge also a check of $5 000, which you sent me through Mr. Alexandre, I suppose this is for the Goya. I think you have received now your pictures and also the Greco. If for any reason you rather not keep it, please return it to me, without the least hesitation whatever.

When writing the words, "I met Mr. Widener," Nardus assumed that Van Horne knew who he was referring to. We know Van Horne did know about Widener, at least as a defecting

Harry (1885-1912) were among the 1 517 of the 2 223 people that drowned at the occasion of the Titanic disaster on April 15, 1912.

shareholder, because Knowles (2004: 334) calls Widener, "the former butcher and Philadelphia entrepreneur who had giant holdings in public utilities," and mentions him as one of the subscribers of the Cuba Company that Van Horne had established in 1900. Knowles also lists Widener as one of the "defectors," who in 1902 bailed out of the company.

The reason for the "disagreeable meeting" was that George, Widener's son, had seen in one of Hofstede de Groot's publications that the latter had omitted the three Vermeers in his father's possession.[114] Widener Sr. and/or his son Joseph must have subsequently proposed another meeting with Nardus in Paris, whereupon Nardus temporarily moved his Paris family, his daughter and his five-month pregnant wife, to Baarn, because his wife "needed a rest," and went back to Paris for the meeting.

Lopez (2007) reports the following on this second meeting between Nardus and Widener:

> According to a letter by a third party [i.e. Van Gelder], dated 6 May 1908, Widener came to France to sort things out.
>
> When I arrived to take lunch with Mr. W., Mr. Nardus was there, and it seems they had in the morning quite a discussion about pedigree, etc. Mr. W. was much disturbed and I took him out for a drive with Harry [Widener's grandson] to give him some distraction; before he left, he arranged with Mr. Nardus to meet Hofstede de Groot who

---

114   This book is volume I of *Beschreibendes und kritisches Verzeichnis der Werke der hervorragendsten holländischen Maler des XVII. Jahrhunderts*, a revision of John Smith's *Catalogue Raisonné of the Works of the Most Eminent Dutch, Flemish and French Painters, (1829-37)*. An English translation can be found at https://archive.org/details/catalogueraisonno6hofsuoft. Also see Qoudbach (2002) on Widener's collection.

is in Paris, to explain to him about his Vermeers of Delft about which he is writing a book.

. . . .

Lopez (2007) writes that the meeting between Nardus and Hofstede de Groot indeed happened and "that De Groot agreed to suspend judgment on the Vermeers until he had seen them in person." Lopez continues about Van Gelder, who "came out of the Widener negotiations with his reputation more or less intact."

Upon arrival back in America, the *NYT* of July 10 reported that Peter A. B. Widener, the Philadelphia traction man and art collector, returned to America yesterday, "after having spent five months at various health resorts in an endeavor to find relief from rheumatism." Also, that Widener was accompanied by his son, Joseph Widener, and grandson, H. E. Widener, who were in Europe with him. There is no record of the Wideners saying anything about what happened in Paris. If they had admitted they had been cheated, they might have lost face and been ridiculed.

About the same event, Samuels (1987: 83) writes that while the Wideners were in Paris, Widener's son Joseph took Berenson to see his father. Both Wideners were "greatly tickled at having acquired a Greco [...]." Samuels also does not mention anything else about the Wideners' stay in Paris, which bears witness to the fact that the Wideners succeeded in keeping their misfortune hidden. The senior Widener subsequently invited connoisseur Hofstede de Groot to Lynnewood Hall his 110-room Georgian mansion in Elkins Park, near Philadelphia, to assess the Nardus pictures. Apparently suspecting what lay in store, the Dutchman [Hofstede de Groot] did not come alone: "he brought the English critic Roger Fry, German connoisseur Wilhem Valentiner[115] and the American Bernard Berenson" with him. The connoisseurs valued the Nardus pictures at roughly five percent of what Nardus had charged (Lopez 2008: 36-37).

Hofstede de Groot on the American continent

That Hofstede de Groot "did not come alone" is somewhat true. Perhaps it meant to say that he was not the only one who went to Philadelphia to assess Widener's treasures. For example, Berenson came only in December of 1908. This is apparent from one of Mary Berenson's many letters to Isabella Stewart Gardner. On December 5, 1908, she wrote that Mr. Morgan had said with a grin: "I hear you're going to Phila-delphia to bust up Widener's collection." In the next letter, of December 16, Mary Berenson wrote "Dear Isabella, We spent a most fantastic two days at the Wideners', inspecting their "treasures" (in Hadley 1987: 426-27).[116]

About the "busting up" of the collection, Quodbach (2002: 79) writes that Widener's earliest acquisitions, those that survived the critical reviews of a number of connoisseurs, were purchased in 1894. Referring to Valentiner's article in *Art News* 58 (April 1959), Quodbach (2002: 80 n. 65) notes that one of the dealers:

---

115 *The North Carolina Museum of Art Bulletin*, Volume III, 1959, issued a 'Supple-ment to the W. R. Valentine Memorial Exhibition,' full of tributes, reminiscences. It also mentions that Valentiner founded *Art in America* in 1909 (later named *The Art Quarterly*). Cf.: https://archive.org/stream/bulletinnorthcar13unse#page/20/mode/2up/search/valentiner (last accessed in October 2014).

116 Anyway, before the Berensons were in Chicago, word of what had happened must have swirled around quickly, as had the idea of the importance of engaging or soliciting as a connoisseur in America (in Europe people had paid dues to their naivety earlier on). Already on June 30, 1908, one month after the scandal was exposed, Mary Berenson noted, "Bernhard went to Duveens. They were most flattering, and if 1/10 of what they say is true, a future of affluence lies before us! They said they would never touch an Italian picture but on his advice, and would give him 10% of their profit on sales!" (in: Strachey & Samuels, Ed. 1983: 147).

bought a castle in Suresnes, near Paris, and the other a villa near Brussels. At the moment this information – and the reference to one of the two as a dilettante painter – is only enough to provisionally identify "Nardus" who appears in the provenance of 11 Widener pictures in the NGA [National Gallery of Art], the majority of which were bought under other names [...], three in 1897 [...], three in 1898 [...]

From Quodbach we might infer that Nardus had only been Widener's dealer from 1897 on. This might explain that purchases prior to 1894 survived the expert eyes of the connoisseurs. Quodbach also quotes (2002: 80) German connoisseur Valentiner:

In these early days P. A. B. Widener appears to have been the primary victim of an infamous Belgian dealer duo, also known to have swindled the collector's friend Johnson, the Canadian Sir William Van Horne (1843-1915), and others.[117] According to Valentiner, it was Joseph Widener who first became suspicious, mistrusting the fantastical provenances the Belgians had supplied for their pieces.[118]

Once the scam had been uncovered, Hofstede de Groot was called in to rid the collection of forgeries [...]

---

117 John G. Johnson (1841-1917), a corporate lawyer, had Widener as a client. Also, Widener's purchases of art went through him. For example, Turner's *Junction of the Thames and the Medway* was sold to Agnew & Sons, London, in 1892, to Wallis in 1893 and in 1894 to Widener, through Johnson.
        See: http://www.philadelphiabar.org/page/TPLWinter07Johnson?appNum=4 (last accessed in October 2014).
118 Joseph Early Widener was the youngest of the three sons of Widener. George Widener was the father of grandson Harry.

"Although Valentiner did not give the dealers' names," Quodbach continues, "further information Valentiner provided enables *one* [italics added] of the two so-called Belgians to be identified tentatively as Leo (or Leonardus) Nardus, 1868-1930, a Dutchman." After all, Valentiner, hired in 1906 by Bode, had started his training in 1905 as connoisseur under the guidance of Hofstede de Groot in The Hague (Scallen, 2004: 194). In other words, Valentiner had had an opportunity to unveil the identity of the "Belgian" dealers.

Because in 1896 Van Gelder was profiled in the *New York Times* of February 14, 1897, as an artist, it's reasonable to assume that both Nardus and Van Gelder could have been described as dilettante painters. Valentiner does mention the name Nardus, but not the name of the elusive booted bantam breeder Van Gelder. From 1908 Van Gelder continued to sell fine arts, but now with Nardus as his silent partner in Europe.

It is time to continue reading the letter Mary Berenson wrote to Isabella Stewart Gardner on December 16, 1908, in which she mentions the "fantastic two days at the Wideners." She went on (in Hadley, 1987: 426-27):

> I can't help being indiscreet and telling you various things that may amuse you (and delight if you are human!). They have really nothing of importance among their Italians, and their best other picture, outside of the Van Dyck, is a fine Frans Hals. But to stick to the Italians – we could not leave one single great name. When you forget how he had made his money, it was rather touching to have old Mr. Widener (he is very broken) trotting round and saying meekly: "Mr. Berenson, is this a gallery picture, or a furniture picture, or must it go to the cellar?" (That is their formula and about 160 pictures are already in the cellar!). He was very pleased whenever we would allow a picture to stay in the gallery, even if shorn of its great name. But we had to banish several. Then the prices!! Jo Widener told us all. They have paid on an average for their Italians

from $10 000 to $40 000 for pictures worth at the outside $500! Their "Titian" – a late copy of the Madonna of the Cherries at Vienna – cost them $40 000 and so on. By that scale, you have scarcely a picture that isn't worth millions [...] We weren't there for the Velásquez nor the objects d'art, but we could not help feeling they had been done over them quite as badly as over the Italian pictures. But of that, so far, they have no suspicion.

....

Samuels (1987: 427) cites Mary B. as saying that she thought Widener's paintings "about the rottenest we have yet seen. Agnew has just simply dumped off all his unsalable rubbish upon this ignorant millionaire."[119] Samuels goes on to remark that the Berensons were careful not to express their opinion about their host's treasures when a dozen years later, "Berenson was called on to prepare a lavish catalogue of the paintings of the early Italian and Spanish schools of the Widener collection." All in all, somehow Nardus' dealership escaped the attention of Samuels and others.

According to Pijl (2005: 77ff), the assessment of Nardus' pictures led Hofstede de Groot to complain to Nardus, by letter of September 10, 1908, that he (Nardus) had sold "a modern falsification" of Jacob van Ruysdael's *The Waterfall.*[120]

---

119   On the other hand, Samuels (1987: 62) writes a few years later that the Berensons thought that "Fairfax Murray, a partner of the Agnew firm, had unloaded many "worthless things ... for vast sums on Widener."

120   VH 48 Ruysdael, Jacob van (Haarlem, 1628-9 – resided at Amsterdam 1657-81, buried at Haarem, 1682). *Landscape with Waterfall and Church.* ⊞: In the foreground is a cascade falling [...] Canvas. H. 27½ in: W 21¼ in (70 cm × 54 cm). Signed on a rock at the lower left "J.v. Ruisdael." In the coll. of M. Smeth Van Alphen, 1810. In the coll. of M. Le Brun, 1811. In the coll. of Van der Pals, Rotterdam, 1824. In the coll. of M. Nieuwenhuys, 1839. In the coll. of the Count de Narbonne, 1851 – Sale Catalogue no. 53. In poss. of Gimpel and Wildenstein, New York, 1909. The continuing page throws some doubts: "Catalogue no. 207, page 85 and mentioned as being similar in subject to no. 334 and 361, page XXIV and referred to in the text, page 62, on account of its careful composition and

Hofstede de Groot also stated that other paintings Nardus had sold, a so-called Rubens and Vermeer's *The Card Players,* were also entirely modern; of this last piece de Groot commented that the paint was still wet. Hofstede de Groot furthermore had his doubts about Vermeer's *Sleeping Kitchen Maid*, Rembrandt's *The Standard Bearer,*[121] two Memlings, one Hals, one of the seven Cuyps and another two by Adriaen Brouwer van Frans van Mieris, all of which Nardus had sworn were genuine.

Quodbach (2002: 85) also mentions "Raphael's" Portrait of Pope Julius II among the fakes Widener bought from Nardus (in 1897) but that painting was kept in the collection by son Joseph "because it harmonized so well with the other pictures in Lynnewood Hall's Raphael Room."

As mentioned, after the meeting in May 1908 connoisseurs such as Hofstede de Groot and Berenson entered the American art scene. Lopez (2008: 42) writes that after that time, 1908, "It became virtually impossible to sell a major painting to a major collection without first obtaining a signed attribution from one of the top authorities in the field." Also, collectors had their existing collections checked by connoisseurs and had the genuine paintings cleaned. They also went to great lengths to weed out the fakes. Van de Wetering (2008: 83) describes the ability to issue authentications or expertises as "the ability, based on experience, to recognize the hand of a

highly finished manner, as a "hilly landscape with a dark and foaming waterfall and sunlit wheat field before a chapel, in poss. of W. C. Van Horne in Montreal", associated in character with "the picture of Bentheim Castle in the distance and a small waterfall in the foreground, at the Rijks Museum (Amsterdam) (Illustrated plate 133). ▣: 30 000.

121 The Standard Bearer (De Vaandeldrager) is mentioned in Van de Wetering (2009: 101). Private coll., Canvas 118.8 cm × 96.8 cm. On October 23, 2009 Prof. Dr. E. van de Weteringe e-mailed: "The Standard Bearer in the Collection Rothschild in Paris (Rembrandt, The Master and his workshop 1991/2). The painting is attributed to Rembrandt by my colleagues because of style and quality and I agree. There are some other versions of the painting. Because that is why Hofstede de Groot had his doubts."

painter [...]. A connoisseur recognizes in a particular painting the characteristics of the presumed author's work that he has previously seen in other paintings by that painter." The Berensons invented a new verb for these professional activities, "connoshing." [122]

Back to 1908: on September 24, 1908, Nardus replied to Hofstede de Groot's letter of September 10, denying everything. Still, in the period 1910-1911 Widener bought two more paintings (late Rembrandts) from Nardus, which are now, according to Qoudbach (in Pijl, 1905: 78) thought to be imitations. According to Lopez (2007), during the 1890s and 1900s Widener had purchased altogether ninety-three paintings from Nardus. But, by now, one of the most prolific connoisseurs, Hofstede de Groot, had entered the American art scene and Nardus' dealership in America ended right there and then.

Van Gelder continued the business with Nardus as his silent partner back in Europe. Connoisseurs such as Hofstede de Groot, Valentiner, Berenson, Bredius, and Bode, while exposing Nardus, must have privately elevated him to sainthood. Without Nardus' "mistakes," "misfortunes" or "overenthusiasm," the authentication business in North America might never have taken off on the scale it did. Ekkart (1999: 80) comments, in Dutch, on Hofstede de Groot's main source of income:

---

122   In Europe/the Netherlands, engaging connoisseurs was much longer en vogue. Heijbroek & Wouthuysen (1999: 50) write about one of the Van Wisselingh sales that someone had bought: a Mauve and two Blommers under condition that a "Dordt connoisseur would fiat them." Scallen (2004: 219) states that Bode has been credited with having been the first art historian to make a practice of writing his opinion about authenticity, an expertise, on the back of photographs.

It is likely that especially his activities as expert for collectors and art dealers were the main source of his income. Besides issuing art historical consults, these activities comprised the issuing, for a fee, expertises in which he declared authenticity and attribution of separate works of art, especially of course seventeenth century Dutch paintings. These declarations were of great importance for the art business because they got the status of a guarantee that could be given to the purchaser.

That is exactly what happened. As Heijbroek states:

Connoisseurship also became tainted: e.g., through bribery. The whole authentication development is reflected in Van Horne's correspondence. Nevertheless, from Lugt's scribbles on the 1933 catalogue and from notes in the Wickenden catalogue it is clear that a number of Van Horne's paintings were not always by whom they are attributed to.[123]

Which, as Heijbroek assured me, is natural: over time views of or opinions about attributions differ.[124] As said, purchasing art was never the same after the 1908 scandal. From then on,

---

123   Personal communication on July 4, 2011 in Amsterdam.
124   In this regard, the cousin, Patrick Neslias, of the spouse of the granddaughter, Yvette, of Marie Gendreau, the woman with whom Nardus lived after he left his wife Lany Bourgeois, reacting to accusations that Nardus would wrongly have attributed paintings, wonders: "Combien de toiles ont changé d'attrbution depuis cent ans?" (Neslias 2010:111)
      In 1940 Nardus 'collection was confiscated by the Nazi's. Neslias (2010) records its impact on the Nardus family and their and his the efforts for recuperation. In 2010 he booked some success.

no serious collector bought an important work of art unless it had been authenticated. As shown in the following excerpt from the *American Art News*, art experts were quick to offer their services:

American Art News advice as to the placing at public or private sale of art works of all kinds, pictures, sculptures, furniture, bibelots, etc., will be given at the office of the AMERICAN ART NEWS, and also counsel as to the value of art works and the obtaining of the best "expert" opinion of the same. For these services a nominal fee will be charged. Persons having art works and desirous of disposing or obtaining an idea of their value, will find our service on these lines a saving of time, and, in many instances, of unnecessary expense. It is guaranteed that any opinion given will be so given without regard to personal or commercial motives.

After 1908, collectors, Van Horne among them, had to veil their nagging doubts about what they had collected so far. To be ridiculed for spending huge amounts of money on an imitation, a fake or a forgery would have been embarrassing. However, it seems Van Horne was willing to take that risk in order to find out which pieces of his art were genuine. According to Knowles (2004: 293), "Conducting tours of his collections was one way that Van Horne could expose it to a wider audience." After 1908, connoisseurs could be counted among the "wider audience."

Van Horne, knowing about the Widener affair first hand, must quickly have realized that there could or would or might be something wrong with his own collection, so that is why he invited German connoisseur Valentiner to his home. We know about the visit from the note dated July 1, 1908, in which Valentiner thanked Van Horne for the "delightful time" he had spent in his house.[125] Valentiner noted that he "really seldom had so many interesting impressions at the same time as in these days, the impressions of different kind of arts, old and modern painting, Japanese works and European ship models and the wonderful orchids."

It would not take long before the next expert invited himself for a visit to the Van Horne collection. It is a small world after all; it was Hofstede de Groot who had trained Valentiner in 1905.

CORNELIS HOFSTEDE DE GROOT (1863-1930)

Hofstede de Groot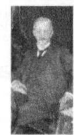

Hofstede de Groot was the The Hague connoisseur that Nardus introduced to Widener. The catalogue of the RKD (*Rijks bureau voor Kunsthistorische Documentatie* / Netherlands Institute for Art History) and Ekkart (1998: 73-95) state that Hofstede de Groot was the not-so-healthy son of Reformed Church minister Cornelis Philippus Hofstede de Groot and Catharina Dorothea Star Numan. Because of his physical condition he was often abroad, where he came in touch with the worlds of history and art history. In 1884 he went to Leipzig to study with Dr. Anton Springer and, later, to defend his thesis *Werken van Hollandsche architecuur schilders in Duitsche verzamelingen (Works of Dutch architecture painters in German collections)*. Back in the Netherlands, there were still no Chairs in history of art (Overmars and Van Veen 2005: 17).

---

125   Letter in VHFF (6/6).

The only person teaching Classical Arts, at the University of Amsterdam, was – of all people – Allard Pierson, Caroline Pierson's grandfather.

Hofstede de Groot's first job was as temporary scholarly assistant of the Prentenkabinet in Dresden in October 1890. In August 1891 Dr. A. Bredius, director of the The Hague Mauritshuis, invited him to become his Assistant-Director. After a cooperation of five years, Phillip van der Kellen invited Hofstede de Groot to become his successor as director of the Prentenkabinet of the Rijksmuseum in Amsterdam. He accepted and held this position for a short period, but handed in his resignation in July 1898. According to Pijl (2005: 10), this was due to arguments with Victor de Stuers of the Department of Arts at the Ministry of Interior Affairs.

From then on Hofstede de Groot made a living by authentications, writing articles and books, and participation in committees. His major publication was an eight-volume oeuvre about Rembrandt that he published with Wilhelm Von Bode and his *Beschreibendes und kritisches Verzeichnis der Werke der hervorragendsten holländischen Maler des XVII Jahrhunderts*. Its ten volumes were published between 1907 and 1929. As mentioned, Widener's son read volume I of it and asked Hofstede de Groot to inspect his father's collection. From that point on the "connoshing" business, as the Berensons called it, was a thriving business for Hofstede de Groot as well.

During his rather short life Hofstede de Groot also made many notes about the lives and works of various artists, and left these notes, combined with photographs of paintings, art historical notes, and other documentation, to the Dutch government under condition that the government would manage his estate. It would become the basis of the 1932 establishment of the RKD in The Hague, i.e. the institute that sent me the 1933 catalogue with Lugt's scribbles.

On September 11, 1908, Hofstede de Groot introduced himself to Van Horne, writing: "Although not being known personally to you, I venture to write you this letter, hoping that you may know my name as a critic of old Dutch art from Holland." [126] He went on:

I am now on a tour through America and after having visited Washington, Chicago, Detroit, the Niagara I intend to go to Montreal to visit you & your collection. Would you be kind enough to allow me this? And also to introduce me to the other collections of your city: Messrs. Drummond, Ross & Angus of whom I have heard a great deal? Perhaps there are still others, which might be worth visiting. [127]

A few years ago when there was the first talk of my trip to your country Lord & Lady Aberdeen whose acquaintance I made at the house of Lord Reay (Dutch Baron Mackay) in London were kind enough to allow me to authorize me to use their name as an introduction to you & also does Mr. P. A. B. Widener at whose house I am staying now, making the new catalogue of his Dutch & Flemish pictures.

---

126   Letter in VHFF (4/6).
127   Sir George Alexander Drummond (1829-1920) was a financier, industrialist and banker: "In the course of their travels and through artists and dealers the couple acquired one of the finest collections of paintings on the continent, including at least five Turners, a Corot, a Velasquez, a Van Duck, a Rubens, and a Lorrain. Drummond, who had a fine eye for art, was president of the Art Association of Montreal from 1896 to 1899, in http://www.biographi.ca/009004-119.01-e. php?BioId=40805 (last accessed February 2014).

James Ross (1848-1913) was a railway entrepreneur, director of many banks and member of even more associations. When he died the *Gazette*, Sept. 22, 1913, wrote: "At a time when Montreal had not many men who both appreciated and possessed the financial ability to purchase splendid specimens of the best art which the old world has produced, James Ross entered that field, and soon made his private collection one of the things of which Montréal were proud."

Richard B. Angus (1831-1922) was one of the railway entrepreneurs who oversaw the construction of the Canadian Pacific Railway. He served as president of the Montréal Art Association, to which he gave substantial donations and also purchased a number of valuable paintings, in http://en.wikipedia.org/wiki/Richard_B._Angus (last accessed October 2014).

Hofstede de Groot was discrete. He writes nothing about "busting up" Wideners collection, but drums up business by mentioning something collectors would come to desire – having a catalogue of one's collection drafted by a connoisseur. On September 16 Van Horne cabled back that he would be "delighted if you will be my guest during [your] visit [to] Montreal." [128] Through Hofstede de Groot's next batch of letters we can follow him on his collections' inspection tour, which shows the interconnectedness of the collectors' world.

In his September 22, 1908, letter from Chicago, Hofstede de Groot thanked Van Horne for his invitation to stay at his house, but mentioned that he first had to go to Toledo, Detroit, Buffalo, and the Niagara.[129] Van Horne, obliging Hofstede de Groot's request to introduce him to other collectors, instructed his secretary, Mr. Lynch, to ask Mr. T. C. Hall of New York City to allow Hofstede de Groot to see the pictures belonging to the estate of the late General Samuel Thomas.[130] But alas, as Lynch informed Hofstede de Groot one day later, these pictures were in storage.

By the end of September or start of October, Hofstede de Groot was at Van Horne's mansion and had been put to work there. On October 5, 1908, he let Van Horne know how much he had enjoyed his stay and how much he felt indebted.[131] Hofstede de Groot added that he had meanwhile met with [his former pupil] Mr. Valentiner and seen interesting things and collections, "Mr. Frick's,[132] Shaw's, Bartlett's, Evan's etc., but

---

128   All RKD letters are from the Hofstede de Groot archives (1853) 1880-1930 (1942).
129   Letter in VHFF (4/6).
130   Letter in VHFF (4/6). General Samuel Thomas (1840-1903) became a manufacturer of iron and railroad supplies after a career in the American army: *New York Times* of January 12, 1903.
131   Letter in VHFF (4/5).
132   Henry Clay Frick was one of the robber barons, or 'squillionaires' who gave up his career 'to collect paintings' (Boser 2008: 49-50). With people such as J. Pierpont Morgan and Henry Vanderbilt, Frick "began to bid against one another for the

not Mrs. Gardner's! She asked me to come back towards the end of November!"

From the rest of the letter it is clear that Van Horne had told Hofstede de Groot about Valentiner's inspection of his collection as well, because Hofstede de Groot added in his letter that Valentiner thought that the Roger Van der Weyden head was "totally wrong." He (HdG) regretted that he did not have a look at it "without glass." Hofstede de Groot went on to say that Valentiner had suggested "that the monks might be by Allessandro Magnasco by whom are two pictures at The Hague in a quite similar scale of colour. I believe he is right." Hofstede de Groot thereafter went on as a salesman:

I ordered Bruckman to send you Pigmentdrucke of the Jacob Backer in the Herengracht collection at The Hague, The Melanchton at Hannover, the Mariakerk at Utrecht by Saenredam by which your S. v. Ruysdael is inspired & the Jan Davidz. de Heem at The Hague, which is similar in style with your C. Fabritius. [133]

spoils of European civilization in a passionate quest to demonstrate not just America's wealth but also its increasing cultivation" (Gross 2009: 69).

133   VH 127 Holbein, Hans the Younger (Augsburg 1497–London 1543). *Portrait of Philip Melanchthon.* ◰: The high forehead, thin aquiline nose and refine features of this learned reformer of the Sixteenth Century are shown almost in profile, turned to the right [...] Circular on wood. 4⅛ in diameter (10½ cm). Probably painted during Holbein's third stay at Basel (1528-32). On the circular frame is the following inscription in Latin: 'QUAE CERNIS TANTUM NON VIVA MELANCHTONIS ORA, HOLBINUS RARE DEXTERUTATE DEDUT' composed probably by Melanchthon as a tribute to the painter, translated: In what thou seest here, Holbein, with rare skill, has given us the all but living features of Melanchthon." In the coll. of Horace Walpole, Strawberry Hill, and sold from there in 1842. In poss. of Dowdeswell & Dowdeswell, London, 1909. ◱: 5 000, Not Holbein.

    VH 50 Ruysdael, Salomon van (Haarlem, 1600). *The Marien-Kirche at Utrecht.* ◰: The high square-topped tower of the Marien Kirche – Mary's church – dominates, with its quaint gables, on the river-bank at the left, and a group of fishing boats flying Dutch flags appear beyond it at the right, where the water extends to misty horizon [...]. Canvas H. 25 in, W. 22 in (63½ cm × 56 cm). From ~~Leo Nardus~~." ◱: From Leo Nardus, Paris 190[?], 3 000.

Van Horne must have been told, or perhaps have asked around, about paintings that were more or less similar to the ones in his collection. During that same visit Van Horne invited Hofstede de Groot to authenticate a picture featuring "a lady seated, dressed in a red, fur trimmed jacket, yellow petticoat and white apron, talking with a maid about the fish [...]." This is how de Groot authenticated the picture: "The undersigned considered it to be a genuine & fine work by Jacob Ochterfelt. October 1908." [134] At some point in time, Van Horne must have sold the Ochterfelt (1634-1682) since this fine work is not listed in the Wickenden catalogue. In Cat. 1933 Ochterfelt's *Mistress and Maid* was no. 57 (behind it Lugt scribbled: Lady buys Finch. Good").

Covenhoven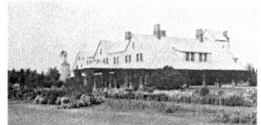

Van Horne was far from finished having his collection inspected and appraised. From Covenhoven, his New Brunswick estate, he replied on October 15, 1908, to Hofstede de Groot as follows:[135]

I have delayed acknowledgment of your note of the 5th hoping to be able to send with it the photo's you wanted but it appears that some of them were not good enough and had to be taken over again.

Please let me know at Montreal where I shall send the photo's and I shall be glad to learn at the same time that you have postponed the date of your sailing so that I may

134 Letter in VHFF (8/14).
135 Letter in RKD.

hope for the pleasure of seeing you again on this side of the Atlantic.

I am naturally much interested in what Dr. Valentiner says about the so-called Roger van der Weyden. I am unable to understand what he means by "Totally wrong." I can hardly believe that he means anything ... a late imitation. If it is a copy or a modern imitation my head will shrink materially. I hope you may have an opportunity to have a closer look at it. My son tells me we looked at the wrong place for the signature on the still life – the so-called Fabritius. I shall take another look on reaching home. Your visit gave me very much pleasure and I shall be delighted if you may be induced to come again.

It is strange that Van Horne looked in the wrong place for Fabritius' signature because Conway (1905: 140), discussing Fabritius' *Still-life,* contends to have already found the signature during his visit to the Montreal mansion:

Another Dutch Painter – no less fine in his way than Frans Hals – was Carel Fabritius, who was killed by a gunpowder explosion at Delft at the early age of thirty-four. As an artist he is most closely allied to Vermeer, on whom he exercised as powerful an influence as Rembrandt had had upon him. Genuine pictures by him are rare. Sir William van Horne possesses a "still-life" on which I was fortunate enough to detect the traces of his signature. It is one of his earliest works, more patient and laborious in executions than those made in the fullness of his power, but thoroughly painter-like in conception and handling.

Hofstede de Groot must have been induced; he paid one more visit to Montreal. On October 28, 1908, he wrote Van Horne:[136]

> A few minutes after I had left you I found at my Hotel Prof. Huls' answer to my letter in which he writes, "Although it is impossible to give a certain opinion from a photograph I will tell you that my first impression was: either totally modern or over painted in a high degree, especially the face. In no case by one of the well- known painters but showing at a certain degree Dirck Bouts influence."
>
> I was sorry our meeting today was so short.

From the following undated letter (but most likely 29 October), it appears that Van Horne must have been feeling the weight of his collection and have asked for a clarification about the Van der Weyden assessment.[137] Hofstede de Groot answered that he was leaving America and hoped to be back in The Hague, by November 5 or 6. He added:

> "Totally wrong" means "absolutely false" i.e., a modern imitation. I am sorry I did not take the trouble of taking off the glass. In that case I would have been able to decide whether this is right. As soon as I have seen the Magnasco-pictures at The Hague again I will write you, whether they seem to be by the same hand as your "Greco."
>
> I succeeded today in getting admission to Mr. Borden's Gallery & was much pleased by the visit.

136 Letter in VHFF (4/6).
137 Letter in VHFF (4/6).

The Yerkes, Schwab & Gould collections remained closed for me, but I saw the Thomas pictures at the storehouse. [138]

As he states in this letter, Hofstede de Groot was much pleased by the visit to Mr. Borden's gallery. In the following year, 1909, it became obvious that Mr. Borden was also much pleased about Hofstede de Groot's visit!

On October 30 Van Horne replied from the Manhattan Hotel in New York,[139]

My dear Dr. de Groot,

I am taking the liberty of sending by my secretary the little picture to look at again. I am very much puzzled to know where are the indications of its being a modern imitation. I am in a position to turn the picture back so it does not matter to me from a money standpoint whether it is right or not. I am glad to learn something I can and I

---

138 Matthew Chaloner Durfee Borden (1842-1912) was the New York owner of a thriving cotton mill industry who "amassed a large and important collection of art," in http://www.nycago.org/Organs/NYC/html/ResBordenMCD.html (last accessed in February 2014).

Charles Yerkes (1837-1905) was a Chicago trolley-car king. According to Saarinen (1958/68: 109) he spent most of his fortune indulging in a chain of love affairs and lived in a grand style in an Italianate palace in New York. "Here he rested his corpulent body in an $80 000 bed that once belonged to the King of Belgium." After he died only one million dollars was left.

Apart from being a great businessman, Charles M. Schwab (1862-1939) was a "gambler, union buster and businessman of dubious ethics," in http://www.bethlehempaonline.com/schwab_bio.html (last accessed in February 2014).

This could refer to George Gould (1864-1923), son of Jason Gould (1836-1892), one of the American railway/robber barons. Gould left his estate to the Georgian Court University, in http://research.frick.org/directoryweb/browserecord.php?-action=browse&-recid=6697 (last accessed in February 2014).

139 Letter in RKD.

should not like to turn the picture back unless it actually is wrong.

It has occurred to me that Mr. Valentiner had in mind the little picture of the woman hanging in the hall, an imitation of Flemish work which I keep as an object lesson and which I bought as an imitation. He seemed to be considerably interested in that.

I hope it will not bore you to look again at the so-called Rogier van der Weyden. I shall value very highly your frank opinion of it and shall be under deep obligations to you. I don't wish to get "stuck," at the same time I don't wish to be unfair to the party from whom I got it.

Trusting that you may have a pleasant voyage and that we may see you again in America.

VAN GELDER FIGHTING OFF JOHNSON, 1908

During his American tour, Hofstede de Groot had also visited collector John Johnson, as was to be expected. According to Saarinen (1958/68: 103-04), "Widener and Johnson were good friends. They played poker together and they served together on the Fairmount Park Art Association Saarinen." Johnson wrote to Nardus, on October 15, 1908, about Hofstede de Groot's visit:[140]

Dr. de Groot has shown me your letter in reply to the one he wrote you, in which you say you are ready to answer a letter from me immediately. I had hoped that you would save yourself the very serious consequences that threaten

---

140   Letter in PMA (JGJ, 5/5,6).

by voluntarily endeavoring to do all in your power to make good the outrage you have perpetrated upon me.

I had hoped that through Dr. de Groot's intervention you would see what was your duty and would do it. In infer from your letter that you intend to do nothing. This being the case, I will now pursue the course I had contemplated. I do not intend that you shall carry away and continue to enjoy the money you have obtained from me under gross false pretenses.

There is not the slightest good in your trying to brazen out the matter by acting and talking as if it was a question about which experts might differ, whether what you sold me was attributed sold truly or falsely.

There is not the slightest possible question of fact. In various ways you have obtained money from me under false pretense. The prices you obtained were excessive, even had the pictures been all you pretended; but that, of course, is a matter for which I claim no redress. What I do intend to obtain redress for is that, after charging what would be excessive prices for genuine pictures, you supplied me with false ones.

Some of the pictures which I obtained from you were exchanged with dealers in Europe, who have condemned the same in the most unreserved manner and have offered to sell back to me the pictures at about one-twentieth of what I paid for them. All these pictures were falsely attributed. A few were old pictures, wrongly labeled. Many of them were modern imitations.

I append a list of these pictures, all of which are now in Europe. There is no trouble, therefore, in obtaining plenty of testimony as to these pictures. I send you another list of pictures, which Dr. de Groot has most unhesitatingly and unqualifiedly condemned. A few of these are wrongly attributed. Many of them are moderns.

These pictures I intend to send to Europe in order that the proof may be on hand there to be obtained from the experts, who will be called, of the facts. Before I commence my legal proceedings I give you this warning of my intention, in order that you may save yourself what will happen. If I do not hear from you within one month from the date of this letter, giving me reasonable assurances of some prompt settlement, I will do what I have said, viz, send the pictures to Europe and will then proceed.

There are many other pictures, which are under examination at the present time, and I fear the results in many cases will be bad. Until this thorough examination, however, I do not deal with these pictures.

I will not now deal with the Italian paintings, because Mr. Berenson is about to examine these and I will await his report before I make my demand upon you for anything wrong in that respect.

The Flemish pictures will be subjected to examination by a competent expert.

I hold your guarantees of genuineness and upon these I will rest my civil suit.

Besides this, however, the obtaining of money under false pretenses is a criminal act, and I will put the case in the hands of counsel in Europe to take such steps criminally as they shall advise me to take.

Johnson got a reply from Van Gelder, from Zeecrabbe, Uccle.[141] Van Gelder was taking care of Nardus affairs at that time, and Johnson was taking care of Widener's mishaps. On November 18, Van Gelder replied, saving neither paper nor ink:[142]

---

141   Most of Van Gelder's correspondence is from (his chateau) Zeecrabbe. If not, it will be indicated. Zeecrabbe was demolished in 1937 and rebuilt; it now serves as the Russian Embassy in Brussels, Belgium.
142   Letter in PMA (JGJ, 5/5,6).

I received today your letter of 9th inst. I am extremely sorry I did not receive your letter of 23rd.

I was very much put out when I received word from you [...] wherein you state: you only could qualify the things you heard as shocking. I assure you I do not know as yet what these things were.

I am very sorry indeed that Mr. Geo W. will go so far as to take proceedings. I think it quite wrong to accuse Nardus of dishonesty. It may be that he made errors but out of ignorance or rather over-enthusiasm. This occurs even yet, it happens quite often that he, intending to purchase a painting runs it up higher than it ought to be through his enthusiasm of which many a dealer has taken and takes yet advantage.

Anyhow if mistakes of his part may have taken place he ought to do everything possible to straighten things out and make right what has been wrong as well with Mr. W. as with yourself. I shall be the first to advice him in that way and to insist of him doing so.

If there could be found a way that Mr. Jo. W. would take some pictures out of Nardus collection which he would care to possess and which would be recognized by experts to be correct, in exchange of the doubtful ones, things could be settled perhaps at once in that way and eventually if you would care such could be arranged with you. I would bear every influence with Nardus that way and assist him as much I could. A financial settlement would be a ruin to him and a process would be extremely annoying for both parties.

I do not want there to be a scar on our name, not for anything in the world. I wrote you in that spirit twice when you were in London. I regret not to have gotten your reply.

I do not see how Mr. W. could take proceedings against me. I have not been instrumental in purchasing for nor selling to Mr. W. I wish Mr. Johnson, you would feel that I am not to be mixed up with the name swindle and that

I have the most serious intention to help in making good there, where possibly wrong has been done either through, as I said, ignorance (Nardus was still young in art matters when he came to America and in the hands of dealers more clever than he) or through over-enthusiasm. I therefore feel warranted to asking you to reply to me as soon as possible.

If you could get Mr. W. and his son to arrange for an amicable settlement in the way I indicate I think a great deal of mischief would be avoided. I will see Mr. Nardus in a few days and advise him in the way indicated.

Yours Truly M. van Gelder

P.S. If you deem it necessary you might show this letter to Mr. W.

On December 10, Van Gelder replied to Johnson, who was in Philadelphia again:[143]

I received your letter of 30 Nov. and did not want to answer you before I had seen Nardus. He expected to go to Phila., but unfortunately he cannot leave at present. His wife got a baby two weeks ago and she is not so well as to be left alone.

However much it would have been desirable for these gentlemen to meet I doubt of the practical result. Nardus assures that these pictures are not copies and I think that he is **absolutely right**. Mr. Widener believes the assertions of De Groot and others, it seems thus of no use of Nardus going to Phila. to contest their opinion as he has done before. That the attributions are wrong **may** be possible, but this, of course, must be proven and the opinion of the

---

143   Letter in PMA (JGJ, 5/ 5, 6).

experts of both parties would be weighed. If it could be shown that Nardus is on the wrong side, I don't doubt for a moment that he would want to make good what is wrong. I am perfectly sure of his absolute good faith.

And then, why could this not be amicably settled by giving in exchange some picture of the collection of Mr. W. of value and of unquestionable attribution. All this could be arranged if either Nardus could go to Phila. or **better still** if Mr. Widerer could come next summer to Paris where an eventual exchange must anyhow be arranged.

I suppose that, if Nardus is absolutely and most sincerely convinced of the absurdity of some of De Groot's opinions and when he can prove so, that it would be ridiculous for him to take back a picture as a copy, which is not one!

So for instance the two Memling portraits, it seems that when these were purchased by Bourgeois that they sent to Brussels to be compared to replicas of the museum there and, several experts declared the two Widener portraits as to be the better pictures!! Some of these experts are yet of that opinion, can Nardus accept De Groot's assertion as to be **copies**?

The Rembt. Standard Bearer a copy, Mr. Johnson, this is not possible! Call replica, a repetition made in the studio or what else, but a copy! Would you [think] Mr. Bourgeois and Nardus stupid enough and dishonest enough to sell bogus and so spoil their reputation!

The Rubens (or Van Dyck), Gevartius most wonderful painting of extraordinary technique, a copy! Dr. De Groot must have been either blind through jealousy or pedantry. So also with the master Brouwer, which because it is a rep.

is not a Brouwer or is there any other rep. of one of the Brouwers in the Kann collection.[144]

There exist some 4 or 5 replicas each excellently painted and recognized to be by the master. What with the Sleeping Servant recognized and illustrated by Burger himself as you know and the Young Man with the Hat as work which I would be **proud** to possess. As to the Card Player, I don't remember it well enough to say anything about its qualities, but it is certainly not a copy.

"One who hears but one clock hears but one sound," so please Mr. Johnson, think of what I am writing you in an unprejudiced spirit. I do not write you this to justify Nardus; I assure you he doesn't need it. He has been of good faith all the time, he has treated you with honesty sometimes perhaps a little too enthusiast or too confident but he took always a most sincere interest in your collections. I write you this as my own personal opinion.

I was, I assure you, most chagrined to read that you labeled your splendid Van Dyck a **copy**, there exist in Brunwich the replica of your picture but **with another expression**, the man as well as the dog and there exists also **two [illeg.] of both pictures, both equally different of expression.** Why for heaven's sake call your picture a copy! Is it not well painted? Are the craquelures lacking? Are the colours so hideous? Is that noble man with his superb dog of such an awful character? Well, Mr. Johnson, if my recollections of the pictures are right, I would be most **happy** to possess them.

The Rabbi never appealed to me and the Q. Metsys I do not recall, but your little Hals I always loved exceedingly,

---

144 The Kann collection was bought by the Duveens, who put up the money, 23 million francs by a loan from J. P. Morgan "who was to have first choice of the Kann's treasures" (Goldstein 2000: 84).

that little beautiful girl with her spirit fully painted bonnet, laughing so innocently yet so intelligently out of her clear eyes, this a copy! It is terrible to think that you despise it, because Mr. De Groot have [an] easy task to show his superiority by running down a splendid work because there exist another.

Could you arrange so as to let me have that picture and also the Van Dyck? I would gladly make any exchange you may propose.

As to the attribution of the Bouts and little Memling, I think that the opinion about the primitives is yet so much guesswork that one should not mind about the exactitude of names, provided the works are fine. That you should have some 35 pictures wrongly attributed seems to me incredible, did I read right? If so which are they?

What to say about the 12 à 15 Nardus pictures which Mr. W. treated [traded?] on his Van Dyck. I heard that these were **thrown** on the market in a time that purchasers were not plentiful and alas that a quantity have been picked up in Paris at prices below their value.

Now Mr. Johnson, please don't consider this as a refutation of your letter. I write you this as my **sincere** and honest opinion in the matter. I think it ridiculous to speak of taking criminal proceedings against Nardus, such are words intended to frighten one who feels guilty, in this instance this does merely make Nardus more bitter and furious.

I am convinced that nice ways could carry things much quicker to result.

I repeat that I was not financially interested in Nardus' sales and that I don't see how Mr. W. could take proceedings against me.

I hope Mr. Johnson that you may come to some better and calmer consideration of the situation, especially as far as yourself are concerned. You say something about the little Peter Christus which I could not possibly decipher, it being written in the margin, please repeat same if you judge it necessary.

....

Nardus must have blessed his second daughter Flory more than once. First, in 1908, before she was born, she had given him an excuse not to go to America after the Widener meeting. Now, in 1909, his wife did not feel well after giving birth and it excused him from going anywhere, including Philadelphia. He did not leave Europe for several years.

The name Bourgeois comes up in this letter; this is Stephan Bourgeois, Nardus' wife's cousin.

It is as Lopez (2007) writes that "the increasingly important role of bona fide experts in the decision-making of American collectors seems to have received direct encouragement from the Nardus matter." [145] Letters by or on behalf of American collectors trying to get redress from their highly cultured European dealers travelled back and forth over the Atlantic Ocean.

From an official letter, letterhead Land Title Building, Chestnut-Sansom and Broad Streets, Philadelphia, we know that Nardus had indeed been unable to find the time to come to America and face the music.

On January 4 1909, Johnson wrote a letter to Van Gelder on Widener's behalf. By this time, Van Gelder was Nardus' silent partner and charge d'affaires.[146] It reads:

....

I am in receipt of yours of December 18th. I am very sorry Mr. N. was unable to come to Philadelphia as young Mr. W. had delayed his departure under the information of such

---

145 Scallen (2004: 185) lists earlier trips to the American continent for collection-evaluation purposes, for example Bode's 1893 trip during which he had not been shy to challenge "attributions he found in New World collections, many of which seemed inflated to him."

146 Letter in PMA (JGJ 5/5,6).

intention, which he had received. Learning that Mr. N. would not arrive, he sailed last week and will there press his claims.

I am very desirous that an amicable settlement shall be made and hope something will be done to save any further trouble. It is not merely Dr. de Groot; but Mr. Fry, Dr. Valentiner, Mr. Berenson, and others have united in their opinion.

Where dealers took at a value of $125 000, pictures in exchange and offered to sell them for $23 000, they gave the best possible guarantee of their good faith in condemnation [?]. There can be no doubt as to the fact in the matter of those works.

Mr. W. is sending to Europe several of the works, and I have not a shadow of a doubt that the condemnation is well founded.

As far as I am concerned, I wish it distinctly understood that no claim of any sort or kind is made.

It is with Mr. W.'s matter that I am interested and I want to see him put right. When he is dealt with satisfactorily, you may consider the episode closed as regards myself.

I am very certain that before young Mr. W. returns, some satisfactory arrangement will have been made, or there will be some very serious trouble. I gave to the Park, to be marked as old copies, the Van Dyck, the little Frans Hals and the Rembrandt "Rabbi." The matter, as far as those three pictures are concerned, is closed.

The Antonello and one of the Van der Neers, are modern beyond all question. The Matsys is not very old. The photographs of most of the German and Flemish pictures have been submitted to Friedländer. Some to Bode. All agree in their opinion.

Let me give you a list of some of the wrong attributions.[147]

Hoping very much that you will be able to make a satisfactory arrangement with Mr. W. on his own account, I am Yours &c.

On January 29, 1909 Van Gelder replied:[148]

I received your letter of 4th inst. and waited with answering until I had something to say about the meeting with Geo. Widener, which you wrote about.

I just arrived from parties and am glad to say that I have succeeded in getting Messrs. W. and N. to settle in an

147   This list is:
- Paul Potter – Small White Horse.
- Paul Potter – Large Green Landscape.
- Memling (should be David).
- Van Eyck, head – school of.
- A. Durer – old Dutch – copy of engraving.
- R. van [der] Weyden – portrait – school of.
- Francesca – minor artist
- Botticelli – Amico Sandro.
- Van Eyck, (Madonna and Child) – School of – unknown.
- Van der Goes – a Master of Bruges.
- Van der Neer (Street of Sunshine), minor artist ≠ unknown.
- Brower (Large Landscape) – Claes Molenaer.
- Mantegna (Portrait of Doctor) – minor artist – Salviati?
- G. Metsu (Woman in Window) – Frans Mieris.
- Dirk Bouts (St. Catharine) – minor Flemish artist.
- L. Tom Ring – minor artist.
- Dirk Bouts (Large Master of Stadel Work).
- Durer (Erasmus) – old copy.
- Terborch (Old copy of Berlin picture).
- Fabritius Palamedes (Still Life), – J. Streek.
- Brauer – Fisherman and Boats – minor artist.
- Vermeer (Landscape) – minor artist.
- L. van Leyden (Portrait) – small ≠ minor artist.
- Hobbema (Large) – Ruysdael.
- Etc. etc.

148   Letter in Letter in PMA (JGJ, 5/5,6).

amicable way the question pending! Before the meeting I had persuaded Mr. N. that if the 12 pictures questioned were of good quality and that the judgment of De Gr. was preposterous, he could not lose in exchanging some of his pictures for those on which a doubt was thrown. Well, after a lengthy discussion it was agreed between the two gentlemen, that Mr. N. would make the sacrifice and give some of his fine pictures in exchange on the formal condition: that all questions would then be settled and that no more claims would or could anymore be put forward hereafter for other pictures sold by Mr. N.

Hereupon Mr. N. consented to give the two little Rembrandts (which he exchanged for his Portr. of a Lady by Memling, actually in the Louvre from the Kann collection.[149]

Then he proposed to give a most superb portrait of the Countess Arundel by Rubens (collection Borgès), this I consider the finest work of N.'s collection.

Then he proposed the two small heads by Rogier v.d. Weyden, exposed at Bruges 1907, which we saw together (St. Catherine and an Old Man). Both are illust. and

---

149   Cf. Quodbach (2002: 80 n. 65): "In 1910 the Wideners also had two small "Rembrandts" [...] in their possession which had been part of Nardus' own collection a short time before." According to Van Gelder's letter, the Wideners acquired ("were given") these two Rembrandts in 1909. Quodbach communicated by telephone on March 16, 2010) that they are now in the National Gallery of Washington. According to its provenance, both paintings are by a follower of Rembrandt and were *sold* to Widener in 1911: "Hofstede de Groot 1907-1927, 6: 255, and also provenance card index in NGA curatorial records, list Nardus as a previous owner of the picture, but his name is deleted on the Widener Collection file card for the picture." Also according to the provenance, *The Head of St. Matthew* came through the Duveen Brothers in 1907 to Kleinberger & Co in Paris, then to Nardus. *The Head of an Old Woman* came possibly via Bourgeois, Kann, Duveen, Kleinberger in 1909 to Nardus, who sold them (read: gave them) to P. A. B. Widener. Joseph Widener inherited them in 1911 and gave them to the National Gallery of Art in 1942.

described in the work "Les Chefs d'Oeuvre a l'exposition de la Toison d'Or à Bruges."

Then he offered de Madonna & Child & Angel by le Maître de la Legende de St. Ursule also exposed at the Toison d'Or and illustr. and described in same book. The cost of these 6 pictures will balance the 12 to be returned. These 6 pictures shall be looked over by someone at the discretion of Mr. Geo. W. who suggested Sedelmeyer, which was agreeable to Mr. N.

The 12 questioned works have not yet arrived from Le Havre, they shall be looked carefully over by Mr. N. and I have promised both gentlemen to come again to Paris to see them.

You see, Mr. Johnson that I have kept word and done all possible to adjust the matter and the solution is fair to both parties.

To answer your letter, I repeat again, that I am much chagrined at your having marked the imposing vDyck and the charming little Hals copies. I predict that there will come a day that these labels shall have to be taken off!

If the Antonello, one of the Van der Neers are modern, there should be done right to you and so with the Matsys and 2 Dürers.

And so Van Gelder went on and on about nine more questioned works, ending this seven-page letter by promising "to make it my duty to get you together with Mr. Nardus" (who for the time being did not intend to set foot on American soil). On Feb. 25, 1909, Johnson received the following reply, to his reply, from Van Gelder:[150]

-----

150   Letter in PMA (JGJ, 5/5,6).

I received your letter. Since I wrote you that things were being arranged between Mr. Geo. W. and Nardus, the matter has been stopped till the arrival of his father next month. Mr. W. will ask me to meet him in Paris. I will do so and then try to bring everything to an end. I think that my presence would be entirely useful between both parties, the more so that, as you say, the English pictures have been questioned and this may lead again to difficulties.

I saw the 12 pictures on their arrival together with Mr. W. and N. I must say that some (not all, fortunately!) were not of the quality expected, if opportunity presents itself I would like to explain to you why I am still convinced of Nardus' good faith.

At this point in his reply to Johnson, Van Gelder shifted tone and topic and continued in an effort to cement his relationship with Johnson: "Did you show Berenson the photo I sent you of the Niccolà? If this unfortunate matter had not disturbed our pleasant relations, I would have send you a photo of a superb portrait of a lady (bust) *en profil* again a [illegible] by Vittor Carpaccio. Do you expect to come to Europe this summer?"

We see that Van Gelder was making big progress with Johnson. He had also progressed from addressing him as Sir, to Dr. Sir, and then to Dear Sir. The following letter of June 16, 1909, starting with My Dear Sir, went on:[151]

Today I found a letter, which I had written you the 15th of May and which unfortunately had not been forwarded

---

151   Letter in PMA (JGJ, 5/5,6).

but waylaid between some papers. I told you all about the binding up of the matter with Mr. W. and Nardus, of course you know all about it now and it is useless to repeat again all what has been arranged. You said in your last letter that you expect to be in Paris the 7th of July, will this letter reach you yet? I expect to leave the 15th of July for Canada to be Sir William's guest for some time, on my return I would be quite happy if I could pay you a visit and see again, after so many years, your collection. When do you think to be back at Phila? Perhaps could I meet you in Paris.

After receiving a reply from Johnson, Van Gelder wrote again on July 6, 1909, to say that he had received his letter and wanted to send him a word of welcome in Paris.[152] He continued:

You probably have heard of the sale of Mr. W.'s (Nardus) pictures at Amsterdam. I am sorry that the prices for some were not as high as anticipated, especially the little Rembrandt, a lovely work that brought 25 000 frs, 5 200 doll.!

I have done everything possible to have the matters between W. and Nardus settled in an equitable way to both parties. I feel unhappy that the sale has not been more favorable. I don't understand why Mr. W. decided to sell the little Rembrandt. I hope you will get it for your collection. I expect to leave for Canada the 2nd week in August and return beginning of September.

I hope Mr. Johnson, now that the W. matter has been settled, that our acquaintance will not be broken off; the pleasant hours we have spent together cannot be

152　Letter in PMA (JGJ 5/5,6).

forgotten; what has happened with Nardus (in whose honorability I persist in believing) cannot be ascribed to me; Your collection will always remain dear to me.

We leave Johnson and his troubles for a while (his troubles were also Van Horne's troubles because he had referred Nardus and Van Gelder to Johnson). On January 25, Gimpel, of Fifth Avenue 636, New York, confided to Van Horne, by way of a sales pitch:[153]

> You know that I have always been very anxious to have you possess my Ruysdael. If I could I would do anything to tempt you, but the picture having passed in public sale, as I told you at the time, and as the price which I paid afterwards and which has been recorded will show, the picture costs me more than $12 500 and it is only to show you my good will, that I will make you a reduction of $500 on the special price named you at the time which was $14 000. You know the prices of Dutch pictures and you will readily realize how cheap this exceptionally fine picture is.

The painting that Gimpel offered could not have been *Bleaching Grounds near Haarlem* because Conway saw it in Van Horne's mansion in 1905. It was neither *Landscape and Waterfall* (estimated at $13 500 on the 1940-1984 Estate Insurance list), nor *Landscape near Arnheim* (estimated at $2 500) at the same list. Anyway, Van Horne apparently went for the Ruysdael.[154] As shown in the footnote, Henschel did

153 Letter in VHFF (6/2).
154 VH 35 Ruysdael, Jacob Van (Haarlem 1628/29-1682). *Dutch Fishing Boats at Sea.* Two boats with extended sails rolling on a choppy sea, under a grey sky broken by

not appraise it, and it does not appear on the Estate Insurance list of paintings. In the Wickenden catalogue he transcribed something that was written on the back of its panel: "This beautiful scrap undoubtedly from the pencil of Jacob Ruysdael was purchased by me purposely to present to my beloved daughter Johannes Smith, in full belief that she will keep it as long as it shall please God to allow her to live. (Signed) John Thomas Smith, Keeper of the Prints and Drawings in the British Museum. September 24th, 1825."

Johnson, Van Gelder, and Nardus were not the only men who went through some upheavals during 1909. Hofstede de Groot had his share of troubles as well. He was not pleased with an article in the Dutch *Handelsblad (Commerce Newspaper)*. While the authentication business thrived, doubts had arisen. On April 10, 1909, Hofstede de Groot addressed a long letter to Mr. Feith, editor-in-chief, agreeing with most of the article about fakes in Dutch art, but not with the following line.[155] Translated from Dutch this reads: "The expert, we have in mind, is so conscious about his expertise of art (of old art) that, for himself, he excludes all doubts about real or fake art."

Hofstede wrote that he inferred that the "expert" was him, and that therefore he felt that he had to explain what he had meant to say on the occasion the press was alluding to. A translation of his explanation reads, "According to my opinion, using all available resources, to decide whether a painting is real or false, a modern copy or original old, but I never wanted to say that I for myself exclude every doubt."

---

a touch of light near the zenith [...] Canvas mounted on panel. H. 5¾ in, W. 8 in (12.5 cm × 20 cm). ⊞: –."

155   Letter in RDK.

In that same month of April, Van Horne had Hofstede de Groot certify Rembrandt's *Landscape*.[156]

On May 20, 1909, Van Horne, now staying at the Amstel Hotel in Amsterdam, let Hofstede de Groot know that he would drop by on the following day while his wife and daughter would be sightseeing.[157] Van Horne wrote that he would be glad "to look in on you for a few minutes should you chance to be in town; but I beg you in advance not to waste any time on me for my day will be ... too long with the pictures at the Museum."

Van Horne must not only have dropped by at Hofstede de Groot's in The Hague, because in that same month of May he received Gimpel & Wildenstein's $10 000 invoice for a painting by De Witt.[158]

Petrus Christiaan Eilers (1864-1936), manager of Van Wisselingh & Co, Spui 23 & 27 Amsterdam, sent a letter on May 24, 1909, mentioning Van Horne's trip, shows that the two

---

156   Letter in VHFF (8/4). The certification reads: *Le soussigné, declare quill a examine attentivement et a plusieurs reprises le tableau qui est photographié ïc-contre et qui est peint sur bois de chêne, haut 25.5 large 39 c.m. et signé authentiquement à gauche et en bas, ainsi que date 1654. Il considère ce tableau comme une oeuvre authentique de Rembrandt. Elle provident de la collection qui a été réunie au moitié du XVIIIe siècle par Jennens à Gopsall et qui a passé par heritage aux Earls Howe. Ce tableau sera décrit par le soussigné dans le catalogue des oeuvres de Rembrandt qui paraîtra dans une des prochaines volumes de sa nouvelle edition de Smith, Catalogue raisonné.*

        April 1909   *Corn. Hofstede de Groot*

        The Service des archives du BAM [*Musée des Beaux Arts de Montreal*] gives the dimensions of Rembrandt's *Landscape* (which was bequeathed to them in 1941 and obtained in 1945) as 25.4 × 39.37 cm and the date as 1654. In 1945 this painting was bequeathed to the BAM. As mentioned, this painting was stolen on September 4, 1972.

157   Letter in RKD

158   Letter in VHFF (4/19). VH 72 De Witte, Emanuel de (Alkmaar, 1606 – Amsterdam 1692). *Interior of a Church in Holland.* ▣: Through a dark arched opening from before which a long green gold-fringed curtain has been drawn to the right, the white-walled interior of a church is seen, illuminated in places by rays of brilliant sunlight [...] Panel H. 28⅞, W. 23½ (73½ × 59 cm). In the coll. of Baron Edmond de Rothschild, Paris. From Gimpel and Wildenstein, Paris and New York, 1909. ▣: 20 000.

knew each other, perhaps from 1906 on.[159] According to the Wickenden catalogue, only Maris' *Girl Knitting*[160] made it to Montreal, but it was bought in 1906 from Wallis & Sons. Perhaps that was bought during Van Horne's visit to the Van Wisselinghs in March 1906. Van Horne was then in London and had visited Matthew Maris, who temporarily lived with the Van Wisselinghs in their little castle in Northwood.

Anyway, Eilers started the May 24 letter by informing Van Horne about the water colour drawing, which was a representation of Mrs. Neuhuijs 25 years ago, by [Albert] Neuhuijs (1844-1914). He promised to send it to Van Horne's London House and said he would write Mr. v. Wisselingh to "keep it for you till you would require it." Eilers went on to wish Van Horne and his family a nice trip to Paris, adding, "After our last meeting about the three paintures, two of J. Maris and the Mauve, I kept them a little aside for you, hoping you will be able to cable me about them and to bring them over to Canada as three of the finest examples of modern Dutch art."

Eilers had started his career in the art business as a student of the The Hague Academy of Fine Arts; at the age of fifteen he was employed by Goupil & Co, which was also in The Hague. During his apprenticeship he had prepared canvasses for Jacob Maris and painted *en plein air* with Vincent van Gogh. In 1892 he was charged with the sales of water colours, drawings, and pictures at E. J. van Wisselingh & Co, and from 1903 he paid 15 000 guilders to become Van Wisselingh's partner for

---

159   Letter in VHFF (3/27).

160   VH 174 Maris, Jacob Hendrikus (The Hague 1837-1899). *Girl Knitting*. ⬛: Sitting on a bench before a shuttered window at the right, she looks down at some flowers near the lower left and quietly continues her knitting [...]. Panel. H. 12½ in, W. 10¼ in (33 cm × 26 cm). Signed on the wall at the lower right, J. H. Maris. From Wallis & Sons, London, 1906. ▣: 2 500.

  Data about the visit are from a letter of March 20, 1906, by E. J. Van Wisselingh to Eilers in the Van Wisselingh & Co Archives that Ester Wouthuysen kindly shared with me.

2/8 of the profits (Heijbroek and Van Wouthuysen, 1999: 40, 51). Also according to Heijbroek and Van Wouthuysen (1999: 58), during a dinner at the Van Horne's, Eilers saw a vase that he himself had painted. He challenged Van Horne, saying that he knew which initials were underneath. A servant was ordered to fetch the vase and yes, there they saw Eilers' own initials. After that, Van Horne frequently recommended Eilers to his circle of collector friends.

In those days, Van Horne's dealers kept him very busy. Van Horne received a letter dated June 16, 1909, from Van Slochem about Delft tiles.[161] Van Slochem was apparently put in charge of Van Gelder's affairs while Van Gelder was busy with Nardus' affairs. Van Slochem must have known Van Gelder and Nardus since their time in New York.[162] In the letter about the Delft tiles, Van Slochem also mentioned that he had cabled Van Gelder and asked him what he thought of that "railway thing." He also asked, "Should I engage a lawyer at once to protect you if anything can be done, so as to arrange it before I leave."

More about the "railway thing" later on, but first let's look at how dealers and connoisseurs networked and protected one another after the 1908 affair.

VAN GELDER PARTNERS WITH HOFSTEDE DE GROOT

Van Gelder, still fighting Johnson's charges, no longer took any chances and started to partner with Hofstede de Groot. In his letter of June 11, 1909, sent from Hotel des Indes in The Hague, Van Gelder thanked Hofstede de Groot, for his "letter

---

161   Letter in VHFF (7/9).
162   Van Slochem advertised his wares at least from January 14, 1896, on in *The New York Times*. He then offered for sale, at the Fifth Avenue Auctions Rooms, a collection of Dutch marqueterie chests, beaded fans, and old paintings by well-known artists.

with expertise." [163] (Of course, all their correspondence was in Dutch, so these letters are translated.) He noted that Hofstede had forgotten Vermeer's *View on Delft*,[164] Rembrandt's *Ox Tongues and Tail*, Snyders' *Tortoises and Fishes*, Flemish school: *David and Harp*. He further wrote that he and his wife hoped to visit another day, and he enclosed the one hundred francs that were "still lacking from the agreed price." From a little addition in this letter, we see that 2 000 francs were 956 guilders, 100 francs were *f*47.80, so the agreed upon price (for work already done?) was *f*1 004.20.

On July 4, Van Gelder thanked "Dr. de Groot" for instructing the Dowdeswell Company to send him a photo of the Jan Steen:

> I thank you very much for your interference in this matter. The painting seems to be of beautiful quality, the price is though much too high. I received the photo of your beautiful Fabritius for which I also thank you. When you visit Zeecrabbe again, I will remind you of your promise to sign the photographs.
>
> I was so bold to send you two of my paintings from Paris, two landscapes by Ruysdael and by DeKoninck; you have seen the photos thereof at my place. I bid you to be so friendly as to give me your opinion and to return them to me [...] you advised me to remove from my collection the piece [the landscape by Cuyp, was hung in Van Gelder's bedroom] as well as the so-called Van Dijck (oval).

---

163   Letter in RKD.
164   This work, a smaller and slightly modified copy on panel of Vermeer's View on Delft, is now attributed to Pieter Ernst Hendrik Praetorius (1791-1876). In the 1930s it was still part of Van Gelder's collection. Its current location is unknown. Thanks to Esmee Quodbach (info in e-mail of November 2, 2014).

On July 16, 1909, Van Gelder wrote Hofstede de Groot that he had received both his letters, thanked him for the information in it and said that he had never heard of Gerrit van Hees[165] "so will keep that painting in my collection, and will put away the so-called Hp. Koning." About Hofstede de Groot's fee, Van Gelder wrote that he (Van Gelder) had considered:

> That these two paintings were part of my collection when you visited me and I even showed you the photographs, and you inspected them as being part of my collection, so an extra honorarium would be out of the question. In the event you have a different opinion and find it fair to invoice me for this advice, please tell me.

Van Gelder's last lines read as if private collectors got their expertises free or for a lower price than charged to art merchants. If that were the case, it would have paid off to profile oneself as a "gentleman (collector)" rather than a merchant. Van Gelder went on in this letter with news about his purchase of [Rembrandt's] *Petronella Buys*, through Kleinberger (Collection Jefferson-De Ridder-Bode Vol. II no 118): "I would appreciate your expertise of this painting that right now is being rid of the layer of yellow varnish. The Jan Steen is too expensive, I believe that Kleinberger will purchase it."

On July 20, 1909, Van Gelder wrote Hofstede de Groot that he agreed with the fee for the expertise of the Rembrandt and enclosed a cheque for 250 francs.[166] He said he hoped that Hofstede de Groot would repeat a visit to Zeecrabbe so he could then also see for himself how beautiful the *Petronella Buys*

---

165   Letter in RKD. Gerrit van Hees' (1629-1702) works were often attributed to Ruysdael or Vroom.

166   Letter in RKD.

had become![167] In a p.s. Van Gelder added that he thought that Kleinberger had bought the Jan Steen and urged "you would certainly keep Rembrandt's Saul & Sara in observation for me."

By the end of the year, on November 30, 1909, Van Gelder, now travelling through Italy, advised Hofstede de Groot, that he had ordered a Parisian photographer to send him (Hofstrede de Groot) about twenty-five photos of his (Van Gelder's) paintings and that more were to follow.[168] Van Gelder hoped to learn whether the photographs indeed had reached Hofstede de Groot.

On December 12, 1909, Van Gelder thanked Hofstede de Groot for his remarks on the photographs. He also confided that since buying *Petronella Buys*, he had not bought any more Dutch masters, just a few Flemish and Dutch primitives and some Italian paintings.[169] Furthermore Van Gelder announced his upcoming visit to Mr. Schwab, who would show him his Rembrandt, "I also believe that it is best to visit that gentleman alone, as you proposed, and then communicate my findings to you."

Meanwhile, in the midst of his dealings with Hofstede de Groot, Van Gelder advised Van Horne by letter of August 3, 1909, of his upcoming visit to Van Horne's estate in St. Andrews.[170] Van Gelder confirmed that he had received the

---

167 Cf.: *The New York Times* of April 28, 1906, sub headline about this painting: A Rembrandt is bought by a Hollander and will be taken home by him ... Portrait of Petronella Buys, Wife of Burgomaster of Cardon, Rembrandt van Rijn; to A. Pryor for H. Texeira de Mattos of Holland ... $20 600 Buys. *The Burlington Magazine for Connoisseurs*, Vol. 25, No 136 (Jul, 1914), p. 261 reads: Dutch, Spanish and Russian Periodicals. Dutch. Oud Holland, 4th issue. No 31, 1913: "Dr. Hofstede de Groot writes on Rembrandt's portraits of Philips Lucasse and Petronella Buys [...] is now in the Van Gelder at the Ukkel coll. at Brussels." A. Pryor will have been Amsterdam art dealer Abraham Preyer who in 1893 served as general manager of the Dutch contributions to the Universal Exhibition in Chicago (Dekkers 1896).

168 Letter in RKD.

169 Letter in RKD.

170 Letter in VHFF (7/2).

photos of Van Horne's superb Halses, and that "the book was already printed," but that he would arrange for Schmidt-Degener, director of the Boymans Museum in Rotterdam, to publish it. Van Gelder ended with expressing the wish that his wife and babies, could join him, but that would have to be arranged later.[171]

Also, on November 5, 1909, banker Morgan, Harjes & Cie informed Van Horne that "at the request and for the account of Mr. Nardus we are these days sending you three certificates of 100 shares of the Laurentide Company." [172] Perhaps Nardus had given Van Horne's address as the one to mail the certificates to. Van Horne must have grabbed his pen right away to let Nardus know that the certificates did not have to be sent to him (perhaps Van Horne no longer publicly wanted to be associated with Nardus), and advised Nardus what to do in case he wanted to subscribe to more stocks or to sell some. As the Laurentide Company had always been a profitable company, Van Horne might very well still have been pleased with Nardus' stake in his ventures.

On November 29, 1909, Eilers – still representing Van Wisselingh & Co – wrote, from Toronto, to Van Horne, who was just back from Cuba, that he had taken Mr. Shepherd of Scranton and his friends to Van Horne's house where a good time was had by all.[173] Eilers had it known that he had sold one Daumier to Mr. Jam. Woods of Ottawa but had kept the best one for Van Horne "as you are the only art-collector in Montreal who can appreciate this picture." Eilers proposed to send Van Horne the Daumier ($7 000) to his house – for viewing we might assume – and let him know that when he would get it back from Van Horne and would take it to Holland, he

---

171   According to the Civil Registry, these babies were Sonia (September 31, 1906) and Wotan (April 4, 1908), both born in Uccle.

172   Letter in VHFF (5/4).

173   Letter in VHFF (3/27).

would set a higher price on it. A flattering and at the same time urging letter!

The next letter throws light on the warm relations Van Horne must have had with customs officers. Establishing a collection is not just a matter of purchasing; there are additional costs such as crating, shipping, insuring, and custom duties. Van Horne often tried to avoid paying his import taxes, but he was not the only one.

On December 8, 1909, Van Horne's secretary, W. F. Lynch, addressed a custom agent as "My dear Postans." [174] Lynch wrote that Sir William was expecting a case, marked "F. M. 0 4979." Lynch kindly requested its transfer to Van Horne's residence, to be opened and examined there "as usual." A handwritten note on this letter indicates that the shipment came from Van Gelder.

In his last letter of 1909 to Van Horne, Nardus apologized for the trouble with the shares and congratulated him with his new Rembrandt.[175] He went on, "I said to Mr. Kann that I consider that Rembrandt one of the most typical and it is an extraordinary work."

As mentioned, according to the members of the RRP, this was the only genuine Rembrandt in Van Horne's collection. Nardus ended his letter with the hope that Van Horne would come over in February. According to Saltzman (2004: 204), in 1907 the entire Kann collection in Paris was bought by the

---

174   Letter in VHFF (7/22).
175   Letter in VHFF (6/4). VH 53 Rembrandt Van Rijn (Leiden 1606–Amsterdam 1669). *Portrait of a Young Rabbi* (or *Young man with Black Skull-cap*). "Leaning slightly forward, wearing a dark brownish robe, a young man of about thirty looks inquiringly out of the picture [...] Signed about at the right "Rembrandt f. 1661." Canvas H. 26 in, W. 22¼ in (64 cm × 57 cm). In Cardinal Despuy's coll. Rome (Presented to him by the Pope (Benedict XIV) in 1750. In the coll. of the Count of Menenegro, Majorca, by inheritance from Cardinal Despuy. In the Cotaner coll. In the coll. of the Marquis de la Genial, Spain. In the coll. of Rudolphe Kann, Paris, 1907, catalogue no. 70, illustrated. In poss. of Duveen Brothers Paris. In poss. of M. Knoedler & Co., London. ⊞: 150 000."

Duveen Brothers, which shows that the sale must have been through Duveen, Knoedler, Nardus and Van Gelder.

Also, 1909 was a great year for connoisseurs. German connoisseur Max J. Friedländer (1929: 2, 9), who is mentioned in Johnson's letter of January 4 (see above), would much later express a very skeptical opinion about *Atteste* (expertises). He would worry about the consequences of the blend of commerce and science, for the quality of the collections, and the morality of this business. He also hands out some tips for collectors, "trust your own eyes," "go to the dealers," and also, "look for connoisseurs." This last piece of advice might have taken the collectors back to square one. Alas, by the time Friedländer's advice was published in 1929, the great collectors of the first decade of the twentieth century had all passed on.

According to Heijbroek and Wouthuysen (1999: 55) Eilers travelled tirelessly from town to town on business. The year 1910 started out well for him. In January Eilers became excited about an article he had read. He told Van Horne about it in the following letter.[176] Instead of the usual Dear Sir William, Eilers started the following letter of January 7, 1910:

> Sir, together with this, I beg to send you a copy of one of our monthly papers *"Onze Kunst [Our Art]"* containing an article by Dr. Hofstede de Groot concerning the last discovered Rembrandt-paintings, which are not mentioned in Dr. Bode's book about Rembrandt.
>
> As your landscape by Rembrandt is reproduced in this copy together with a reproduction after a pen-drawing by Rembrandt (reproduction no. 9) of which Dr. Hofstede de Groot says in the same article: this pen-drawing seems to be a true sketch from nature after the same farm of your picture (he wrote "of Sir William van Horne's picture")

---

176   Letter in VHFF (3/7).

and which proves that Sir William's picture is one of the
very rare paintings painted by Rembrandt directly from
nature. I thought it would interest you to have a copy of
this paper.

....

On January 10, 1910, Van Gelder, sailing on the steamship
George Washington, wrote Van Horne that he had been thinking about the Constable, "for which you paid such a big sum." [177]
There must have been a delay in Van Gelder's plans as he had
already announced his upcoming visit to the American continent in August 1909. Anyway, Van Gelder said that Van Horne
should not "bear such a tremendous loss through the fault
of Nardus or me." He also said he was convinced that Nardus
would do the right thing and that he, Van Gelder, would see to
it that the right thing did happen. Van Gelder then discussed
the start of the Borden affair: "I look forward with great interest towards the result of your visit to Borden and your advise
at what should be done." (More about this affair in the next
chapter.)

On January 21, 1910, Van Horne received from E. Gimpel &
Wildenstein of 636 Fifth Avenue one more invoice for a picture
by Dewitte, "sold to you in Paris last September." [178]

----

177   Letter in VHFF (4/11). Was this VH 13, Constable's *View on the Stour* (▣: 1500),
      which was the only Constable in the collection and purchased in 1900 from Nar-
      dus and Van Gelder? Or was it a Constable that had to be removed?
178   Letter in VHFF (4/19). VH 72, Witte, Emanuel de (Alkmaar 1617–Amsterdam
      1692). *Interior of a Church in Holland.* ▣: Through a dark arched opening from
      before which a long green gold-fringed curtain has been drawn to the right, the
      white-walled interior of a church is seen, illuminated in places by rays of brilliant
      sunlight. Panel H. 28⅞ in × W. 23½ in (73.5 cm × 59 cm). In the collection of Baron
      Edmond de Rothschild, Paris. From Gimpel and Wildenstein, Paris and New
      York, 1909. ▣: 20 000.
          Another note on the Henschel sheet says that Sir William paid $10 000 or
      50 000 francs. A note dated April 9, 1964, said "Fine! Should perhaps keep? May
      increase 3 times in value." This painting was no. 29 at the 1933 exhibition in
      Montreal.

Nardus' next letter, of February 4, 1910, shows his multi-tiered relationship with Van Horne. He expresses regret again for the trouble with the shares, by saying "you will oblige me to have them sold. Please deduct $1 000 you have advanced from the proceeds of the shares." [179] He expressed disappointment that Van Horne couldn't come in the middle of March, but he hoped to see him later. "Because Paris was inundated," Nardus went on that he had settled at Hotel De l'Europe for the time being. Also, he would not forget about the flower picture he had promised. At the end of the letter, Nardus mentioned that it was difficult to write because he had a blister on his thumb from fencing.[180]

Nardus, Van Gelder, Van Wisselingh, and Eilers were not Van Horne's only Dutch dealers. On February 10, 1910, art dealer P. J. Zürcher, from FINE ART GALERY, VILLA ERICA, 25 SCHEVENINGSEWEG, THE HAGUE, wrote:[181]

I received a letter from Mr. van Tol saying that you bought the drawing by Toorop entitled "Le jardin des douleurs" and have herewith much pleasure to inform you that this drawing carefully packed is forwarded to your address

---

The other De Witte in Van Horne's collection was VH 73, *Portrait of Spinoza*. Ⓦ: Under the dark arches of a temple, with a landscape opening beyond a column seen in perspective at the right, the subject is depicted half length, life-size, the gloved right hand, held across the body [...]. Canvas H. 30½ in, W. 23½ in (77.5 cm × 59 cm). From the sale of the collection of Herman Linde, New York, 1910. Ⓜ: 5 000.

179 Letter in VHFF (5/4).
180 Later on the SR/Olympic Sports Website published the following results of Nardus' fencing efforts:

Games	Age	City	Sport	Event	Team	Rank	Medal
1912 Summer	44	Stockholm	Fencing	Épée, Team	Netherlands	3	Bronze

181 Letter in VHFF (7/20).

with the Steamer Potsdam, from the Holland-America line, sailing the 6th of this month and [I] shall be pleased to hear from you the good arrival [...] I also have a very fine and important work by Jan Steen and when you are interested...." [182]

On April 2, Zürcher thanked Van Horne for the draft of $390 (in sterling) and confirmed that he had written Toorop "to ask him to give me all particulars about its meaning." [183] Heijbroek (2008: 102-107) notes about the Toorop that it had been missing since 1910 and that the Rijksprentenkabinet of the Rijksmuseum had bought it in 1977. About the Old Garden of Tears's provenance, Heijbroek notes it was at an exhibition in Belgium, Ghent, and Antwerp in 1892, then bought by Van Wisselingh & Co., who sold it to a Dutch family. So, in 1910 Zürcher had it for sale. Because Van Horne wanted to know about the drawing, Zürcher asked Toorop, who had replied that *The Old Garden* was the start of a series of symbolic drawings.

Back to the North American continent. Nardus had not been forgotten in the American art world and neither had Van Gelder; his return to New York was mentioned in a short article in the *American Art News* on February 19 under the heading WITH THE DEALERS: "Mr. M. Van Gelder, of Brussels, who some years ago when associated with Mr. S. Nardus, of Paris, sold many old and modern foreign pictures to prominent American collectors, is again in New York for a visit after a lapse of many years."

---

182 P. J. Zürcher's artist brother, Jan Zürcher (1851-1905), had married into a rich family and might have had the Steen in his collection. Cf.: http://www.dbnl.org/tekst/molh003nieu08_01/molh003nieu08_01_2159.htm (last accessed March 2014).

183 Letter in VHFF (7/20).

Then, on April Fool's Day, Van Horne's secretary wrote Van Slochem, who was staying at 477 Fifth Avenue, that Van Horne had telegraphed him (Van Slochem) that very morning, as follows: "Increase limit Rubens to twenty thousand, Reduce number one sixteen to four hundred [and] buy little Romney number one twelve if goes under two hundred".[184] Three days later, April 3, 1910, Van Slochem replied to Van Horne that he had shipped the Meister der Weiblichen Halbfiguren (referring to an early Flemish master) and the Van Orley: "your son will be also delighted I am sure."[185] Furthermore Van Slochem expected to meet with Van Horne that same week. A handwritten statement details part of the sale (and much of the rise of Van Horne's collection):

Rubens	*Feast of Herod*
Hals (?)	*Portrait of D*
Master of Half-length Female Figures	*Scene from the Cross*
B. van Orley	*King bearing Gifts*
Also misc. pictures from Wickenden sale.	

The *Feast of Herod* seen by Caroline Pierson, having survived the 1933 fire, deemed an unimpressive schoolwork by Frits Lught later on in 1933, was obviously removed from the collection. From 1910 on, another *Feast of Herod* by Rubens – rather Studio of Rubens – was going to deck the Van Horne

---

184 Letter in VHFF (7/9). VH 4, Romney, George (Becksdie, Daltin-in Furness 1734–
     Kendal 1802). *Jane, Duchess of Gordon and her son George, Marquis of Huntly.*
     ☒: In a white dress, seated near an open window, three-quarters-length turned to
     the left, leaning towards a circular carved table at the right on which she rests her
     left arm, the head is turned full three-quarters to the left supported lightly by the
     hand [...] Canvas 49¾ in, W. 40⅜ in (126 cm × 102 cm). In the coll. of Sir Herbert E.
     Maxwell, MP 1891; in poss. of Mr. Charles Wertheimer, London, 1896; in poss. of
     Messrs. Sulley & co. London; in poss. of T. J. Blakeslee, NY. 1910. ☒: 15 000, would
     have cost 60 000.
185 Letter in VHFF (6/18)

mansion walls. It is now at the Nasher Museum of Art at Duke University.[186]

The April 13, 1910 invoice reads:[187]

Painting

The Feast of Herod by P. P. Rubens	$5 250[188]
Portrait of a man by Frans Hals.	$225[189]
Express charges to Montreal	$16.11
Packing and shipping.	$22
. . . .	$5 513.11
Credit by Cash	$5 500
Balance	$ 13.11

In an April 11, 1910, letter to Hofstede de Groot, Van Gelder thanked him for the postcard, the letter, and the photo.[190] He went on about an extraordinarily colourful and bright painting that sizzled and was far above his *Toper*: "It cannot be compared with my woman's portrait that is simple, earnestly, nearly colourless, a studied work, but my impression is that

---

186 See: http://emuseum.nasher.duke.edu/view/objects/asitem/items$0040:1535 (thanks to Edmee Quodbach for the information).
187 Letter in VHFF (5/11).
188 VH 137 Rubens, Peter Paul (Siegen, Westphalia, 1577–Antwerp 1640). *The Feast of Herod*. ⊞: Max Rooses in his monumental *L'Oeuvre de Rubens* (Vol. II, page 11, no. 242) entitles this picture *Le Festin d' Herodiade*, and follows with a detailed description which we here translate: "The King Herod is seated at the head of the table, under a canopy of a seat covered with a red cushion [... four pages]." Panel H. 28 in, W. 40¾ in (71 cm × 103 cm). In the coll. of Sandrart [...] Purchased from one of Sandrart's descendants, 1885. In the coll. of Hermann Linde of Berlin and Pittsburg [...]. Purchased by Sir William Van Horne in New York, 1910. ⊞: 30 000.
189 VH 66 Hals, Frans (Antwerp 1584–Haarlem 1666). *Portrait of a Dutch Gentleman*. ⊞: He is shown standing, three quarters length life size, dressed in plain black, with body in profile to the right [...] Companion picture to the *Portrait of a Dutch Lady*. Canvas 36⅝ in, W. 27⅛ in (92 cm × 68 cm). Inscribed on the background to the right, "AETAT. SUAE. 37. Ano. 1637. In the coll. of the Count de Thiennes. In the coll. of the Countess Van Limburg-Stirum. In the coll. of M. Van Gelder, Uccle, Belgium. ⊞: 125 000 (pair 250 000).
190 Letter in RKD.

I do believe that it well keep up with the portrait. It is from a very important English collection. I have the piece in option and can show it to you in Paris."

Next, a seven-page letter, dated April 17, 1910, from Van Gelder to Van Horne.[191] He wrote that he was beginning to believe that Van Horne would not come to Europe, that he (Van Gelder) did not know when he would return to America and that it would depend on Van Horne's reply to this letter. He went on:

As to the Frans Hals I will arrange everything to your satisfaction, I hate to think that the two Rembrandts don't please you; the Hals is now at Decock. I will communicate later on with you about the picture.

I heard with great satisfaction about your purchase of the Rubens – the Master of the Half Figures, the Van Orley. I am happy that Van Slochem has been of service to you and see with very much pleasure that you trust him with your interest. I thank you most sincerely for the interest you take in our new venture; V. Sl. writes me a great deal of your kindness and the very valuable advice you are giving him. What V. Sl. needs is first of all experience and then I can think of getting him some works of art, which will bring him at once to the front.

Van Gelder went on about being anxious to see the Rubens, raved about the Master of the Womanly Half Figures, discussed the Van Orley, and advised that he had sent the photo of his DeKeyzer to Kronig,[192] who was writing an article about

---

191   Letter in VHFF (7/15).
192   Joseph Otto Kronig (1887-1984) was partner with Abraham Bredius (1855-1946), Director of The Hague Mauritshuis museum from 1889 to 1909. In 1907 Kronig moved in with Bredius, "when he was appointed in 1910 as Director of the Frans Hals Museum in Haarlem. Kronig held this position for one year. In 1912 he

this painter in *l'Art Flamand et Hollandais*: "Do you get that publication?" he asked. Then Van Gelder got serious – as he should have:

> Now Sir William, I want to ask your opinion on a very important matter. Through special circumstances I got quite strongly interested in the British Columbia and Alaska R. R. (or Br. Col. R+R. Dev. Co.); they cost me 10 dollar per share. What do you think of the enterprise? Do you know some of the Directors? It being a matter of much interest to me, I would ask you to kindly to give this your careful consideration, perhaps you could let me know about this, as soon [as] possible. If you think favourable about the Cy., I may come over to Canada and get in close touch with the Direction, if not, I will have to get out quickly. I ought to have asked your advise before, but valuable time would have been lost; I am told the Cy is in very good hands, the Can. Government has given it a large subsidy and enormous grants of land.

Next, on April 25, 1910, Van Horne, back from Cuba and more or less on his way to Europe, was still agonizing about his collection.[193] He apologized to Hofstede de Groot that he was:

> very much in default to you in the acknowledgement of a very kind note you sent me many months ago but I have been running about in the Tropics and everywhere and lately have been from week to week on the point of sailing

---

moved to London, moved in with Bredius again in 1916. In 1920 he moved to Florence where Bredius had bought him a house. It is said that Bredius in 1919 moved to Monte Carlo in Monaco due to a sexual scandal" (Blankert 1978/80/90: 24, 27).

193   Letter in RKD.

for your side of the Atlantic and hoping then for the pleasure of seeing you at The Hague.

I write now to ask if you will permit me to send for your examination and opinion in a professional way an occasional picture and permit me to pay the usual fees. I have one or two now on which I should like your opinion and I am anxious to keep out of my collection anything of a questionable or second-rate character. If I may do this. I shall be glad if you will let me know how the pictures should be addressed.

You may be interested in knowing that I have made some important additions to my little collection since your visit. Aside from the Rembrandt Landscape study of which you know I have added Rembrandt's "Young Rabbi" from the Rudolphe Kann Collection (Bode (509); a very fine Church Interior by Emanuel de Witte; Rubens "Feast of Herod (Max Rooses' "Oeuvre de Rubens PP Vol. I and Rubens" Vol. 2, p. 591 + 612) (Cat. Duke of Leuchtenburg gallery 1852, no 102 + Burl. Magazine Vol. 10, p. 96), a Jacob Ruysdael (Smith sup. P. 709, no 83) another J. Ruysdael, the one in the Gardner's coll. "Maria mit dem Kinde" by the "Master" of the Deaths of Mary (Bode cat. Hainanan coll. No 62); a very fine "Descent from the Cross" by the "Master of the Half-length Female Figures," and a number of English pictures (XVIIICX), Hoppner, Romney, Hogarth etc. which may not interest you.

By the way, I noticed that you have included one of my Cuyp's in your revised Cat. Raisonné – the "River Scene with Cattle,"[194] but that you have omitted the other

---

194   See footnote 14: 🅦: In poss. of L. Salomon 1894. 🅟: $3 000.

one – the "Stable Interior." [195] Was it because you regarded the latter unfavourably that it was omitted?

Dr. Friedländer thought the omission must have been an oversight. I mention it because in such a work as yours an omission has the effect of a condemnation. To enable you to recall the picture I am sending you a photograph of it.

I trust that we may have the pleasure of seeing you again on this side of the Atlantic before long.

As for Cuyp's *Stable Interior*, it seems that this painting is omitted everywhere, even in publications about Abraham van Calraet, 1642-1722, who also signed his work with AC. Cuyp.

✕

---

195 In his soothing letter of March 14 of 1907, Nardus wrote to Johnson: "The Stable by Cuyp is a second rank work."

PEOPLE & A PLACE

M.C.D. Borden
Source: History of Fall River,
Fenner/Harper & Brothers
P.D.
➔

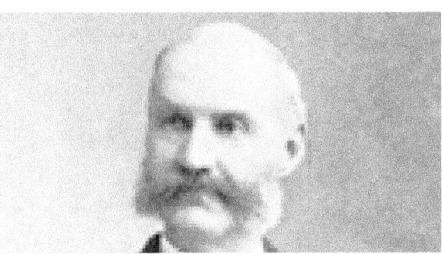

Cogels-Osylei 7, Antwerp
(Cogels Avenue)
Photo: Mary Eggermont-
Molenaar
➔

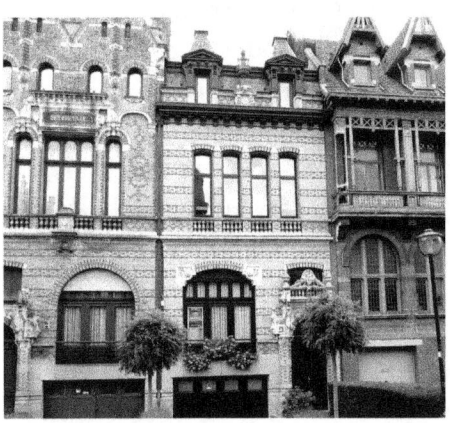

Berend Berenson
➔

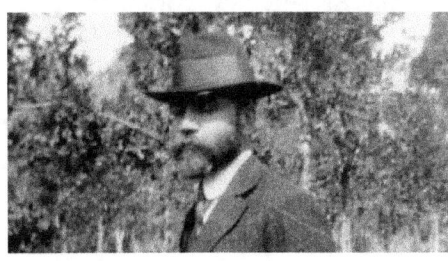

CHAPTER 5

THE BORDEN MATTER / 'FINE ART AN EXTRAORDINARILY DIRTY ART?'

REMEMBER WHAT HOFSTEDE de Groot wrote on October 29, 1908: "I succeeded today in getting admission to Mr. Borden's Gallery & was much pleased by the visit." And also remember that on January 10, 1910, Van Gelder added, "I look forward with great interest towards the result of your visit to Borden and your advise at what should be done."

It looks as if Mr. Matthew Ch. D. Borden, the largest producer of printed cotton in his time, had consulted Van Horne and was not happy with the outcome. On April 27, 1910, the cotton baron wrote the following letter to John G. Johnson using a most impressive letterhead (American Printing Company, above a photo of an aerial view of a number of mills, 34 Thomas Street, New York):[196]

> Some years ago I purchased from Messrs. Nardus and Van Gelder a number of paintings, and I have just discovered that some four or five of these are fraudulent. One attributed to Rembrandt, one to Metsu, one to Velasquez, one to Corregio and one to Rubens. Having been informed that you had had transactions with these men to a considerable extent, I write to ask if you can give me any information

---

196   Letter in PMA (JGJ (5/5,6).

that will be of service in prosecuting my claim against them.

Johnson must have forwarded Borden's request to Van Gelder. We see that Nardus again stayed out of the loop. Van Gelder replied to Johnson on May 10:[197]

I received your kind letter today. I was much astonished to learn from what you wrote about Borden's disposition. I did not think possible that any of his pictures should be disputed and suppose that he might have heard about the Widener affaire and thus became ready to listen to over jealous dealers.

I will at once communicate with Mr. N.[Nardus] and advice him to treat the matter with nicety and dignity and try to avoid proceedings.

I thank you very much for your timely advice. I personally have not sold to B. anything nor ever signed a bill.

I have written Mr. Van Slochem about the matter asking him to pay you a visit before his departure for Europe. I hope you will kindly receive him and talk with him about this business. I am dear Sir, very surely yours.

It looks as if from now on, perhaps from earlier on, Van Slochem, also born in Amsterdam and also residing in Belgium, in Antwerp, partnered with Van Gelder and Nardus.

Next, on May 9, 1910, Hofstede de Groot, writing from Heerengracht 5, The Hague, replied to Van Horne that he would await with pleasure the (photo's of) the pictures about which

197   Letter in PMA (JGJ, 5/5,6).

you want to have my opinion.[198] He went on about the complaint regarding the missing "Cuyp:"

> My "Cuyp" was finished long before I went to America. Your river scene I knew by Jacacci's photo. This is the reason why it came alone in the book. Of course there is not the slightest doubt about the horses. Did you receive my album with Rembrandt-drawing-reproductions, I send you through Valentiner? I am glad to hear you made such important new acquisitions. Are you coming to Europe this summer & shall we have the pleasure of seeing you here?

Van Horne's art- and affair-related correspondence picked up, envelopes whirled one after the other on his doormat. Van Gelder wrote to Van Horne on June 8, 1910, advising that he had received a copy of the letter Van Horne had written to Mr. Borden.[199] He said he assumed that upon Van Horne's return from Cuba he would have found his (Van Gelder's) letter to Mr. Borden. Van Gelder enclosed a photo of the paintings by the Master of the Female Half Figures endorsed by Friedländer (who in 1929 would write so critically about the authentication business). Van Gelder went on to write, "the exact translation of what he [Friedländer] writes is: The pictures after which this photo is taken I consider to be a characteristic work of the Master of the Female Half Figures." [200]

---

198   Letter in VHFF (8/1).
199   Letter in VHFF (7/22).
200   "De Meester van de Vrouwelijke Halffiguren" or "the Master of the Female Half-Lengths" is an anonymous Flemish artist who worked in the first part of the sixteenth century. In part XII of Friedländers' *Die altniederländische Malerei* (published between in German in 1924 and 1937; in English between 1967 and 1976) Friedländers pays attention to this painter" – Suzanne Laemers (RKD),

Van Gelder, not a merchant, but a self-labeled gentleman, went on in this letter about a bill he had come across and had now enclosed of "your chairs and candelabro's, which we bought at Madrid." From the rest of the letter we learn that Van Gelder also engaged Friedländer for authentications.[201] Van Gelder continued this same June 8 letter about Lady Van Horne's visit to Van Slochem, and about a Morales with a most impressive composition and colour. He then changed topic and stated that he still worried about the Brit. Col. Cy & Dev. Cy, "against which you cautioned me. Here is no market for the shares at present and every effort to sell would hurt my and the Cy's interests."

Van Gelder enclosed some information about a Fifth Avenue bank that would show how seriously the officers of this Company took matters and apologized for bothering Van Horne again about it. He continued, "but the amount involved means terribly much for me." This last piece of business had nothing to do with the rise of Van Horne's collection, but it affected his relationship with Van Gelder. Van Horne would show a near inexhaustible amount of patience with Van Gelder and Van Slochem, and he would be a tremendous help to them.

On the same day Van Gelder penned his lengthy June 8 letter to Van Horne, Nardus penned Van Horne that he had "taken" tickets for Quebec on July 28th.[202] Perhaps Van Gelder had convinced Nardus that he could feel safe on the American continent again. Nardus complained that he could not get the stateroom and asked Van Horne to recommend him to

e-mail of September 16, 2009. See also: ww.mbam.qc.ca/bibliotheque/micro-site_seac/Maitres_anciens_Old_Masters_ENG_ONLY.pdf (page 124).

201 As Friedländer (1929: 4), would write, in German, later on, "the man in Detroit or Toledo (USA) whom is offered paintings does not turn to a dealer or a connoisseur, no, the dealer turns to the connoisseur. The dealer fights his doubts with certificates."

202 Letter in VHFF (5/4).

the captain. Whether Van Horne felt ordered around by this request is unknown.

Nardus also mentioned that he wondered what to do with the triptych, which was now with Decock (the restorer). And he announced that he would bring the Magnasco[203] to sell to Van Horne for $5 000, and pay Van Horne $2 500 for the Turner. He went on about Bourgeois being very ill with rheumatism and finished with the promise to bring along a picture of the *Moulin la Galette* by Arnoud Hucké as a present, and some of his own "good painting." There are numerous paintings by Nardus in the 1959 list of paintings at Covenhoven (Sullivan 2007: 171-173 and appendix 1 in this book).

Just one day later another letter arrived, this one from Van Slochem, telling Van Horne that he could send a cheque to his bank at 530 Fifth Avenue.[204] The statement he enclosed shows Van Horne's latest purchases in pounds, shillings and pence:

Statement

To. Painting, *Descent from the Cross*[205]

    by Master of the Weibliche Halffigures £9 000

To. Painting, *A King Magi* by P. Van Orley £3 500

To. Balance for packing and shipping

    Anderson and Leeds, sale pictures £13.1.1

. . . . £12 513.1.1

Credit by Cash £7 500

Balance due £5 013.1.1

---

203   VH 119 Magnasco, Alessandro, called "Il Lissandrino" (Genoa 1661-1741). *Franciscan Monks in their Refectory.* ▣: A group of brown-robed monks are gathered about a white cloth spread on the floor to the right [...] Canvas H. 16 in, W. 25 in (41 cm × 61 cm). From the Ehrich Galleries, New York, 1911. ▣: $5 000, Not signed, questioned.

204   Letter in VHFF (8/11),

205   *Descent from the Cross*, Oil on panel 17¼ in × 11¼ in was no. 73 at the 1860-1960 exhibition in Montreal. The provenance reads: H. van Slochem, 1910; van Glede [sic], Belgium; Sir William Van Horne, Montreal. Montreal Museum of Fine Arts, 1945, Adaline van Horne Bequest.

VAN GELDER'S WOES

On June 11, 1910, Van Horne wrote to poor Van Gelder, not
so much about fine or fake arts, but about his poor business
judgement.[206] The letter gives insight into Van Horne's ideas
on establishing a profitable railroad and shows that Van
Gelder should have stuck with breeding booted bantams. Van
Horne wrote that he had just returned from Cuba and had:

only time at this moment to write concerning your railway matter. The prospectus you sent me bears on its face
clear evidence of intent to deceive and it has no date or
signature and contains many misstatements. The original
scheme was one of those, which burst the Sovereign Bank
of Canada. It was sold for a song among the assets of the
bank and turned into the present company. Mr. Villard
was probably put in as a figurehead because of his father's
name having been so well known in railway enterprises.
He amounts to little and the rest to nothing.

I asked Sir Thomas Shaughnessy yesterday about the
subsidies and I enclose his reply.[207] I do not think that
they have even a promise of subsidies either in lands or
money. A land grant would not, in any case, carry the
precious metals. If there is any coal or iron these would
have no value for a long time to come because there is no
market for them and there is plenty of these things where
the people are. There are no people along the route save
occasional Indians, and there is hardly any land suitable
for agriculture. The line as described lies through a sea
of mountains and would be enormously expensive to
build – far more expensive than the mountain section

---

206   Letter in VHFF (7/22).
207   T. G. Shaughnessy (1853-1923) was a Chicago storekeeper: in 1882 he became a
      CPR purchasing agent, in 1891 CPR vice-president in 1891 and in 1899 he suc-
      ceeded Van Horne as president.

of the Canadian Pacific – and the mountain section of the Canadian Pacific has never earned the interest on its costs notwithstanding its large through traffic [...] I do not hesitate to say that the enterprise, if it may be so called, is not worth a damn and that any money you may get back may be counted as clear gain. I am exceedingly sorry that you have fallen into such a hole and I should be glad to do anything possible to help you out, but it is as impossible to help you, as it would be if you had lost your money at Monte Carlo.[208]

Cogels-Osylei 7, Antwerp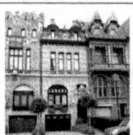

Next, Van Slochem solicited business in his letter to Van Horne of June 14th, 1910.[209] While still staying at 477 Fifth Avenue, he wrote: "I am leaving for Antwerp on the SS Lapland. If I can attend to anything for you or your family – my address in Europe is 7 Avenue Cogels, Antwerp."

208 On June 16 Van Gelder got a long letter, a copy of which he forwarded to Van Horne, from J. Wolkenstein, a member of the Company's board, that ended with: "Needless to emphasize that the largest benefit of this enterprise will accrue to the holders of the capital stock, and you, being one of them, will have every justification to be highly pleased with your investment." Underneath Van Horne scribbled to Sir Thomas that he had advised his Belgian friend "that Wolkenstein's project was not worth a damn."
209 Letter in VHFF (7/9).

Van Horne must have cabled Van Slochem right away that he would attend to Van Gelder's unfortunate affair, and consulted him about a lawyer. Van Slochem's reply on June 16, 1901, reads: "Nusbaum is a lawyer. I know personally: but as to his capabilities in such a case, I know nothing! I believe that no time should be lost, as I do not know if V.G. has written you; how much he has invested? As far [as] I could learn from that so-called friend Gerhardus. I hear it is eighty thousand dollars; isn't it awful!" [210]

On the same day, June 16, Van Slochem gave Van Horne a Delft address for tiles, Joost Thooft, and advised that he had cabled Van Gelder about the railway matter. [211] Things moved quickly. By June 21 Van Gelder had let Van Horne know, in agitated handwriting, that he was thankful that Van Horne had looked into the matter so soon after his trip to Cuba. [212] Thereafter Van Gelder quickly moved on to business:

I was quite stunned with your opinion! Before leaving the States, April last, I confided to a friend (?) the right to invest some money, which he did as you know. I have made a fearful mistake. I have received a lesson, which I will probably remember for years. I am thankful to you for having looked into the matter so soon after your arrival from Cuba!

Now Sir William, although your letter reads hopeless, let us see if there can be done something and save what can be saved.

210   Letter in VHFF (7/9).
211   Letter in VHFF (7/9).
212   Letter in VHFF (7/22).

Van Gelder went on to explain that, while he was in London, he had tried to see Wolkenstein, the vice-president of the development company. However, this was not possible because Wolkenstein was on his way to Victoria to meet the premier and arrange for the application for the subsidiary grants. Van Gelder wondered what Van Horne could do to favourably influence the legislative decision.

Things got tough. On June 24 Van Gelder subsequently wrote to Van Horne in a sulky tone saying that, he had "been feeling blue and worrying and furious about having been so indelicately taken advantage of." [213]

One wonders whether this letter shook Van Horn's confidence in his dealer. Van Gelder ended this letter requesting that Van Horne ask one of his friends or lawyers to look into the matter. Obviously, he was not ready to give up. On June 28 Van Gelder wrote to Van Horne again, from Hotel Regina in Paris, that he still thought that the railway people were "reliable people," and that it would help if Van Horne would help them "instead of making war to them," which would destroy his chances of getting his money back.[214]

On July 4, 1910, Van Slochem reported that he had arrived home safely and had visited Van Gelder.[215] In his four-page letter he expressed his anxiety about Van Gelder's misadventure. He ended with a confidential note: "I must tell you in confidence Van Gelder thinks, that if the Columbian Government grants them this subsidy, and the Canadian Pacific Railway would be lenient with them, there may be still a hope – and – as soon as I hear about the tiles [...]"

This whole unfortunate affair did not end until 1911.[216]

---

213   Letter in VHFF (7/22).
214   Letter in VHFF (7/22).
215   Letter in VHFF (7/9).
216   The conclusion can be read under a very elaborate headline in *The New York Times* of May 16, 1911: NAMES LEADING MEN IN A FRAUD SUIT. INDUCED TO INVEST

Fine art dealers and their mishaps formed a big part of Van Horne's social life during this period! Nardus sent Van Horne a cable in July 1910 with the short message: "When are you coming." [217] Nardus was actually asking at what date Van Horne was planning to go to his New Brunswick estate, Covenhoven. On July 14 Nardus sent another brief message to Van Horne: "Sailing today 14th Empress Ireland." [218]

Apparently, Van Horne was in Covenhoven by July 16 because he wrote to Hofstede de Groot in The Hague on that date.[219] From this letter it is clear that dealers were not the only ones who sometimes took care of publications of their clients' purchases; connoisseurs, at least Hofstede de Groot, did so as well:

> I was away in Cuba when your letter of the 9th of May came. I did not know until recently that the beautiful album of Rembrandt's drawings came from you. It had merely a New York post-mark. A thousand thanks for it. And I fear that I may have failed in acknowledging in thanking you for your paper from "Onze Kunst" on the newly discovered works of Rembrandt which you were so

---

$80 000, PLAINTIFF SAYS, IN A PROMOTION TO WHICH THEY GAVE THEIR NAMES. VAN GELDER COMPLAINANT DECLARES DIRECTORS OF BRITISH COLUMBIA RAILROAD WERE FALSELY REPRESENTED AS HAVING PAID FOR STOCK THEY HELD

A suit that has been brought in the Supreme court by Herman Van Slochem, as assignee of Michael Van Gelder, against Jean Volkenstein and Roscoe Conklin, son of William G. Conklin, President of the Franklin Savings Bank, bids fair to involve the names of a number of well-known men in the financial community, with a complicated chain of circumstances connected with the promotion of the British Columbia railway & Development Company, which attracted much attention a year ago. Van Slochem declares in his complaint that Gelder was victimized to the extent of $80 000, which he paid in good money for an allotment of 8 000 shares [...] on the basis of a glowing story told to Lloyd S. Gearhart, as his agent, by Volkenstein and Conclin.

217 Letter in VHFF (5/14).
218 Letter in VHFF (5/4).
219 Letter in RKD.

good as to send me a long time ago. I can only plead as an excuse my long absences from home in distant countries.

I have not had time since my return from Cuba to send you the pictures I wrote you about for examination but shall do so very soon.

There is one, which may be sufficiently recalled to you by a good photo, a portrait of "a lady holding a poodle dog" by Bart. Van der Helst.[220] I shall send you the photo when I go up to Montreal and you can then say if I shall send the picture itself. As I remember you had no doubt concerning it but in these days "vouchers" are important and I am anxious to have my little collection so far as I can beyond dispute.

I hope to have the pleasure of visiting Holland during the coming autumn and of seeing you there.

On August 5 Van Slochem replied saying he was glad that Van Horne was comfortably settled at St. Andrews (Covenhoven). He also mentioned that he was pleased to learn that Van Horne now had the tiles and that the enlargement and improvements had given such satisfaction to his dear family.[221] He thanked Van Horne for the remittance of $5000.

From the rest of the letter, it appears that Van Slochem – perhaps thinking about Van Gelder's railway mishaps – did not intend to steer far from the art business:

---

220 Perhaps Hofstede de Groot did not go for the *Lady with the Poodle*; the only Van der Helst that made it to the collection was VH 45, Helst, Bartholomeus van der: *Portrait of a Dutch Officer, Admiral Cornelius Tromp*. ▣: Wallis & Sons, London, 1910. ▣: 15000.
    Lugt scribbled on Cat. 1933: "no, not Tromp, but excellent, here en fond, painted in yellow jerkin."
221 Letter in VJFF (7/9).

I will now write you something about my business. I may safely say that Van Gelder has secured some very beautiful and important works and I hope to do some fine business this fall. He invested a considerable amount in these pictures. We have been for a trip to Munchen, Vienna, Dresden, Brunswick, London, Paris and Bruges; in all those places we visited the museums and also some private collections. This trip has been of great benefit to me, as you can well imagine to be with someone that knows so much and has such taste was a great treat. We were together for several weeks and spoke of your collection very often. I mentioned to V.G. that you bought a portrait by Moroni. He told me that he knew of a very fine portrait by that Master and described it as follows [...]

Van Slochem ended with: "I wonder if this is the picture?" From this letter, one would assume that Van Horne had sent the two gentlemen on a scouting trip. It comes across as if Van Slochem was contrasting Van Gelder's bad luck in investing with his (Van Gelder's) good taste in fine arts. Also, Van Slochem was taking the opportunity to remind Van Horne that he was often thinking of the Van Horne collection.

On August 17 Eilers wrote another letter to Van Horne; this letter was also signed by E. van Wisselingh.[222] Eilers, Van Wisselingh's junior partner, also wrote a passage in the letter informing Van Horne that the director of the Mannheim Museum had asked them whether: "the Daumier – *Deux Bachantes poursuivies par des Satyres* was still for sale," as he was almost sure that the committee of his Gallery would allow him to buy this painting for the museum. "Although we got the impression that you surely would buy it, we never got your

222   Letter in VHFF (8.1.1.)

confirmation, so we couldn't answer him and should be greatly obliged if you would give us any decision about it."

Eilers added that they had mounted a very important exhibition in The Hague during the last four weeks. In the exhibition they had seven Jacob Maris pictures for sale, and their prices had gone up so much that they were "nearly equal to the Corots." He also said he planned to visit Canada but had not let other dealers know, "hoping to prevent to be there in the same time together with all the other dealers, it is very cosy, but doesn't pay." [223]

The dealers were not the only ones who were very busy with their business. Van Horne was much engaged in their businesses as well. On August 21, 1910, he finally shows some annoyance when replying to Van Slochem by saying that it was quite impossible for him (Van Horne) "to do what you suggested in Mr. Van Gelder's railway matter for I do not know the Premier of British Columbia, besides, I could not afford to have my name mentioned in any way in connection with such a rotten scheme." [224] Van Horne went on to say:

> The manipulators of this scheme put somebody of my name in New York into their Board of Directors, a man whose wife's name was Shaughnessy. With the object as I am told and believe of creating the impression that Sir Thomas and I were in some way connected with it.

---

223   In this regard it is remarkable to read the letter Eilers would write much later, in 1929 to Klaas Groesbeek, then his business partner in the Van Wisselingh business. During his May 1929 trip to Canada, he had met London art dealer Wallis who also traveled to Montreal. "I don't believe that he liked to see me go to Canada, but such is life, a regular fight. I hope he has good luck as long as I have it as well!" (cited in Heijbroek and Wouthuysen 1999: 200, 201). Wallis might have had the same thoughts about traveling together.

224   Letter in VHFF (7/9).

This is quite in line with the rest of their operations and is further evidence that the whole thing is a thin confidence game [...]

I am very much afraid that Van Gelder's delay in this matter may destroy the possibility of his recovering one cent for as soon as those people find out that they are not likely to get anything from the Government, Mr. Whistlostein will probably pocket all the money he has got and let Van Gelder whistle [...]

My Moroni is not the one you describe. Mine is a full-face bust portrait of a similar quality to the "Tailor" in the National Gallery and probably painted at about the same time. Dr. Bode, in addition to certifying to it, speaks in very high terms of its quality." [225]

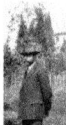

Bernard Berenson

With regard to Bode's certification of the Moroni, this was preceded by some upheaval in the bosom of the Berenson family. Samuels (1987: 159) cites Mary Berenson's letter to her family of April 9, 1910. She wrote that upon her and her husband Bernhard's return from London:

B.B. found a letter that made him perfectly furious. One of the big Paris dealers had sent him an enormous

---

225   The Wickenden catalogue does not list a Moroni, but Cat. 1933 no. 78 does: Giambattista Moroni, 1520-1578 (School of Brescia). Portrait of a Young Italian Nobleman. *From the collection of the Count de Montbrison*. Mentioned by Dr. Bode.

photograph and two thousand francs, asking him to write
on the back of the photograph the opinion he had already
expressed when he saw the picture in their shop, that
it was a portrait by Moroni. As B.B. had never seen the
picture, and as in any case it could never be said it was a
Moroni, for it wasn't, he at once returned the money and
told them they were under some delusion. The picture
is better than a Moroni, but not by anyone we know by
name. Last night came a letter partly bullying, partly
cringing, saying that the dealer, his son and his nephew
all distinctly remembered B.B.'s pronouncing the picture
a Moroni, and that on this guarantee, they had sold it to
Sir William Van Horne who now required B.B.'s written
guarantee, that they wouldn't for anything have had such
a mistake happen with one of their important clients, that
they would pay B.B. 15 000 (fr) and more for getting them
out of the business, and so on, they wanted to present him
with various objects d'art and traiter des grosses affaires
in the future and so on – evidently an attempt at intimida-
tion and bribery at the same time. To which B.B. replied
that he certainly [had] never seen the picture, that if he
had he could never have called it a Moroni, that their letter seemed a very strange one to him and that if such a
misunderstanding ever happened again he would be afraid
ever to go to their shop, that he could not accept presents
from them and so on. It is rather disgusting to have one's
nose rubbed in them and so on. I hope Van Horne will
return the picture on their hands.

On September 19, Eilers thanked Van Horne for his letter,
saying that he was glad to learn from Van Horne's letter of
August 27 that Daumier's "Deux Bachantes poursuivies par des
Satyires" would remain in his collection: "I am glad that you

got it and hope that in the meantime the ladies have come at peace with the subject." [226]

Whether "the ladies came to peace with this subject" or not, this painting also survived the 1933 fire and was featured at the exhibition that same year.

In the same letter Eilers went on to say that he expected to visit Montreal in October and would bring, besides some good specimen of the Dutch school, "a few first class Corots and a very strong Marine painting by Dupré & some Rembrandt etchings." His enclosed invoice reads:

> One oil painting by Honoré Daumier
>
> *Deux Bachantes poursuivies par des Satyres,* Salon 1850/51. $6 500 –
>
> Nov. 14 cheque on a/c $4 000).
>
> The receipt (8/1) of November 28, 1910 reads: Ontvangen van [received from] Sir William C. Van Horne, Montreal, de somma van six thousand five hundred dollars for one oil painting by H. Daumier.
>
> *Deux Bachantes suivites [sic] par des satyres.*
>
> [Signed] E. van Wisselingh.[227]

VAN GELDER PRESSURES HOFSTEDE DE GROOT

October 1910 was a quiet month in Montreal, but back in Uccle "gentleman" Van Gelder was too busy to have his merchandise authenticated. On October 5 he wrote to Hofstede de Groot asking him to write on an enclosed photo of the Frans Hals that the painting would be described in his (HdG's) *Smith Raisonné* supplement and include the measurements of the painting.[228] Van Gelder added that he couldn't find his fountain

---

226   Letter in VHFF (8/1).
227   Heijbroek and Wouthuysen (1999: 58, 75) note that Van Horne paid over 16 000 guilders for it.
228   Letter in RKD.

pen and thought perhaps he had left the thing at Hofstede de Groot's place the last time he had visited.

Hofstede de Groot must have returned the photo and the pen, because, on October 13, Van Gelder thanked Hofstede de Groot for both items.[229] Van Gelder said Hofstede de Groot should expect to receive the invoice for the Van Goyen expertise any day, and then he commissioned another expertise: "I would dearly like your personal impression of my "Toper" by Frans Hals!"

The "personal impression" Van Gelder talks about is reminiscent of what Mary Berenson wrote on October 25, 1913, from her villa I Tatti. While complaining about the Duveens,[230] she simultaneously gave a glimpse of the cold war raging in dealer/connoisseur circles when she mentioned that the dealers were: "continually at him [husband Berenson] to make him say pictures are different from what he thinks, and are very cross with him for not giving way and "just letting us have your authority for calling this a Cossa instead of school of Jura" or "allowing us to take it you will approve us calling this by the master's hand, as it is so close [...]" (in Strachey & Samuels 1983: 192).

Still, Mary B. might have been disgusted by the sheer thought of bribery. Goldstein (2000: 153) mentions a contract – discussed in E. Gimpel's *Diary of a Dealer* – between Berenson and the Duveen Co., conducted in 1912, which allowed "Berenson a quarter of the profits of all items of Italian origin sold by the firm."

---

229   Letter in RKD.

230   During the Napoleonic wars Henoch Jeseph fled from France to Holland, taking the name Duvesne, which he later changed into Duveen. In 1863 his grandson Joel started a business in England where he later sold his grandfather's blue-and-white pottery. In 1877 Joel set up shop in New York, selling porcelains, silver, furniture, tapestries and Dutch portraits (Goldstein 2000: 80 ff.). Goldstein goes on about the relationship of the Berensons with the Duveen brothers. See also Secrest (2004: 247)

In the meantime, Van Slochem planned to return to America. The *American Art News* of October 15 reported under the heading AROUND THE DEALERS' GALLERIES: "Mr. H. Van Slochem writes from Belgium that he has secured several fine pictures, which he will show at the galleries, no. 477 Fifth Ave., this winter. He will return next month." On the 5th of November *American Art News* expanded on the good news: "Mr. H. Van Slochem had returned last Saturday from Europe with many new finds. His galleries, no. 477 Fifth Ave., are now open for the season."

As mentioned, this book focuses mainly on the contributions by Dutch dealers and the involvement of connoisseurs in the Van Horne collections, their interactions with him, with his fellow collectors and among each other. The following letter shows that, more than once, Nardus and Van Gelder bought paintings through or from other dealers before selling the works to Van Horne. One of these dealers was Duveen. The next letter, of November 7, 1910, shows this.[231] It is from dealer A. H. Fisker, Strand on the Green, Chiswick, England. He wrote that he had enjoyed "four hours of delight" among Van Horne's pictures and promised not to forget about Cranach's *Luther with a Beard*[232] and the little medallion of Melanchthon[233] from the Strawberry Hill. Fisker signed off with: "Hoping you keep good health, and in lively recollection of the

---

231 Letter in VHFF (6/2).
232 VH 128 Cranach, Lucas the Elder (Kronisch, 1472–Weimar 1553). *Martin Luther with a Beard*. ⊞: Wearing a black gown he is portrayed half-length standing under a clear azure sky [...] Panel H. 12½ in. W. 11 in (31 cm × 28 cm). At the extreme lower right in black somewhat obliterated, is the emblematic device of the winged serpent, ranted Cranach in 1508 by Electoral Edict, and with it which he signed his works after that date. From the coll. of the Voordauw family, Holland. Purchased from L. Nardus and M. van Gelder, 1900. ⊞: $15000. Final 6000; consid. doubtfull.
      On Cat. 1933 Lugt scribbled a question mark behind the title of no. 73: Maarten Luther ? with a Beard.
233 See the letter by Hofstede de Groot of October 5, 1908. In it Holbein's *Melanchthon* was already mentioned.

great pleasure you gave me in Montreal." But, the Wickenden catalogue again has the date of purchase as 1900 (error?) and states that the dealers were Nardus and Van Gelder.

In his letter of November 14, Eilers, now in The Windsor in Montreal, thanked Van Horne for his $4 000 cheque and offered him another Daumier, this time *3rd class Railway*.[234] This painting "would complete the four you have got and in case you would get tired of it, it should be easy for us to take it back, as they are very rare and not difficult to sell in Europe."

A handwritten note shows that Van Horne was not left much time to decide as Eilers added that he would leave that morning for the King Edward Hotel in Toronto and would stop over for one or two days in Montreal, on his way back home.[235] Subsequently the E. J. van Wisselingh & Co. invoice of November 26 reads: "For inspection. 1 picture (oil painting) H. D. Daumier. *Wagon 3-ième classe.* $ 4 500."

Next, Van Horne's purchase of a frame for a Frans Hals started out with a value problem. Poor Van Slochem had thought that he had complied with Van Horne's instructions, but, as he wrote to Van Horne on November 19 "I found today the frame of the picture you bought a little while ago and have

---

234   Letter in VHFF (3/27).

235   On November 12, 1909, *The New York Times* featured an article about the Borden pictures and so did *American Art News* of November 20, 1909. It described the Borden pictures shown at the Union League: "the star pictures of the display were unquestionably the Daumier, about mentioned, entitled, "An Interior–Third Class," a truly remarkable study of French peasant character and expression as seen in a railway carriage, and exceedingly rich and strong in its color scheme of warm reds and browns." Actually, Daumier painted this scene twice. The one in Borden's possession was sold after his death to the Havemeyer family. See:

   http://www.metmuseum.org/Collections/search-the-collections/436095?rpp=2 o&pg=1&ao=on&ft=Daumier&pos=1 (last accessed March 2014).

   Heijbroek and Wouthuysen (1999: 199) have the following text under their photo of a painting that Van Horne bought: "H. Daumier. Le wagon 3me classe, ca. 1862. Canvas 65 × 90 cm. This important painting was purchased by Eilers at Reid & Lefèbre in London. That same year it was sold to the Canadian collector Gordon C. Edwards. National Gallery of Canada Ottawa. Photo archives E. J. van Wisselingh & Co."

forwarded same by American Express today. I have put a shipping value of $50.00 on the picture. You will understand I do not mean to charge you $50.00 for the frame, as the price was figured on the picture when you bought it, and the frame is perhaps not worth $50.00." [236]

Two days later Van Horne's secretary, W. F. Lynch, replied testily that Sir William had received Van Slochem's letter in regard to the price "which you have put on the frame of the picture, which he purchased from you last week. Your reference to the picture in your letter makes your letter valueless for the purpose for which it was wanted." [237]

The picture that Van Horne "bought a while ago" (see the letter above of November 19), was a Frans Hals. Under the heading A HALS FOR MONTREAL, *American Art News* of November 19, 1910, wrote:

Sir William Van Horne of Montreal has purchased from Mr. H. Van Slochem for his noted collection, an unusually fine and important example of Franz [sic] Hals. The canvas a half-length of a red-faced man holding a cruche or earthen pot is entitled "The Toper," [238] and comes from the Duke of Hamilton's collection. The figure of the sale is not given. The picture was expertised by Dr. De Groot of The Hague last summer who pronounces it a fine example of the master and who will include it in his forthcom-

---

236 Letter in VHFF (7/9).
237 Letter in VHFF (7/19).
238 VH 68 Hals, Frans (Antwerp 1584–Haarlem 1666). *The Jolly Toper*. (Man with a jug). ▣: Hals painted this from the same rubicund quaintly-featured model as appears in the 'Allegro Concerto' of Sir Frederic Cook's Richmond coll. and the Joueur de Rommelpot in that of M. Van Gelder [...]. Canvas H. 26¼ in, W. 21¾ in (67 cm × 54.5 cm). In the coll. of Mr. A. R. Severn, whose family was connected with the late John Ruskin. In poss. of Sir Guy Francis Laking, Bt. London, Keeper of the King's Armoury. In poss. of Sir George Donaldson, London. In poss. of M. Van Gelder, Uccle, Belgium" [and sold to Van Horne by Van Slochem]. ▣: 60 000.
    Further comments on the accompanying sheet are: "1962: Brandt said "Doubtful," thinks by Frans Hals's son. 1964: Hubbard said by J. Leyster."

ing Catalogue Raisonné of the works of Hals. Sir William is to be congratulated upon the acquisition of the picture, and Mr. Van Slochem on its sale.

On November 22, 1910, Van Slochem, still staying at 477 Fifth Avenue, apologized about the frame matter and said he sincerely hoped that this did not mean that Van Horne had to pay the duty on that amount: "My purpose of putting on a value of $50 was merely to be sure of the prompt delivery by the Express Co., and I fully admit that the frame was not worth over $10." [239] He added that he would leave it to Van Horne to ask him for a refund or to protest and have some of the duties refunded: "I regret very much to have made this mistake."

In a letter stamped November 28 from the Metropolitan Museum of Art, New York, Valentiner apologized to Van Horne for not coming, since he was "in the midst of the preparation of the catalogue of Mr. Borden's collection." [240] Valentine wrote furthermore that he had "to use the Thursday for work as they are in a great hurry." He expressed hope that the invitation could be renewed as he was "extremely sorry to miss the breakfast" in Van Horne's house on Sunday. Also, that he had very much enjoyed "the dinner and the breakfast at the Manhattan last week." [241] Perhaps Van Horne wanted to keep an eye on Valentiner's work because Valentiner's job at Borden's will have caused some anxiety among his dealers.

For example, Van Slochem arranged to have an interview with Nardus. By letter of December 13 Van Slochem guessed that:

---

239   Letter in VHFF (7/9).
240   Letter in VHFF (6/2).
241   The Metropolitan Museum has no correspondence between Valentiner and Van Horne, Nardus or Van Gelder in its archives (e-mail of October 4, 2009).

Dear Sir William, you would no doubt be surprised to hear that I am probably in Paris by the time you receive this! I am going to have an interview with Nardus! Re: the Borden matter; Van Gelder will explain you everything when you meet him. I further hope that you are in the best of spirits. [242]

Van Slochem ends this letter with the usual best wishes for the family and, as it is December, a Merry Christmas and a Happy New Year.

From the letter above, it seems as if Van Slochem, Van Gelder, and Nardus acted as a trio. Consider the following: Van Gelder intervened on Nardus' behalf in the Widener case in 1908, and Van Slochem – on Nardus' behalf – intervened in the Borden affair in 1911.

In the last letter of the flurry of 1910 letters, dated December 19 and written in French on the letterhead "Steinmeyer & Stephan Bourgeois, 3 Place du theater Français, Paris, Maison à Cologne," Bourgeois tells Hofstede de Groot that he (Bourgeois) would send him three more pictures by Ruysdael and asked his opinion about a winter landscape in the Emile Goldschmidt de Francfort collection, which he (Bourgeois) had attributed to Jacob Salomon Ruysdael, even though it had no trace of a signature.[243] Bourgeois suggested that Hofstede de Groot should mention these paintings, if they were worthy of his interest. Bourgeois already had the photographs under his personal name, meaning under the name of M. M. Steinmeyer in Paris. In other words, Bourgeois had his wares authenticated before trying to sell them, and had even suggested

---

242   Letter in VHFF (8/1).
243   Letter in RKD.

to Hofstede de Groot that he should mention said paintings in some publication.

Here is one more example of Van Gelder instructing Hofstede de Groot: on January 24, 1911, he sent Hofstede de Groot a reproduction of a life-size portrait of De Keyser, which Hofstede de Groot had authenticated a few years earlier.[244] Van Gelder now wanted some words of appreciation on the back of the photograph because "As you know for sure, this painting is from the Baron Nieserwand, Cologne collection. Van Oldenburg also described it in his latest publication. Recently Dr. Friedländer and Dr. Graul[245] from Leipzig visited me; both have admired and praised the painting to the fullest." Did these recommendations persuade Hofstede de Groot to follow orders?

THE BORDEN MATTER REARS ITS HEAD

On January 3, 1911, Van Gelder, who was aboard the steamship *George Washington,* wrote a letter to Johnson that began: "My Dear Mr. Johnson" [246] The letter does not leave any doubt about Van Horne's warm relationship with connoisseur Valentiner, and also with the maligned dealers, Van Gelder among them:

> After a delightful stay with the family Van Horne at Montreal, I returned to N. York two days ago and am now on my way to Europe.
>
> I went to see Mr. Borden on the 1st. He received me quite cordially and told me that Mr. Robinson of the Met. Museum and Mr. Jaccaci had questioned four of the pictures

---

244 Letter in RKD.
245 Dr. Richard Graul (1862-1944) was a Leipzig art historian.
246 Letter in PMA (JGJ, 5/5,6).

he got from Mr. Nardus. He was much pleased to see me and wanted to know what I had to say.

I assured him of my very best intentions to get to an agreeable solution between him and N. I told him that I had been waiting for Mr. N.'s reply at Montréal and that I was glad to say that Mr. N. proposed to clear up for once this whole transaction. He would take back all the pictures sold to Mr. Borden and give him the money back for them.

Mr. B. now replied that he would not accept this proposition as his Lucretia, which had cost him 60 000 doll. was now worth 250 000 according to an offer made to him a short time ago and thus alone would be nearly worth what all the light pictures sold to him amounted to.

I then said that I felt quite sorry that he would not accept such a very fair proposal and that I had nothing else to say for Mr. Nardus. Mr. B. said he expected to send these 4 works to Europe to have them expertised and would then communicate the result to Mr. N.

Sir William wanting to see his collection would come soon pay him a visit and I promised Mr. B. also to communicate with N. again.

So Mr. B. is quite willing to wait for a while before doing any step forwards. I then went in the Gallery with him; we had a pleasant chat and departed most cordially.

I thought, Mr. Johnson, well to inform you how things are and also to show you that I am trying to get this Borden matter out of the way as nice as possible. I have some hope as to an ulterior settlement.

While at Sir William's, I had the pleasure to meet Dr. Valentiner with whom I had some pleasant chats. I expect to arrange Mr. Van Slochem's business in good shape on my return, so that he can get back by the 1st of February.

On January 26, Van Slochem, still staying at 477 Fifth Avenue, let Van Horne know that he had received Van Horne's letter of the 24th with the enclosed cheque of $2 500.[247] He noted that the pictures had been sold the previous night and that no. 1152 by J. W. Morrice had sold for $550. The rest of the letter shows that Van Slochem was keen not to irritate Van Horne again with a mistake such as undervaluation or double billing:

> I did put it in with a start of twenty, when an angry voice shouted two hundred and fifty and so on, so I was not in it. Today the bergères are being sold. I noted that you do not want the big lounge; what I have bought is packed and I will not ship until the sale is over! So if you do not approve of the prices I invoiced them as per letter mailed. You will oblige me to let me know and I will change the prices according to your instructions.

On February 4, 1911, *American Art News* reported Van Slochem's return under the heading AROUND THE GALLERIES. The article mentioned that he had brought with him "a few choice old masters, which are now at his galleries, No 477 Fifth Ave. All come from famous private collections and are well worthy of attention of the discriminating connoisseur." One of these paintings which were worthy of attention was one that Conway (1905: 137) described as follows when discussing the Van Horne collection:

> Amongst the old masters my own special tastes were gratified by the sight of one of the most charming early sixteenth century Flemish pictures that exists. It is a little panel-painting of the Magdalen in a charming landscape, painted no doubt, at Antwerp or Bruges about 1520, perhaps by Adrian Ysenbrandt.

247　Letter in VHFF (7/9).

No. 135 in the Wickenden catalogue is Adrian Isenbrandt's: *Lady Reading her Breviary* (vSlochem, NY, 1911). Wickenden starts his description with: "seated to the right of her praying-desk or feldstool [sic], on which is an opened vase of chiseled gold, a richly-attired lady reads from the illuminated breviary, held in her finely formed hands. She wears a thin white veil-like cap, and two necklaces with jeweled pendants."

There is nothing in the description about a charming landscape, the background is described as a dark alcove. Also, in *Maria Magdalena Reading*, in the Prado in Madrid, attributed to Isenbrandt, Maria Magdalena is not reading in the foreground of a landscape and her necklaces lack "jewelled pendants." The Prado description states that this work is "a replica of a much-repeated prototype with which this artist achieved a certain success." Wickenden goes on to say that Dr. Max Friedländer attributed "this masterpiece of Bruges art to Adriaen Ysenbrandt, whose supreme skill in the perfecting of detail is here evident."

Henschel appraised it at $3 500. A 1964 scribble says that it is catalogued as a replica of one in the Ben Witz collection ($1 500). And, much later, on December 6, 1972, at the sale of a number of pieces from the Van Horne collection, no. 12, the title *Lady Reading her Breviary* is upgraded to: *Portrait of a lady as the Magdalen* (Acquired in 1911 from Van Slochem). This Isenbrandt in the collection is a puzzle.

Where were we? First, remember Nardus' letter of May 2, 1906, about selling a Velasquez to Van Horne? Van Horne must have been grinding his teeth in anger while replying to an employee of *American Art News, America's Only Art Newspaper* who had asked Van Horne to send the paper details of that particular Velasquez. As well as the size and description, the employee wanted to know who Van Horne had purchased it from. How dare he doubt a picture purchased from Nardus! The gnawing was heard by those on high in the art world. On February 25, 1911, Van Horne got a long letter from James B. Townsend, the president of the said newspaper, in which he apologized for the "almost impertinent request of February 23, by an overzealous employee." [248] Townsend went on to say:

> It appears that on Feb. 22, what would seem to be an AP dispatch from Montreal was published in such a reliable journal as the *NY Evening Post* and, other good journals here, to the effect that you had stated that you owned a portrait of Philip IV by Velasquez and that you did not credit the report – as we did not either – that Mr. J. P. Morgan had purchased a similar portrait, also by Velasquez.
>
> You were quoted in this presumed AP dispatch in about the words above given, and the employee, in this youthful enthusiasm, thought it a good idea to get from you, if possible, the details regarding your picture – or the one attributed to your ownership. I can only hope that the incident did not too much annoy you and I have issued orders that no such message be sent in future to your good self or other collectors without my approval, or that of some older person.

The incident would linger. On March 2, 1911, Townsend wrote that he would publish Van Horne's "indignant denial of the unfortunate statement," in the issue of March 11.[249] In a way Van Horne's indignation is understandable: a collection that contains fakes or forgeries enhances neither its value nor the owner's reputation. Meanwhile the promised notice in the *American Art News* of February 25, 1911, was elaborate. Under the heading FAMOUS VELASQUEZ HERE, it read:

---

248   Letter in VHFF (43/9).
249   Letter in VHFF (43/9).

On the *Mauretania* last week arrived Mr. C. R. Williams of the London house of Agnew & Co., who brought with him for the joint account of Knoedler & Co.,[250] and Scott & Fowles, the "Portrait of Philip IV of Spain," by Velasquez, in the uniform of a Field Marshal, and which is said by Mr. Williams to be worth $440 000. Mr. Williams was obliged to pay an extra freight charge of some $2 000, the Cunard Company, while accepting no responsibility, exacting a charge proportionate to value on valuable painting.

The history of the painting, which has been called the lost Velasquez, has been told in the *Art News*. A similar portrait in the Dulwich Gallery where it has hung for many years, was supposed to be a Velasquez, but was adjudged some time ago as a copy by Maso, the son-in-law of Velasquez, and this led to a search for the original. It was finally discovered in the collection of one of the Bourbon Parma family in Austria. The portrait now here is a full length standing presentment boldly and strongly drawn and the face full of character.

Right under this news item, under the heading ANOTHER VELASQUEZ, a lame statement followed: It began with, "Sir William Van Horne owns a portrait of Philip IV of Spain, by Velasquez," and went on to comment on the recently published report that such a portrait had been purchased by Mr. J. Pierpont Morgan. The *Art News* statement went on to say that the writer of the report said: "I have good reason to believe that Mr. Morgan has not acquired any picture by Velasquez."

Next, *American Art News* of March 4, 1911, page 1, had under the heading FRICK BUYS VELASQUEZ: "The famous portrait of

---

250 Knoedler & Co. in New York started when the Parisian firm Goupil started its New York branch with Michael Knoedler heading it. In 1870 Knoedler took his brother John into the firm and in 1877 "he gave his eldest son, Roland, a partnership and renamed the firm M. Knoedler & Company" (Goldstein 2000: 26, 54).

Philip IV of Spain, by Velasquez, recently imported by Scott & Fowles and Knoedler & Co. on joint account from the Agnews in London, had been sold to Mr. Henry C. Frick, and now hangs in one of the drawing rooms of his Fifth Avenue house."

Something else was brewing as well. On March 2, 1911, Van Slochem wrote Van Horne that he would like to have a chat with him before his (Van Slochem's) return to Europe.[251] But, shortly after, on April 28, Van Slochem was still in New York from where he wrote that he received a letter from Van Gelder who had informed him that:[252]

> his [Van Gelder's] proposition to you re the Greco (*la Grada Tanulia*), no doubt this will be to your entire satisfaction. As I told you all the pictures have been returned to Europe but I have kept here the frame of the El Greco, so if you will be kind enough to wire me to send you the frame before I leave. I will arrange for the packing, and as soon [as] I arrive in Europe will ship the picture. You will then find the Greco on your return from Cuba in your home.

Van Slochem duly asked Van Horne to please state in a wire "at what figure" he should invoice the frame for the duty. What he was really asking was by how much he had to under value the painting in the fake invoice. Van Horne was not the only collector trying to cheat the government. Lopes (2007: N 28) notes: "There is also evidence Johnson colluded to evade import duties in bringing some of his Nardus pictures into the country." Regarding a supposed Ghirlandaio Johnson bought for $16 000, Van Gelder wrote on 16 February, 1908: "I am

---

251 Letter in VHFF (7/9).
252 Letter in VHFF (7/9).

sorry I cannot send it to you as before. I would suggest to ship it as 'Italian School' and invoice it at $5 000." [253]

April 1911 was quiet; apparently Van Horne was in Cuba, from where he paid for an Elsheimer.[254] He was back in Montreal on May 4 from where he wrote the following letter to Hofstede de Groot in The Hague:[255]

Mr. Herman Van Slochem of New York, who is just now sailing for Europe and who is going to The Hague soon after his arrival on your side, had kindly offered to take with him the two pictures which I wished to submit for your opinion. I have told him that I would arrange the matter of fees directly with you, and I shall promptly send the amount if you will be so good as to let him or me know what it is. You will perhaps be interested in knowing that I have acquired from Mr. Van Gelder his Frans Hals, the "Toper", which bears your certificate. I am sending you by this mail a photograph of a fine B. Van der Helst[256] which I

---

253 Letter in PMA (JGJ, 5/5).
254 VH 126 Elsheimer, Adam (Frankfort 1578–Rome 1600). *Leto (or Latona) with Apollo and Artemis in the Isle of Delos.* "Under a tree near the banks of a river or lake, the goddess-mother Leto, in blue dress and yellow shawl, invokes the protection of their father Zeus for her two children Apollo and Artemis on the ground before her. [...] Oil, on copper. H. 8¾ in, W. 13⅜ in (22 cm × 34.5 cm). From the late Langton-Douglas coll. no. 2 Hill St. London. He was formerly Director of Dublin Museum + an authority on Da Vinci + Fra Angelica. ▣: $ 12 000)."
255 Letter in RKD.
256 VH 45 Helst, Bartholomeus van der (Haarlem 1613–Amsterdam 1670). *Portrait of a Dutch Officer: Admiral Cornelius Tromp.* "Against a background of dark bluish-gray clouds the sturdy figure of the doughty Dutch officer is shown three-quarters-length, life-size, high about the horizon [...] The eminent Dutch critic and painter, the late Jan Peter Veth on seeing it for the first time declared in Sir William's and the writer's [R. J. Wickenden] presence, that its exceptional quality "made it necessary for this to revise his opinion of Van der Helst" as it seemed finer than any of that painter's works he had yet met with. Sir William himself said, 'It was the most satisfying portrait he had ever seen.' [...] Canvas H. 40½ in, W. 33 in (103 cm × 84 cm). In the coll. of James Whatman, Esq. 'Vinters,' near Maidstone, Kent, England. In poss. of Messrs. Wallis & Sons, London, 1910. ▣: $15 000."

acquired not long ago, and I shall take the liberty of sending you a little later photographs of a number of Dutch
and Flemish pictures which I have added since your visit.
Pardon a typewritten letter, for I am leaving for Cuba in an
hour or two and have only time to dictate it.

I was so much hurried on my last visit to Europe that I
did not have time to visit The Hague as I had hoped. I trust
that we may have the pleasure of seeing you on this side of
the Atlantic again before long. A great many good things
have come over within the past two years.

On May 17, 1911, Hofstede de Groot congratulated Van
Horne on his Hals: "I think a very fine acquisition." [257] He
continued that he had heard from Jan Veth about Van Horne
having been in Paris and in London, which shows that the art
world closely watched Van Horne's moves. Hofstede de Groot
went on to say that he had seen the Van der Helst when it was
sold in London not long ago: "He wears a yellow costume, if I
remember right." And he let Van Horne know that he himself
had bought some very fine Rembrandt drawings, "which I am
very proud of. I hope you will have a pleasant & not too warm
stay among the Havana's, which we both like so much!"

It seems that he was feeling quite positive when he wrote
that letter, but there were more mishaps in store for Van
Gelder. On May 19th Van Slochem, who was back in Antwerp
after having taken care of Van Gelder's railway affair, wrote
to Van Horne that he had seen the Van Gelder family for a few
moments only "as there was some sickness in the family.[258]
They were all in bed owing to some poisoning [...] I believe
it was some fish." It appears that, due to the sickness, Van

---

257   Letter in VHFF (5/8).
258   Letter in VHFF (6/2).

Slochem could not attend to the shipping of the El Greco and the Goya. But, he had been attending to the Durighello sale of the Arabian Glosses and bronzes and also secured thirty pieces of glass for about 3700 francs. He invoiced twenty pieces at 50 francs and ten smaller pieces at 20 francs, making the total for the invoice 1200 francs. Van Slochem added that (while in Paris) he had been spending his evenings with Nardus and his wife, who were looking forward to their trip to St. Andrews. He concluded by saying that Van Horne would soon hear from him about the Goya as well as the Fabritius' landscape.

On June 8, 1911, Nardus, now from Luzerne, confirmed his upcoming visit to Van Horne.[259] He regretted that it was impossible to get the stateroom on the Empress of Britain[260] and asked Van Horne–again–to recommend him to the captain. He went on:

I shall send you the Magnasco with pleasure at $5000, if this is satisfactory to you and I take back the Turner at $2500. I am very sorry to say that Bourgeois has been very, very ill; he had a severe attack of rheumatism and is already two months in bed. I think in 3 weeks he will be all right again. I enclose herewith a letter of Mr. Borden, as you advised me to do nothing I shall do so. I sent you a picture of the Moulin la Galette by Bernard Hucké, which I make you a present of. I bought 2 of him. I did some good painting lately, and I hope to show you soon at St. Andrews.

---

259   Letter in VHFF (5/4).
260   Apparently the *Empress of Britain* did not work out. On July 14 Van Horne was
      notified that Nardus was "sailing today 14th *Empress of Ireland.*"

By letter of June 15, Van Slochem wrote that he had just returned from a trip along the Rhine with his wife and that upon his return he had found Van Horne's letter with the draft.[261] He went on about Nardus, who was preparing his trip to Canada and looking forward to it, but:

> I alas noted that you traded your Master of the Death of Mary for a Murillo, am glad to hear this makes you happy.[262] Nardus told me that he was attending to shipping the El Greco and the Goya. I have not seen Van Gelder yet; they are all well. I have had a chat with him through the phone. He told me that he was in Paris and that he has attended to the shipping of the El Greco and the Goya, he has secured another frame for the Goya; the price of the Goya is fifteen thousand dollars, $15 000. You will no doubt remember the price he wanted at first. No doubt this will be to your entire satisfaction, as to the Fabritius landscape, this being part of [a] private collection he does not wish to part with same.

It reads as if Van Gelder, through Van Slochem, was trying to make Van Horne eager to own the Fabritius. Van Slochem went on about the Flemish church lamps for St. Andrews that he could send on or, he wondered, "shall I wait till I hear from

---

261   Letter in VHFF (7/9).
262   VH 100 Murillo, Bartholome-Esteban (Seville 1617-1672). *A Spanish Gentleman.* "Half-length, in oval with landscape background, his body turned three-quarters to the left, his right hand with wide lace cuff is placed against his breast, as he inclined his head and looks out of the picture. [...] Canvas H. 34¾ in, W. 24½ in (88.5 cm × 62.5 cm). In the coll. of Prince Eugene de Beauharnais. In the coll. of the Duke of George Leuchtenberg. In the poss. of M. Knoedler & Co., London June 1909. Presented as a wedding-gift to Napoleon's step-son Prince Eugene de Beauharnais on the occasion of his marriage to Princess Augusta Amelia of Bavaria in 1806. Upon the downfall of Napoleon after 1815 they returned to Munich. ⊡: 25 000."

you. Perhaps you wish me to attend at the same to have them fixed up for the electric lighting or ..."

On July 3, 1911, Bourgeois wrote Van Horne that Nardus would certainly have told him about his illness and that he had received the Turner safely. Also, at Nardus' request, he had forwarded the different pictures and added the Magnasco.[263] He went on about a visit from Friedländer who had examined the Roger van der Weyden very carefully:

> and although he thinks the picture very fine and most near to Roger v.d. Weyden, he cannot give the attribution with certitude and neither can he attribute it to another master. I had a talk with Nardus about it and he thinks as we have to do here with an exceedingly fine picture, and as Nardus is convinced it is by R. v.d. Weyden, he encouraged me to send you the picture. When he will be with you he wants to talk it over with you [...] PS: I enclose an invoice of your purchases and you will oblige me to send the check to Nardus.

Van Horne again had to rely on Nardus' judgment. Did he? It looks as if Nardus was now also partnering with Bourgeois, his wife's cousin, and that Van Gelder and Van Slochum, in Belgium, were beginning to do more business together as partners.

Meanwhile, on July 6, 1911, Bode wrote from Berlin thanking Van Horne for the four pictures he had received through Mr. Herman van Slochem:[264]

---

263 Letter in VHFF (2/7). This Magnasco will have been no. 24 in Cat. 1933: *Capuchin Monks around a Refectory Fireplace*.
264 Letter in VHFF (8/11).

With great pleasure I will give you my opinion about the pictures or photos [illeg.] you are sending me. And, if you like I also will recommend you one of the other fine picture salable which we do not want or are not able to pay. As money is always wanting here [...] I send you in another cover the 4 photo's with my opinion on the back. Amongst us, I do not think the 3 Dutch or Flemish dealers who sold (mostly together) so many pictures to American collectors are dealers to depend on, though Van Gelder knows Dutch and Flemish masters of the XVIIth century well.

Bode acted as connoisseur as well as dealer. After this letter Van Horne must have harboured more doubt about his collection. He turned again to an expert, even though this expert was one of his dealers! Knowles (2004: 293) writes that Van Horne reacted vigorously when the authenticity of one of his works was disputed "as he had little faith in the infallibility of judgments delivered by most of the so-called experts." Van Horne's actions in engaging experts to chase out fakes from his collections as vigorously as Captain Ahab chased the white whale contradict what Van Horne is said have felt on this issue. The chase for fakes went on. Van Horne's "little faith" may also be explained by the next letter. On July 13 Hofstede de Groot wrote that he had had the pleasure of seeing Mr. v. Slochem, who had brought along the two pictures:[265]

which I have examined very carefully. The "Van der Helst" looks not so good as when I saw it under glass in your house. I am now persuaded that it is a little too coarse for the master; also it comes very close to his later period. I am sorry I can't find a positive name to the picture. The

---

best name is Dutch School under strong influence of van der Helst about 1660.

The "Frans Hals" is a very clever portrait, much admired by Dr. Bredius and others who saw it. It is still a puzzle. The style of painting is Dutch under Italian influence, could be painted by a Dutchman in Italy, by a man like du Jardin or Michiel Sweerts, but it is by neither of them. I will keep it in my memory by the photo you sent of it and as soon as I know something positive, I will write you again. I congratulate America that Mr. de Wild,[266] our best picture restorer, is going there in the service of Mr. Knoedler. He can do an immense deal of good to art treasures there! It is a great loss for us.[267]

---

266 Dutch restorer Carel Frederik Louis de Wild sr. (1870-1922) settled in New York in 1911.

267 Enclosed in this letter was a "Pedigree of a picture representing The Toper by Franz Hals." Transcript:

This Picture represents a middle-aged man in a happy and smiling mood. Before him stands a brown stone pitcher, the handle of which he holds with his left hand and with his right one he seemingly caresses it as if expressing: "How good it does to feel it, and how well it does to drink it!"

On his head he wears a striking red felt bonnet, which falls on his ears right and left in picturesque folds. In the bonnet sticks a wooden spoon, symbolizing that with good drinking, eating should not be neglected; and thus lives this Toper, with but one thought, get the best of everything in life.

On the background, to the right, are chalk marks characteristic of the epoch meaning, in this instance, that our customer has been enjoying two whole jugs and three halves.

He wears a gray dress with red sleeves, his white shirt is open at the neck, its strings hang loosely down to give him more ease to degustate his drink.

This Toper may be considered as the most spiritful expression of a smiling man ever painted by the genial Franz HALS. It can therefore, without hesitation, be placed in the Master's last and best epoch, around 1640.

These little eyes so full of gay mischief, these big cheek bones drawn upwards in the effort of smile and shining with contentment, this big nose breathing the fumes of the delightful beverage, this mouth opened with a self contented smile, ready to swallow the contents of the beloved pitcher, these impressive hands seemingly safeguarding his pitcher as a treasure all his own, what more deep and subtle study could there be given of a being so human and of such impassioned temperament!

If one looks at the wonderful combination of colours, varying from the deep carmine red of the bonnet, the rosy flesh tints of the face and hands, the lovely cool

Van Gelder's situation, with the railway scam being out of the way, wrote to Van Horne on July 30, 1911, that he had received the $15 000 draft for the Goya.[268] He continued to suppose that Van Horne had gone to Montreal when the Greco and the Goya arrived: "How superb will this picture look in your

grey of the dress, to the superb brown tone of the pitcher with its deep brown black lacquered shadows, all this against a light brown transparent background, there is only one expression to be used to resume this Work, painted in this most extraordinary dashing and vigorous manner ...." A Master Piece"!!!
This Picture comes from the Collection of:
The Duke of Hamilton.
It was sold in December 1823 at Christie's under the number 33 of the catalogue.
It was further in the possession of:
The Family Severn, in England,
Who were related to the late John A. RUSKIN.
Afterwards it became, though a sale at Christie's the property of:
Mr. Laking, in England,
Keeper of the Armour to the late King Edouard the seventh, from whom it past [passed] in the hands of:
Sir George Donaldson, in England,
Of whom it was indirectly acquired by the present owner.
This Picture is well known by:
Doctor Cornelius Hofstede de Groot, the well-known Expert on Dutch Art of the XVIIth century.
A photograph, with on its back an endorsement of this gentlemen as to the genuiness of this Work, goes with the Picture.
Signed to the left in monogram F.H.
Height   ... 21 1/2 ...
Canvass: Width   ... 26 1/4 ...
Frans Hals – Born in Antwerp in 1576 – Died in Haarlem in 1666.

This ringing endorsement was complemented with "A copy of an expertise from Doctor Hofstede de Groot about a Picture representing 'The Toper,' by Frans Hals.

The undersigned has carefully examined the Picture of which the endorsed photograph has been taken, which is painted in life size on canvas.
He considers it to be a perfectly genuine Work of Frans Hals.
October 1910 (signed) Corn. Hofstede de Groot.
P.S. This Picture will be described in my supplement of the Catalogue raisonné of Frans Hals" Works (signed) C. H. de Groot.

268 Letter in VHFF (7/15). VH 109, Goya y Lucientes, Francisco Jose de. Fuentetodos (Aragon 1746–Bordeaux 1828). *The Horrors of War* (an incident of the French Invasion 1808-12). 🖾: A Spanish home is being raided by Hussars and Cuirassiers [...] Canvas H. 15¾ in, W. 19 in (40 cm × 48.25 cm). From Gimpel & Wildenstein, Paris and New York, 1909. 🖾: $20 000.

hall! You have now the Spanish school magnificently represented; it will be a real treat for the connoisseur." Van Gelder
went on and on and on about this treat and continued to express the hope that Van Horne would take Nardus to Montreal:

> He will certainly enjoy your acquisitions of those last
> three, four years. How is little Willem getting along? You
> see I am living with my thoughts fresh to you, when for
> a moment I throw the cares off; my great happiness con-
> sists in thinking of you in that hopeful promising land of
> Canada.
>
> In two days I will be in another charming country:
> Holland I feel always happy when I go there where I was
> born,[269] where our great masters in philosophy, literature
> music and painting have live, were every road every river
> every farm is familiar to me. I will walk around in the
> country with its long distant horizon, its lovely skies, it
> fresh pastures, its superb cattle, and I will feel careless
> and young again.

Van Gelder wrote this letter of July 30, eleven days after his
father had died in Amsterdam. Perhaps his father's house
had to be cleared out as his mother had died a little earlier, in
October 1910.

Meanwhile, Van Horne wrote to Hofstede de Groot, addressing him as "Dear Dr. de Groot" on August 20:[270]

> I am greatly obliged by your letter of 13 July. I am not sur-
> prised at what you say of the "Van der Helst." I had thought

---

269 As said, Van Gelder was born in Amsterdam, in 1864, the son of Leon van Gelder
     and Henriette Swelheim.
270 Letter in RKD.

it right but very much over-cleaned. However, I have never cared much for it.

As to the "Frans Hals" portraits of Spinoza, so called: I only told Van Slochem that it was attributed to Hals by the former owner but I did not buy it as such. I have thought it Flemish and probably by J. B. Weenix. What say you to that? There was a picture by Weenix in the Dutch exhibition in Paris about 3 months ago, very liked it in many ways. Perhaps you may recall it.

I have made a good many additions to my collection since you saw it – Rembrandt's "Young Rabbi" from the Rud. Kann collection, the Rembrandt Landscape you described, "The Toper" of Franz Hals of which you know, two Jacob Ruysdael's, a remarkable Emanuel de Witte and some other early Dutch pictures; two easel pictures of Rubens and some earlier Flemish things; two Murillo's, a large and fine Greco and a number of other early Spanish works and several early Germans and an occasional early Northam and XVIII century English. I hope I may have an opportunity to show them to you before long.

The coming of Mr. de Wild to New York, while a disadvantage to you is not likely to help us here in Canada very much for we find it easier to send pictures to and from Europe than to or from New York.

I trust that you will permit me to pay your usual fees for the examination of the pictures I may submit to you so that I may feel free to do so when I am in doubt. An adverse opinion is of about as much value to me as a favorable one for I want to keep my collection clean.

Next, on August 26, 1911, Van Slochem, as always keeping an eye on his business, wrote that he had forwarded a lamp to Covenhoven that he had bought so reasonably that he did not

want "to trouble you to send me a check for such a trifle." [271]
With reference to the trouble with Van Gelder, Van Slochem
went on, "I can inform you that I have seen him, told him flatly
what I wanted, but we cannot come to any arrangement, his
intention is, to come over himself. I advised him to consider
everything well before going over. I have concluded to do
nothing until I have seen Nardus as I have written you in my
previous letter; whatever the result may be, I am coming over
anyhow."

On September 17 Van Gelder instructed Hofstede de
Groot:[272]

Just having returned from the journey I found your letter
with enclosed invoice. I ordered my banker to pay your
bill, $f1$ 370 – and I hope that you will receive my "remise"
one of these days. About the little painting by Rembrandt,
I totally agree with you, to send it along with you, so you
can compare it with the little work of Johnson. I do have
to advice you to forward it to a friend or acquaintance,
because even of such a little thing, custom officers can be
troublesome upon your arrival in New York.

It is too bad that you can't find the necessary peace of
mind to dedicate yourself to your interesting paper for
"Onze Kunst." However, you say that work is being done.
Hopefully you get it done prior to your departure. I did
not receive a reply to my question whether it wouldn't
be better to have the photogravure of my Rembrandt by
Buschman. Please let me know, so I can eventually order it
at Braun.

271 Letter in VHFF (7/9).
272 Letter in RKD.

On September 22, 1911, Van Gelder continued his correspondence with the Most Esteemed Dr. [Hofstede] de Groot.[273]

> Please advice me about your conditions for the authentication of two portraits by Frans Hals, about which I talked during my last visit. I was a bit sick so could not come around the time I had planned. In the meantime I sent both portraits to Dr. Bode who replied with a beautiful letter; which I might show you. I also value much your appreciation. I hope however that your demands will be reasonable so I will be encouraged to further purchases and to continue our friendly relationship. In case we agree, I will come to The Hague next Tuesday.

It looks as if Van Gelder, perhaps still reeling from the $80 000 loss, acknowledged that it no longer paid off to purchase without prior authentication and therefore tried to compare the experts' fees and their expertises by shopping around. On October 5 Van Gelder wrote to Hofstede de Groot once more, saying he was sorry to have missed him and was returning both his 'expertises:'[274]

> Enclosed I send them back with the request to repeat them at the back of the photos of both paintings. I don't know whether you plan to include both Masters in your Catalogue Raisonné. If this is the case, it would please me if you mention this in your expertise and then I will be pleased myself to send you another picture of both paintings for your studies. [...] I also received your letter with regard to the reproduction by Braun of my Rembrandt. As

---

273 Letter in RKD.
274 Letter in RKD.

said, I have been at Braun's who will send me the samples. I would have liked so dearly the results of your research with regard to the date of the painting of my grey-haired old man. As you saw in Bode's letter, he places it in the époque of the L'Enfant Prodique.

After comparing it with the range of late portraits, I am personally of the opinion that my work belongs to the very latest period of the Master and this is just what the big Master had tried to accomplish during his entire life. The broad idea of modeling with a palette knife into the paint, blended by shadows in black lacquer, all this done so simple and sure and self-conscious; with this the great feeling, put in the stammering mouth and in those eyes, that speak of suffering and deep questioning. In short, watching my grey-haired old man for me is completely separated from the natural tendency of each proprietor of a work of art to give this a place as high as possible [...]

I had also expected a few words about your idea about the date of the painting of the grey-haired old man, about which I wrote extensively. The study evokes time and again the same emotion as when I saw this work, cited by Bode, in Petersburg. It also made a great impression on Bode; his enthusiast description of it is proof thereof. I am convinced that it also would have made a deep impression on you in the event you would have seen it after cleaning.

After having instructed Hofstede de Groot how and where to appreciate the Halses (at the back of the photographs), Van Gelder left for America. On October 10, 1911, he cabled Van Horne that he was sailing Saturday 12 with Mrs. Van Gelder, on the *Mauretania*, and asked Van Horne to contact him at The Manhattan Hotel (in New York City).[275]

On Oct. 31, Eilers, who was staying at the The Queens in Toronto – and as always wishing to be the only player around – also announced his upcoming visit to Van Horne.[276] He informed him, as well, that he thought it better to start in Toronto "as the other dealers are going usually first to Montreal, to be together in one town. We Dutch people call that 'fishing behind the net.'"

Eilers, not only a good, trustworthy dealer, but apparently also a good father and obeying husband, entrusted Van Horne with some personal disappointment in this letter. He said he had wanted to bring his seventeen-year old daughter along, but his wife felt she was too young and she did not trust him to look after her well enough: "I thought she knows it better than I and went alone." Eilers went on about waiting "for a good consignment [of] very good paintings, between them an important picture by Turner." He regretted to have missed Van Horne the previous Sunday and announced that he would be back in Montreal in early November, when he would show his pictures at Messrs. Roberts & Son, Young Street, North 729. Apart from the Turner, of which he was going to send Van Horne a photo, Eilers then noted that he had obtained:

a beautiful Monticelli,[277] some Fantins, and Corot's, besides works of our people such as a Maris, Mauve, Bauer & Breitner. Bauer is very improving, we can see him sell him

---

275   Letter in VHFF (7/22).

276   Letter in VHFF (3/27).

277   VH. 247 Monticelli (Adolphe Joseph Thomas). Marseilles 1824-1886. ⬚: Mountainous Landscape near Algiers." In the distance the sharp white crests of mountains, and on the nearer hills, under an overhanging dark cloud, fortifications or monastery buildings. From E. J. Wisselingh & Co. Amsterdam 1911. ⬚: 3 000.

all over; it was difficult to me, to save 5 works by him for Canada.

I couldn't get one Daumier, they are getting very rare and high prices. I saw a small picture at Paris, as large as the one I had last year "Wagons third classe." They asked me dealer price frs. 38 000. – Perhaps you saw it at Paris at Bernheim, June. The title is L'amateur d'Estampes, very sketchy!

Not long after Hofstede de Groot had seen the two Halses, *Onze Kunst* on November 1, 1911, published his article "Two Newly Discovered Portraits by Frans Hals." [278] The copy in the Van Horne Family Fonds mistakenly attributes this article to *L'Art Flamand et Hollandais*, but does contain a quite faded English translation of this article:[279]

The portraits of which the reproductions are published herewith are the property of Mr. M. van Gelder, Castle of Zeecrabbe, in Uccle, who a short time ago purchased them from the Count of Limburg Stirum. The Count had inherited them from the family de Thiennes, which should have been related to the family of Hals. These portraits would, according to legend, represent personalities of the nearest surroundings of the Painter.

I have not succeeded in finding amongst these a married couple of the year 1637 of which the man was born in 1600 and the wife in 1601. However the legend might be true because the persons here pictured belong to the same simple class to which Hals also belonged. Both wear the simplest dress as the fashion was then. No lace ornaments to the bonnet, collar and cuffs, no

278 Letter in VHFF (2/24).
279 This article is translated into French as "Deux portraits nouvellement attribués à Frans Hals," published in *L'Art Flamand & Hollandais, Revue Mensuelle Illustrée*, vol 17, 1912, pp. 1-2, reproduced.

flowered silk or velvet, no embroidered bodice or gloves, not a single golden ornament, even no wedding ring wears the wife dressed in nothing but black and just as simply dressed is the husband, who wears his heavy mantilla thrown over his left and under his right shoulder, so that the left arm in which he holds his gloves rests as in a sling, while he points with the right towards himself with strong self-consciousness. Are these perhaps Mennonites, who thus purposely show their repulsion of worldly pomp?

But precisely on account of their simple dresses which the Artist has painted with large yet careful touch – look for instance at the richness and variety of tones in the black of the costumes – the attention of the spectator is drawn on the flesh tones; on the healthy blushing face of the motherly wife and on the air-tanned features of her husband. Both look at us with their sympathetic eyes straight in the face. We receive the impression of the glory-day of their life, the day on which they, the simple gentry, went before their then already far and near famous citizen to have themselves perpetuated for their children. And these children will certainly have kept proudly in honour such portraits from such parents and left them in succession to their children and grand children. This circumstance explains probably the fact that these portraits have been always inherited, never have come into trade and thus so far could have remained totally unknown.

As regards the relation of these portraits to the other Works of Frans Hals, the woman has probably the most analogy with the portrait of Reyna van Steenkiste, now in the Rijksmuseum, while the man recalls some figures on the big Amsterdam Archer piece by Frans Hals, painted in the same year of 1637.

Hofstede de Groot should have added that it was Van Gelder who had told him about the provenance. As it was, it seemed as if the Count had given him (Hofstede de Groot) that story; two years later, this omission would lead to an event in which Hofstede was not shy to embroil Van Horne. Anyway, as shown in the footnote, Hofstede de Groot made two similar statements about the male and the female pictures in September 1911.[280]

On November 12 Bourgeois cabled Van Horne, then at Railroad Co. Habana, Cuba that Bode would come to New York. Bourgeois fixed his visit to Montreal on Monday, "as Bode will be back in New York to see some other collection he could not see before and [also because] he will start Europe the 23rd he declared that he could not make a change of his tour in United States and has fixed his visit Montreal Monday." [281] On the same day, Van Horne received one more cable from Bourgeois: "I am very sorry but think you will see him when you come back from Cuba." [282] Ten days later, Bourgeois, then staying at The Plaza in New York, apologized to Van Horne about forgetting to give him a receipt for his cheque of $6 000. On December 8 Bourgeois, now from Hotel Netherland, New York, wrote:[283]

....

Coming back from Montreal I couldn't have a room in the Plaza and stay now for a few days in the Netherland. From next Monday I shall be definitively [be staying at]

---

280   The undersigned declares that he has carefully inspected the picture of which this is a photograph, which is painted on canvas, high 0.92, large 0.68 meter (36 6/8 × 27 1/8). He considers this picture to be a perfectly genuine & splendid example of the art of Frans Hals. Sept. 1911, The Hague (signature) Corn. Hofstede de Groot). This picture will be described in the Supplement to my Catalogue raissonnée of Frans Hals's works CHdG.
     With these photo's went a "copy of a declaration:"
     Portrait of a Dutch Gentleman
     " " " Dutch Lady by Frans Hals:
     Photographs of same endorsed on back by C. Hofstede de Groot and Letter from Dr. W. Bode, Kaiser Friedrich Museum, Berlin Produced translations from L'Art Flamand & Hollandais, Nov. 11, Oct. 15 and letters from Mr. Van Gelder and Mrs. M. T. Dowkjig in regard to the same.
     Stamp of H. van Slochem, Dealer in High Class Old Masters, Paris – 15, rue de Rochefoucauld. F. Hals. Photo's.
281   Letter in VHFF (2/7).
282   Letter in VHFF (6/2).
283   Letter in VHFF (2/7).

389 Fifth Avenue and hope to have soon the pleasure of seeing you there. As for the pictures by Monet, I can you give one, as I promised you, the exact prices, fixed by Nardus. He writes me in his letter: "If Sir William likes the "Quais of Paris" which is wonderful, you can sell it to him for $8 000. The "Marine with cliffs" is also splendid, is $7-8 000. The landscape "spring" you can sell for [more] than $4 000.

As I personally believe that the later picture is as to the quality of colour and facture the finest of all. I think it is not expensive."

Around this same time Van Slochem wrote in an undated letter that Archer Huntington had asked about the *Holy Family* that Van Horne had bought from Van Gelder.[284] He had told Huntington that Van Horne had another important Greco in his collection [*Head of St. Maurice*]. About the two Rembrandts, Van Slochem noted that Townsend wanted to write about them in a special Christmas issue.

Bode, back in Berlin, wrote Van Horne on December 8 that since he had returned from New York, he had spent nearly all the time in bed because his veins were again inflamed.[285] He added that he had obtained:

---

284 Letter in VHFF (7/12). VH 102. A description by Wickenden is lacking. Instead there is a newspaper clipping: "*El Greco and His School*, by Harold E. Wethey, Excerpt from pages 188-189, *Holy Family with the Magdalen*. ⊞: no. X-101 *Holy Family with the Magdalen* (Type III). Oil on canvas. 48 × 40 in (1.22 × 1.02 m). Montreal, Sir William van Horne, Heirs of Jorge Manuel (?), ca 1620-1630. A free replica of the Cleveland picture painted in a very mannered way. The poor quality of the drawing is particularly noticeable in the hands and also in the Magdalen's head [...] Other dating: Mayer 1604. Collections: Private Collection, Gijón (?); Mietke, Vienna; Van Gelder, Brussels. Bibliography: Mayer, no 29; Camón Aznar, no 240, fig. 429. [On the accompanying sheet: *Holy Family + Dish of Fruit*.] ⊞: $400 000-500 000. From Van Gelder.
285 Letter in VHFF (7/12).

the photo of the picture by Magnasco of which I spoke to you; I sent it enclosed.[286] It is about 4½ feet large and 3 feet high, in best condition. The subject is a scene of Don Quixote, as I believe. The picture is very strong in treatment and fine in color. The proprietor, Baron v. Windland in Munich, is disposed to sell the picture (though he is a rich man, he always wants money) if he gets it for two thousand dollars. If you like, please let it know me, if you do not [illeg.] to write to the owner directly (his address is Schloss Bernried, Starnberger See, Bayern).

You told me in New York that you bought 2 examples of *Monks in the Refectory* by Magnasco, a smaller sketchy one and the larger original. If you would be disposed to part with one of them, I should like very much to get the smaller one for our Gallery in exchange occasionally.

As shown, both Nardus and Van Gelder invested in some of Van Horne's businesses, the sardine plant among them. Reports in the *Beacon* allow a look at the other side of the railway track, so to speak. On December 1911 the *Beacon* reported that a modern canning plant would be erected "upon the lands recently purchased at Chamcook" and that Van Horne, his son Benedict, and railway men Shaughnessy and Bosworth were among its backers. The *Beacon* report on the rise and the fall of this cannery gives a rare glimpse into people's struggle for even their basic needs. The plan for the plant would start with building piers and workmen's cottages; prospects were to sell the produce – sardines in oil – to the navies of the world. Van Horne not only put his capital into the enterprise, he also showed an interest in the design of the future workmen's town site.   ✕

---

286   This painting was?/is not mentioned in the Wickenden catalogue.

PEOPLE & PLACES

Museum Bredius
Lange Vijverberg 14 Den Haag
Courtesy Pauline van Till
➔

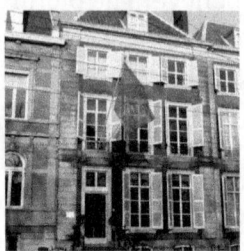

Abraham Bredius
Collectie Veenhuijzen,
Centraal Bureau voor
Genealogie, Den Haag
➔

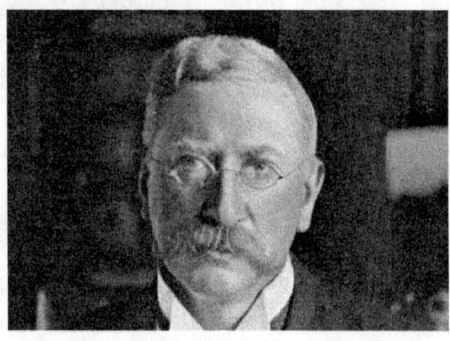

Cornelius Hofstede de Groot
(1863-1930)
photo RKD
➲

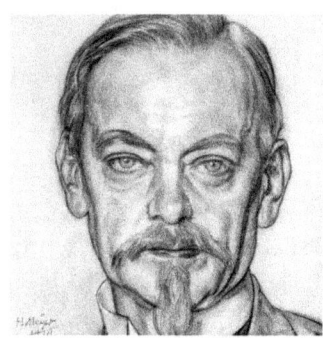

RKD archives.
http://www.codart.nl
➲

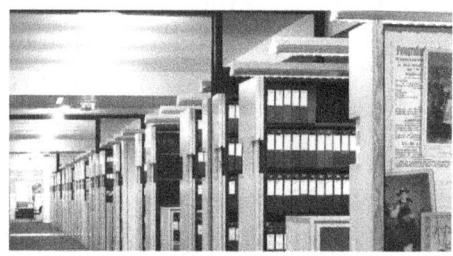

CHAPTER 6

HEYDAYS OF COLLECTING / SARDINES / ANXIETY

WE HAVE ENTERED the year 1912, which, for Van Horne, would turn out to be a glorious year for collecting. At the start of the year, on January 5th, two people wrote to Van Horne.[287]

The first one was Eilers, who thanked him for the "kind letter concerning the painting by Turner, it was just what I needed." [288] He went on to tell Van Horne about a sale of the collection of the late Mr. Weber of Hamburg that was going to be held on February 20. "I am going to assist that sale, if I can do something for you, please let me know by cable."

Next was Nardus. We saw that Van Horne was now abreast of Bode's opinion about Nardus and Van Gelder, who he called the Dutch and Flemish dealers (even though neither of them was Flemish). Nardus' letter shows that while Van Horne had admonished Nardus, he had still not lost his trust in him. On

---

287 Letter in (3/27).
288 VH 21. Turner, Joseph Mallord William, London 1775–Chelsea 1851. *Launch at Chatham*. ▣: (On the Medway-Kent) In NY February 1969. Note: This painting water colour hung in the large living-room on the top floor of 1139 Sherbrooke St. West, together with the Cotman water colour which proved to be so important in London. Sold to Sotheby's. There has never been a reason to doubt the authenticity of this water colour, but it must now be verified by experts as it has not been recorded in recent publications on Turner. One must always remember that the Van Hornes did not encourage publication of their paintings. It has hung in the above location since before the death in 1915 of Sir William Van Horne. Watercolour H. 10 in × 16½ in.
      Cat. 1933 only lists no. 93, Turner: *Shakespeare's Cliff*, Dover.

January 5 Nardus wrote from Paris, and it seems that business went on as usual:[289]

It was delightful as well for Mrs. Nardus as for myself, to receive the picture you painted for us at Covenhoven. It has given us the charm, and atmosphere of your island.

I have been at Mr. Decock to see about your pictures and happy to say that he save the Goya. That picture has been awfully spoiled, the others are also well progressing, and at the end of next month, they will be ready for shipment. On my return from Spain I have send to Bourgeois 2 photos of a large family picture by Goya, which is in the Prado. That picture is very similar to the one I sent you. I have studied it carefully, and I can say without hesitation, I didn't see any pupil of Goya who could have done it. As I told you before, that evening when we were walking together at Montreal, this picture is an early work by Goya, and after my return from Spain, and the comparison I made there, I am convinced still, it is by Goya. I am very happy to write you that I have succeeded in obtaining 2 portraits by Goya, these I bought at Valencia from the family Montesinas. The 2 portraits presumed to be the *Marquis and Marquise de Castelfort*, which are remarkably painted in his ripest period. The lady portrait is painted with an exquisite charm and with astonishing simplicity; the portrait of the man is audaciously executed, as really a man ought to be painted. They represent the highest expression of Goya's art. I have never seen any better.

Bourgeois wrote me about the kindness you show him, which encourages him very much, and I thank you sincerely for all that. I have thoroughly understood your last

---

289   Letter in VH (6/2,3).

letter and I hope you feel sure that I shall send him only high-class works.

....

After apparently having met with Mr. Borden, Van Horne instructed Van Gelder how to go about the Borden matter on January 17:[290]

....

The enclosed letter is written with a view to sending a copy to Mr. Borden, which I have done.

You will I think discover my meaning between the lines. He was rather offish at first – perhaps suspicious but we soon got on very good terms and at the end he gave me his very expensive two-volume catalogue. While he showed some feeling about the condemned pictures he was not so hot as I expected to find him and he freely admitted that he had **no legal claim**. I need not tell you of all our long talk. I extolled the value of his Lucretia and the little Hals and he holds them in great esteem and I am pretty sure that he feels inside that on the whole he has not done badly.

Now I would suggest you writing me a letter expressing gratification at mine enclosed; expressing an earnest wish to do what you can to recover a place in Mr. Borden's confidence; point out that at the time the pictures were sold you did not pretend to any precise knowledge on the subject; that since that time you have studied much and have come to realize what they were; that Nardus has lost so much through the Widener settlement and otherwise that he can't be counted upon to help much if at all in this matter; that you were acting only as an Agent and were in no way legally responsible for the transaction with Mr. Borden;

----

290   Letter in VHFF (7/22).

that you wish to re-establish yourself financially through your present knowledge of Art and therefore do not wish to have the ill-will of anybody in starting and carrying on your business; that you wish to give Mr. Borden substantial evidence of your good faith; that it is quite impossible for you to redeem all of the condemned pictures; that it is impossible after so many years to put these back to the dealers from whom they came – most of these dealers being now dead and out of business; that while it would be a severe strain on your heart-strings and an equally severe strain on your resources you are willing to sacrifice even your de Keyser to please Mr. Borden and secure his good opinion.

Then go on and make as strong as you can the point about the impossibility of your getting anything back now for the condemned pictures from those from whom they were bought. If you had known of any objections to them within a reasonable time after Mr. Borden bought them this could have been done but now when you have lost all right of recourse you are sure that Mr. Borden could not expect you to take them all back and burn them etc. etc.

I mentioned the de Keyser because of something Van Slochem said to me, which I assumed you had talked with him about. Be sure to send me a good photograph of the de Keysers and its size.

....

This letter also reads as if Van Horne had a stake in keeping Mr. Borden quiet. What stake? His name? Did he fear that Borden would go public with a condemnation of Van Horne's beloved dealers? Knowles (2010: 152) states that the diversions of Van Horne's collector's instinct and artistic bent "distracted him from the many worries" about his CPR and other businesses. Could it be that it was the other way around, that his business worries distracted him from his collector's worries?

214 | The William Van Horne Collection

Van Slochem's letter of January 23, 1912, to Van Horne casts light on the path of the two Halses' purchase.[291] Apparently he (Van Slochem) tried to purchase the Halses from Van Gelder for Van Horne:

I have just received a reply to the long cable I sent yesterday. The reply [by Van Gelder] says:

Lowest price for Sir William for the two Halses and four pictures one hundred and fifty thousand dollars. Now Dear Sir William, it is for you to decide. I must say this; that I had already written to Van Gelder a long letter when I was with you in Montreal. In this letter I told him already that you like the Halses so much and that you had told me that if you close a certain business and V.G. would make a different [difference] for the Halses to you, that you would like to own them, no doubt he has received this letter. And yesterday my long cable on top of that, he came probably to the conclusion that as I cabled him your offer, that your transaction must be closed and as he knows you would like to own them, he came down that much in price to you. If you will kindly let me advise you. As I know the kind of letter I wrote in Montreal. I hope you will do this much for me! and close the two Halses and the four pictures for $150 000 – and upon my own responsibility I would arrange to have you give the small Guardi in payment for $15 00 fifteen hundred dollars bringing it down to one hundred and forty eight thousand five hundred $148 500. Now I like to suggest to you that the Halses should be shipped to you to Montréal. And that you do not show them in my place in New York until the Borden matter has been settled which may only be now a question of a few weeks.

---

291   Letter in VHFF (6/2).

When you decide to make that exhibition in New [York] you can arrange that with me. Hoping to have the pleasure to get a favourable reply.

p.s. if you rather have me come over to see you in Montreal Sunday to talk the matter over I will gladly do so. As regards the hanging I have just come back from the sale and I have secured eight of [them?]. I shall put the number together with prices on the other page. All those I bought I consider cheap and like to hear so from you.

Only one day later, January 24th, Van Slochem wrote from #2 East 41st Street, New York to tell Van Horne that he had taken the liberty of sending him a pair of candelabras, a pair of andirons, and ten lamps. He added, "should you not like them at all, you may return them." [292] On that same day, apparently after a telephone conversation with Van Horn's secretary, Lynch, Van Slochem wrote Van Horne one more letter, this time from 477 Fifth Avenue:[293]

I presume that Mr. Lynch has perfectly understood our conversation by phone and do hereby confirm same.

I received your telegram saying that your letter about Hals should have read seven hundred thousand francs instead six hundred. This telegram will be destroyed as per your request. I wrote you in my previous letter that V.G. has cabled me his lowest price for the two Hals portraits: Jan Steen, Nursing Cat; Van Goyen, Winter Scene; Guardi, Storm; Young Lady writing, Half Length Figures is one hundred and fifty thousand dollars.

---

292 Letter in VHFF (7/10).
293 Letter in VHFF (7/10).

I have written you that on my own responsibility would I act for V.G. by taking the Guardi from your collection in payment at $1 500 making it $148 000 but to avoid this responsibility. I rather would you leave it as V.G. has cabled me, as I also have had a cable this morning from V.G. saying that he had an offer of the Halses from Berlin for six hundred thousand Marks. Besides this there is a letter from me on the way to V.G. in which I am enclosing your letter and **saying alas**, that you offered me for the four pictures for which he asked ($26 000) you offered $20 000 dollars and your Guardi: therefore if you will be kind enough not to consider the proposition I make taking the Guardi in payment from the $150 000 I shall be much obliged to you.

I would suggest to you that you figure the Halses bought for $130 000 thousand and the four other pictures for $20 000 and your Guardi. No doubt the letter I wrote to V.G. while I was in Montreal and my strong advise in my cable has had a very strong effect upon V.G.

I am most happy that the Halses are yours and congratulate you with such an important asset to your so worthy collection. I have written V.G. a long letter about your intention to have the Halses exhibited in my place in N.Y. but in the mean time I cabled him today to ship them to you this week to Montreal as it would be much better, to keep quiet for a few weeks yet. Perhaps the Borden matter will be settled before exhibiting the Halses! Don't you think yourself this would be better?

I am now awaiting your letter, to hear from you if you want me to ship the four pictures. The lamps I shall number with an individual number and will explain you on a separate list, which number I gave the catalogue numbers. I will arrange for the packing tomorrow, and ship them this week. I asked you for check of 1 500: thinking I may get the cabinet or the settees in that sale.

If you have no appointment for Sunday I should like to leave Saturday evening and spend an hour with you Sunday, just coming for the day leaving again Sunday evening. So if you can let me hear from you in time I shall be delighted.

In the end, on January 27, 1912, Van Horne asked Van Slochem to "forward the things you bought for me at the Grisby Sale with invoices as you suggest." [294] In a P.S. Van Horne added that he would try to keep free from any other engagements the following Sunday. Van Slochem replied that he would wait with his visit until he had heard that the Halses had arrived.

Next, Nardus, still residing in Chateau Lea-Flory at Suresness au Seine, received the following (typed) letter from Van Horne dated January 31.[295] It must have shaken him up.

Confidential

Dear Nardus

I got your letter two weeks ago but have been too busy until now to acknowledge it. I am glad to have your good report of those pictures Decock has in hand and particularly glad that the Goya is coming out well. And we are all much pleased to know that Mrs. Nardus and the little ones are well and that they are none the worse of their visit to Canada.

Bourgeois was here a week ago with some pictures but they were not the kind to appeal to our Montreal collectors and he sold nothing. They were too high in class

294 Letter in VHFF (7/9).
295 Letter in VHFF (5/4).

for some and not high enough for others. I am very sorry that Mr. Bourgeois did not make this; his first business visit with something better for it is not easy to overcome first impressions. I am afraid that you do not realize the great change that has occurred in the picture business on this side of the Atlantic in the past 12 or 14 years. Don't get angry at me for saying what I think, for it is said only because of the interest I feel in your success and in that of Mr. Bourgeois. He must either be a Connoisseur-dealer and have only high-class and unquestionable pictures or must be a general dealer with a large variety of pictures of a cheaper class. He is well fitted for the former in every way, but the latter would be far below him and a waste of his fine taste and great knowledge and his pride would be in constant revolt. The kind of people he is best fitted to deal with want really fine and high-class pictures, not necessarily all old masters, but if modern pictures they must be of the very best. And don't forget that old masters can't be sold on this side except on recognized authority. Too many have been bitten and so much has been written about rich Americans having got "stuck," that everyone is suspicious. Mr. Bourgeois ought not to offer or show one doubtful picture, much less sell one, for that would be fatal to his business. Van Slochem has now **only** fine and high-class pictures, all of them certified by Bode, Friedländer or some other recognized authority and if he sticks to such he will succeed, although he may not know how to sell pictures or know a hundredth part as much about Art as does Mr. Bourgeois, who is certain to fail with the pictures he has. Really fine works are absolutely necessary and, to start with, moderate prices. With these he can succeed for he is much liked by everybody he meets. He has not said so to me, but I feel sure that he is ashamed to show the most of the pictures he now has, to anybody who knows anything of pictures. So I beg you to provide him with something better and give him a chance. (Sgd) W. C. van Horne.

Don't forget that "Artist pictures" which appeal so strongly to you do not appeal so strongly to collectors.

....

This letter is typical of Van Horne's style, even though this one was not hand-written. Vaughan (1920: 355) described Van Horne's letters as follows: "He had been always been a fastidious letter-writer, and observed the graceful custom of answering private letters in his own original and distinguished hand-writing. His business and private correspondence was terse, clear, and direct – free from literariness and every kind of affection."

This same letter by Van Horne also contains one more example of how much he must have enjoyed the diversions collecting fine arts gave him. However, it throws some doubt on a Lopez statement (2007: n 33): "The only overseas customer with whom Nardus appears to have remained on good terms was Van Home [Horne]."

Van Slochem, by letter of February 2, 1912, replied to Van Horne's letter as follows: "I have send the two Hals photo's to Miss. Van Horne with your request to place them on the bottom of her truck so that they will not get bent." [296] He also gave Van Horne the measurements of the two Halses (36⅝ by 27⅛)[297] and a copy of the photos endorsed by Mr. Corn.

---

296 Letter in VHFF (7/16).
297 VH 66 Hals, Frans (Antwerp 1584–Haarlem 1666). *Portrait of a Dutch Gentleman.*
    🅦: He is shown standing, three quarters length, life-size, dressed in plain black, with body in profile to the right [...]. Canvas H. 36⅝ in, w. 27⅛ in (92 cm × 68 cm). Inscribed on the background to the right, "AETAT. SUAE. 37. ANo. 1637. In the coll. of the count de Thiennes. In the coll. of the Countess Van Limburg-Stirum. In the coll. of M. Van Gelder, Uccle, Belgium. 🅦: 125 000.
      VH 67 Hals, Frans (Antwerp 1584–Haarlem 1666). *Portrait of a Dutch Lady.*
    🅦: Standing, three quarters length life-size, turned slightly to the left, she wears a white ruff and close fitting coiffe above a full and squarely cut black dress, with

Hofstede de Groot. Van Slochem further wrote that he would gladly send the four pictures and come to Montreal to fetch the Halses for his exhibition, "in the same way as Mr. Knoedler has sent for your Rembrandt and your Murillo." Van Slochem also announced that he would make inquiries about how to deal with the customs house with regard to taking pictures from Montreal to New York, for exhibition purposes, without having to leave them in the public stores.

Van Gelder's next letter, of February 4, reflects Van Horne's aid in the Borden matter.[298] This letter, which was in reply to Van Horne's letter of January 31, mentioned that he had received both Van Horne's letters on the Borden matter and was "much elated at the result of your meeting him." Van Gelder continued:

> The letter you enclosed, of which you have send Borden a copy is masterly composed and takes beautifully the pretentions away from him. As you suggested I have written you a letter in which I kept closely to the terms you have indicated and in which I offer my superb DeKeyzer! in lieu of the four questioned pictures. I had the letter typewritten for Borden's sake. I hope you will find it satisfactory, I have sent you two copies, one for Bord. and one for yourself. I hope you will soon find the opportunity to see B. I said in my letter that I was going to send you a photo of the DeKeyzer but I have no more. V. Sl. has them all and he will, of course give you one when you say so. When I get back I will ship the DeKeyzer, so that you may have the Picture at hand when required.

epaulettes [...]. Canvas H. 36⅜ in, w. 27⅛ in (92 cm × 68 cm). Inscribed on the background to the right, AETAT. SUAE. 36. ANo. 1637. In the coll. of the count de Thiennes. In the coll. of the Countess Van Limburg-Stirum. In the coll. of M. Van Gelder, Uccle, Belgium. ⊞: 125 000.

298   Letter in VHFF (5/4).

I said in my letter that, when M.B. would accept the Picture I expected him to sign a statement saying: that he feels satisfied with the exchange and thus discharged Nardus and me from any possible future claims. I hope that you will not find difficulty in getting him to sign this, as without that we might get trouble possibly with B's heirs or from jealous people who may find that the exchange was not so advantageous for Mr. B. and thus my sacrifice would be lost.

The redaction of such a paper can be perfectly left to you or if you wish be gotten up by my lawyers which v. Slochem could eventually arrange, but I don't think that this be necessary. It would be well also that I should get possession of the four questioned pictures and thus have them out of our way.

I have sent a reproduction of the DeKeyzer to Hofst. De Groot and asked him to acknowledge it with his signature (he has seen it before in my house), I expect to find same on my return at Uccle and will then forward it at once to Van Slochem.

I have received a letter you wrote van Slochem about the Halses and what I retain there from is, that our friendship cannot or will not be influenced nor does depend on any question of financial moment. Your wish about the Halses has come to realization and although you cannot own the "syndics" you own now two works which rank perhaps as high in Hals' Portraits as the former with Rembrandt! Van Slochem writes very enthusiastic about the future; he speaks about all the lovely plans you have made out for him, the Borden matter settled! An exhibition of the Halses in his place! A letter you will get up [draft?] for him to be send to the best buyers! A visit with Mr. Borden etc., etc. Well, I got warm in reading all this and I am feeling so grateful and happy to think of what you will do for me. Wasn't it foolish to send you my last letter asking you to help Van Slochem!

Two days ago the Halses left on the "Corsican." I assure you they are never out of my mind and hours at night I lay awake thinking about them and wondering what you will have to say when you seen them. I wish I could be standing somewhere hidden when they arrive, to see your smiling, happy expression in looking at them very, very long. I wish you could see them first of all and afterwards have Lady van Horne come and your children so that in your turn you may watch their feelings! Could you manage that?

Van Gelder ended this flattering letter by assuring Van Horne that he enjoyed all kinds of winter sports, which was so "necessary for both of us to get out of the misty atmosphere and get some highly needed distraction." Certainly an understatement.

German connoisseur William Bode wrote Van Horne, on February 12, 1912, from Charlotteburg, that he was in bed again and that the American trip had been too much for his poor health. [299] He went on about the cheque he got for the Magnasco, "which I sent to Baron v. Windland. I hope that you got the picture in the meantime or that you will get it soon, and think you will be pleased with it. I am very curious to see the photos you promised to send. We have a rather important sale here in 12 days, the sale of the Weber Coll. of Hamburg."

On that very same day Van Horne wrote to Van Slochem to let him know that he was not happy about the Halses' shipment. [300] He complained that, if the Hals pictures had been shipped by the Dominion Express Company "they would have been in my house now." To top it off, Van Horne added, the pictures had not only arrived by freight but were consigned to

---

299   Letter in VHFF (8/1).
300   Letter in VHFF (7/10).

a firm of customs brokers here, "involving unnecessary delay and expense, but also that they had been exposed to extreme cold, the temperature being minus 25 or 30." Van Horne went on with instructions about how to handle his wares:

> As soon as the pictures come I shall have them carefully examined so that in the event of damage Mr. Van Gelder may be able to make the necessary claims under the insurance policy. I hope they will be found all right, but I am, as you may imagine, anxious about them.
>
> If the pictures do not arrive until after I have gone to Cuba it might be well for you to come up so as to see them when they are opened. I will arrange to have you notified by wire. I am leaving here Wednesday evening for New York to sail from there for Havanna on Saturday.

On February 22 Bode wrote Van Gelder in German. The fact that the letter was written in German might have upset Van Gelder, but perhaps not as much as its content.[301] (The following translation of this letter accompanied the German version.)

> I hear that you have bought today at the Weber-Sale the Man with the Fur Bonnet, ascribed to Rembrandt. I congratulate you with this acquisition, and I should be particularly pleased, if you should have bought this Picture for Sir William van Horne.
>
> Frankly speaking I find this picture, which may almost certainly be considered as the masterpiece from Barend Fabritius considerably more beautiful than the undoubtedly authentic Portrait of a Boy by Rembrandt, for which

---

301   Letter and translation in VHFF (51/4).

120 000 Marks has been paid at the sale. I know very few pictures, if any, by pupils of Rembrandt, which have been painted so effectively and so masterly as this portrait, and which so much approaches Rembrandt in his best epoch.

We saw that Bode had informed Van Horne about the Weber sale in his letter of February 12, so perhaps he was a bit annoyed that Van Horne had not commissioned him to buy on his behalf at that sale. If so, maybe his opinion about the Rembrandt was due more to wounded pride than professional observation. On the other hand, perhaps he was right. After all, in 1972 members of the RRP deemed the painting not to be a Rembrandt. Of course Van Gelder did not like what Bode wrote. By letter of February 25 Van Gelder objected to Bode's opinion about the *Man with the Fur Hat being attributed to Fabritius.*[302] Bode subsequently wrote to Van Gelder, again in German, from Charlottenburg. (This letter was also accompanied by the following translation into English):

Our last letters crossed; I think you will have received, while yet in Berlin, my observations about the marvelous portrait by Fabritius.

I must admit, that my opinion about this picture and some similar ones (namely a large Biblical composition in Darmstadt) is not entirely fixed yet! They are really too effective and too strong and they are painted with too much im pasto for Bernard Fabritius. On the other hand they do not show much resemblance with the two authentic portraits by Karel Fabritius (a thorough study of the pupils of Rembrandt is so necessary!). To my great regret I have neither the time nor the ability to travel therefore.

302   Letter in VHFF (51/4).

For almost 19 years I am very much hindered by this miserable affliction of the veins, and therefore could not get anymore to new thorough studies. What I have written in all that time is for the greater part the fruit of previous studies.

[The following note is written on the English translation of this letter:] "Original, which relates to some other matter is returned to Mr. Van Gelder. 30th April. WCVH."

Meanwhile, on March 15, 1912, Van Slochem wrote Van Horne from New York about his ongoing efforts to pacify Borden:[303]

Immediately after you left my place yesterday I had the DeKeyzer put under glass, so everything is ready for Mr. Borden as far as I am concerned. I hope you will have had an answer from Mr. Borden as you anticipated and that you will be able to spare the time to write Mr. Borden that the DeKeyzer is now at my place etc., etc. and if you will be kind enough to draft the invitation for me for the exhibition so that I can commence to write the letters together with the list to whom I shall send them. I shall get busy and thank you very much.

More diversion for Van Horne, but he sent the draft two days later, along with instructions for handling the DeKeijzer. He also announced a transfer of $33 000 from London to Morgan, Harjes & Co. Paris, for the credit of Mr. Van Gelder.[304] An additional amount was going to be sent "from here in a day or two."

---

303   Letter in VHFF (7/10).
304   Letter in VHFF (7/10).

Van Horne had returned from Cuba the previous Friday and had sent Lynch a cable that was worded curiously: "Returned [from] Cuba Found Hals good condition Thanks Fabritius No answer Borden Writing him today." [305]

Lynch relayed the message to Van Gelder a day later, on March 18.

Both Van Slochem and Bourgeois wrote to Van Horne on March 22. Bourgeois, writing from 389 Fifth Avenue, apologized for not replying to Van Horne's letter of the 18th. [306] He had mistakenly thought Van Horne was in New York. He continued: "I am very sorry that the A. Benson is in so a bad state and I cabled to Decock to give us his advice." [307] Bourgeois enclosed the invoice for the little Rhyes and a note saying that Bourgeois still hoped to see Van Horne in New York.

Van Slochem's letter said that, on Mr. Borden's request, he had sent Borden the DeKeyser for "a few days inspection." [308] Van Slochem indicated that he expected that as soon as Van Horne had met with Borden the matter would "finally" be out of the way. He also said that he had had "a visit of Mr. O. H. Kahn who liked my pictures very much, he requested me to send few pictures to his house, which I did, but they have been returned. Since your last visit here, I have received a few pictures, which will give you great pleasure to see."

So, the Borden matter was about to be resolved. What was that all about? Lopez (2007) states that it had taken years to uncover all of Nardus' misdeeds, with most of the detective

---

305   Letter in VHFF (7/22).

306   Letter in VHFF (2/7).

307   VH 139. Benson, Ambrosius, working at Bruges, 1521-1550. *Portrait of a Gentleman.* ▣: Half-length, with distinguished features, strongly-formed brow, nose and firm mouth, his expressive eye indicates both the gentleness and thought [...] Canvas H. 19 in, W. 15 in (47 cm × 37 cm). Initials "A.B." on the cuff of the glove, of sitter. ▣: $1 000.

    On the accompanying sheet are two other notes: "Not Benson, but good!" And "Apr. 64. Not Benson, Franco-Flemish painter of around 1540-1550. Fine quality."

308   Letter in VHFF (7/10).

work being done by Valentiner (see the November 1910 correspondence on page 180):

For instance, in preparing a catalogue of the private collection of the textile millionaire M. C. D. Borden in 1910,
Valentiner discovered that Borden owned six Nardus'
fakes, including a fraudulent Rembrandt self-portrait. He
expunged these works from the catalogue, but the story
has an intriguing footnote. Aside from the fakes, Nardus
had also sold Borden a masterpiece, which had come from
Bourgeois, namely Rembrandt's Lucretia. Neither Valentiner nor anyone else ever entertained any doubts about
Lucretia, but Nardus's involvement with it – not a major
selling point after the Lynnewood Hall incident – was
prudently left unmentioned when Borden's estate sold the
painting at auction in 1913. The National Gallery of Art in
Washington, which now owns Lucretia, has no record that
it ever belonged to Nardus – a man whose name has been
written into history with the point of an eraser.

Lopez subsequently went to the National Gallery in 2007 and
had the provenance changed![309]
Throughout 1912, Van Horne continued to be bombarded
with letters containing offers, flattery, and praise. Many of
these letters were from people whose names and tactics you
are familiar with by now: Nardus, hiding in the background,
Van Gelder, skillfully elusive, Van Slochem, keeping his eye
fixed on business, and Eilers, who preferred to work alone.
And then there were the connoisseurs, who were taking full
advantage of being very much in demand.

---

309   http://www.nga.gov/content/ngaweb/Collection/art-object-page.83.html (last
      accessed in March 2014). See also Lopez (2007: 76-83).

A STAGGERING LIST OF NEW ACQUISITIONS

In December, an acquaintance wrote to Van Horne saying: "You stagger me with the list of your new acquisitions." (Knowles 2004: 292). He was referring to the art Van Horne had purchased during the last twelve months. It was a stellar year for any collector, as the following summary of Van Horne's 1912 acquisition-related correspondence shows:

March 28: Van Slochem wrote from 477 Fifth Avenue to let Van Horne know that he had received the photo of Frans Hals (Toper) and Van Horne's letter re Mr. Borden, who had returned the DeKeijzer.[310] The good news he conveyed was that Mrs. and Mr. Huntington had been at his exhibition and thought the Halses were fine. Van Slochem added that Bourgeois had come in to see the Halses: "He says you write to W. that I like them so much that he likes to steal them!"

March 29: Bourgeois, enclosing an invoice for the Dabo pastel, wrote that he had received Van Horne's cheque for $200 and that the Van Slochem exhibition was very remarkable: "I saw your Hals collection yesterday, will be a big sensation for the art lovers here." [311]

April 5: Eilers thanked Van Horne for the £512, part payment, for Monticelli, and noted that he found the Weber sale very disappointing because the catalogue, and the preface by Mr. Friedländer, had indicated the pictures would be of the highest quality.[312] "It is always the same with the collections in

---

310   Letter in VHFF (7/10).
311   Letter in VHFF (2/7). Leon Dabo (1865-1960) was a French-born American painter whose family had fled the 1870 Franco-Prussian war. Later on, several Dabo's were found at Covenhoven, *Hillscape* (19¾ × 24), *Towards the Bay* (20½ × 31) and *Landscape* (20½ × 31½).
312   VH 247 Monticelli, Adolphe Joseph Thomas (Marseille 1824-1886). *Mountainous Landscape near Algiers*. ◫: In the distance the sharp white crests of mountains, and on the nearer hills, under an overhanging dark cloud, fortifications or monastery building [...]. Panel H. 12¾ in, W. 35 in (31 cm × 87 cm). Signed at the lower left, "Monticelli." From E. J. Wisseling & Co. Amsterdam 1911. ◫: 3 000.

Germany 9/10 procent is usually doubtful or not first rate."
Eilers went on about a very nice picture, a "bend" by M. Maris
and Don Quichote by Daumier, "however, very expensive. We
cannot sell it below $10 500.00." In this letter Eilers offered
Daumier's *The Wagon 3rd classe* for frs. 150 000, "I think Daumier will be paid in the future higher than Millet and there is
some reason for [this]." [313]

April 8: Bode wrote Van Horne from Hôtel de Rome that he
was glad to hear that Van Horne had bought the two Halses
and that he had had a chance to study them carefully while
in his room in the Museum. He added: "They are fine and in
good condition." [314] Bode also said he had heard of Van Horne's
intention to buy Magnasco's and to present one to his museum,
the Kaiser Friedrich Museum in Berlin. He promised Van
Horne that he would keep him posted on some fine pictures
that had been for sale.

April 11: Bourgeois wrote to Van Horne's secretary, "As you
know, Sir William bought from me last week two important
pictures by Goya, which are exposed in this moment at the
Dickens centenary exhibition.[315] I promised Sir William to
bring the pictures myself over to Montreal and to hang them
in the Hall."

April 15: Bourgeois informed Van Horne about the Squiere
sale where he (Bourgeois) bought a green bottle and a *sang de
boeuf* jar.[316] The bottle had been examined by Mr. Freer, "and
contrary to the attribution in the catalogue as Yung-sheng
period (1723-1735) he is sure that it is one of the finest pieces of
the Ming period." He went on about the temple bells being sold

---

313   Letter in VHFF (3/27).
314   Letter in VHFF (8/11).
315   Letter in VHFF (2/7).
316   Letter in VHFF (6/2).

for $425, which he had not bought because Van Horne's limit was $300.

About the Dickens exhibition where, according to Bourgeois, Van Horne's Goyas were not in the best society, he noted: "because there are no first class paintings except yours. Some paintings were cleaned too much, others had great names without being great masters and several were modern imitations." The letter also shows that dealers had to encourage their clients to look for other art than European art. Bourgeois went on to encourage Van Horne to go and see the Freer [and Peters] exhibition of Chinese art, modern American pictures and Persian potteries. About the Velasquez he wrote that Mr. Altman[317] had given it back to Gimpel, and that Duveen[318] had

---

317   Benjamin Altman (1840-1913) had started as an after-school clerk in his father's store, opened his dry-goods emporium in 1865, founded Altman Brothers, purchased in 1882 a pair of Oriental vases and soon became the first American Jew to become a world-class retailer. In 1906 Altman & Co. was a New York City-based department store and closed on December 31, 1989. Altman died in 1913 and left no heirs (Bose 2009). When his third store was originally built, "a niche occupied by Knoedler art dealers was left in the southwest corner (Fifth Avenue and 34th St.).

318   The Duveen Brothers were back in business! *The American Art News* of December 24, 1910, wrote under the heading SUIT AGAINST DUVEENS:

> The government has filed a civil suit in the U. S. District Court against the Duveen Brothers to forfeit their entire stock in trade because of undervaluations of imported merchandise. The goods involved in this proceeding are already under seizure [...]

American Art News of April 11, 1911, reported on the start of this matter:

> The surrender of themselves by Messrs. Joseph J. and Louis Duveen, under indictment of a charge of undervaluation of art imports and consequent defrauding of the U. S. government, the payment of a fine of $10 000 each, with consequent remission of prison sentences and the acceptance by the government of the Duveen firm's offer of $1 200 000 as complete satisfaction of the government's claim for undervaluations and penalty with release of the goods, seized in the Fifth Ave galleries here, does not entirely end the case. The criminal indictments against Mr. Henry J. Duveen, under $75 000 bail and now in Europe and in poor health and Mr. Benjamin Duveen under $50 000 bail and who has remained here, still stand, but if Messrs. Henry J. and Benjamin Duveen plead guilty when arraigned in

bought it but had been astonished to find it so much enlarged. Bourgeois went on to say he expected Gimpel to offer it to Van Horne. On a personal note, Bourgeois mentioned he would spend Christmas with Nardus and family and hoped to be back in New York on January 16, 1913. He finished by recommending a Monticelli for $3 000, a Cezanne for $6 000[319] and a Manet for $15 000.[320]

April 20: Van Horne's secretary replied to Van Slochem: "I intended handing you yesterday the enclosed account for $12.00 from W. Scott & Sons for their work in connection with the Hals pictures.[321] I assume that you will send a check to them direct. I had an engagement last evening, and was unable to see you before your train left, but I may be in New York to meet Sir William, and shall hope for the pleasure then."

April 20: Van Slochem advised Miss Van Horne by letter that he was sending her "today the photo of the Countess by Goya."[322] He asked her to ask Mr. Lynch whether the four pictures had arrived and enclosed a photo of Contessa by Goya. (He asked Lynch the same question on the same day.)

April 24: Van Gelder wrote to Hofstede de Groot that he had learned that de Groot had left for Italy and would like to know whether he had yet returned: "I would like to show you a grey-haired old man by Rembrandt that I bought from Kleinberger

---

October next, the indictment against them will probably be quashed, on payment also of $10 000 fine, by each man.

See also Secrest (2004, 246 ff.)

319 The Wickenden catalogue doesn't record a Cézanne. Cat. 1933 mentions two: 146a *Portrait of the Artist's Wife* and 146b *Roadway in Provence*.

320 Most likely this was VH 248, Monticelli, *The Fountain*. ▣: A series of hill-side terraces are surmounted by a table-shaped basin over the edge of which fall the waters of a central fountain [...] Signed in red at the lower left, 'Monticelli.' ▣: Final 3 000.

321 Letter in VHFF (7/11).

322 Letter in VHFF (7/11).

and that comes from Lesser." [323] Van Gelder advised de Groot that he would take the painting to Paris to have it photographed by Braun and asked whether they could soon meet in Paris.

May 7: James B. Townsend, of *American Art News*, wrote Van Horne that Van Slochem had suggested that he could pay a visit to Van Horne.[324] Van Horne must have replied and asked right away about the Velasquez. In a next, undated cable, Townsend asked him for the size and description. In his 1905 narrative about the Van Horne collection Conway describes this *Philip IV* as follows:

> Sir William's Spanish pictures are amongst his most valuable possessions; they include two that bear the great name of Velasquez, one of these is a splendid full-length of Philip IV, painted about 1644. It does not repeat any of the well-known full-lengths so far as I can remember. It comes closest to the Dulwich portrait in pose and lighting, but the costume is altogether different, and so is the position of the right arm.

May 13: Van Slochem wrote from Cogel Avenue that he had arrived safely in Europe, had met Van Gelder, and that both men were looking forward to seeing Van Horne in Europe soon.[325] Noting that Van Gelder had not yet received the last payment, he went on: "As yet I explained to him that I understood from you that you had send to him $60.00, $30 000 and fifteen thousand dollars. I trust you will look into this, as I must have misunderstood you about the last payment of $15 000 dollars.

---

323   Letter in RKD.
324   Letter in VHFF (43/9).
325   Letter in VHFF (7/11).

I shall be in Paris for six weeks and shall be there at Mori's, where I will show my pictures during the Paris season."

While the above flurry of letters flew back and forth, forboding clouds were gathering over Sardine Town. The *Beacon* of May 2, 1912 reported:

On Thursday the Italian camp declared for higher wages and shorter hours, and threatened to enforce their demand by force of arms. The immigration agent and Town Marshall were summoned to the scene, and to prevent possible bloodshed Magistrate Stoop went out and some twenty-five or thirty husky white men were sworn in as special constables. No. 10, a swarthy son of Italy, with unpronounceable name was said to be the ringleader. He was collared, and placed in charge of the Immigration agent, who deported him to the US by train the same night. But the other Italians would not go to work and Mr. Murray, the Italian contractor, was called down to use his influence.

The article, divided by the inflammatory sub-heading: Italians Open Fire, goes on to say, "The labor troubles at the sardine works nearly culminated in a murder on Friday last." It continues to describe the scene with sentences such as, "people loitering, not moving quickly enough", "a push with a blow", "the drawing of a revolver", and "an Italian taking to the woods and thought to be gone away." One page later the article focuses on the town site: "As Sir William Van Horne undertook the responsibility for the town site plan there can be no question as to its artistic appearance."

May 15: Van Slochem wrote to Van Horne from the Berlin Hotel, Bristol. The letter reads as though Van Slochem was trying to undermine Bode's suggestion that Van Horne buy the Magnasco for his collection.[326]

You will note that I am at present visiting Berlin. I went there with the Karel Fabritius from the Weber sale, a superb acquisition.

When Dr. Bode saw this, he remarked how wonderful this has improved in cleaning. He said he will write to you himself about it and he also handed me a letter for Van Gelder in which he felt most enthusiastic. No doubt V.G. will send you this letter. I also think this a wonderful work and a great addition for your Dutch room. Dr. Bode also showed me a Magnasco, the subject is an alchemist, but [I] would advice you to have him send you a photo of it as I am not so sure that you would like the picture (this is of course confidential) but I did not like to say to Dr. Bode that I do think, you would perhaps **not** like the picture.

I advised him to send you a photo of it first and he said he will write to you about it when he writes about the Karel Fabritius.

I also visited here Professor Von Loga of the Kupferstich Cabinet. He told me that he had not long ago returned from Spain, while there he heard that Nardus bought two very fine Goya's. He asked me, had I seen them? I said not from Nardus but I saw at Sr. William two very fine Goya's and that this very likely will be the two Goya's he referred to. He is most enthusiastic about them and remarked that he would be very happy to know, that they are in your collection. He will write to you asking you for the photos and you will be, I am sure delighted to hear from him.

I also saw Dr. Friedländer, who complimented your purchase of the two Frans Hals portraits. He was surprised,

---

326   Letter in VHFF (7/11).

he said, as he was most aware that you would go in for two such enormous pictures, remarking: "As I presume Sir William paid at least fifty to sixty thousand Pounds for them." Of course, I said, that was the price. Dr. Bode also spoke to me about your two fine Frans Halses and so did Professor Von Loga!

On my return to Brussels with Karel Fabritius I will see to the shipping so that there will be no mistake!

Van Horn might have enjoyed to know that other collectors talked about his excellent purchases and were in awe of the price he was able to pay. Van Slochem's letter must have made him smile. Van Slochem, keeping his eyes open for business as usual, ended this letter with a promise to look for lamps. He added that he hoped the trouble in Cuba [where a fight for racial equality was raging] would not interfere with Van Horne's interests. Van Slochem's invoice of April 20 read:[327]

Invoice

1 picture Storm scene: Guardi

1 Skating scene: Jan Van Goyen[328]

1 portrait half-length figures

1 picture Children playing with Cat: Jan Steen[329]

Value pictures $4 000

Four frames. $50

Shipped May 16th through Day & Meyer, New York.

327   Letter in VHFF (7/1).
328   VH 80 Goyen, Jan van (Leyden 1596–The Hague 1656). *Skating Scene.* ⊡: A wintry afternoon on a Dutch river when the ice is thick enough to bear not only the skaters and people who have come on foot, but also two parties in horse-drawn sleds. [...] Panel, oval. H. 8 in, W. 10¾ in (.20 ¼ cent. x 27 ¼ cent.) Signed at the lower left, J. V. Goyen. 1642. From the coll. of M. Van Gelder, Uccle, Belgium. ⊡: $2 500.
329   VH 77 Steen, Jan (Leyden 1626-1679). *Children Playing with a Cat.* ⊡: A girl and two boys are playing with a grey and white cat, wrapped in a cloth and held on the

Undated [A note written on Van Horne's letterhead reads]: "I received a cable from Van Gelder saying that he will accept from Sir William $150 000 for the two Hals and the four pictures – Van Goya, Guardi, Jan Steen and half length figures. Mr. Van Slochem will destroy Sir William's message of last night. He has received message of this morning which will have no effect in the trade." This note added that he (Van Horne) purchased 10 lamps ($1 052) and a glass (40.00) at the sale.

May 23: Eilers told Van Horne that they (E. J. van Wisselingh & Co., Kunsthandel) had bought a fine Millet, *Pay de Dome*, and had enclosed a photograph.[330] (On June 4, E. J. van Wisselingh apologized for the poor photograph and sent another one.)[331]

May 24: Townsend thanked Van Horne for the two "most agreeable days" in his house and expressed surprise at the extent and high quality of his pictures and the wide range and variety of his collections.[332] Three days later Townsend was in Europe and sent Van Horne a reproduction of a painting from the Dettari collection and an old Greek portrait on a wooden panel.[333] He added that a similar work was in the Metropolitan and said: "I believe any Newman will be valuable in a short

---

girl's lap, while she feeds it porridge from a silver spoon [...]. Panel H. 18⅜ in, W. 15⅝ in (47 cm × 40 cm). In the coll. of H. Phillips, Esq. London, 1833. Hudtwalcker sale Hamburg 1861. M. Neven sale, Cologne, March 17, 1879. No 191. In poss. of H. Van Slochem, New York, 1911. Ⓜ: 12 000.

330   Letter in VHFF (3/27).
331   Letter in VHFF (3/27). The only Millet in the Wickenden catalogue is VH 205, Millet, Jean-François (Greville, Manche 1814–Barbizon, S.-et-M., 1875). *A Smithy in Normandy*. Ⓦ: In a passage-way leading to the smithy seen through a square opening, three horses await their turn [...] Canvas. H. 10¼ in, W. 12½ in (26 cm × 32 cm). Signed with the initials 'J.F.M.' near the base, left of centre. From F. A. Chapman, New York, 1905. Ⓜ: 200.
332   Letter in VHFF (43/9).
333   Letter in VHFF (43/9).

time." So, Townsend, editor of *American Art News*, went art dealing as well!

Meanwhile, back in the Netherlands, Hofstede de Groot was drawing up an authentication of Rembrandt's *Head of an Old Man*.[334]

June 4 (3/27): E. J. Wisselingh apologized by letter about sending a poor reproduction of a Millet painting, and he promised to send a better example.

June 7 (7/15): Bourgeois wrote Van Horne from 226 rue de Rivoli, Paris, that he had spent some time in Spain and Germany. He said he had received his "kind letter" and thanked him for the cheque of £2 111.2.2 on account of the Goya business and the little frames and that he had ordered another very fine one for the little Leonardo-sketch. Bourgeois went on:

> I am very glad to hear, that your pictures look so fine, as you hanged them and you will have seen these of Decock, which will leave Paris for Montreal in 2 days. I gave the Amb. Benson to transfer on canvas, but this work will not be finished before October.
>
> I thank you too for your kind introduction to Mr. T. B. Withney whom I hope to see the next week. I shall write you all the details about his collection.

---

334 VH 55 Rembrandt Van Rijn (Leyden 1606–Amsterdam 1669). *Head of an Old Man*. ▣: Against a dark brown background, light falls from above on the bowed head of an Old Man, turned slightly to the right [...] Panel H. 10½in, W. 8½in (26½ × 21½cm). In poss. of S. Bourgeois, Paris, from whom it was purchased. ▣: 35 000. Bourgeois said Sir. Wm. paid him 30 000.

Hofstede de Groot's authentication: *May. Le soussigné declare qu'il a examine attentivement le tableau, don ci-contre la photographie Il le considere comme une oeuvre authentique et très charactértéristique de Rembrandt, peint dans la manière la plus développée et mûre du maître (vers 1660/1) May 1912. Corn. Hofstede de Groot.*

Le tableau sera catalogue dans le Catalogue raisonné et descriptifs des oeuvres de Rembrandt. CHdG.

I think to go on the end of this month to London, and like very much to see Mr. Dunn's[335] pictures, especially the fine Holbein portrait. Do you think, that he will show me his collection, when I go to see him? Also Mr. Farquar's Tiepolo, which you recommended him to buy, interests me very much, and if I have the time, I shall try to pay him a visit.

I found Nardus in splendid health and form. He is not at all angry about your letter. On the contrary, he thinks exactly as you and is satisfied with the business. I had in the meantime also the chance to sell the little Botticelli and the Van Gogh and Nardus found some very fine things. I hope to bring different masterpieces with me, when I come back to the States and think to be there about the end of Sept. to see in St. Andrews the end of the summer, which must be wonderful.

Please let me know, if you received all the catalogues of Paris, which I ordered for you. I was very astonished over the prices, good pictures bring here in salons and it becomes quite impossible to find something interesting for a reasonable sum.

Enclosed I send you a little article of the *NY Herald* about a Raeburn, which was sold by Blakeslee. If you were so happy to find a masterpiece of the great artist, please send me a photo. Also I like very much to have some photos of you Spanish pictures, which you were so kind to promise me. I would be very grateful to you, if you would send them over, because I am studying in this moment the Spanish school.

....

335   James Hamet Dunn (1874-1956) was a Canadian stockbroker.

June 8: Van Slochem wrote from Hotel Continental, Paris, that he supposed Van Horne had received the Fabritius he had forwarded some time ago, and "also the pictures from Mr. Decock have been sent to you long ago." [336]

He continued:

....

I read in your last letter about the death of Mr. Borden and was surprised; as when he last shook hands with me I thought he was very strong. I told V.G. of it, who said, he hopes the heirs will not bother him!

There has been quite some interest last week in the Taylor sale at Christies in London. No doubt you have read all about this. Everybody was surprised at the prices of the two portraits by Bronzino bought by Knoedler, one sold for about £6 000 and the Memling whom everybody thought would realize the highest price sold only for £3 600 and is held by Kleinberger in partnership with two other dealers so this will eventually be marked up to at least £10 000, if not more. As to Bronzino, I must say that I believe V.G. to be very lucky.

....

Van Gelder, Nardus and Van Slochem and perhaps even Van Horne must have felt relieved with poor Borden's death. Van Slochem went on about the Bronzino in an effort to whet Van Horne's appetite for it and continued:

---

336 Letter in VHFF (7/11). VH 57 Fabritius, Karel (1620 – killed in the explosion at Delft, 1654). *Head of a Young Man in a Fur Cap*. ▣: Turned three-quarters to the right, he looks out of the picture and wears a high red cap, bordered with fur, a black jacket and white neck-cloth [...] Canvas H. 19¾, W. 16½ in (50.5 cm × 42 cm). In the coll. of Jos de Kuyper, Rotterdam, 1895. Catalogue of Weber Coll. of Hamburg. Sold at Rudolph Lepke's Berlin 1912, No 251. ▣: $5 000.

I do not know if V.G. has mentioned anything to you about his Rembrandt. He has paid an enormous sum for that picture. It is a portrait of a man, but once seen this, it is never to be forgotten.[337] This is all I wish to say about it. For the present, he had not made up his mind yet, if he will sell it at all. I hope he will let me have that in New York. Dr. Bode has seen the picture and wrote not only a beautifull letter to V.G. about it but will publish the picture in his next edition.

By the end of this letter Van Horne's appetite for one more Rembrandt must have been sharpened as well! Nevertheless, on June 9 Van Horne cabled Bourgeois: MAKE LIMIT HELLENIC PORTRAIT ABOUT EIGHT THOUSAND FRANCS INSTEAD FOUR IF VAN GELDER THERE TELL HIM YOUR BID FOR ME.[338]

June 11: Bourgeois cabled back to Van Horne: "Hellenic portrait very fine will bring ten thousand francs shall bid till this sum with your permission. Kindly wire Van Gelder not to bid for you." [339] On June 19 Bourgeois cabled that he had bought the Hellenic portrait for six thousand six hundred francs for Van Horne, and again on the 22nd to confirm that he had received seventeen thousand francs from Van Horne. The Hel-

---

337 VH 56 Rembrandt, Van Rijn (Leiden 1606–Amsterdam 1669). *An Old Man with Slashed Black Cap.* ▥: The head and shoulders of an old man, moving into the picture from the right, and whose expression denotes a philosophic acceptance of life's varied experiences. He wears a black flat slashed cap [...]. Canvas H. 24 in, w. 20 in (61 cm × 51 cm). Exhibited at the Tuileries, Paris 1911, no. 123 or 133) In poss. of Lesser, London. In poss. of F. Kleinberger, Paris, Catalogue no 58. In poss. of M. Van Gelder, Uccle, Belgium. ▥: 150 000.

 The American Art News of March 7, 1914, reports that at the Philadelphia Griscome sale, $36 000 was paid by the Kleinberger Galleries for *Head of an Old man,* "given to Rembrandt in the catalogue on the authority of Dr. Bode." We might assume that is was another *Old Head*.

338 Letter in VHFF (2/7).

339 Letter in VHFF (2/7).

lenic portrait was subsequently shipped to Montreal by the S.
S. Montezuma, at a value of £1 650, which was much less than
Van Horne paid for it.

June 13: Van Gelder told Bode that he had asked Van Slochem
to "be kind enough to take the FABRITIUS along to show it to
you, as I have promised you [...]"[340] He continued:

> Sir William is very anxious to have your opinion and
> thinks it also to be by Karel Fabritius, he writes me very
> enthusiastically about it [...]. This Portrait makes on
> everybody a very profound impression, all are struck by
> its strong colouring and its powerful individuality. Many
> connoisseurs compare it to the Picture in Rotterdam.
> Schmidt-Degener (the Director of the Museum in Rotter-
> dam) has asked me for a photo.

June 14: Bode wrote to Van Horne that Van Slochem had
shown him *Portrait of a Man* sold in the Weber-Sale under the
name of B. Fabritius.[341] He continued:

> It became much finer by the restoration. It is now so vigor-
> ous, so fine in color and des à chiaroscuro that it looks
> more like a Karel Fabritius of his later time than like Ber-
> nard Fabritius. Mr. van Slochem also showed me a Portrait
> of young Alessandro de Medici, rich and fine in color and
> of very fine design. It is characteristic work of Bronzino of
> his best early time. Did you get my letter about the picture
> of an Alchemist by Magnasco, which I discovered at a
> dealership here?

---

340   Letter in VHFF (51/4).
341   Letter in VHFF (51/4).

At this point, Van Gelder engages Bode for his expertises.

On June 15: Bode subsequently wrote, in German, to "Esteemed Mr. Van Gelder" explaining that Van Slochem had showed him Van Gelder's Fabritius and that (Bode) would write to Van Horne about the picture. Bode said he would mention how much it had "changed to its advantage, it is so very effective, and at the same time so beautiful in colour and tone. I will also today write to Sir William van Horne about it."

Two days later Van Gelder, obviously elated, reported to Van Horne:[342]

I have a bit of very good news to confirm to you, which expect you know already from Dr. Bode. He has now accepted my views on the Fabritius and given it to Karel! So now you have this extraordinary Master represented in your Collection and how! You remember how curious I was to get for you about two years ago the K. Fabritius from Count Delaroff of St. Petersburg. Unfortunately I had to let it go and it went to Hofst. De Groot who has now two, one of which had just escaped you at Dowdeswells. In a pamphlet about the Rotterdam museum issued not long ago Mr. Schidt-Degener proves that their superb portrait is K. Fabr.'s self-portrait, he then sums up the works so far known to be doubtless as 8 and joins two more, one a woman portrait in Ghent and a composition in my collection, thus ten in all and yours is now the **eleventh**. Of the portraits, yours ranks next to the Rotterdam one, of the compositions is mine, I think the most interesting, while the little bird at The Hague is all by itself.

The landscape, which Bennie liked so much at my house, is not by Fabritius, but very probably by Her. Sêghers. So let me congratulate you one more on this

---

342   Both letters in VHFF (51/4).

superb and indeed very rare acquisition! I am very happy and when you will see it you will, I feel sure, understand why. It is a work just for you and in your style; it is a unique work in the Dutch school, like most of Fab.'s paintings.

This new finding is so much more interesting while it has been made at one of the most important public sales ever held in Europe in the present of most of the superb and dealers in Dutch art. I selected a fine old frame for it, I hope you will like it; you have paid for it with the $8 000. – Decock wants 1 500 for the cleaning and I really think he deserves it for his extremely careful and successful work. I will forward the picture this week to you. I encl. translation of my letter to Dr. Bode and his reply.

June 20: Van Slochem advised Van Horne that the lowest price for the two Halses and four pictures was one-hundred and fifty thousand dollars and that he would arrange that he (Van Horne) could give him the small Guardi for $1 500.[343] So the price would amount to $148 000.

June 29: Bourgeois wrote Van Horne that he was very happy to have secured the fine Hellenic portrait, and continued:[344]

It is the finest, I ever have seen on the market and I think it is very cheap. Dattari paid it in the time F 7 500 himself and was very astonished that it got a so low price in his sale. By mistake, you sent me by wire F 17 000, although the picture cost only F 6 600. Kindly inform me what to do with the remaining F 14 000.

---

343   Letter in VHFF (6/2).
344   Letter in VHFF (2/7).

As the picture is a little broken and on a very thin panel, I wouldn't risk to send to Canada without fixing it on a bigger. Decock will do that, but without repainting the slits, the picture never having been retouched.

With the same mail is going over the catalogue of the Dattari sale and photo of a beautiful Egyptian cat in bronze. You told me in the time, that you like to have one as fine as Van Gelder's one. This one is a little smaller, but finer of quality, and of an intensity of life, as if it is living. The patina is excellent the piece intact, and it measures 7.1 inches. The price is 2000 dollars, which I think is not exaggerated.

In the meantime I saw Mr. Whitney's collection of Rhodian and Damascus plates. I thank you very much that you gave me the opportunity to see all those fine things, the collection is unique in the world.

Mr. Whitney told me, that he gave you a catalogue and I will give the numbers of those, I think they are the best [...]

Nardus wrote you, as he told me, a letter and sent you a photograph of the Rembrandt he found. The picture is small of size, but large in effect. When you look on it, you feel as if a big picture is standing before you, so powerful is the brushwork. I think it is the model for the St. Matthew in the Louvre, and when you compare the photos of the two pictures, you will find, that our picture is much stronger than the other one. Rembrandt painted it with all his ardour and penetration of the human soul, and when you like to purchase it, you will have, Sir William, one of the most characteristic and emotional pictures of Rembrandt, the great master ever painted. I don't know if Nardus wrote you that Hofstede de Groot recognizes the picture and will publish it but it is also signed and it is one of those works of art, which are so great that also somebody who is not a connoisseur will feel instantly that it is one of the greatest of Rembrandt.

When I came back from the States, Nardus showed me the picture and you can feel with, how glad I was, that we are now in the right way. He gave me one of the greatest sensations I had in my life with this beautiful Rembrandt picture. He and I, we bought several very important things, but nothing so fine as the Rembrandt and therefore we thought, that it would be a precious complement of your collection.

Vaughan (1920: 353) writes that in the summer of 1912 Van Horne had "added several rooms to his Montreal house." Vaughan could just as well have written that Van Horne "had to" add several rooms in order to display his rapidly expanding collection. Vaughan also states that Van Horne had set aside a few days in June 1912 to participate in a homecoming festival in the US Perhaps this was also to get away from the construction.

According to Knowles (2004: 408) it was July and it was to coincide with the American July 4 festivities. Van Horne set off with his wife and daughter, Adaline, to Joliet, Illinois. Both Vaughan and Knowles relate the same story about the Van Hornes meeting old friends, including the elementary school teacher, and a visit to Van Horne's parents' home. Vaughan notes that Van Horne came across one of his own paintings at a friend's house. It was a picture of the Weber Valley that he had painted during his honeymoon: "It wasn't half bad when I painted that forty-five years ago," he said when he picked it up. He then asked whether he could take it to Montreal and retouch it "in the light of a more developed art."

July 8: Van Slochem wrote to Van Horne from Paris to say that he expected that Van Horne had received the Karel Fabritius. Then, abruptly switching subjects, he mentioned that he understood that he (Van Horne) had notified Van Gelder about Borden's death. He went on to say that Van Gelder had commented that he hoped not to be bothered by the Borden heirs.[345]

Van Gelder's cynical remark about Borden's death might indicate that his conscience was being haunted by the late collector.

July 10: Van Gelder wrote Van Horne that he had received his letter of the 21st of June and had heard from Van Slochem, "to whom you wrote," about Borden's death: [346]

> The news was quite unknown to me, I was as you thought quite sorry to hear it![347] I hope that you are right in that there will be no more danger from the heirs. I wonder what will become of questioned pictures? All the same I began to feel as if my DeKeyzer was not painted for Mr. Borden! About your acquisition of the superb Hellenic portrait, I knew quick enough as you will see by the encl. letter, I had given order to buy it, with the idea to get it for you; I suppose I was your competition instead! Fortunately I was on a fishing trip, if I had been at the sale I would of course have bid much higher. It is a marvellous portrait and you got it exceedingly cheap. I congratulate you with it. I saw it repeatedly before the sale and Hirsch, the auctioneer, told me that the former owner had paid 10 or 12 000 francs for it, however he thought that there wouldn't be many amateurs for that sort of art; he didn't count on a certain gentleman in far-off Canada!

---

345   Letter in VHFF (7/11).
346   Letter in VHFF (7/22).
347   Cf. Van Slochem's letter of June 8 to Van Horne: "I read in your last letter about the death of Mr. Borden and was surprised; as when he last shook hands with me I thought he was very strong. I told V.G. of it, who said, he hopes the heirs will not bother him!"

Has the Fabritius arrived? And have you seen it; I am quite anxious to hear from you about it. We received delicious maple syrup [...] A few days ago I had a very agreeable surprise in seeing in the European Daily Mail the Laurentius shares quoted at 197! I felt very much elated at this extraordinary size. What is the reason of this, after last years doubling of the shares? Somebody spoke to me about Wayagamack Pulp co.[348] Are you interested in that?

Meanwhile, Van Horne and his investors must have been pleased with the following article about the sardine plant in the July 11 edition of the *St. Croix Courier*:

New Canning Town.
Girls will be imported from Norway and Elsewhere.
Good progress is being made with the canning plant at Chamcook, also the boarding houses. [...] The help problem is to be solved by the importation of girls from Norway and elsewhere. It is expected that 120 girls will leave Norway about the first of August. These girls are of superior type and are accustomed to the handling of fish. In addition to local help, it is likely that men and women will be brought here from Nova Scotia fishing villages.

July 22: Eilers wrote to Van Horne at St. Andrews, Canada:[349]

Your letter of 26th June came duly to hand for which please accept my best thanks. If I don't sell our Daumier before leaving for Canada this year, I will take it over

---

348 This company started in 1912 in Cap-de-la-Madeleine and partners since 2001 with Kruger.
349 Letter in VHFF (3/27).

buying or not buying it, you will not find it empty, but a fine example of this artist, a reproduction gives always a wrong impression of a picture. I therefore do not like to send photographs [...] This morning I received from your secretary Richard D. Harlan a draft for £615.7.9 sterling in payment of balance for which please accept our best thanks.

August 3: Bourgeois wrote to Van Horne at Covenhoven saying that he had received the "kind letter and the $5 000 draft" and also that the Hellenic portrait was still in the hands of De-cock.[350] He went on to say that he had bought paintings of the Tang period in Paris, and he would send a photograph of it.

Bourgeois further noted that he had heard about Dabo's success in America and heard from Van Slochem that Van Horne had invited Dabo to Covenhoven. The next part of his letter sounds as though Bourgeois needed to keep an eye on Dabo because he suggested that "we meet together there, when I come back" [from Antwerp].

August 27: Bode wrote to Van Horne from Charlottenburg to thank him for the present, a Magnasco he had given to the gallery, and continued: [351]

I returned the other day from the country. The first object I discovered in my room in the Kaiser Friedrich Museum was the Magnasco, the very fine present you made to our Gallery. It is just a pendant for a curious picture with small figures by Cerguogni in our Gallery and fits pretty well.

350   Letter in VHFF (2/7).
351   Letter in VHFF (8/11).

Many thanks also for the photo of your pictures. You only began the old Masters since I have seen the Gallery, 19 years ago. How many fine Hals, Goyas, Steen, Helst, Ruysdael, Dekoninck, Rembrandt (!) etc. About the 4 pictures, Reading girl, Portrait of an Old Lady etc. I am not better informed as you are. That the Reading Girl might be by Vermeer, I cannot believe though it has his fine sunshine and is rather very fine.[352] It is nearer to Frans Hals and his school perhaps Versprong? The small print given to A. Cuyp is I believe by A. Coosemans all those print pieces signed A. C. and although to Cuyp, the big landscape with a small lake in the foreground give to Ruysdael I believe to be a very characteristic as fine Z. Hackzant [sic] with figures by his friend A. van de Velden. About a few pictures I have some doubts, but I do not know whether you like to hear them.

On September 3, Van Gelder advised Hofstede de Groot that he had received the photos of Rubens and Vermeer from Haarlem. He also mentioned that he hoped he had arranged with Buschmann for the publication, and continued:[353]

in photographure of my Rembrandt, perhaps it would be better to have Buschmann himself take care of the

---

352   Bode's assessment of Reading Girl did not cause Van Horne to return it to Nardus as Carter (1932) listed it as "VH70 VERMEER, Jan 1632-1675 'Young Girl Reading' 24 × 20. 2000." The Wickenden catalogue states that Van Horne obtained it from Nardus and Van Gelder in 1900.
    On the Index card Hofstede de Groot, no. 1490133 (RKD), it is entitled "Jeune fille lisant," and listed as Utrecht School, seventeenth century. It is also noted that this is the painting sold to Van Horne by Nardus and Van Gelder as a Vermeer. The painting's present whereabouts are not known. Thanks to Esmee Quodbach (e-mail of October 27, 2014).

353   Letter in RKD.

photographs. Therefore I will wait with Braun until I hear from you that you will leave it to Buschmann.

Anyway, I hope that you will be so kind, taking in account as well, the extra expenses which I will put up with, to give a report as beautiful as possible of my magnificent painting, just as you did for my Halses. I will send you today the Cuyp and the Rembrandt and wait your reply.

September 4: Van Slochem wrote to Van Horne that he had found Van Horne's letter with his first impression of Fabritius:[354]

I regret to note you were not very favourably impressed with it. V.G. thought you would be most pleased with it. I did not mention anything to him; perhaps your second impression is a better one. V.G. told me he received another remittance from you of $30 000, that he has replied to you! and has mentioned in his letter about the fine pictures he is going to let me have next season. Probably leaving for New York, second week of October, looking forward to meet you in the best of health.

In Bourgeois' letter of September 11, he said he had received Van Horne's draft of 35 000 francs, and he promised to bring the Fayum picture and the Benson. He also noted that he would love to see Van Horne at St. Andrews and thought it was an excellent idea to invite Dabo. He continued:[355]

---

354   Letter in VHFF (7/11).
355   Letter in VHFF (2/7).

I regret very much that you had some disappointment for me sending the catalogue. When I come over, will you please explain to me the way you like that I declare everything, but I didn't know exactly about the custom duties in Canada. Decock has not at all repaired it, but has strengthened the panel which was too thin for forwarding it without damage as I told you I shall bring it over with me.

Some days ago I sent you a photo of the portrait of Cezanne's wife by the artist himself. You told me last year that you are anxious to get a portrait of this artist [...] I think that he and Manet are the greatest painters of the last century and I am trying to get also an important portrait of the latter to complete your collection of impressionists, because you really need to have two portraits of those most importants.

September 14: Nardus cabled Van Horne from Biarritz: "Kindly secure 40 000 dollars preferred stock. Thanks." [356] It seems that Van Horne was willing to overlook Nardus' obvious failings. Perhaps this was only because Nardus still invested in Van Horne's businesses, or Van Horne perhaps still hoped the scoundrel would find a real gem for him in one way or another?

On September 17 Van Gelder, who had just returned from some journey, wrote Hofstede de Groot that he had received his f1 350 invoice and charged his banker to pay it.[357]. About "the little Rembrandt" Van Gelder noted: "I completely agree to give it to you so you can compare it with Johnson's painting. I advise you to send it ahead with a friend or an acquaintance,

---

356   Cable in VHFF (5/4).
357   Letter in RKD.

because even with such a small thing customs can be trouble-some upon arrival in New York."

September 26: Bourgeois told Van Horne that he had arrived in New York and would come to Covenhoven on Wednesday or Thursday. He added that he would bring Dabo "whom you invited too, as Mr. [Bennie] van Horne told me." [358]

THE SARDINE BUSINESS

As if all this art-related correspondence between Van Horne and his dealers was not enough, these gentlemen also had to keep in touch about the business venture they were all involved in – the sardine factory. A sample of their letters about this enterprise follows:

On October 2, Van Horne cabled (in VHFF 7/22) investor Van Gelder in Belgium: "secured even forty thousand send only balance above amount due you from me. Charge Sardine Co. our half rates."

On the same day, Van Horne cabled Nardus in Suresnes: "secured thirty-four thousand in all. Charge to Sardine Co., sent half rates." [359] Underneath is a handwritten note: "Cable (copy). Nardus, Biarritz. Secured twenty five thousand with forty per cent common bonus, trying [to] get more."

On paper, it looked as though the sardine plant was doing well, and newspaper reports helped to reinforce this idea. On October 3 the *Beacon* reported that the directors of the Canadian Sardine Company had decided to increase their capital from $100 000 to $160 000 to double the capacity. Part of the article reads: "The company of which Sir William Van Horne and Mr. George F. Johnson, Montreal, are the ruling spirits, had

---

358   Letter in VHFF (2/5).
359   Cable in VHFF (5/4).

enough orders booked at the present time to take the output for the next year and are enlarging ..."

But then the *St. John Globe*, (no date) reported that the Sardine Company executives were not honouring their contract with the employees. The newspaper alleged that the company had hired "men and their wives and brother and sisters", but was now seeking "to get rid of the men, or some of them, retaining the women workers." And there was more: Under the subheading Showed a Revolver, the article continued: "There was trouble at the Hatt boating house, Chamcook, last Wednesday, which might have ended in a shooting scrape." The story went on about an assault, a blow in the face, a brother smashing his sister's trunk with an axe, kerosene, and fire.

On November 2: Nardus sent Van Horne a cheque for $34000 for the Sardines Company. In the accompanying letter, he offered sincere thanks "for your goodness and best wishes for your good health and family." [360]

But, trouble kept brewing at the sardine plant. The *Beacon* of November 7, 1912, reported about a certain Mrs. Neilson having thrown a knife at Miss Robertson, but that proved not to be true. She, accused of inciting trouble among the Norwegian girls, had thrown her knife on the floor. The magistrate had "decided in favor of the complainant and a fine of $10 or 30 days' jail was imposed."

Vaughan (1920: 341) noted there had been problems at the plant from the beginning. He commented: when the Scandinavian women arrived, essential parts of the machinery were still lacking and the work could not be begun – the capital outlay was too large – the management was inefficient – when

---

360   Letter in VHFF (5/40). In the margin of this letter Van Horne scribbled: "Your cable Bourgeois. Thirty four thousand is amount cash for that amount preferred and thirteen thousand six hundred common stock, Van Horne."

the plant was in running order, the fish chose to frequent other waters for a season. Van Horne himself had invested $200 000 in the sardine plant and when the Great War broke out, this "upset all business." [361]

Van Horne's cable of November 30 to Nardus reads: "Have stock where send (?)" [362] On the same day Nardus replied: "Deposit stock with Morgan, New York."

From the confirmation by cable of December 3 by Van Horne's secretary to Mr. Leo Nardus, the "Canadian Sardine Co." stock for yourself and Mr. Bouget (six) had been sent by Registered mail to "J. P. Morgan & Co." New York, in accordance with the enclosed letter of November 30th.

Bourgeois was now also one of Van Horne's investors. And, the *Beacon* of November 21, 1912, finally had something good to report about the sardine business. Under the heading, "Chamcool Plant: Steam is Up and Factory will soon be Ready," it reported that the building of the new Chamcook sardine town went on well and:

> The working girls are now comfortably housed, and with little to do except dress themselves, eat, sleep, and draw their pay, they are having a good time. The Company maintains a rigid watch on the entrance of the grounds to prevent strangers from entering. It has been found necessary to erect a lock up to care for any troublesome members of the colony or unwelcome visitors.

One gets the impression that Van Horne is now a Father-Superior of a Norwegian convent besieged by Italian monk(ey)s.

---

361 Knowles (2004: 394) about the sardine plant: "after conferring that summer [of 1913] with the company's bankers, management shut down operations, which, due to a scarcity of fish, did not resume."
362 Cable in VHFF (5/4).

The rest of this article is not as glowing; it goes on to mention alcohol being peddled in the town and the roads in the vicinity being "full of deep ruts and gulleys."

BACK TO FINE ARTS

Sir William Van Horne never had a dull moment. He was probably glad to forget about the social unrest and the alleged lack of road maintenance in the company town by focusing on his art correspondence. Letters continued to fly between him and his dealers, and also between his dealers and art experts.

On October 5, Van Gelder expressed his regret to Hofstede de Groot for having missed him in Paris, but said he had received both expertises, thanked him for them, and continued:[363]

Would you mind repeating them (the expertises) on the photographs of both paintings, which I sent you simultaneously? I don't know whether you plan to include both masters in your Catalogue Raissonné, but in this event I would appreciate it if you would add this to your expertises, and I will then gladly send you another photo of both paintings for your studies. Perhaps you will be so kind as to add a few words of appreciation to the expertise of the Janssens owing to the rarity of an outdoor scene by the Master.

I also received your letter with regard to Braun's reproduction of my Rembrandt. As I mentioned in passing, I have been to Braun's, who will show me the proofs. I would dearly have liked to have learned the result of your quest about the date of the grey-haired old man. As you have

---

363   Letter in VHFF (7/22).

seen in Bode's letter, he places it in the époque of l'Enfant Prodigue.

After comparing it with the range of late portraits, I am personally of the opinion that my work belongs to the last period of the Master and this is really counter to the natural tendency of every owner of a piece of art to give it a high a place as possible.

I regret that I could not show you this splendid portrait after cleaning. This painting gives me the impression that it is the final solution of the problem, the realization whereof the grand Master had tried to achieve his entire life.

The broad approach, plastering of paint with the palette, relaxed here and there by shadows in the black lacquer, all of this done so simply and so surely and self-consciously, with the grand feeling put in the stammering mouth and in those eyes, which speak of deeply felt suffering and life experience; in short by looking at my grey-haired old man the same emotion is evoked as when I saw this splendid work, cited by Bode, in St. Petersburg. It has also made a great impression on Bode, his enthusiastic description is proof of it, and I am convinced that it would have made a deep impression on you if you had seen is after the cleaning.

On October 8 Van Gelder again wrote Hofstede de Groot that he had received his expertise and his invoice and that he would order his banker to send him 600 frs.[364] Van Gelder expressed his disappointment that Hofstede de Groot had not written a bit more appreciatively about the Janssens as "it was an unusual work by the master." Van Gelder had also expected

---

364   Letter in RKD.

to find some words about the date of the painting because the study head was part of his collection and he had decided not to sell anything from it. He added that he had been invited by Van Horne to spend time on his island and that he would be back by the end of November.

On October 15, Bourgeois, who was then in New York, invoiced Van Horne for "one portrait by Paul Cezanne, representing Mme. Cezanne for the amount of $7 000." [365] (A later cable reads: "Received payment March 19, 1913, Stephan Bourgeois.")

October 23: Van Slochem, who was also back in New York, at 477 Fifth Avenue, drafted and sent another letter to Van Horne in St. Andrews saying he was "making sure that we keep in touch [by] letter." [366] He continued:

Van Gelder wrote me telling me how glad he was to see you, and that he met your dear family in St. Andrews in the best of health. It seems so long that I have not heard from you, I am looking after some alterations on the premises, and could not manage it, but I would have loved to have had the opportunity also to see your island, however this pleasure is yet in store for me. My wife who is with me wishes to be remembered to you and the Ladies and I shall be most happy to hear something from you.

On November 12 Bourgeois let Van Horne know how glad he had been to see him in New York on the 16th and wrote a more or less urging letter:[367]

---

365   Cable in VHFF (4/12). This Cezanne is no. 146a in Cat. 1933.
366   Letter in VHFF (7/11).
367   Letter in VHFF (2/7).

I opened yesterday my exhibition, and arranged it very nicely to show the important Tiepolos, of which I told you. As to Nardus' cable, I shall explain you the whole matter in detail, when you come to New York. He found two life-size portraits of Van Dijck, representing a nobleman and his wife with her children. As we are in this moment very short of money and they are pictures of very high price, but as business relatively not too expensive for doing making a very good profit, he thought, you would perhaps like to be interested in it. But as the pictures were offered only for a few days, business had to be concluded in a hurry, we had not the opportunity to talk it over and to come perhaps to an understanding. Hoping, that you had an agreeable trip to Winnipeg.

On November 29 Van Slochem cabled Van Horne: "shall I leave here tonight with Rembrandt." [368]

Perhaps Van Horne felt he was drowning in paintings. He cabled Bourgeois at 389 Fifth Avenue on November 30: "Don't ship Spanish picture yet writing to-day." [369]

December 12: Bourgeois wrote to Van Horne about the course of affairs in Paris:[370]

Enclosed you find the results of the Rouart sale in Paris. The prices are tremendous. The Corots and Puvis de Chavannes went far over the estimations of the experts. Degas got a record price, which is not at all in relation with his artistically value. Manet is booming in a regular and sure way. I was astonished that Delacroix did not fetch higher

---

368   Letter in VHFF (7/11).
369   Cable in VHFF (2/7).
370   Letter in VHFF (6/2).

prices. He was the biggest of that earlier school, but the public does not understand his imaginative force.

I saw in Fisher's exhibition the small Tiepolo, of which you spoke to me on the steamer. The picture is of the latest period of the master. I do not think you would improve your collection by making an exchange with the "studio" picture. Yours is a little too early and the other too late. In Fischer's picture is no any more quality of colour, but only a great virtuosity in using the brush. Also there is often discussion in specialist circles about those late pictures, because, as the master lost in the end of his life much of his character and sensuality, his pupils had it easier, to imitate his manner. My former partner had such an experience with a similar picture, which was at first published by Ventury as an original, and later by Molmenti as a school picture.

On December 13 Van Gelder wrote Hofstede de Groot that he had returned from his trip to Canada and wondered how he (HdG) liked his little painting after comparing it with the pendant at Johnson's, "and please, send it back." [371]

On December 23 Townsend wrote Van Horne that he had hoped to go to Montreal for the opening of the museum on December 9th, but that he had to go to Kalamazoo to appraise a collection of pictures. [372]

In Miss Chesley's article in "last Saturday's *Art News*," Townsend went on, he had discovered that "there are three new Rembrandts, a landscape, young rabbi and head of an old man." Townsend noted that he had seen the last two at

371 Letter in RKD.
372 Letter in VHFF (43/9). The Montreal Museum of Fine Arts was opened in December 1912 and welcomed some 50 000 visitors in 1913.

Knoedler's and Kleinberger's in Paris and had asked Van Slochem for photographs of the last two for reproduction, but the latter had been unwilling to oblige. Townsend continued:

> And I could get little or no information from him. As you know, I would not wish to annoy you, I then told him that I would write you at once so that you would hear tomorrow and ask you whether you would not kindly wire him to let us have the photograph of the old man [with black cap], at least. As the pictures are on public exhibition and it is known in Montreal they belong to you and as you see I my-self discovered it, the news of this important acquisition, will almost surely leak out to the daily papers and it would injure us to have it published before we make notice. There are books here in which we could get these pictures, but as I have said above, I would rather have your author-ity. I should be personally very much indebted if you could grant this favor and we will not say anything about the pictures having come through Van Slochem, unless you are willing. A wire of authorization to him, and if not ask-ing too much, to us, would be greatly appreciated.

Back at the sardine plant, things were looking better. The *Beacon* of December 26, 1912, ended one of its articles with a far more upbeat note: It noted that in the new sardine town of Chamcook the first baby was born: "to brighten up the humble cabin of Mr. and Mrs. Longa. The father of the child to whom this honor belongs is the Italian foreman at the new works. The baby boy has been christened Casarco, this combination being made up of the first letters of the Canadian Sardine Company."

The stellar collecting year of 1912 finally ended, but, as the 1913 correspondence shows, the art business was still thriving.

January 2, 1913: In response to Van Horne's request of December 31st, Van Slochem sent the invoice of the Rembrandt and acknowledged Van Horne's receipt of "NY exchange for $10 000 and a New York cheque for $15 000 making $25 000 on account of the 100 000." [373] Van Slochem, as usual trading in lamps as well, also thanked Van Horne for the $130 for the lamps and the church candlesticks.

Van Gelder had managed to stay out of trouble since his questionable deals with Johnson, Widener, and Borden, and he had not been burned himself since the railway scam. But, by the end of January, Van Gelder was in trouble again.

Old Man with Black Cap questioned

Old Man with Black Cap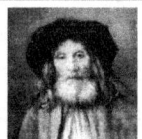

January 24, 1913: Van Horne wrote to Van Gelder in Uccle: [374]

I have something startling to tell you.

The Rembrandt, "Old man with Black Cap" which was in the recent Montreal exhibition with my other pictures attracted much attention and favorable comment; but one visiting connoisseur made a remark about it, which was to say the least, disquieting, and I arranged as soon as I got my pictures home and hung to have Dr. de Wild come

373   Letter in VHFF (7/12).
374   Letter in VHFF (51/10).

up from New York and examine all of my pictures with a view to deciding as to which of them required attention. After he had spent something more than a day with them, I asked him how he liked the "Old Man with black cap." He answered evasively and I insisted on knowing what he meant, and he finally said that the picture was an extraordinary fake, made within comparatively a few years and made in France.[375]

I was more than astonished at this and insisted that he must be mistaken and I told him what Dr. Bode and Dr. de Groot and Dr. Friedländer had said about the picture. He replied that he was absolutely certain and that he felt sure that Dr. Bode had never seen the picture itself and had been misled by the photograph, and that such was probably the case with Dr. De Groot; and he said that with the picture in his hands, Dr. Hauser would confirm his opinion in five minutes.[376] He said further that he did not pretend to be an expert in art in the sense that Dr. Bode and Dr. de Groot were experts, but that he did claim to be an expert in painting and in the materials of painting and that he had no hesitation in saying that the work and materials were not those of Rembrandt or of the time of Rembrandt, but of a quite recent time, probably within ten or twelve years, and he thought that even the canvas was not old, but that this fact had been largely hidden by the relining.

He said that not being a professional expert in art, he did not wish to mix in such a matter, or to have his name

---

375   As already mentioned, on May 12, 2009, Mrs. Oomen, assistant of the Rembrandt Research Project, communicated that Prof. Bruyn later attributed *A prophet*, or *Old man with slashed black cap* to Titus van Rijn.

376   Dr. Friedrich Hauser (1859-1917) was a German archeologist and art historian. Cf.: http://www.dictionaryofarthistorians.org/hauserf.htm (last accessed July 2014).

used, but that the question could be quickly settled by sending the picture to Dr. Hauser and at the same time submitting it to Dr. Bode.

He suggested that all this should be quietly done, so as to cause as little trouble as possible in making reclamation, and this suggestion I took to mean that if I had occasion to make reclamation against one party, that party would probably have to do the same against another and so on.

What is to be done? Shall the picture be sent to you to be submitted to Dr. Bode and Dr. Hauser, or shall it be sent directly to them? I am obliged to go to Cuba by tomorrow's steamer and shall be gone about four weeks, but if the picture should require to be shipped before my return, I suppose it will be best for Mr. van Slochem to go up and attend to it. I have explained the situation to him quite fully. I am under pledge to Dr. Wild not to use his name, and I beg you not to let it go beyond yourself.

I am greatly distressed over this matter because I loved the picture very much and it seems almost beyond belief that such a beautiful thing can be wrong. I am writing you without delay so that you may, if need be, take the earliest possible steps towards protecting yourself as against the party from whom you got the picture.

Of course, it is hardly necessary for me to say to you that I have not the remotest shadow of doubt of your good faith in this matter or of your absolute belief in the picture, and I am very sorry to write you a letter, which must bring you so much unhappiness.

....

"How can such a beautiful thing be wrong?" Van Horne wondered. A good question that will not be answered here, or anywhere else as long as beauty is valued in terms of money, name recognition and prestige.

January 27: Bourgeois wrote to Van Horne's new secretary, Mr. Richard D. Harlan, that Van Horne had given him permission to exhibit three of his (Van Horne's) impressionist paintings during his February exhibition in New York.[377] The three paintings were Cezanne's portrait of his wife, Toulouse Lautrec's red-haired women, and women drinking absinth. Bourgeois went on with instructions for shipping and handling, asked for the measurements because of the catalogue, and noted that he had given the organizer of the exhibition the values of the paintings: Cezanne 8 000, Toulouse Lautrec 5 000 and 3 000.[378]

After more letters about the upcoming exhibition, with regard to shipping and insurance, Bourgeois informed Van Horne on January 31 about the insurance rate "in case you would send your pictures to a restorer in New York. I think the rates are very reasonable." [379] He went on:

I received my Goya, and several other pictures, which you will see at your return. The Marquez de la Vega Inclan[380] paid me two visits with Mr. Archer Huntington. I showed

---

377 Letter in VHFF (2/7).

378 In Cat. 1933 these Cezanne's are listed no. 147 *In the Garden* and no. 148 *At the Café*. The Jan. 30 letter by Secretary Harlan gives the measurements of *Madam Cezanne* (15 × 18 in), *Red-haired Lady* (21½ in × 25½ in) and *Absinth Woman* 21¾ × 18½. A letter by Hamlin & Co., a New York insurance company informs (letter in VHFF 2/5) about insurance and location: the paintings could be insured for "30% per $100 for the trip from Montreal to New York and return to Montreal, and 30% per $100. Additional to cover the period of three months that the painting may be at the premises of Messrs. Knoedler & Company, #556 Fifth Ave."

379 Letter in VHFF (2/7).

380 In 1910 the government of Spain charged Marques de la Vega Inclan (1858-1942) with setting up a network of hotels. See: http://www.paradores-spain.com/comments/ (last accessed February 2014). Archer Milton Huntington (1870-1955) was a stepson of railroad magnate and industrialist Collis P. Huntington, was a lifelong friend of the arts and is best known for his scholarly works in the field of Hispanic Studies and for founding The Hispanic Society of America in New York City. See: http://en.wikipedia.org/wiki/Archer_M._Huntington (last accessed February 2014).

him the photos of your two Goyas, which he admired very much. [...]

I think it would be very interesting to send him the photos of your Spanish pictures, because he seems to have a good knowledge of this art.

I was very glad to sell to the imperial museum in Vienna the little Jean de Flanders, the primitive, which you had for some time in Montreal. But here in New York business is very, very quiet. I am going next week for a few days to Canada, to see, if there is some chances for my beautiful Tiepolo's.

February 6: Van Gelder, writing from Hotel Capar Badrutt in St. Moritz, replied to Van Horne's "welcome letter Jan. 18." He said he was extremely sorry to read of all the sickness in Van Horne's household soon after he and his family had left.[381] He continued:

I was much interested in your description of the Montreal exhibition, what a pity that these beautiful pictures were so badly hung. Your participation was most important: 4 Rembrandts, 4 Hals, 4 Goya's etc. I thank you for your promise to find me a catalogue; I hope you will get me one! I was much pleased to read of the change you have made in the hanging of your pictures, your reception must be superb and well worth coming from far to see; I suppose the Old Man got the honour place? Your second hall must be also extremely interesting with the impressionists. Before resorting to extreme measures, I have proposed to V. Slochem to send the figurines to Berenson, if the latter persists in giving it to a pupil, I will put his judgment as

381   Letter in VHFF (6/6).

against Bode and Friedländer. As to Mr. Savidge, I recently received the encl. copies of the references, which give more ample information about him; however as soon back to Belgium, I will ask him to come and see me and see what stuff he is made off. I will then ask him the questions you mention and will write you fully what impression he made on me. I laughed heartily about your reference to help in connection with probably Sunday work! I am staying with the family in St. Moritz and feeling all well and happy. I send a photo, which shows you our pastimes [...]

P.S. I have received a month ago $25 000 on the Rembrandt.

February 7: Van Slochem cabled Van Horne that he had received a cable "that Dr. Bode and Hauser had both seen picture – you will hear from both." [382] It sounds as if dealers no longer contented themselves and their clients with the opinion of just one expert. And on February 28 Bourgeois, wrote to Van Horne, from 387 Fifth Avenue, saying he was sorry to have not seen him that afternoon, but that he understood that Van Horne was busy and had not sufficient time to see all "what you like to see." [383] He continued:

The reason I write you is to know if you will be in Montreal next Tuesday. I would like to talk with you about the catalogue, several propositions I received from Paris and about the documents you know will be necessary to make a scientific and perfect edition [...]

I did not get the fine Chou bronze; it fetched $1 200. This and all the other prices are much higher than I

382   Letter in VHFF (7/12).
383   Letter in VHFF (2/7).

supposed. Enclosed photo of my fine B. de Bruyn, which I would like to show you, especially as I give you always the first look at my best purchases.[384] They are a unique pair and in excellent condition. Friedländer sent me a splendid letter about the authenticity and they came from the collection of councilor Schnitzer in Cologne

Van Horne, busy as he was, was still as involved as ever with dealers and connoisseurs. On the third of February 1913, he had turned seventy. Doubtless, his friends marvelled at his energy and his ability to keep up with his varied ventures in business and art. Vaughan (1920: 352) observed that:

no one was ever better equipped with resources for his leisure hours. In Montreal or Covenhoven, when he was freed from his correspondence and the entertainment of his guests, he had his romps with his grandson, his farms and stock, the sardine plant at Chamcook, and his painting. His thirst for collection was keen as ever.

Thirst for collection? Was he still thirsty, or was he being water-boarded with art but enjoying the challenge?

March 3: Van Horne, confident and with the audacity of hope, wrote a long letter to Van Gelder.[385] From his words, it becomes clear that Van Horne is convinced that the Rembrandt Van Gelder had sold him was authentic.

384   For De Bruyn, see http://de.wikipedia.org/wiki/
Bartholomäus_Bruyn_der_Jüngere.
385   Letter in VHFF (7/2)

By now you will have had my cable to the effect that I am quite satisfied and that I suspect a conspiracy in the matter of the Rembrandt. I am now pretty well satisfied that the whole thing was worked by Carstairs, who used Wild as his dirty tool.[386] I can't mention Carstairs by name yet outside for I have no evidence as yet – only a strong suspicion; but I think I shall soon know. The enclosed copies of letters to Carstairs and Knoedler explain themselves and express my feelings so clearly that I need not add to them. I am not going to let the guilty parties get off easily. I suspect Carstairs of the original doubt; but that by itself made no impression on my mind. I did not get Wild's opinion until I had left home for New York and Cuba and had no chance to look at the picture again or to refer to the papers and I thought that perhaps Dr. Bode and Prof. Hauser had only seen photo's, improbable as that might be. I can now see why Wild did not give me his opinion until I had left home and can see just how the whole thing was worked from the time I asked to have Wild sent up to examine and report upon the condition of the Dekoninck and several other pictures. Really picture dealing has become a wonderful art – not a fine art but an extraordinarily dirty one.

If Roland Knoedler is the kind of man I have always thought him I feel sure that he will send Wild home and, if my suspicions of Carstairs are well grounded, that he will put him out of the firm. We shall soon see. Meantime don't mention any names. I shall let you know what occurs.

I don't know just what course this thing may take and although I have no shadow of a doubt I should like, to make my case quite complete, a letter from Decock to the effect that he cleaned the picture and that the statement that the

---

386 Charles Carstairs was head of the London branch of the New York gallery M. Knoedler & Co. (Saltzman 2008: 169).

paint was modern had not the least excuse. I have anticipated this in one of the enclosed letters because of what
you told me of Decock's remark.

I am very sorry to have caused you so much unhappiness
in this matter but there are so many differences about
paintings between experts and so many mistakes have
been made, that I feel bound when a question is raised, to
go to the very bottom of it with regard even to the seal of
the Almighty.

March 24: Van Slochem wrote to Van Horne to tell him
that he had a visit from Dr. Hillwell, who had said that he was
pleased to hear:[387]

That those who tried to do some mean thing, have not succeeded! I have been very careful not to say anything, he did
not mention any name, nor did I. I have been expecting to
hear from you what Knoedler replied to your letter. I suppose you were busy and forgot to write me about it. I have
just received a letter from Van Gelder in which he writes
that he has received your cable and had also written to you.

April 28: Bourgeois thanked Van Horne for his kind letters from Cuba and announced that he would go to Montreal
on Tuesday to see Dr. Shepherd, "who likes to see the same
pictures in which Sir Edmund Walker is interested." [388] In a

---

387　Letter in VHFF (7/1).
388　Letter in VHFf (2/5). Dr. Frank Shepherd (1851-1929) was an American collector
　　from Scranton, Pennsylvania (and later was elected president of the Art Associa-
　　tion of Montreal in 1906-1911 and 1918-1929) (Heijbroek and Wouthuysen 1999:
　　58).
　　　Sir Byron Edmund Walker (1848-1924) was president of the Canadian Bank
　　of Commerce from 1907 to 1924 "and a generous patron of the arts [...] Walker's

postscript Bourgeois added: "Your Bourdelle bronze is in my office, in which way do you like it to go to Montreal, bring it, send it or as luggage?"

April 30: Van Slochem sent Van Horne the *New York Times* of April 13th in which Van Horne would "find the photo of your fine view at the St. Andrews." [389] Van Slochem's accompanying letter sounds as if his warm business relationship with Van Gelder was cooling off:

> I cannot get a reply from you in New York and I shall be most happy to hear from you in Antwerp, 7 Avenue Cogels. Perhaps you will be so kind as to write confidentially the contents of the letter you received from Van Gelder, about which he cabled me to remain in New York! And await your reply. I suppose you will explain him everything as to the future of my business and hope you will advise him not to discontinue the business. Looking forward to see you this summer in Antwerp.

May would be quiet month. On the 5th Van Horne wrote to Bourgeois about his upcoming visit to New York: "Must be New York Wednesday, Thursday possibly Friday." [390]

---

relationship with George Agnew Reid led to the founding of the Art Gallery of Ontario. On March 15, 1900, Reid, then president of the Ontario Society of Artists, brought a group of citizens together to consider the formation of an art gallery for Toronto. At that meeting, a Provisional Art Museum Board was set in place with Walker as chairman and Reid as secretary. Through effective lobbying and fundraising ($5 000 each from 10 benefactors), the Ontario Legislature later that year passed a bill incorporating the Art Museum of Toronto [renamed the Art Gallery of Ontario in 1996]. Walker became president of its Board of Trustees and served until his death," in http://en.wikipedia.org/wiki/Byron_Edmund_Walker (accessed October 2014).

389 Letter in VHFF (7/12).
390 Letter in VHFF (2/5).

On May 26 Van Gelder wrote Hofstede de Groot that he had received both of his letters (June 8 and 24) and that he had not responded to the first letter because he had been away.[391] Van Gelder mentioned he was interested to learn that Hofstede de Groot in all likelihood had found the pendant to his Petronella Buys. (Some time earlier, Van Gelder had mentioned this painting to Van Horne, but he had not bought it.)

Apparently Bourgeois had left New York after Van Horne's visit.

June 2: Bourgeois wrote to Van Horne saying that he had enjoyed a splendid crossing and had found Nardus and his family in very good health and humour.[392] He added:

> Nardus and I, we hope that we shall have soon the pleasure of seeing you in Paris. The season is progressing splendidly here, and there are a lot of exquisite things to be seen in the moment, in exhibitions and collections [...].
>
> There is especially in this moment a fine exhibition of Chinese art in the Cernuschi museum, this you ought to see. Nardus has an exhibition in Rosenberg's Gallery, and has much success. But we have just now so many exhibitions, that I cannot explain you all by letter. You have to come over for that, and I shall be very glad to see them with you together. I did not buy for you the Rembrandt drawing in Amsterdam. The quality was inferior and the price higher as your limit (2 000 dollars). I received the photo of the Lotto and sent it directly to Berenson asking his opinion.[393] I think to have in a few days an answer and shall then write you about the matter.

---

391   Letters in RKD.
392   Letter in VHFF (2/7).
393   Lorenzo Lotto (1480-1556) was a Northern Italian painter.

But the most important is, that you will kindly send me the notices concerning your pictures for the catalogue, or when you come over, please bring them with you. I would like to begin as soon as possible with the descriptions, that we may discuss the matter when I come back in the fall.

I am going tomorrow night to London, to see if I may find some very fine pictures. Nardus found in the meantime a very extraordinary Goya, a portrait of the artist himself, dressed as toreador, in green, brown and with a large head. He is looking out of the frame in a marvellous attitude. It is really a masterpiece and very unusual. You will see this picture as also [well as] the fine Greco portrait of the Rouart sale.

June 2: Bourgeois again wrote to Van Horne commenting: "business is not so bad in Europe, but it could be better." [394] Dealers had started to gently nudge their clients away from the European Old Masters. In this letter, Bourgeois tries to interest Van Horne in oriental art:

I had some good chances and bought a lot of fine things, especially in England. I saw Fearon in London and did some business with him. Sir Edmund Walker is there too, but I did not yet succeed to see him. I would like to show him a life size portrait by Drouais representing the marquis of Ossun, and which was painted on order of Louis 15th. I think it could be interesting for Ottawa, which has not yet anything of that kind.

As for the Buddha head, please decide after you have seen it. The piece has not yet arrived and will be sent directly to N. York where I shall find it coming over in the

---

394   Letter in VHFF (2/5).

fall. Bing offered me to take it back, but my opinion is, that we have to do with a unique piece of Chinese sculpture, as never was found before, and I would not miss such an opportunity. The reason why Bing is interested in it, is because lately one of the curators of Boston saw the photo, and would like to buy it. Kindly wait till it will arrive and if you do not like it, I shall take it for myself. The price I paid for it is 4 000 dollars, and I do not think, that it is a high price for such a piece.

I saw in London Binyon, the well-known writer about Chinese paintings and spoke to him about your paintings.[395] I shall give him a photo of your horsemen, but as I have no reproduction of your Japanese painting and the letter, please send me two, one for Binyon and one for me. I would like to discuss with him the matter, and see what is his opinion. He showed me the marvelous painting of Ku-Kai-chi in the British museum. It is a very extraordinary painting, but the silk begins to break and for that reason they do not like to show it to anybody. When you come over, I would like to show you this and several others. In any case, I bought a fine reproduction for you, which gives an excellent idea of it and which is made by a very clever Japanese in London. It will be ready in a few weeks and I shall send it you. You will also receive the reproduction of Persian drawing by Bihzat (about 1507), representing a horse, and which I bought lately. I think you find in Migeons book about Persian art some indications concerning Bihzat. This artist is regarded the greatest master of Persian miniature and Martin calls him in his history of that art the Rafael of the East.

---

395 Binyon, [Robert] Laurence (1869-1943) was a poet, Assistant-Keeper of Prints and Drawing of the British Museum and author about a number of books on art-history. See: http://www.dictionaryofarthistorians.org/binyonl.htm (last accessed October 2014).

I have not yet found a new place in New York, and intend to come over early in September to see what I can do. I have a very fine gallery in view corner 57th street and Fifth Avenue, but as the proprietor will not give the concession that I am the only art dealer in the same building I do not think to take it.

....

June 13: Van Slochem acknowledged the letter Van Horne had written in the train to St. Andrews, informed him that he had just returned from Paris and been present at the sale of the famous Steengracht collection.[396] Van Slochem wrote that the piece that went for the highest price was a Rembrandt, secured for Mr. Altman and that the Jacob Adriaen Backer, the Hobbema, Jan Steen, Terborgh, and Paul Potter were secured for the Rijksmuseum in Amsterdam. He also mentioned that the Brouwer went to a German collector, and that the Govert Flinck and the Gerard Dou's to a dealer, who said he was buying them for Senator Clark of New York. Van Slochem finished with a wry comment about all those present having been satisfied to see the competition between German, Dutch, and American collectors.

As mentioned, the Van Horne collection was catalogued by Robert J. Wickenden. However, it seems that Van Horne had originally asked Bourgeois to do it. From Bourgeois' July letters (which follow) it certainly seems as though Van Horne and Bourgeois had an understanding about this arrangement.

_____

396   Letter in VHFF (2/5). The Steengracht collection was brought together by
        Jonkheer Johan Steengracht van Oostcappelle (1782-1846), the first director of
        the Mauritshuis, The Hague; Jonkheer Hendrick Steengracht van Oosterland,
        The Hague (1808-1875); Jonkheer Hendrick Adolf Steengracht van Duivenvoorde,
        The Hague (1836-1912). On June 9, 1913 the estate was sold at Galerie Georges
        Petit in Paris.

June 14: Bourgeois wrote Van Horne that he had received the photographs and had talked with Mr. Gerona, an art publisher, about the catalogue. Bourgeois went on:

He considers the photo's satisfactory, (I am speaking of the Greco portrait, the Zurbaran St. Elisabeth, van Goyen, de Witte and Hals' Toper), but as he would like to do his best, he asked me, to lend to him for a short time the negatives of these photo's. The first preproduction will be frs. 100 a piece, and about 5-600 frs. for the five. Thinking that this proposition is fair, I gave him order to begin. Waiting for your decision concerning the negatives, I am with the kindest regards.

July 4: Bourgeois was supplying Van Horne with painting materials such as "colours, brushes and canvasses." In one of these shipments, he enclosed a letter from Sedelmeyer, "who is asking a photo of the little Rembrandt, which you bought from me and which Bode wishes to publish in his last volume."[397] Bourgeois continued:

Please send me some reproduction made by your photographer of Montreal, because those made in Paris show the picture before it was cleaned. Did Bode publish your little landscape before? If not, please let me know, have sent a whole lot of colours, brushes and canvases you will receive soon.

---

397   Letter in VHFF (2/5). Charles Sedelmeyer (1837-1925) was a Paris art dealer (Saltzman 2008: 93)

July 11: Bourgeois thanked Van Horne for his two letters of June 25 and the $35 000, which he "had received safely." [398] He added that he was very glad to have such good news about De Witt, N. Maes, Tintoretto and the large Ruysdael. Bourgeois went on about a Chinese painting he was going to give to Van Horne and mentioned his visit to Mr. Walker: "I showed him photos of several of our last purchases and he was extremely impressed by the Goya Toreador [399] and Cranach's portrait of a young man." [400]

In this letter Bourgeois does not mention which Maes he is talking about, but it has to be the *Old Woman Reading,* the picture about which Lugt scribbled, "no, not a Maes." [401] Nevertheless, Bourgeois said he was happy to have "heard good news about it."

Under his description of Maes *Old Woman Reading* Wickenden first cites de Groot's *Catalogue of Dutch Masters of the XVII Century*, Vol. VI. Section XXXIII. Page 475: "... in the first ten years he [Maes] painted masterpieces..." and then cites Conway (1905: 139):

....

But there is a portrait of an old lady reading, by Nicholas Maes, which is impossible to forget. The subject was a favourite with the artist; a well-known picture in the Brussels gallery is of this type; a drawing in the Albertina may be connected with it. Maes' best pictures all belong to his early period, when he was strongly influenced by

---

398 Letter in VHFF (2/5).

399 Goya's *Toreador* is not listed in the Wickenden catalogue.

400 The only Cranach listed is VH128, *Maarten Luther with a Beard*, sold by Nardus and Van Gelder in 1900.

401 VH 61 Maes, Nicolaes (Dordrecht 1632–Amsterdam 1693). *Old Woman with Bible.* ⊞: Seated in an arm-chair at the right, three-quarters-length, before a table at the left, the freshly-coloured face and expressive eyes of this interesting old Dutch woman turn toward the spectator as she holds the red-edged leaves of an illustrated Bible with her right hand, the left resting across her waist [...] Canvas H. 39¾ in. W. 31 in. (1.01 m × .79 m). Purchased from Knoedler and Co. ⊞: 8 000.

Rembrandt. Many may remember the admirable representation of an old woman saying Grace, which is in the Amsterdam Gallery. Sir William's canvas is no less excellent, and appears to be of about the same date."

The sheet on which Henschel valued Maes' *Old Woman with Bible* for 8 000 also features scribbles, such as: From Knoedler New York... Sir W. paid 6 000... De Groot doubts att. to Maes... Dr. Friedländer (1909) pronounced it by Maes, but painted in an unusual manner...

A 1964 scribble by Bourgeois reads: "better than appears! Worth restoring." All in all, perhaps the good news for Van Horne was that Dr. Friedländer pronounced the Maes to be a Maes. And the large Ruysdael a Ruysdael? Could this have been the Ruysdael that Conway (1905: 140) describes in his article as follows:

A fine landscape, a view of Haarlem from the bleaching grounds, so favourite a subject with the local painters, is ascribed to the great Jacob Ruysdael. It resembles, but is not identical with, a view of the same subject in the Hague Gallery [Mauritshuis]. Another has found its way into a private collection at Philadelphia. In all three the sky goes for much in the general effect, the earth being little more than foreground to it.

July 14: Van Slochem, who was in Berlin at the time, wrote to Van Horne explaining that he had approached Dr. Bode.[402] However, Dr. Bode had not been able to receive him owing to serious illness. Van Slochem continued:

402 Letter in VHFF (7/12).

I therefore could not arrange anything about the Vivarini, which he [previously?] said was undoubtedly an original and fine portrait by the master and, as you will remember I told you Berenson said was not a Vivarini! Dr. Friedländer whom I showed the picture compared it in my presence with an important picture by Vivarini, hanging here in Kaiser Friedrich Museum, agrees with Dr. Bode. And advised me to go to Cassel to a Director of the Museum there, a gentleman who has also written a book on Italian art and get his opinion. After that I should send Berenson the picture as he thinks that it is rather difficult to give an opinion of a picture of that character on the photo only.

Van Gelder has also written me saying that he received from you the entire balance on the Rembrandt Old Man with Black Cap. I also thank you for this. In the Kaiser Friedrich Museum I have seen here the Magnasco you presented to the Museum. It hangs there very nicely amongst the Spanish picture and looks very well indeed, And on a very neat plate in black and gold it reads: gift from Sir William Van Horne of Montreal. So this looks to me, that dr. Bode thinks very well of the picture. I noticed there another Magnasco, but I do like yours better [...]

P.S. Dr. Bredius whom I met in Holland intends to visit you in the fall, he told me so.

July 23: Bougeois thanked Van Horne for his kind letter of July 13th and kept him posted about the colours and brushes shipped to St. Andrews.[403] He also thanked Van Horne for the invitation to come to Covenhoven, agreed with Van Horne's advice about a new gallery location in New York, and told him not to work too hard on the catalogue.

---

403   Letter in VHFF (2/7).

So, it seems that Van Horne worked on the catalogue as well.

Bougeois continued that he would see Bode and then give orders for the printing. He ended by promising that the first volume would be ready before spring.

August 1: Van Gelder wrote Van Horne that he had received his last letters. He then went on about investor matters and sleepless nights – it seems life was not dealing kindly with this dealer/friend/gentleman/investor:[404]

Through my absence from home these last three weeks I could not answer you before, I was on a painting trip with two friends. I received $1 000 through Morgan, Harjes & Cie., sixty thousand dollars, which squares your account with me altogether. I want to thank you very much indeed for this remittance, especially as I know how much you need the money at present for your various enterprises and how scarce money is at present. I was a little startled on reading the copy of letter about Sardine factory to M. Meger. Truly said I did expect something of the kind, although not so bad as you show it to be. I remember quite well your grumbling at Mr. McColf at St. Andrews last year about the exaggeration of his initiative expenses but thought him wise enough to take at heart what you said and go easy and carefully. However do not doubt for a moment but matters will change as soon you have taken more direct touch with the administration, especially you being so close at hand and able to give the enterprise much of your thoughts and time, during your stay at St. Andrews. You had had to deal with matters more difficult than this before and come out on top and surely you will this time; I have unlimited confidence in you. Perhaps I could be of

404   Letter in VHFF (7/22).

some use to you in one way or other, if so please dispose of me, [I will put myself at your disposal] when at St. Andrews. I suggested to Bennie my willingness to serve as a director in the concern, I don't know if he transmitted this to you. Could I do something to help you and relieve you in something please count on me. I received a circular of the Laurentide Co. about a new issue of shares to increase the capital. I regret that such an issue has been made at a moment that money is so scarce and business so bad. I personally cannot afford to take more shares at present and will sell the rights to my great regret. I read with great interest your opinion about my picture business in the States, which has given me numberless sleepless nights; I will deal with that more fully later on when writing you again.

My wife and I we had hoped to see you in Europe in the spring, we would have given you a lovely time. Perhaps you may get over next spring as I suppose your business will keep you going for some time to come. If possible try to make yourself loose from business worries for some time, a little relaxation is often wholesome! The machine cannot always keep running without oiling! We received the delicious syrup and sugar with delight, we cannot be anymore without it, accept please our best thanks, the children love it. Yesterday Dr. Stillwell from New York came to see me with a friend, they seemed greatly pleased with their visit. Dr. S. is a very intelligent man of a generous appreciative nature.

Van Slochem went to Germany and England and is elated with the success of his beautiful Vivarini, which is everywhere highly admired, as it justly deserves. I think that Berenson's popularity is a thing of the past. How is the painting getting along? Have you found time to do some.

August 11: Bourgeois, after thanking Van Horne for his letter of July 27th, wrote that he was glad that Van Horne liked the pictures he had sent photographs of.[405] He added: "I sent Sedelmeyer the photo of the old man's head and to Bode the photo of your little Rembrandt-landscape. Berenson wrote me about your Italian pictures. He says he cannot judge the pictures without seeing the originals." He then referred to finding a gallery location in New York: "I think we have found now the real standard for a fine business, more a connoisseurs' business as dealers do usually." Then he mentioned Van Horne's catalogue, saying that he worked on it "every day a little." He also mentioned that Nardus was painting in Scheveningen, that Mrs. Nardus was taking baths in the Pyrenees and ended with:[406]

Business is very quiet, but I had some nice chances and cannot complain. I saw Bode in Berlin and he received me in a very charming way. With the time everything about Nardus' misfortunes in America will be forgotten and Bode and also Berenson will help us in any way. Some good clients in America, a fine place in New York and those people behind us and we cannot otherwise than to have big success.

Bourgeois' confidence was misplaced. Nardus' "misfortunes" are blog material one hundred years later.

August 13: Van Horne received a thank you letter from Mrs. Isa van Wisselingh.[407] He must have sent his condolences upon hearing about the death of her husband of many years. Van

---

405 Letter in VHFF (2/7).
406 According to the "official" Leo Nardus website (http://www.leonardus.fr/0) he divorced his wife in 1911, but the procedure took twelve years.
407 Letter in VHFF (3/27).

Horne must also have made a remark about Mr. Maris, which explains why Mrs. Van Wisselingh added: "I shall tell Mr. Maris what you say about his way of working, spent a day with him last Thursday. He was very well."

August 16: Van Slochem, writing from Antwerp, confirmed that he had received Van Horne's letter of August 2 and in reply would "explain particulars about the Vivarini:" [408]

From Berlin I went to Cassel with an introduction from Dr. Friedländer to Dr. George Gronau, Director of the Museum, who is very well posted in Italian art. His first impression was it [is] not Antonello de Messina, this is Vivarini, and after careful examination came to the conclusion this to be Luigi Vivarini.

I than told him that Dr. Bode and Dr. Friedländer were of the same opinion, which pleased him very much; I did not mention anything to him about Berenson, but he suggested that I should show the picture to a friend of him who is at present in London, namely Dr. Berenson, and he gave me his address in London. I than had to tell him that Dr. B. had seen the photo and said it was not Vivarini, but he strongly urged me to go to him with the picture, as he felt quite sure Berenson would agree with him, when he sees the picture.

I decided to go, and I found Berenson in the hotel, but he refused to see me, I finally got him on the phone but when I told him whom I was, he said he had no time, and dropped the receiver. This proves that he has heard something that did not please him; and therefore refused to see me, while in London. I decided to take the picture to the National Gallery, and inquired from the secretary who was their expert on Italian art, and I was introduced to

408   Letter in VHFF (7/12).

Mr. Collins Baker, connected with Nat. Galleries. I showed him the picture and he was very much interested, taking the picture in my presence to the room where the Italian pictures are exhibited, amongst which there is a portrait from the late Mr. Salting collection and two other portraits belong to the National Gallery. He than requested me to leave the picture with him, and to call in him the next morning, when he will give me his opinion, the result was for him this to be a work by Alvise Vivarini.[409] I ask him to give me this in writing, but he said, before he gives anything in writing, he would prefer also to have the opinion of a gentleman, Dr. Tancred Borenius, residing in London, who formerly lived in Italy to study Italian art, wrote books on Italian art and is very much interested in that master, and whose opinion is very much thought off by the committee of the National Gallery on Italian art.[410]

I was glad to hear such and preferred that this gentleman should by all means see the picture, the picture remained there an other day, and the next morning I met Dr. Borenius in the presence of Mr. Collins Baker who congratulated me to possess such a fine work by Alvise Vivarini and both the gentlemen than gave me their opinion in writing and I am perfectly please to know that Dr. Berenson is not the only man that knows Italian art. Last week Dr. Stillwell visited me in Antwerp and during our conversation I told him of this. He said that he heard of Dr. Borenius and thinks much of him, and he remarked that he wished I would make this public on my return to NY as Berenson refusing to receive me would count very much against him.

---

409   Luigi Vivarini (c. 1446-1502) is also known as Alvise Vivarini.
410   Dr. Tancred Borenius (1885-1948) was a Finnish art historian.

I have however decided to do nothing until I get to New York but I learned from Dr. Stillwell that he is not a believer in Berenson; I was also surprised to note in your letter that Mr. Johnson is also one of the collators that does not believe Berenson to be the final authority on Italian art, although I always thought the contrary. Mr. Altman should know your opinion and Mr. Johnson's about Berenson and the other collectors are sure to follow; than the great Italian expert Berenson will lose some of his power. I should like to hear from you what you think of this result!!

October 6: Van Slochem confirmed that he had received van Horne's letter of 8th of September, noted Van Horne's remarks about Berenson "and the difficulty in dealing against the strong influence he had acquired with the Duveen clique!" [411] Van Slochem went on:

However some European collectors, and art critics know well of his doing and are very much against him indeed. No doubt this will make itself felt in America sooner or later. When I say critics I mean men such as I mentioned to you in my last letter, like Dr. Borenius, Dr. Gronau and many others of their standing all students in Italian art, Dr. Borenius has openly recognized a certain picture where Berenson agreed upon as having made some error in the attribution. On my next trip to London I shall find out something more about that. Now Sir William some thing else in strict confidence, I write you, that Van Gelder is very much discouraged! I intended to sail on the 4th of October but a few days before my sailing we talked over the situation and Van Gelder urged upon me to postpone my

---

411   Letter in VHFF 1913 (7/12).

trip till January as things do not look so brilliantly in the States, and besides he wants to curtail the heavy expenses. He has not made any additional purchases and says if I can not sell pictures such as the fine Vivarini, Rubens, P. de Hoogh, Vermeer of Haarlem, Tiepolo, Goya and many others that he than is at a loss to know what to buy for America. Unless the outlook is a little better, I expect to follow his suggestion and will not sail until late in January. **I would however very much like to hear from you how things are in America and if you would advise me to come before that time!** Owing to this change I regret very much to postpone my departure as I thought surely of spending a few days on your island in St. Andrews.

DR. ABRAHAM BREDIUS STEPS IN

As we already learned – on July 14, 1912, from Van Slochem – Dr. Bredius planned a trip to Canada. On August 27 Bredius informed Van Horne about his upcoming visit to America and said that he would be sailing on October 4. He also mentioned he hoped to see Van Horne's "celebrated collection" on 20 or 25 October, and went on: [412]

May I ask you for a great kindness: two lines, to tell me if you will be at home then? I am traveling now home from Contrexéville where I make a cure every year! My address is always Prinsegracht 6, The Hague. I have got some new pictures and fine Rembrandt drawings. Whenever you come to Europe I should like so much to know. You ought to come to The Hague then, and see your friends. I think there is time still for an answer before Oct.

---

412 Letter in VHFF (2/16).

Yours very sincerely Bredius.

One of the best connoisseurs, Mr. Kronig is travelling with me.

....

Bredius did not introduce Kronig as his life partner because mentioning this kind of relationship was not done at that time. Bredius added a note to this letter: "I have found new and very strong proofs for my attributing Mad. [Madame] Elis. Bas to Ferd. Bol. I am publishing them in the Burlington Magazine."

It is not clear why Bredius thought that his attribution of Madame Elisabeth Bas to Ferdinand Bol would be of interest to Van Horne.[413] Did he think that Van Horne was abreast of this quarrel with Hofstede de Groot about this attribution? Perhaps this note was meant to convince Van Horne of his skills and to lay stepping stones for a trusted relationship.

Abraham Bredius

Abraham Bredius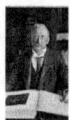

Barnouw de Ranitz (1978/80/90: 13-26) writes that Bredius, a collector of 17th century Dutch paintings, was the son of a wealthy manufacturer of gunpowder. Young Bredius did not feel he was a merchant. Instead, he went into music but then felt that he was not good enough. During travels through Europe he found his niche in fine arts. In 1880 he was appointed

---

413   From 1906 to 1909 Bredius had argued for attribution of this painting to Jacob Backer. More interesting details on this question are in Scallen (2004: 220).

Assistant-Director of the Netherlands Museum for History and Arts in The Hague, the museum that merged into the Rijksmuseum in Amsterdam. In 1888 he left this position and became Director of the Mauritshuis in The Hague. (About two years later Hofstede de Groot became his Assistant-Director but left five years later to become Director of the Rijksprentenkabinet in Amsterdam.) Due to health reasons Bredius resigned in 1909, which gave him the time to collect, write, issue expertises, and travel widely. The Bredius collection and Bredius' house were bequeathed to the Municipality of The Hague.

How much their lives were intertwined is apparent from the following overview of their lives.

Abraham Bredius Bredius (1855-1946)	Cornelius Hofstede de Groot (1863-1930)
1855: Son of a rich Amsterdam gunpowder manufacturer	
	1863: Minister's son from Dwingeloo (east Netherlands)
1880: Assistant-Director of the Dutch Museum for History and Arts in The Hague. (Later this would merge with the Rijksmuseum.)	
1888: Director of the Mauritshuis, The Hague.	1890: Assistant of the Prentenkabinet in Dresden.
	1891: Assistant to Dr. A. Bredius, director of the Mauritshuis.
	1896: Director of the Prentenkabinet of the Rijksmuseum in Amsterdam.

Abraham Bredius Bredius (1855-1946)	Cornelius Hofstede de Groot (1863-1930)
	1898: Resigned Directorship. Made a lot of money by issuing expertises, had to travel in order to do this, started a collection of his own.
1909: Resigned Directorship. Made a lot of money by issuing expertises, had to travel in order to do this, started a collection of his own.	**1930:** After his death his estate was bequeathed to the Dutch State.
	1932: Establishment of the *Rijksbureau for Kunsthistorische Documentatie* (RKD).
1946: After his death his collection and his house were bequeathed to the Municipality of The Hague. The collection is now at Lange Vijverberg 14.	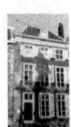
	Photo RKD
Photo Bredius Museum http://www.museumbredius.nl/	

Of course Van Horne said he would dearly love to have two more connoisseurs visit him and his collection. Bredius replied (no date) from the Central-Hotel Berlin.[414]

---

414   Letter in VHFF (2/16).

How kind of you to invite us to stay in your house. May we really accept this?? We would be in Montreal about 18 Oct. and stay first in New York in the new Van der Bilt Hotel. Parting the 17th in the evening. The Bol question interests me very much. The couple Havemeijer[415]/man/and Lord Iveagh[416] /wife/ are certainly Bol's and I can prove with photo's which I will carry with me. I do not understand Dr. Hofstede de Groot who does not accept Mad. Bas and believes it Rembrandt. But not many more with him.

With thanks for your kindness and looking forward with great pleasure on the favour to meet you soon

Only for one day here to fetch a picture, which Professor Hauser has authenticated (for the Rijks Museum).

The painting of the widow Elisabeth Bas was one of the first Rembrandts acquired by the Rijksmuseum. Manuth (2005: 58) writes, in Dutch, that the Madame Bas affaire started in 1911, when Bredius argued in two articles that this painting was not by Rembrandt, but by his student, Ferdinand Bol. Hofstede de Groot did not agree. The disagreement between the connoisseurs lingered on about details in the painting, the golden ring, and Rembrandt's handwriting. In the end Hofstede de Groot pointed out that Bredius was an auto-didact (while he had "studied" art history). It is amusing and puzzling at the same time to see this controversy carried on in Bredius' correspondence with Van Horne.

415 The Havemeyers were Louisine (1855-1929) and her husband Henry O. Havemeyer (1847-1907) of the American Sugar Refining Company. Louisine was known to be an art collector, feminist, and philanthropist. Their art collection is now in the Metropolitan Museum in New York (Saltzman 2008).
416 Edward Cecil Guinness, 1st Earl of Iveagh (1847-1927), was a voracious collector himself (Saltzman 2008: 105).

Quodbach (2005: 74) explains, in Dutch, the ongoing different opinions of Bredius and Hofstede de Groot due to their different approach to connoisseurship. Hofstede de Groot's approach was scientific; for him paintings were "preaparates," while Bredius trusted his intuition. Manuth (2005: 56) makes the same argument, but also quotes Hofstede de Groot's praise of one Rembrandt, *Seelenmalerei* (Painting of the soul) as psychologizing. At the end of his article Manuth cites Hofstede de Groot's own opinion: "Bredius rather values the judgment of eighteenth century connoisseurs and I rather what my eyes teach me."

Perhaps art historians should look into the question of whether Hofstede de Groot, within the parameters of his professional ethics, phrased his authentications in such a way that they were pleasing for the ears of his client. After all, Hofstede de Groot, himself an ambitious collector, made his living by his authentications.

Back to Montreal and the next letters of October 1913.

Undated: Bredius wrote to Van Horne from the Vanderbilt Hotel in New York, probably in early October.[417] His letter shows that he still had not let go of the Madame Bas affaire (and wouldn't until 1922!):

> May we now arrive next Saturday evening, with a train that leaves here 8.45 and arrives 8.20 at Montreal or would it be more convenient for you Monday? We arrived safely here yesterday. We are so delighted with your kindness to allow us to see your beautiful pictures in such a generous way. I have to tell you new surprises about Rembr-Bol & bring you proofs of the certainty as Mad. Bas being painted by Bol!

417   Letter in VHFF (2/16).

The question about why Bredius continued to keep Van Horne abreast of the Bol matter is puzzling. Was it meant to show his mastery? To keep in touch? Or both?

Van Horne must have replied that he had not understood something in Bredius' letter, because the following week Bredius (n.d.), who was still at The Vanderbilt Hotel in New York, wrote: "Did I write so badly? I am sorry to trouble you again, but we intended to leave here Saturday morning to arrive 8.20 in the evening. If this suits you, we will come directly to your house and no answer is expected. What a fine museum here and what splendid art treasures." [418]

The letter above reads as if Bredius had been visiting the Metropolitan.

Apparently, one week later, on a Thursday, Bredius (n.d.) wrote from Chateau Frontenac in Quebec that they had arrived safely.[419] From this letter is clear that the Van Horne visit had gone well. Bredius said that Kronig and he were,

still fully rememorizing the kind reception in your house, family and beautiful things we have seen there. You have given us hours of happiness – that is a great thing to do. I hope you will be convinced that we shall never forget these charming days under your roof. Mr. and Mrs. Van Horne were also very kind – please thank them again for me! We will stay after tomorrow – and 5 or 6 days more – in **Boston**, in the Touraine Hotel. Kronig discovered here in a private collection two really **marvellous** pictures of **highest rank**!

---

418   Letter in VHFF (2/16).
419   Letter in VHFF (2/16).

October 23: Van Horne cabled Bredius, who was still at Chateau Frontenac: "Where shall I forward your mail?" [420] Bredius' reply: "Hotel Touraine, Boston."

October 23: Van Horne received the following letter from Kronig, from the Chateau Frontenac:[421]

I don't know how to thank you for all your kindness and for the most pleasant and instructive time I spent at your delightful house. I shall never forget it and if there is anything I could do for you I hope you will dispose of me [put me at your disposal]. You know of course monsieur Pinauld's pictures. *The portrait of a lady* he attributes to school of Rafael is a very fine Sebastiano del Piombo and the *portrait of a lady* attributed to Lotto looks more like a Vicenzo Cateno. You should keep an eye on these pictures.

October (n.d.): Bredius, still in Chateau Frontenac, and still not in the habit of dating his letters, wrote to Van Horne as follows. This letter reads as if Van Horne offered Kronig a job but Bredius, of course, did not want to lose his special friend: [422]

We heard of Mrs. Charpels here who must have a Botticelli but will not show them to us, afraid that we shall find her house in disorder. Having just arrived from the country where she left some of her best pictures. As I could observe, the proposition to Kronig has still a possibility of being accepted, **all** will depend from the time allowed to him to stay in Europe every year. He would be **the** man to make and **arrange** you a perfect Gallery in O. We always

---

think of your great kindness, how glad I will be to see you once in The Hague.

A. Bredius, (A, not S.)

ABOUT TWO PORTRAITS ATTRIBUTED TO FRANS HALS

In *L'Art Flamand* of October 1913 a follow-up to the September 1911 article about the two Halses appeared. This article forboded another little storm in the art world.

....

In our January 1912 number we published an article by dr. Hofstede de Groot on "Two portraits recently attributed to Frans Hals" belonging to Mr. Van Gelder, at Uccle. The previous owner of these portraits, Madame la Comtesse de Limburg Stirum having heard of this publication, requests us to rectify some of the information imparted. It is said that according to the tradition these portraits are supposed to represent members of the painter's family or household and that they never went outside of the painter's family; consequently they never went to the trade and always remained unknown. Madame la Comtesse de Limburg Stirum informs us that the portraits were simply purchased in the 19th. Century by Count de Thiennes, her grandfather, for his amateur collection of tableaux, and there does not exist any tradition connecting them with Frans Hals. On the contrary, these portraits were not considered in her family as having been painted by this Master and they were not sold as such. Furthermore, there never was any alliance between the Thiennes and Hals families.

Evidently these observations will not in the least alter the opinion of our eminent collaborator as regards the attribution, but we wish to transmit Madame la Comtesse de

Limburg Stirum's declarations, which are very important from the history point of view of these two portraits.

On November 1, this time dating his letter, Bredius wrote to his former assistant Hofstede de Groot in The Hague from Hotel de Touraine in Boston. It starts with Bredius expressing his regrets that Hofstede de Groot adhered to his supposedly wrong opinion. The letter also seems to reflect, as Scallen (2004: 219-232) describes it, 'their contest for authority' during the first decade of the twentieth century. Bredius went on as follows: [423]

> But of course, as long as you don't recognize that E. Bas cannot possibly be a Rembrandt and always refers to the Bol's, which don't resemble her, you will not get any further.[424] The **Havemeyer-Iveagh** Rembr's/Bols are the real **pendants** of the Rothschild Bols, *anerkannt* by you and Bode. I would declare that one also as a real Rembrandt, despite the fake signatures. Investigate Iveagh and pay attention to the hand (without glass). The 2nd Bol of H. Lane is quite later that Bas, still the techniques of the handkerchief look like it. Wait until my booklet about Bol will be published.
>
> Truth, also in matters of fine arts sometimes has to wait for some time, but will triumph in the end. So it will go with that nasty bogus-thing, Weber's adulterous woman. Too bad that Bode, in order to spare Valentiner, sings like that, he completely agrees with me!! It came out that it was a campaign against him in order to veil Valentiner's

---

423   Letter in RKD.
424   Blankert (1978/80/90: 22) argues that Bredius was the first one to attribute Elisabeth Bas to Bol, "a top piece that had always been considered to be a Rembrandt."

mistake!!!! Mel Bierman, his secretary confessed to me, I now saw the photographs, one really **cannot distinguish difference** with the old one and the thing remains as nasty, senseless *machwerck* as it was. I regret that you and Valentiner are not convinced of Rembrandt's greatness and keep this soulless & unsentimental work of the painter of S + D & of Jacob's Seger in Cassel.

I have seen much & everywhere people are very nice and friendly. Kronig discovered here very big **main work** by C. Fabritius. You will read about it in Reports of the Museum of Boston.

Buy now, **on my account**, (I will get it later), a Braun photo of 853, Bol, Petersburg and put them next to Havemeyer's man's portrait + the wife of Rothschild / Bol next to Iveagh!!'s pendant. And then turn at the same time! We were in Worcerster where they started a very nice museum and now go to Providence. On November 2, I hope to have lunch with Mrs. Gardner & see her home on November 3. Therefore we have to especially return.[425]

In Quebec is a party Cole with **very rare** Italians, completely unknown. Sir W. v Horne's Rembrandts are not as beautiful as the one's of Ross or Angus.

I direct your attention to a 2nd Bol Bas article in the Burlington that will be issued soon. I think to be able to proof that Remb. already ± 1636/37 had Bol as a "fertig" painter. Where is **all** Bol's works from the 1638-1650 period?

---

425   With regard to this visit Scallen (2004: 201-02) writes that Gardner first refused Bredius "a special viewing," so Bredius was forced to go to Boston a second time and "was only permitted access along with the general public for the usual admission fee." Scallen assumes that this may explain Bredius' "surprising – and tart – dismissal of her three Rembrandts" (the *Christ on the Sea of Galilee*, stolen in 1970, among them).

Just in Petersburg are 4 or 5 Bols with fake Rembr. signatures!!! The so-called Bol at Holford is a Flinck, as you can compare with the **Flinck** in Darmstadt. Those two portraits came across as very Bol-like, are not Fincks either.

There is much to see here! Had dejeuner with Denman Ross,[426] who has a few nice things; we saw the mixed coll. Evans. De Wild also does not understand that Bode or you believe in that Woman with Hare. It will be a Drost, assisted by Rembrandt in a hurry. 1676.[427]

Did you see that strange thing at Kappel.[428] Did you then turn around again (make volte face).

I hope that you will not try to find that thing of Kappel through Kleinberger.

When can you finally show me a photo of Rembrandt's hands / real ones / that look a bit like those of E. Bas.???

Did the poultry business by Drost come across?

The infighting among connoisseurs caused the following rather ironic alert in the *American Art News* of November 1, 1913:

"EXPERT" BERENSON COMING

Mr. Bernhard Berenson, the "expert" on early Italian painters, is expected this month in New York, to remain for the winter. He will follow the Dutch "expert" Dr. Bredius, at present on an

---

426 Denman Waldo Ross (1853-1935) was an American painter, art collector and professor of art at Harvard University and author of *A Theory of Pure Design, Harmony, Balance, Rhythm*, published by Forgotten Books. See: http://en.wikipedia. org/wiki/Denman_Ross (last accessed in February 2014).

427 For Willem Drost (1633-1659), see: https://rkd.nl/en/artists/24317

428 Marcus Kappel (1839-1919), a German corn dealer, who built up his collection with Bode's help. See: http://de.wikipedia.org/wiki/Marcus_Kappel (last accessed in February 2014).

"expertizing" tour of the leading Art Museums and private collections in the United States and Canada.

Back to Van Horne: Van Horne's private secretary wrote
to Kronig, at The Vanderbilt Hotel, that his boss would be in
New York on Tuesday morning.[429] This cable was followed by
another on the same day about Van Horne's whereabouts: he
would be in New York from Tuesday to Friday, reside in the
Manhattan and hopes "to have the pleasure of seeing you and
Dr. Bredius while there."

SIR WILLIAM VAN HORNE'S ILLNESS

November 17 turned out to be a bad day. Van Horne had been
persuaded to give an address to the Canadian Club luncheon
in Toronto, but it did not happen. He had a chill, fell ill and left
for Montreal where a horde of reporters awaited him at the
railway station. Pierson (1929: 85) and Knowles (2004: 418)
report that upon arriving in Montreal Van Horne was besieged
by a crowd of reporters, which made him walk "the length
of St. James Street to demonstrate how well he was." His inflamed joints however rebelled and once home he had to go to
bed. The bad news soon reached art circles in New York.

On November 22 *American Art News* reported that "sir Wm.
Van Horne, whose reported illness in Toronto early in the
week made quite a stir in the art world and greatly alarmed a
host of friends, was only slightly indisposed it transpires and
is happily himself again."

----

429   Letter in VHFF (2/16).

November 28: Van Horne's typed letter to Bourgeois makes it clear that Van Horne was far from "residing happily in bed:" [430]

> I have not sent a cheque for balance of account, because my right hand is involved in my rheumatism and I can't sign anything. I hope however, within a day or two to be able to do it. I had hoped to be able to answer your kind enquiries with my own hand, but there is not a very good prospect of it yet. [A note added to these lines reads: "dictated."]

November 29: Bourgeois replied from Hotel St. Regis in New York to say that he was very sorry to hear about the arthritis attack.[431] He continued about a treatment with hot lamps, information about his exhibition in the St. Regis, and, of course, the latest opinions about the paintings he was displaying:

> Bredius came to see my Dutch pictures and was highly interested in the "Rabbi," which he admired very much. His opinion is, that it is the work of a Rembrandt pupil whose name was entirely lost although he was a man of great talent. Several of his pictures are authenticated as Rembrandts. Bredius discovered lately his name through a signature Carel van der Pluym.[432] Until [now] he has not published his discovery he does of course not want that our traders know about it. He prepares a little surprise for his colleagues.

---

430   Letter in VHFF (2/3).
431   Letter in VHFF (2/3).
432   Carel van der Pluym (1625-1672) was a painter, second cousin and a pupil of Rembrandt (Scallen 2004: 251).

Another visitor was Dr. Valentiner whom I never could induce to come and see me, as you will remember although you gave me such a fine introduction to him. [...]

Valentiner will introduce me to the curator for the modern paintings in the Met. Museum and that will be excellent thing for my business with the impressionistic pictures. I write you all those details knowing your kind interest for Nardus and my enterprise which begun under such difficult conditions. I feel that the ice is now broken as we say on the other side and that when I shall open February 1st. We will have a big success. Wishing you a speedy reestablishment of your health I am with the kindest regards.

Van Horn's secretary, referring Bourgeois "to his favor of Nov. 29th," wrote on December 1 that Sir William wished him to forward the message that he is "greatly obliged for your suggestions, but the doctor is not yet disposed to attempt the [hot lamp] heat treatment, everything is going very well so far." [433]

More letters from Bourgeois followed, in which he offered advice and suggested a doctor. But Van Horne's secretary let him know that there are many types of rheumatism and that Van Horne was still in a lot of pain and had to do what his doctors told him to do.

By December 10 Bourgeois had announced his upcoming visit to Van Horne.[434] Apparently he had to see for himself.

December 16: While still in bed, Van Horne dictated the following letter to Van Slochem:[435]

433   Letter in VHFF (2/3).
434   Letter in VHFF (2/3).
435   Letter in VHFF (7/14).

I appreciate your kind telegram very much. It was a surprise to me because I did not think that you were yet in New York. I have to send you a typewritten letter, because I am yet unable to write, having been suffering from a sharp attack of rheumatism for the past four weeks. I am looking forward to the pleasure of a visit from you soon and I have a good many things that I should like to talk over with you. Just now I can only lie on my back and swear occasionally.

December 18: Bourgeois sent Van Horne's son, Bennie Van Horne, a puzzling cable from the St. Regis Hotel: "Rumor here that VH is ill kindly answer at once." [436] On this cable are the following notes: "phoned," and "awkward." Awkward it was, as Bourgeois had already offered advice on the treatment of rheumatism. However, Van Horne would soon get news that might have cheered him up a bit. *American Art News* of December 20 announced that "the noted authority," Dr. Bernhard Berenson, accompanied by his wife, had arrived, as had Mr. H. Van Slochem, who had sold to such prominent American collectors as Messrs. J. G. Johnson, Benjamin Altman, Sir William Van Horne and others.

On December 20, *American Art News* had an eerie, but true news item, on page 1. It was about Van Slochem, but Van Horne's name was again mentioned along with other prominent men:

Mr. H. Van Slochem, who arrived from Amsterdam last week, tells of a most remarkable happening at his Gallery, no. 477 Fifth Ave. In a narrow entrance hallway, leading from the outer Hall to the Gallery, and which is closed

---

436   Letter in VHFF (2/3).

up during Mr. Van Slochem's long Summer absences in Europe, there have hung and hang a number of framed photographs of some of the important and valuable Old Masters, which he has sold, the past few years, to such prominent American collectors as Messrs. J. G. Johnson, Benjamin Altman, Sir William Van Horne and others. Among these was a photograph of a fine Van Orley, a "Virgin and Child," sold to the late Mr. Altman and now in the collection bequeathed to the Metropolitan Museum.

When Mr. Van Slochem, last week, unlocked the doors of this hallway, not entered during his absence, he started with surprise, for on the floor, fallen from its nail, and face downwards, with shattered glass, lay one photograph only – that of the Van Orley sold to the recently dead Mr. Altman. This is a true story!

On the 29th December Van Horne's secretary asked for the price of *la jeunesse inaltérable et la vie eternelle*[437] that E. van Wisselingh Jr. had sent him. Perhaps the secretary had overlooked it, but the price, $50, was mentioned in the accompanying letter. The secretary should instead have asked for this fine little book's genesis! Then he would have heard an interesting story. Heijbroek and Wouthuysen (1999: 140) would later note that Van Wisselingh had early on financed Marius Bauer's (1867-1932) travels to Eastern Europe and Turkey. On one of his journeys Bauer had met the author William Ritter

---

437   Letter in VHFF (3/27). On the 13th of January 1914, word came that the book would cost $50. Perhaps it was not good timing with Van Horne in bed, facing the fact that his vigour was wasting away and that his life would not be eternal. Therefore the secretary replied on January 28, 1914, (VH 3/27) that Van Horne "had been on his back with a severe attack of rheumatism for the last nine weeks and [been] unable to look over any of his correspondence." And, Van Horne already had the book and it would be returned the same day. The question remains, why did Van Horne ask about the price when he already had the book?

(1867-1955), who was then employed at the French delegation in Bucharest. He had Bauer read the story he (Ritter) had recorded from the vernacular (from "de volksmond"). Bauer was so touched that he illustrated it with nineteen sketches. Later he asked Groesbeek – who was, with Eilers, partner in Van Wisselingh & Co. – whether publication would be possible. It was a problem because there were too many sketches and too little text. However, in the end it was published as a bibliophile publication.

✕

PEOPLE & A PAINTER

Sir William in 1915
(Pen drawing by Musamjé)
➔

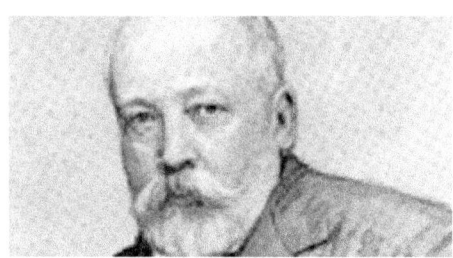

Lady Van Horne in 1920
(nee. Hurd)
Montreal QC, 1920
Photograph – Wm. Notman &
Son | II-235277
© McCord Museum
➔

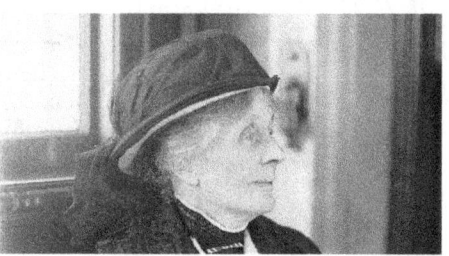

Willem Witsen, circa 1893
(Self portrait)
Ede, The Netherlands
Public domain
➔

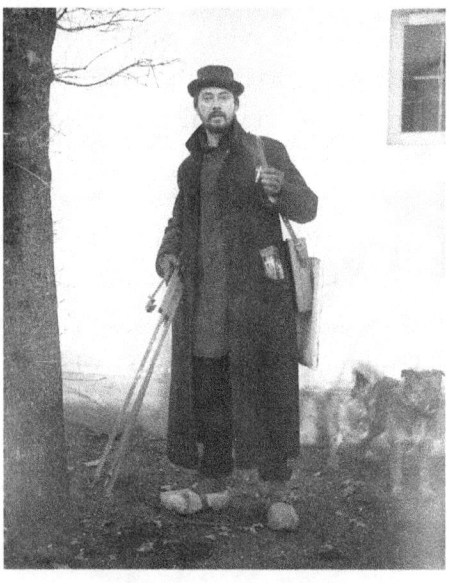

CHAPTER 7

THE GREAT WAR ROARS IN / WITSEN'S LAST ADDITION TO THE COLLECTION

FOR VAN HORNE, 1914 started miserably from a health standpoint, though he would recover somewhat. But then, in July, the Great War broke out, which would prove to be absolutely not great for the art world. For most people, this was the least of their worries, but for collectors and dealers it proved to be disastrous.

Bourgeois, now staying at the Hotel Blakestone in Chicago, was keeping track of Van Horne's illness. On January 3, 1914, he wrote that it had been his pleasure to hear through Miss van Horne that Sir William had changed "his position in bed."[438] A bit later he wrote "that owing to important business matters upon return from Chicago it had again been impossible to pay the proposed visit."

Van Gelder, staying at the Parkhotel Sonnenberg, Engelberg, Switzerland, wrote to Hofstede de Groot on January 7 to thank him for his brochure about Rembrandt's *Petronella Buys* and [the painting of] her husband.[439] He noted that he had followed these discoveries attentively and "found it too bad that both spouses were hanging so far from each other" and that he had hoped to take possession of the man's portrait.

---

438   Letter in VHFF (2/3).
439   Letter in RKD.

Van Gelder suggested that Hofstede de Groot publish about it in the *Burlington Magazine* as it could be of interest to English art lovers.

As I have said, dealers not only took care of crating, shipping, and double billing, but also of publications that might please their customers. However, publications did not always please the customer. Poor Van Gelder, in trouble again, went on to complain about "the two Halses" that Hofstede de Groot had written about:

Last week I heard that the Countess Limburg Stirum had send an article to the *l'Art Flam. et Holl.* about the provenance of the two Halses. Yesterday I received the issue which article had escaped me. It is pure libel! It seems that the Countess had regretted that these two works got such reputation; she turns, twists and pulls back what she contended earlier to me. I regret very much that you did not consult me before you added a few words [to her words]. You must understand that I have no reason whatsoever to invent these fabrications. For me it was enough to know that both paintings came from the Limb. Stirum and the Thiennes families. When you asked me whether I knew how these paintings had ended up in these families, I answered you that the countess, on account of her deceased father De Thiennes, had contended that it were portraits of Hals' father and mother (which hypothesis appeared not to be valid because of your comparison with the data) and that there was a relationship between the families Hals and De Thiennes. These contentions I got from the countess herself and a lady on her account, Mrs. Dowling, one of the countess' friends, who declared such in a letter to me. I write you all of this in order to convince you that I gave you these contentions in good trust. As you know, I have enough experience that pedigrees are highly valued and that one has to be very cautious with contentions. Again, I regret that you did not first consult me about the countess' article. Upon my return in Brussels I will pay the countess a visit and urge her to revoke that article; I do not wish to be known as the inventor of lies.

If Van Gelder had told Hofstede de Groot that the contesse Van Limburg Stirum was the source of the story, but that her story was later twisted, he would have been able to stay out of trouble; however, trouble seemed to be Van Gelder's constant companion.

Meanwhile, Bredius was faring much better than Van Gelder. *American Art News* of January 10, 1914, reported:

Dr. Bredius in Chicago

"The recent Altman bequest to the Metropolitan Museum, in which twelve excellent Rembrandts were included, and the addition of the Frick collection, which Mr. Frick intends to present the New York Museum, will make America and the Metropolitan one of the art centers of the world," said Dr. Abraham Bredius in a published interview in Chicago. "America has been grossly misjudged on the continent," continued Dr. Abraham Bredius. Commenting on his three months in America: "American collectors are spoken of so often over the water as bags of gold who buy indiscriminately and know almost nothing of their expensive collections. I come over here, and what do I find? With one or two exceptions, the makers of your great collections are connoisseurs, who have bought their pictures with rare discrimination. Your collections are selected."

Dr. Bredius has just returned from Minneapolis, where he made a special visit to the collection of James J. Hill. "It is," he said, "a magnificent collection, the best perhaps in the world of

the Barbizon school – Corot, Troyon, Millet, Daubigny and Courbet. Of each master he had perfect specimens." [440]

Finds one exception

"Occasionally, of course," said Dr. Bredius, " I find a collection that is full of imitations, presided over by a superfluously
pedantic owner who corresponds to our European tradition of
the American art collector, but I have really found only one such
man. Once in a while I find a bad piece, the imposition of some
dealer, in the midst of a really fine collection. Here in Chicago, for
instance, I found a tray with the head of a woman on it with her
hair done after the Napoleonic mode of 1840, which the owner
bought for a Van Dyke of the wife of Charles I. But, on the other
hand, imagine my delight when in discussing Rembrandt with
young Mr. Widener of Philadelphia we spoke of a picture now in
France, and he told me he suspected it was by a pupil of Rembrandt's. I had thought I was alone in that discovery." [...]

Americans original

"American artists," according to Dr. Bredius, "show a direction
away from French imitation that is vital. He admires their brushwork and careful technique as contrasted with the slap-dash effect of some modern continental work. The failure of the futurist
and cubist school to attract young Americans away from "a due
perception of nature" he regards as indicative of the strength of
American independence."

"Painting is dying in France," said Dr. Bredius, who regards the
pictures shown in last Winter's futurist exhibit as the would-up
kinks of lunatic fancy, and shocking symptoms of disease.

440　The Jerome J. Hill collection is in the Minneapolis Institute of Arts.

It must have been a tremendous pleasure for young Mr. Widener and a host of budding American painters to read this article, despite its sometimes awkward wording.

We have to return to chapter 1: Mary Berenson's January 10, 1914, letter (in Hadley 1987: 504-05) to Isabella Stewart Gardner about her visit to the Van Horne mansion. Van Horne was in bed and Mr. Berenson nursed his cold on the couch. In the same letter Mary B. commented on the Van Horne collection:

> The usual acres of Barbizon output greet us here, some of your beloved Rembrandts, a few real Goyas and false Velásquezes, endless "English School" and French XVIII Century" pictures, Japanese knickknacks enough to bury you – and all dreary and horrible, and affording unending satisfaction to the owners.

After the Berensons' visit, Van Horne's secretary informed Bourgeois, on January 12, that Van Horne was not yet able to sit up but was so much improved that he expected from day to day to see the end of his troubles.[441] The secretary proudly added:

> He had had a visit from the Berensons on Friday, Saturday and Sunday, but unfortunately he was not able to see much of Mr. Berenson for he did not wish to keep him too long in his room. However, he was most favorably impressed by both Mr. and Mrs. Berenson. While he does not feel quite sure that he correctly understands your letter, he takes it as meaning that he may expect the pleasure of a visit from you next Sunday, [and] hopes by that time to be able to move about the house.

441   Letter in VHFF (2/3).

As we saw, the "favourable impression" was not reciprocal, the Berensons had not enjoyed their visit. However, let's return to someone who certainly had enjoyed visiting Van Horne in Montreal – Abraham Bredius. On January 17 the *American Art News* reported Dr. Bredius' departure for Europe as follows: "Dr. Abraham Bredius, and his colleague, Dr. Kronig, who have been on a tour of inspection of American Art Museums and private collections, will sail for Bremen en route to The Hague, Tuesday next on the Kronprinzessin Cecilie."

By the end of January, Van Horne was feeling much better. On January 29 he replied to Van Slochem's letter of the 27th saying that, for the past week, he had been able to sit up for part of each day, "now seven or eight hours, and attend to a little business." [442] Van Slochem must have conveyed some concerns previously, because Van Horne went on:

If the bulk of the Morgan things are sold I can well imagine the effect on the Art Market but I can hardly believe that Mr. Morgan has any serious intention in that way yet.[443] Anyway, I hope it is not going to result in driving you out. I am glad to hear that you are coming up a week from Sunday. I expect to be hobbling about the house by that time.

Meanwhile, nothing much had been heard from Nardus. He seems to have been seriously out of the loop allowing others

---

442   Letter in VHFF (7/14).
443   It could well be that the Morgan sale did indeed put lots of porcelain on the money-tight market. According to Gross (2009: 117) in 1913 Duveen sold to Junior [Rockefeller] the best of the Garland – J. P. Morgan Chinese porcelain collection.

to take care of his art-dealership while he engaged in playing chess. Winter (2009) has the following:[444]

Another win by Nardus, played at the Café de la Régence, was published on pages 103-104 of *La Stratégie*, March 1913:

Paris, January 1913

"Hunt Opening"

1 b4 d5 **2** Bb2 Bf5 **3** d4 e6 **4** a3 Nf6 **5** e3 Bd6 **6** c4 c6 **7** c5 Bc7 **8** Bd3 O-O **9** Bxf5 exf5 **10** Qd3 Ne4 **11** Ne2 Qg5 **12** g3 Nd7 **13** Nbc3 Ndf6 **14** f3 Nxc3 **15** Bxc3 Rae8 **16** Bd2 Qh5 **17** Kf2

On February 6 Bourgeois wrote to Van Horne's secretary, Anslow, about another attempt to visit. He said it would be on Sunday 8th, but that he would have to return to New York the same night.[445] "Therefore I am writing to ask you if you will be good enough to get me a ticket and drawing-room, if possible via the Rutland road, for Sunday night."

Van Slochem must have written again to say he would visit on Sunday 8, the same day as Bourgeois, but from the following letter it seems he did not make it after all. On Monday, 9 February, Van Horne wrote to "Dear Mr. Van Slochem" to let him know that he was sorry he had not been able to make it on Sunday. He added that he himself, "was getting on as well as can be expected and for the past four days I have been able to take a drive about town." [446]

Van Slochem still kept in touch and reported some good news on February 17.[447] He said he had had the pleasure of a

---

444   See: http://www.chesshistory.com/winter/extra/nardus.html (last accessed in October 2014).
445   Letter in VHFF (2/1).
446   Letter in VHFF (7/14).
447   Letter in VHFF (7/14).

visit by Sir Edmund Walker, "who also liked the Goya very much and upon his return would see Mr. Shepherd." He continued:

> I took it upon my responsibility to ask less than V.G.'s price to me "so as to receive some cash in hand." When I meet you again, I will than explain to you, my intention! As to my final settlement with him if that sale goes all right. No doubt you will hear from Sir Edmund Walker. Glad you have done away the crutches.

The next day Van Horne dictated the following letter to his secretary for Van Slochem.[448] He said that he [Van Horne] was glad to hear that Sir Edmund Walker would talk with Dr. Shepherd about the Goya, "for I should like much to see it go to Ottawa. I am still using crutches but to-day I have been able to walk a little without them."

The secretary – we might assume it was still Mr. Anslow – asked Bourgeois on February 22 to please forward the address of Mr. Berenson and let Van Horne's secretary know whether Mr. Berenson was still in New York.[449] (It might indicate that Van Horne still had more paintings he wanted to have inspected.) The letter ended by saying Van Horne hoped that Bourgeois was keeping well and that his exhibition of paintings would prove to be a decided success.

A bit earlier that month, on February 14, *American Art News* reported under the heading NEW PICTURES AT DEALERS that: The new Bourgeois Galleries, no. 668 Fifth Ave., at 53 St. will open to the public next Tuesday, Feb. 17. The galleries occupy the top floors of the handsome new gray stone building, just

---

448   Letter in VHFF (7/14).
449   Letter in VHFF (2/3).

opposite St. Thomas Church, and are exceedingly well appointed and lit."

Probably because Bourgeois had been very busy, more than
a week went by before he replied to Van Horne on February 26
from his new location. Obviously elated, he wrote:[450]

I opened my new galleries last week, of which I sent you
enclosed a catalogue. I think it a great success and all the
articles in the papers are very enthusiastic. People are especially interested to see old and modern art together, and
when you see Van Gogh's landscape which I have hanging
between two Monticelli's, you will be convinced he was an
absolutely classical master.

The primitives are a sensation for everybody and especially the Patinir and the Balding Green provoke general
admiration. From morning till evening there are people
coming and especially last week when I saw nearly every
day one hundred visitors and had the chance to meet
some very fine people who, I think, in time will come to be
clients.

I also have some business in view, which I hope will be
settled when the exhibition is ended. But for one thing I
am very sorry, that you were not here when I opened and
that you had not the first glance at the exhibition. You
have encouraged me during the last years so much and
helped me with your valuable advice, that I owe you very
much and sincere thanks. It would have been for me the
greatest pleasure to have your criticism, which I value
higher than that of anyone else in this country. The idea to
hang old and modern together comes really from you in-
sofar as I have seen in your house that you dared to do that
for years against the opinion of all the other collectors.

---

450   Letter in VHFF (2/1).

That is not only an original but a logical one and it will help people to understand the way art developed in the last century and that the point here we are today had to be reached logically.

You find in the *American Art News* and in all the other papers, descriptions of the galleries so I do not need to give you an account of that. The things really look fine and some of them better than ever before. The Chinese head, which arrived, is in the entrance room and people who understand this kind of art are overwhelmed by its quality. The piece is far better than the photograph I showed you could make me believe and when I unpacked it I was myself astonished that I made such a fine stroke.

I just heard that your Han Kan is published by Binyon, in his new edition. I have written to get it. As more and more I see Chinese painting, I begin to understand how rare such a piece is and how difficult it is to get anything finer. The Metropolitan Museum just bought over a hundred Chinese paintings from Mr. Ferguson. Matsuki, who is here in New York, and I went there last Sunday and we agreed that in the whole lot there are only four that are worth while to be considered as art. Chinese painting seems now to be the fashion in New York because everybody is asking about them and as there are more clients, the greater will be the difficulty to find them. Therefore I am very glad you bought your painting in a time when but few had the appreciation of this kind art.

I heard that Sir Edmund Walker, who was here last week and was very much pleased to see my exhibition, speaks with great enthusiasm about painting I sold him. I think you must have helped him a little to understand it because at the time they bought it, I don't think they really knew how valuable the piece was they were buying.

I wanted very much to come to Montreal to tell you all that has happened in the last week but visitors keep me so busy that I don't think it will be possible. I hope that you will soon be able to go out and that you will come over to New York to see the exhibition.

I hope you received my letter concerning Berenson's address. He is now, as far as I know, away on a trip and I don't know when he is coming back. That is also the reason why I have not seen him at my exhibition. I am just reading his book, "The Study and Criticism of Italian Art," in which he published so many interesting things and started the famous discussion about Amigo di Botticelli. I wrote to him a few days ago, inviting him to come and I think that at the beginning of next week I shall have the pleasure of seeing him.

Fourteen days later *American Art News*, of February 28, under the heading NEW BOURGEOIS GALLERIES, published a lengthy description of its five rooms, giving a vivid impression of the gallery's ambiance. The writer gave readers a "tour" of the exhibition, starting with the ride up in the elevator, which was "draped with red hangings" and then led readers into a room "hung with a soft pinkish gray brocaded silk." This was the room where the Chinese and Japanese paintings and sculptures, including the head of Buddha, were exhibited. At this point, the reporter commented that the Buddha was "extraordinary in expression and modeling."

The writer then guided the reader into the Room of Moderns, where the walls (also covered with a pinkish gray brocaded silk) were covered with Manets, Monets, Van Gogh, Toulouse de Lautrec, Monticelli and Van Gogh. Commenting that visitors' appetites had now been "whetted for old masters," the writer described the third room, where "old Masters of Quality" such as a Tiepolo, were displayed against a background of rose mauve brocaded silk. Finally, the writer described the two smaller rooms, one in red and one in green, that contained Flinck, Moreelse, Puga, Van Dijck, El Greco, Brouwer, Van Scorel, Patiner, Tiso and Tintoretto.

The article concludes with: "Mr. Bourgeois has certainly made an auspicious entry into the ranks of leading New York dealers, with this initial display."

Van Slochem's letter of March 3, written from 477 Fifth Avenue, sounded a bit desperate. He obviously wanted to stay in touch with Van Horne, even though the latter was going to leave for Europe on April 8.[451] After asking after Van Horne's health, he wrote that "if I do not hear anything soon from Sir Edmund Walker or from Dr. Shepherd, I shall give up all hopes of selling to the Museum [in Montreal]; can you give me any encouragement? I have written VG quite a letter; have you heard anything from him and have you written him? We have had a big storm here, the heaviest snowfall for years."

On March 4 Van Horne replied to Van Slochem that he was improving but was still on crutches, so he couldn't hope to travel to New York until the end of the month at the earliest.[452] About the business Van Horne added:

> Doctor Shepherd came in to see me the other day and spoke of your Goya "A Man's Portrait," with which Sir Edmund Walker had been much impressed. I told him that I regarded it as a very important example of Goya and hoped the Government would buy it. They will soon be able to do so because they have got a grant of $100 000.00 and their disposition is to buy important things rather than little things. I have been so busy to clear up my old business matters, that I have not yet written Van Gelder, expect to so within a few days.
>
> P.S.
>
> I have just learned that Doctor Shepherd will be in New York, at The Belmont, on Saturday and for some days, and

451   Letter in VHFF (7/14).
452   Letter in VHFF (7/14).

that Sir Edmund Walker will be in New York at the same time. It may be interesting to you to know this but don't let them suspect that you know that I have made any recommendation to them about the Goya.

Perhaps fearing that his last letter would not reach Bourgeois, Van Horne's secretary wrote Bourgeois on March 5 that Van Horne wanted him to know that Sir Edmund Walker and Doctor Shepherd would be in New York Saturday and for a few days thereafter: "He thinks you may not wish to be away from NY during their visit."[453] Sick or not, Van Horne kept looking out for the interests of his dealers. A few days later, on March 10, Van Horne dictated another letter to Van Slochem, telling him that Doctor Shepherd and his associates were considerably interested in the Goya:[454]

I urged them by all means to secure it, which seemed to clinch the matter so far as he was concerned. I am very glad they have taken it. I am shocked and grieved at poor Blakeslee having shot himself. I had seen nothing of it in the newspapers. I am surprised as well because I thought he had been very prosperous in the past few years. I have always had a warm regard for him and I am very, very sorry.[455] I am much pleased to hear that you have made a

---

453 Letter in VHFF (2/3).
454 Letter in VHFF (7/14).
455 Blakeslee's suicide was not so much the result of not being prosperous anymore: "In the early twentieth century, my father, Robert C. Vose, bought several eighteenth-century English portraits from the leading New York dealer in that field, T. J. Blakeslee. That contact ended in 1913 when Blakeslee sold a Thomas Lawrence portrait of Lady Mellville, with a fine provenance, to the great collector George Hearn. Within weeks, Blakeslee sold Robert Vose an excellent copy of Lady Mellville accompanied by the same provenance. When this dishonesty was discovered, it led to Blakeslee's suicide by gunshot," in http://www.vosegalleries.com/tips/index.cfm#h_5 (last accessed in March 2014).

favorable settlement of Van Gelder's BC matter. I feared that he would not get a cent out of it. My second carbuncle gave me something of a set back, trust it will quite eliminate the rheumatic poison. Aside from that I am feeling as well as ever.

The increasing unrest in Europe – 1914 would not be a good one for Van Horne's European friends. Fortunately, in March 1914 Van Horne still got good news from them. On March 11 Bredius, writing from the Hotel Cusset in Paris, thanked Van Horne for his letter.[456] After saying he hoped Van Horne would "be more careful for himself," Bredius continued:

You may not forget you have so many friends who want to see you still many, many years healthy and strong. I must tell you what happened these days in my house. A man, Austrian, living in Brussels came to The Hague with a picture, master unknown, dirty and looking unimportant. It was Bacchus and Ariadne, small figures, near a rock, with a dark sky and the sea to the right.[457] Much the disposition of my Andromeda by Rembrandt, Rembrantisk in colour.

According to *American Art News* of March 14, 1914, the strain and anxiety that had led to Blakeslee's death by his own hand was caused by "an over-extended line of costly foreign pictures," and the "leasing and furnishing" of his new galleries in the expectation of a good season, "which proved the reverse."

456 Letter in VHFF (6/2).

457 Blankert (1978/1980/1990: 222-23) lists, in Dutch, Ariadne en Bacchus under no. 169: "Origin about 1912 [should be 1914]; provenance acquired by J. O. Kronig about 1912 [...] Kronig published the piece as a newly discovered Rembrandt [...] "According to me the piece mostly resembles a Van Uyttenbroeck." After cleaning, his *"signature and date 1631 appeared."* On December 30, 2009, Albert Blankert e-mailed (in Dutch): "Currently one thinks that this painting is by Pieter Potter (father of Paulus). The attribution by Kronig is only in my Bredius catalogue." See: http://www.museumbredius.nl/schilders/potter_nl.htm (last accessed in February 2014). Also see Blankert (2006: 47-59) about Bredius' "alarming pace" of discovering "new Rembrandts and Vermeers and Kronig's "discovery" of Vermeer's *The Emmausgangers*," which caused the Han van Meegeren scandal.

I told the man, that I believed it to be by an unknown scholar of Rembrandt and that I did not want it. Mr. Kronig who is in London, but visits me now and then, was just staying in my house. I went upstairs to show him the picture. **At the same moment** he saw it, he exclaimed that is the Great Man! I said: look carefully, there are weaknesses, it is not good enough for himself. He declared: I **must** buy that picture, will you lend me the money? He bought it **1 500 francs**. We went then to the Mauritshuis to compare it with my Andromeda, which is painted in a stronger bolder way. But the picture **could** stand its neighbourhood. Kronig went then to our present best restorer and had the varnish revived/regenerated/ and . . . the picture **signed** R 1631. Perhaps the whole name has been on it, but the R is perfectly genuine and clean. Kronig will publish his picture in *Onze Kunst* and send you a copy of it. I bought a very fine Rembrandt drawing **signed** and dated 1632. Bode has published in *Der Kunstfreund* of February an article on newly discovered Rembrandts. **Six** of these "Rembrandts" are not by the Master, e.g a large picture, in the last volume of Sedelmeyer's booklets, he calls it Simson, but it is a David, with white Turban. This is a **true early auto**-portrait by Ferd. Bol. The same as in Mr. Taft's coll. You have only to compare them. Mr. Taft has sent me a photo of that interesting picture. As they try to sell that large early Bol as a Rembrandt in America, I **warn** you, I saw it in New York, but know the picture since **8 years** when I saw it in London. **A fine Bol**, a young Lady in red, with red hat and feather, inspired in Rembrandt's Saskia, was sold last week in London (I was there) at Christies for **2 100 guineas**. I am going to write a book on Bol, but cannot find the time for it. With kindest regards to your son and daughter and with many thanks again for the charming days in your house.

Please tell Dr. Shepherd of Mr. Kronig's good luck! He has also a pastel by Latour which he found in a shop in

Florence for 25 francs and one of the **finest** Rembrandt drawings (£20) and an immense easy but very fine picture by Metsu (£2!! in London) etc.

Bourgeois apologized on March 13[458] for not having been able to stay a few days after his visit the previous Sunday and announced that he had sent Van Horne two photos, "exquisite in drawing" by T. Lautrec. He added that he had also bought a fine pastel by the same artist. Bourgeois subsequently asked whether Van Horne had heard about Blakeslee's death. "I was very much affected, when I read it, I am so sorry for Mrs. Blakeslee. Business picking up slowly in N.Y. but I have confidence that we shall have a splendid spring season."

Van Slochem, seemingly unaware of the war clouds gathering around Europe and the fact that the war would affect America, proudly told Van Horne on May 19, 1914, that he had just arranged something, "that may surprise you.[459] I have taken a lease on the premises for another year at a reduced rental: for my own account. It worried me considerable to break up the place and I finally made a proposition to the landlord, which they accepted. I should very much like to pay you a visit and shall be pleased to hear from you which day next week will be convenient to you, and also let me know how you are getting on."

Only two days later, March 21, Van Horne told Van Slochem that he had received his letter of the 19th, had had many visitors, would be glad to see him anytime, and was also glad that he would stay in New York for another year.[460] Van Horne

---

458   Letter in VHFF (2/1).
459   Letter in VHFF (7/14).
460   Letter in VHFF (7/14).

added, "I shall be glad to be of use to you in every way possible. I still have to use my crutches but am getting better day by day."

The previous day, March 20, Van Horne apologized to Bourgeois for neglecting to reply, saying that he had had many visitors, but would be:[461]

> delighted to have you come up. I am so much better, that I have been able to get about the house to-day with a walking stick in stead of crutches. I have received the two T. Lautrec pictures and am very much impressed by them – by the young woman particularly, and I hope soon to have an opportunity to see the originals.[462] I may possibly be able to go as far as New York within two or three weeks. I want very much to see your new quarters.
>
> Doctor Mayer remained two days with us. I think I have already told you that Mr. Berenson regarded my so-called Murillo, Young Man with a Stick as a Velasquez and not by Murillo. Doctor Mayer confirms this, and says there is no possible doubt about it and he thinks the picture is probably the long lost portrait of Fonseca who appears in one or two of Velasquez' compositions.

One day later, on March 21, Bourgeois wrote Van Horne that he was delighted to hear that his knees were better, that things were quiet in New York, and that most of the dealers were leaving for Europe: "I shall possibly stay till the beginning of May; having several good business in view, I don't want to miss opportunities." [463]

---

461   Letter in VHFF (2/1).
462   The Wickenden catalogue does not mention any work by Toulouse de Lautrec (1864-1901). Cat. 1933 does in no. 147: In the Garden and no. 148: At the Café.
463   Letter in VHFF (2/1).

Back to Van Horne's sick room. Bourgeois, who had made an earlier appointment to visit, mentioned on March 26 that he could come on April 3rd.[464] His announcement sounds as if he had missed opportunities, or there had been no opportunities. His letter suggests that purchasing is akin to investing:

> The Metropolitan Museum has in the meantime taken the Head of Kwan-on in stone and also the Japanese wood statue of Bodhisattva as the trustee refused the funds for the marvellous drawing of Bezat, which you probably re-call, and Dr. Valentiner did not want to give back to me. I presented it myself as a gift to the Metropolitan Museum.
>
> I think that is a very nice start here in New York and I am only sorry that you did not take the Head because it is everywhere regarded now as the finest piece of sculpture [that] has ever left China. Dr. Valentiner intends to pub-lish the piece now in "Art in America."
>
> I have some other things in view especially with the Patinir and the Puga, which probably will go to other American Museums. Also I have several clients on my modern paintings and I would be very happy when I would sell some of those because they are not only wonderful and selected things, but also not expensive, and will rise in value from year to year.

On March 28, 1914, Van Horne replied to Bourgeois in his usual way, saying that the postponement of the visit was fine with him, that his general health was excellent, that he had discarded his crutches and was glad that the Metropolitan had taken the Buddha head.[465] He also agreed that he should have

---

464   Letter in VHFF (2/1).
465   Letter in VHFF (2/1).

taken it himself, "but the first photo you brought from Paris gave no idea of size and importance." Was Van Horne backing off because he had no idea about the size, or did he doubt how much a Buddha head would enhance his collection or, could it have been that finances started to restrain him a bit?

After having spent a few days with the Van Hornes, Bourgeois, writing from his gallery on April 6 said that he had arrived in New York that morning:[466]

> And the first thing is to thank you for your kind hospitality. I passed not only three exquisite days in your society but was especially delighted that you were so much better and that you will soon be as well as before.
>
> I have quite forgotten to receipt my statement as I wanted to do it and I beg you to send it to me in order that I may promptly acknowledge the receipt of your last check.
>
> I would be very glad if you would take the Puga as you told me yesterday. I send you enclosed a copy of the arrangement, which we did before in which you see that the Puga was counted as $5 000. Perhaps we could make another arrangement if you would consider the purchase of some other things which interest you so much before you became ill or which I have bought in the meantime. I do not dare to recommend anything to you because I would not have you think that I wish to induce you to do some business. It might however interest you that I recall to you the things about which we had some correspondence and for that reason I am sending you with this letter a list with descriptions.[467] The prices are fixed and lower than those pictures of the same kind brought in public sales in Paris:

---

466   Letter in VHFF (2/3).
467   This is the list of "things" Bourgeois had for sale – none of them made it to Van Horne's collection.

Rembrandt 4 000

Album 8 paintings (Chinese) 3 000

Painting, lady, Ming period 1 000

Antonio Puga 5 000

. . . . 49 000

In payment Del Mazzo 4 000

So: 45 000

April 17 Bourgeois wrote to "Dear Sir William" that he had sent him a cutting from the *New York Herald* about his newly discovered Velasquez:[468]

You cannot imagine how all New York is stirred up. Thank you very much for your kind letter and the letter of Mr. Greenshields, which I am returning with this. It was very kind of you that you took this matter up and I am very thankful to you for that.

I think that Mr. Greenshields makes a mistake by saying that he has seen the picture in New York. He must have mistaken it for another picture that he has seen; this picture of which I gave you the photograph is to day in a private collection in Boston and was bought in the time directly in London from Colnaghi & Obach.[469] It is

---

• VGogh: Orchard of Artist House 5 000
• G. Flinck: Rabbi (recog. by Hofstede de Groot) 25 000
• Paulus Moreelse: Elizabeth Stuart 12 000
• Lucas: Bull fight 12 000
• Cezanne: Self-portrait.. 6 000
• Lautrec: Portrait of woman 25 000
• Puga: Old woman in kitchen 5 000
• Pacchiarotto: Madonna and Child + Jerome 12 000

468   Letter in VHFF (45/7).
469   Colnachi & Obach was founded in London by Giovanni Battista Torre in 1760. In 1894 the company took in Deprez and Otto Gutekunst, in which company Gustave Mayer was partner. In 1911 both London companies merged. See: http://www.

as stated in the picture itself on the upper left corner a Portrait of Isabella Angus.[470] The picture is an exquisite work of Art and I regard it as one of the finest examples of this man and it surpasses in skin quality anything I have ever seen of Matthew Maris. What Mr. Greenshields calls "Fairy Quality" is more of a literary conception of Art and cannot be applied to a Portrait, which is painted after life.

Business in New York is very quiet as it probably is everywhere in the world. Hoping that your knee and your general health are progressing...

Van Slochem, back in Antwerp, wrote on April 27 that he hoped Van Horne would now be underway to Cuba. As usual, he started about lamps, but then he went on about furniture. "While looking for these, I found a bureau [...] a fine old Louis XV bureau, has three long drawers with carving of the period.[471] I am going to give it to a cabinet-maker and it will look fine; when he is through with it! This will take about a fortnight; it needs overhauling and cleaning; this all will be done by the time I hear from you, where you want me to forward this bureau! As I do not know if you want this for Montreal?"

Meanwhile Van Slochem had received Van Horne's letter of April 21 with the enclosed letter from Mr. Abbot. Van Slochem

britishmuseum.org/research/search_the_collection_database/term_details. aspx?bioId=128766 (last accessed February 2014).

470   Van Horne must have decided not to buy *The Portrait of Isabella Angus* (1887) by Matthijs Maris. In 1939 it was donated to the Stedelijk Museum of Schiedam. Cf.: http://www.stedelijkmuseumschiedam.nl/nl/component/content/ article/9-uncategorised/171-de-periode-van-1938-tot-1952 (last accessed February 2014). Isabella Angus, daughter of art dealer Craibe Angus, was the widow of art dealer E. J. van Wisselingh. M. Maris lived in London from 1888 until his death in 1907. The Van Wisselinghs gave him a monthly allowance and he had the "good soul" Mrs. Briggs take care of his modest household. (Heijbroek and Wouthuysen 1999: 60).

471   Letter in VH (7/13).

replied on May 8 saying that he was sorry that the board had not yet made up their minds about the Aart de Gelder, and that he was delighted to hear that Van Horne was leaving for Cuba. He thanked Van Horne for the Maple syrup and the sugar, and went on: [472]

> Now something in **confidence**, in settling my account with V.G., this depends upon payment for the Goya I sold to the National Gallery (Ottawa)! If you upon your return from Cuba should think of it perhaps you could mention something to Dr. Shepherd that they do not keep me waiting for that till the fall of course when V.G. asked me to wait till the Goya was paid. I could not very well insist so I said all right! I have so far seen him only once since my return; and then he felt very much worried and not at all pleased with that I have done! I shall have to wait till I get to Paris to arrange something for my American business and if you could advise me in some way I shall thank you very much! Hoping this will reach you in good health.

This sounds as if the relationship between Van Gelder and Van Slochem was becoming even cooler.

Anyway, on May 11 Bredius thanked Van Horne for his letter and mentioned he had found something in a document about Van Horne's family: "The father of the clergyman had a very high position one of the Chief Director of the West Indian Company." [473] He then said he hoped that Van Horne would again be in perfect health and went on about his partner Kronig who had had "very good luck, through his eminent eyes he discovered and bought at small prices! **Three Rembrandts,**

---

472   Letter in VHFF (7/13).
473   Letter in VHFF (6/2).

one Titian and a **magnificent** Hercules Seghers!! He is making now for himself quite a nice gallery!! Hoping to hear soon from you."

Meanwhile, Bourgeois had returned to Europe, but had left J. C. Kindlund behind to take care of his gallery. On June 3 Kindlund wrote to Van Horne:[474]

> We are sending your painting c/o Blaiklock Bros. the painting of the Madonna and Child, which Mr. Bourgeois had transferred from panel to canvas. It has been at the Lincoln Storage for some time and through a misunderstanding that it was not sent to you before Bourgeois departure for Europe. Will you be kind enough to inform us as to whether or not you wish the Bronze Head which you asked Mr. Bourgeois to keep for you, sent to Montreal and if so, what value we will have to place upon it.

However, on June 6 Van Horne's secretary replied to Kindlund that he should not ship the Bronze Head because Van Horne was now on his way to Europe and would likely not be back in Montreal for five or six weeks.

On June 13 Van Slochem wrote from Amstelhotel, Amsterdam to Van Horne, who was staying at the Carlton Hotel in London to say that he was looking forward to their meeting in Antwerp:[475]

> In reply to yours from Montreal with reference to the Hohan (Buddhist apostle) of the Tang period, I beg to say that I attended to it at once. I have send it in the Burlington Magazine and have secured also the Ostasiatische

---

474   Letter in VHFF (2/3).
475   Letter in VHFF (7/14).

Zeitschrift containing Dr. Kummel's article and wrote to a friend of mine in Paris who asked me to come over! But unfortunately as I was about to leave I received a telegram from Amsterdam with the sad news that my father was very ill and slowly passing away. I than left immediately for Amsterdam and arrived in time to be present while he died. The funeral is taking place tomorrow, Sunday and shall go to Paris Monday and shall be in Antwerp Tuesday evening late. I telegraphed to the Carlton Hotel asking about when I may expect you in Antwerp. I could perhaps then stay in Paris a day longer...

As is apparent from Van Slochem's letter, Van Horne went again to Europe. According to Vaughan (1920: 363) he went with his son "and M. Klechkowski, a member of the French diplomatic service who had held the French consulship in Montreal, he travelled through the châteaux district along the Loire – a treat he had long promised himself [...] He bought a few pictures in Paris and purchased an exquisite screen by Matthew Maris." Vaughan goes on about Van Horne, "being crowded with invitations and financial consultations."

On June 17, Mr. Reid, manager of the E. Wisselingh Gallery, 14, Grafton Street, Bond Street, London W., wrote that he had just heard that Van Horne was in London and had taken:[476]

the liberty of inviting you to see our W. Willem de Zwart's pictures which we have just completed hanging. W. de Zwart has now recovered from a long illness and is doing excellent work and we think his pictures will interest

---

476 Letter in VHFF (3/27).

you.[477] Mr. Eilers would be very much obliged of you would let him know when you propose visiting Amsterdam.

As Vaughan said, Van Horne was "crowded with invitations." On June 21, Van Slochem let Van Horne know that he had reserved a fine room and bath for him in the Grand Hotel and that he would wait for him "if you let me know time of arrival." [478]

On June 24 Van Gelder wrote to Van Horne and his son:[479]

A few lines to welcome you in Belgium. I would have come personally but am laid in bed with a swollen face, it will be all-better by tomorrow. I wish you would feel that there is a friend in Brussels ready to receive you with open arms if you would care to rest for a few days under his roof. My wife asks me to say to you that she would be but too happy to have you and Ben come, there is room enough and no bother. I am also anxious to talk with you about our misunderstandings of late and clear things away. I have been suffering the last two months with rheumatism in a slight degree but sufficiently to have my doctor advise me to spend three weeks at some Spa, we might perhaps combine. With kindest regards from my wife and a kiss from Sonia [Van Gelder's daughter, born in 1906].

After Van Horne had been visiting and purchasing in Amsterdam, Eilers wrote him on June 27:[480]

477 For Willem de Zwart (1862-1931) see: https://rkd.nl/en/explore/images/195392 (last accessed October 2014).
478 Letter in VHFF (7/14).
479 Letter in VHFF (7/22).
480 Letter in VHFF (3/27).

The next day of your visit, the owner of the Satsuma bird you purchased – Mr. Westendorp – telephoned us up and was desperate, that he sold his bird, his talisman, as he called it, which he had from his boyhood. He offered it for sale in a moment of extremely down feeling, as soon as he realized that his bird was gone, he felt that his best friend was going to leave him ... he does not know that you are the purchaser as we never mention the name of our clients, but he will lose 1 000 florins, he will give for nothing the best piece of his pottery, if he can get back his talisman. I told him that I would write the purchaser and await his answer before sending off the bird. Please let me know what I have to do in this business.

P.S.: Mr. M. Schildt of Rotterdam forwarded us an oil painting and a drawing, which we will join to the pictures you kindly bought.[481]

Isa van Wisselingh's letter of July 9 to Van Horne from Frithwood House, Northwood, Herts, shows that news of his whereabouts was spreading like wildfire.[482]

Miss Cary, art critic from NY was here about a fortnight ago. She here liked the picture I have by Daumier. I said you were interested in his work. I thought you would like to see it. This would give me great pleasure. If you cared to see it, and have not the time to come here, I could send it to Mr. Reid in London, so you can see it there.

481 For Martin Schildt (1867-1921), see https://rkd.nl/nl/explore/artists/90085 (last accessed October 2014).
482 Letter in VHFF (3/27).

Two days later Isa van Wisselingh thanked Van Horne for his kind letter and said she would to be glad to see him on Monday or Tuesday:[483]

> I much regret that I have a business appointment on Monday in London from 12 o'clock to 3.20 afternoon, but I will return to Northwood with train of 3.20. Lunch on Tuesday. A good train leaves the Great Central Station at 12.35. Kindly tell me the train you will come by! I shall send to meet you.
>
> I should like Mr. Maris to meet you sometimes; as a rule it is difficult to get him from home – I could if you like accompanying you to see him after Tuesday. Just to call on him.

Isa van Wisselingh's English was far from perfect, so perhaps her phrase "to meet you sometimes," when referring to Mr. Maris, should have been "to meet you again." As we know, Caroline Pierson quoted Van Horne's daughter, "Papa *was a personal friend of Maris on whom he always called when in London.*"

On July 12 Bode wrote to Van Horne and enclosed a photo of the four pictures Van Horne must have been asking about. Bode was unable to give an opinion but used the occasion to boost Kleinberger's New York location:[484]

> You will see how little I know! Not for one of the pictures I am able to give you the name of the master with certainty. I hear from Dr. Friedländer that Willems [illeg.] & Kleinberger in Paris bought lately the marvellous [painting] by

---

483   Letter in VHFF (3/27).
484   Letter in VHFF 8/11).

Rubens (Virgin with the child and several young female saints). It is one of the finest and most charming pictures of the master. But they ask f400 000. Kleinberger has 2 portraits by Titian, bought from the Giustiniano Barbaryo family. A member of the Barbaryo family bought these and other pictures (now in the Hermitage) immediately after the death of Titian. One is probably only finished by Titian (the Dogen Gritt), but the pupil of a Dogen Barbaryo is by Titian's own hand entirely. You should try to buy it from Kl., who did not pay a very high price for the 2 pictures. I think you could get the pupil portrait at about DM18 000 or even a little less. If you like to have photos of the pictures write the Kleinberger's place at New York.

Isa van Wisselingh sent an invitation to Van Horne on July 13 in which she said if Van Horne would meet her on Wednesday, he would be sure "to find Mr. Maris at home." [485] That Van Horne duly accepted the invitation is evident from the July 15 copy of the bill of lading from E. van Wisselingh. (The Van Wisselings took care of Maris' upkeep and sold his paintings for him.) It concerned two cases of pictures which were to be shipped to Montreal.[486] The original of the bill of lading was

----

485 Letter in VHFF (3/27).
486 Copy of bill of lading in VHFF (3/27). One of these "pictures" is listed as VH 175, M. Maris (Amsterdam 1837–London 1917). *A Service to Isis*, (four paneled screen). Sir William showed this work to Matthew Maris in London after its purchase and received from his full assurance of its authenticity, and of his pleasure in seeing it again. From E. Van Wisselingh & Co. Amsterdam, 1914. ⊞: 10 000 (probably cost more). [Note dated April 9, 1964:] Sir W. paid $17 500 shortly before his death."

In September 1915 *The New York Times* reported that the four panels were painted for Daniel Cottier some thirty years ago, and that these came from the collection of the late Hamilton Bruce.

The panels, now in the Amsterdam Rijksmuseum, go with the following text: "In 1878, art dealer E. J. van Wisselingh took the advice of the painter Matthijs Maris and bought a four-panel screen in Paris. However, Van Wisselingh's employer, Cottier, was less than pleased with the purchase. So he got Maris to work

sent to Sir William at Piccadilly Hotel, London: "+ Draft on London £600, for equivalent of $3 000. Order E. J. van Wisselingh. Enclosed bill value $500 – Weight 116 kg."

Obviously, the Van Wisselingh hospitality paid off for them, as had Van Slochem's. This is apparent from the following documents of July 21:[487]

Enclosed please find particulars of shipment and also bill of the seven lamps and the chest of drawers. The three cases have been shipped by this week's steamer from here per Dominion express Co. Until the present I have had no news from Mr. Perzynski in answer to my last letter to him from London and very likely the incident is closed.[488] The expense of my trips to Paris, London, Berlin telegraphing etc. amounted to £50.0.0. I hope you had fine trip across and that the family are all having a fine summer at St. Andrews.

A few days later, on July 25, Van Slochem let Van Horne know that Mr. Perzynski offered the Torso for DM35 000 and if he wished to make an offer, "it would be best to cable me. In my letter I forgot to write that Max Rooses died a few days after

on the panels and sold the pictures as genuine Marises to a Scottish collector. In 1913 the Dancing Figures – by now framed as separate paintings – came up for sale again. A Dutch collector [that was Van Horne] bought them for the enormous sum of 38 000 guilders. Once again the panels disappeared from public view for years, until they were recently presented to the Rijksmuseum. The owner realized that the paintings were by Matthijs Maris, but not that they formed a famous work, long presumed lost: the only piece of furniture Maris ever decorated." As said, *A Service to Isis* is now part of the Rijksmuseum collection under the name *Dancing Figures* (BK-2000-9) (Heijbroek 2008: 105).

The other painting Van Horne had bought was *View on Freiburg* that Maris painted in 1861. It is now in the Montreal Museum of Fine Arts.

487   Letter in VHFF (7/14).

488   Dr. Friedrich Perzynski (1871-1965) was art-historian for Japanese art. See: http:// de.wikipedia.org/wiki/Friedrich_Perzyński (last accessed February 2014).

we had seen him.[489] I suppose he was feeling bad already when we visited him." Van Horne was apparently still in a spending mood as Van Slochem went on: "As to Mr. Perzynski I had given up hopes to hear from him at all and I personally think that we may perhaps get it by making him an offer of 30 000 marks. Have you received the photos from M. Venier? Trusting to hear from you."

As we see, the description of Van Horne's collection as "eclectic" is justified. Not just Barbizons, paintings by Old Masters, bronzes and Buddha heads, but also ship models! On July 29 Van Slochem, staying at the Hotel Palais Royal, Amsterdam, informed Van Horne about a ship model. For a long time this item would sail through their wartime correspondence:[490]

By this you will note where I am at present. I have been asked to come here to see a fine ship of the **Period (1600)**. The same buyer who bought that ship at the last sale at Frederic Muller promised me that should he come across a fine ship he will let me know and so he kept his promise! And as to style and period it is not to be compared with that one sold at Fred. Muller.

This, which I have secured for you, is much finer! Probably you have still the photo of that one sold and by comparing the two you will come to the same conclusion. I had very little time to take it, or leave it, as there were many others after it [...] I am enclosing the receipt of what I paid and I am convinced that the man I got this from had not made too much profit on it and further more, some one

---

489 Letter in VHFF (7/14). Max Rooses (1839-1914) was a Belgian linguist, literature critic and from 1876 on curator of the Plantin-Moretus Museum in Antwerp. He wrote books on Rubens and Jordaen. See: http://www.dictionaryofarthistorians.org/roosesm.htm (last accessed in February 2014).

490 Letter in VHFF (7/13).

that was after it also was thunderstruck when he heard that it had been sold and wanted to know if he could get it by paying a profit. But I answered, this is out of the question; as I know that you do not wish me to devote my time and trouble going to Holland etc. etc. I leave the matter of commission entirely to you!

I would not have mentioned it at all, but I know your feeling in regard to that. I am enclosing receipt of payment of £275.0.0. And hope that it arrives in good condition and that you are delighted with it. I need not mention that the dealer asked me much more but I kept daggering on the price; and did the best I could; the cash payment had a great deal to do with it, owing to the European war scare. The outlook being very critical in Europe. Today here the stock exchange closed and at several exchange offices they refused me to change Belgian paper money into Dutch. Hoping the outcome will be better than it looks and that you and your family are enjoying a fine summer with best regards...

P.S. will invoice it for £100.0.0.

The invoice of July 29 reads: "Antique model of a sailor ship in wood frs. 2 500. Two thousand five hundred francs cost of packing included. Forwarded per Holland America Line from Rotterdam." And, on that same day Van Horne's secretary had Bourgeois know that, "in further reference to yours of June 3rd Sir William Van Horne had just returned from Europe. He would like the bronze head kept in New York until Mr. Bourgeois' return when some arrangements can be made to bring it to Montreal." [491]

491   Letter in VHFF (2/3).

GERMANY INVADES BELGIUM

That same day, July 29 Van Slochem, occupying himself with invoicing the sailing ship, did not know that on the previous day WWI had begun when Austria-Hungary declared war on Serbia. This war soon became a global conflict, affecting everyone and everything, Van Slochem's business included. His little sailing ship would never make it across the ocean as the war also affected Van Horne's purchasing. On Aug. 11 he wrote to Van Slochem:[492]

> I have your letter of July 25th. I am afraid that Dr. Persynski has to keep his Torso until the war is over, for nobody that I can think of can get any money now. I am exceedingly glad, as matters have turned out, that I did not load myself with his Lohan. If I had any ready money now I should lock it up and sit on the box. I have been very busy since my return as yet.

About money, Vaughan (1920: 367) writes that Van Horne had clung "for a score of years to some shares in a Vermont Powder company, which had been continually on the verge of liquidation. The necessities of the Allies now made these shares very valuable, and he [Van Horne] was able to sell them at an unexpectedly high figure." This might have been of some help to his cash flow, but it would prove not to be enough to his liking.

Van Slochem did not fare any better. His letter of August 17 contains an eye witness account of the war exploits in Belgium:[493]

---

492 Letter in VHFF (7/14).
493 Letter in VHFF (7/13).

Enclosed please find bill for the ship. Owing to the war the same could not be shipped from Antwerp. I instructed the shipper in Amsterdam to have it insured for three hundred pounds. This being two-hundred pounds above the cost price but this has been done in case the same should be seized while on the way to Canada by Germany or England. I hope nothing of the kind will happen and that the same will reach you all right. As you note, we are still in Antwerp! Terrible fighting taking place, a few hours away from us, a big battle is expected any moment! The military authorities are keeping everything as quiet as possible; here in Antwerp all Germans had to get out! The most prominent German businessmen have proven to be spies; several have been shot. Now and then troops of German soldiers with their officers pass our door as prisoners of war. I hope that we will have a good many changes on the map and that Germany will be the lower of all the colonies and that France will get Alsace Loraine back. From them! I note that Canada is also coming to our assistance. Lots of people say here in Antwerp that we are quite safe here!

And that the Germans will never be able to take Antwerp, therefore we remain where we are.

Another thing owing to the moratorium I have to be careful with expenditure from Van Gelder I heard nothing. A few days ago it looked as if Germans would be able to get to Bruxelles and a good many people left. Probably he also left. Very likely to London, this being the safest place to be. Since you left for Canada I have not heard from you. I hope a letter is on the way telling us that you are all well, same as this is leaving here. Hoping that those barbarous Germans will soon be wiped out and for centuries to come will remain powerless.

The month of August was not yet over. On August 24 Eilers Jr., writing from The Netherlands, thanked Van Horne for his letter "with enclosed London exchange for £2 000 in partly payment for the pictures you kindly bought." He went on:[494]

I am sorry that there is any misunderstanding regarding the little Corot, I thought you would take it but not pay it this year, therefore we sent it you together with the other pictures, but whatever you might decide in this matter, we always will agree.

I quite understand that reaching home you found financial matters in chaos, it is the same all over and what will be the end!

Who could have suggested at the time you were in Holland that in a few weeks whole Europe should be in war, the most terrible war ever came over the old country. Until the present our little country is free from war, but the greater part of our country is in a state of war. All over soldiers, no business, no money. The first week of the war it was very difficult to get exchanged bank paper from early in the morning until 4 o'clock a long file was standing before the Bank of the Netherlands to get their bank paper exchanged in silver or gold, the people had nearly lost their mind and made it very difficult to the bankers. Now all is more or less managed in the usual way, but there is a down feeling through the whole country, we do not know what the future will bring us and we do not get any trustful news from the battlefields.

Poor Belgium, which had nothing to do with the whole movement, wishing nothing else than to live in peace, has become the center of the battles. What we hear from fugitives is terrible, not to believe in a time that we might expect the people living in Europe too civilized to kill and

494   Letter in VHFFF (3/27).

murder each other like savages. And they do it in the name of God and with the Bible in their bloody hands.

I hope you will not get any trouble in Canada, your island is so near to the ocean, we feel however England too powerful on the sea to allow any foreign battleships in their waters.

You will understand that our kind of business is entirely dead, nothing doing. It was my intention to visit this fall Canada, but for the present I do not see how to get my pictures forwarded, and besides . . . is there any chance of doing business in Canada or America?

For the present I understand there is not, but suppose the war is over then I think there will be more chance to do business in your country than in Europe, if possible you would greatly oblige me to give me your opinion and advise in this matter. Hoping ...

Because Van Horne had planned to sit on his money, he did not want the torso, he did not want the ship model, and he did not want the Corot. Correspondence from this period on merely shows how the Van Horne collection could have looked if the Bosnian Serb student Gavrillo Princip, on June 28, 1914, had not assassinated Archuke Franz Ferdinand of Austria.

On August 25 Van Slochem, now staying at 115 St. Marks Road, North Kensington W., London, wrote Van Horne to confirm he had received both his letters of August 1 and August 7 with the enclosed draft £50.0.0:[495]

for which I thank you very much as I admit it came very useful, especially being payable in Pounds and in London, where I have taken a home at the above address with the

---

495   Letter in VHFF (7/13).

entire family. We all have been so nervous and upset of the pitiful scenes in Antwerp that I suddenly made up my mind, to get out of it! That what I personally witnessed of those poor refugees, you will no doubt read in the newspaper. If we only would have the satisfaction that those barbarous Germans would undergo the same tortures from other powerful nations, such as they have inflicted on the poor Belgians. They are paying bitterly for their bravery!! In order to protect Antwerp the most superb homes, and parks, outside of Antwerp, had to be sacrificed, especially near the frontier of Eschen, on the way to Holland. The homes had to be burned up and some of the finest trees cut down, a sight that nobody can picture. This will take years and years to recuperate.

I left with the entire family just in time to get the last boat from Ostend to Folkstone. The boat was packed, where there is only accommodation for about 800 passengers, there were about 3 000 including about half of them refugees of Gent, Bruges and Ostend, who all left their home; when they saw entering some Uhlans![496] Shooting brutally down old and young people that they met on the road before they entered these towns!

You are quite right, by saying no one can foresee this end! We all reached here safely and found a fine home with members of our family who had big enough home to take us all in and I left my Antwerp home in charge of trustworthy people, not to enter Antwerp again until the trouble is over.

---

496 Uhlans (in Polish: "Ułan;" "Ulan" in German) were Polish light cavalry armed with lances, sabres and pistols. The title was later used by lancer regiments in the Prussian and Austrian armies. Cf.: http://en.wikipedia.org/wiki/Uhlan (last accessed in February 2014).

As to coming over to America, I am not thinking of anything in the way of business and being settled down here, I shall have to make some plans.

Now Dear Sir William, I do not think that the ship for which I laid out £265.0.0 have reached you yet, as far as I understand the Dominion Express Co. in Amsterdam has forwarded it to you by the Holland America Line, but I need not explain to you the difficulty in exchange.

On July the 23rd the Fifth Avenue Bank has forwarded me a check to Paris of $14 000.00 and until today [the] same has not reached me yet. I cabled about it and they are looking into the matter. I am so sorry to ask you, but if you could send me a draft for that 275.0.0 it would come very useful. I took plenty of Belgium money here to London, but under the present conditions some banks here refuse to exchange it and those money changers are willing to change it at about 20% or 25% less than the actual value, and I have been advised by a banker, not to change it, if I can carry myself over for a few months, when it will surely be alright again!

As to Van Gelder, I have not heard or seen anything from him since the fourth of August. I have inquired right and left, but the post is very much mixed up on the continent! It takes four to five days before a letter from London or Paris reaches Antwerp or Holland. I hope he has gone somewhere where he and his family are safe and that those horrible Germans will leave Zeecrabbe alone, although regiments of Germans passed Uccle!

We all were delighted when your letters came and I must thank you! for your lovely offer inviting us to come to St. Andrews. Here in London we all feel much better! and hoping ....

While Van Horne worried about Van Gelder, Van Slochem wrote another letter from London to Van Horne on September 3: [497]

I received your letters of 11 and 13th. I have inquired in every direction about Van Gelder and I presume that he has not left Uccle or else his bankers Morgan, Harjes would know. From them I heard that they have no other address, but Zeecrabbe Uccle and as he usually leaves his address with them when he goes travelling he must have remained at Uccle. When I last saw him on the 3rd of August Van Gelder told me that he had put his treasures in an archway cellar under the chateau and that they took in enough provisions to last them several months.

I urged upon him to leave Brussels, he said he may and will let me know but all the communications with Antwerp were cut for four or five days after; and what ever I tried has been in vain up till now! Knowing how anxious you are; I will cable you as soon as I hear something; I may hear something within a few days as I am trying to trace his secretary! A young Englishman who will have to come to London as the Germans having control in Brussels ordered all Englishmen to leave!

Van Gelder being a Dutch subject may after all be all right in Brussels! At least, I hope so! But we all here worry about him and his family! If he would be in Holland or France I surely would have heard from him although it takes a full week to get letters from these places! I surely would have heard from him; same as your letters arrived to Antwerp have reached me here, therefore I am sure he remained in Uccle.

---

497 Letter in VHFF (7/13).

Kindlund, manager of the New York Bourgeois gallery, wrote Van Horne on September 5 to say that he had heard from Dabo that Bourgeois (who was of German stock) had left his home.[498] (Although Bourgeois was of German ancestry, perhaps he was a French national. Regardless, Dado's phrase "leaving for the war" did not mean that he had been forced to fight for the Germans.)

....

The letter that Dabo sent me from London (dated Aug. 23) told of his arriving in Paris "three weeks ago today" and finding Bourgeois in the midst of preparations prior to leaving for the war. If Dabo was correct in stating dates, then Bourgeois left Paris on Aug. 2nd, two days before he cabled to me from Brussels (on Aug. 4th), saying "Everything all right, gallery closed till further instructions." I feel confident that Bourgeois is somewhere in neutral territory and that we will hear from him in the course of time. If you have received my news, which would lend to corroborate my deduction I should be greatly pleased to hear of it.

I am trying to be optimistic but, frankly, my position (in relation to the business) is an exceedingly perplexing one. I have been associated with Mr. Bourgeois since he opened his New York galleries and, during his absences, have acted as manager but have not been given power of attorney. The monies I have handled (deposited by Mr. B. in my name as "cashier") have been used to pay bills, salaries etc. I received one remittance from B. since he left NY and he was to send me another check the middle of August but of course was unable to attend to it, with the result that I am without funds with which to carry on the business.

---

498   Letter in VHFF (2/3).

The paintings I still have in New York (having sent most
of our stock to Paris) approximate in value $100 000.00
but unfortunately I have no authority to use the proceeds
from sales. I am stating these facts to you, knowing your
friendly relations with Mr. Bourgeois and in the hopes
that you may possibly be able to offer some advice.

I presume that Dabo will see you before coming to New
York and perhaps you can discuss the situation with him.
It was through Dabo that Mr. Bourgeois secured my services and, as you know, Dabo has taken a very great interest
in the New York galleries, which I have understood are
partly the outcome of your encouragement.

On September 11 Van Slochem wrote Van Horne from his
London address to say that he still had no news from Van Gelder and his family and had come to the conclusion that he had
remained in Uccle.[499] He continued:

I met here some friends who told me, that when the Germans entered, they escaped, but they heard nothing of
V.G. but in the environs of Ixelles [Elsene] and Uccle the
Germans demanded all horses and motorcars! From those
that possessed any; and those that could not accommodate
them, had to take in Germans to feed them, let us hope
for the best. Thousands of Belgians have come to London
the last few days, but very few from Brussels. They mostly
come from Antwerp and towns near Ostend.

The Bank of England exchanges Belgian money into
English at full value, but only to those that can prove that
they lived in Belgium and not over £20.0.0 every two weeks
for each family.

---

499 Letter in VHFF (7/14).

I wonder how the situation will be by the time this reaches you. If the Allies will keep going as they did during the last few days, the Germans will be crushed much sooner than they thought! But it will take some doing!

I just received a letter, while writing this, that my servants in Antwerp were terribly shocked at half past three in the morning. They were thrown up and down in their bed and several windows in my house broken through the throwing of the bombs to this kind of warfare the neutral powers should protest, this is awful news to get and I wonder if I will see my home back again, this letter took nine days before it reached me.

Belgians fleeing to England, people in Antwerp. Protection of Antwerp, burning homes. 3 000 on boat, half of it refugees. Shipment I laid out for you (£275.0.0) will not have reached you, please send draft. Did not hear from Van Gelder since 4th of August. Thanks for invite to St. Andrews.

Van Horne had always shown concern for his dealer friends' woes, and was really worried now that they were living with the terror of war. On September 17, he replied to Kindlund's letter of the 5th, saying that he had heard that Dabo had passed through Montreal a few days ago on his way to New York, so he assumed that Kindlund had seen him by now:[500]

I am quite in the dark where Mr. Bourgeois is nor what his plans are. Last I heard from Dabo is that he had been put in the army and sent to the front on very short notice, heard nothing of him nor of Nardus since I left London

---

500   Letter in VHFF (2/3).

in July, quite at a loss how to advise you concerning the
subject of your letter of the 5th.

Van Slochem, we may assume still in London, wrote Van
Horne on the 18th that he had received a letter from Antwerp
informing him "that several letters have been returned to my
house in Antwerp, amongst them one which was written to
you!!" [501] He went on, again about the ship:

I do not know, which letter that can be, but that letter
must have been written about the first week in August! in
which I had enclosed to you an invoice for the model of the
old ship that I sent you. The price of the ship for which I
bought it for you, was £100.0.0 but I explained to you in the
letter that owing to the war risk at sea! and especially the
North Sea! and same having been shipped from Holland, I
had same insured for the sum of **three hundred Pounds.** I
hope that you are not having any trouble on account of not
having received the invoice!

I have instructed the return of the letters but owing to
the Censor all letters from Holland are delayed for several
days. As soon as this letter is returned to me, I will re-
forward same to you.

This clears up, why I have not heard from you all that
time! I hope that through the delay of that letter with that
invoice you are not having any trouble with clearing that
case. As to my going to New York, I have nothing decided
as yet. From Mr. Van Gelder I have not heard anything. I
have written to some of his relatives in Holland, but they
replied that they have heard nothing from him and they

hope that he is safe with his family in Uccle! Same as we all hope here about them!

I hope you will excuse me for what happened with the Antwerp letter! But owing to the war so many things and especially business matters are in a muddle! I shall be glad to hear from you upon receipt of this!

Van Slochem, continued about the ship on the 25th:[502]

I received yours of Sept. 12th and I herewith enclose letter I wrote you long ago, with enclosed bill for the model of ship. The letter was returned by the Antwerp port office on account of having been sent closed; same should have been left open. However I hope that you do not have to pay duty at the rate the ship has been insured for as I mentioned in my last letter, why this was done!

I have received a letter from a relative of Van Gelder informing me that they are all right at Zeecrabbe and shall cable you today. I have written a few letters to Bourgeois but received no reply. The news to you from Mr. Dabo accounts for him, let us hope for his safe return. I am very much relieved to have heard that Van Gelder and family are all right, although I would like to hear from him. It seems not to be possible, as he does not know that I am in London.

I hope that there will soon come an end to this wholesale slaughtering of human souls! I am sending you different illustrations of the war by the same post and trust they will reach you. I trust that the ship has reached you by now and that you will agree with me that it is a very fine one.

502   Letter in VHFF (7/13).

Again about the ship; on October 20 Van Slochem advised Van Horne:[503]

I received yours of the 5th with enclosed draft for which I thank you very much. I am however very much disappointed with your opinion on the ship and hope you will not leave it in the Customs.

Owing to various reports about my Antwerp home, which may not have gone entirely, I am about to go over there. If I can succeed in securing a pass to enter and to leave from there, I will try to go to Amsterdam and see the dealer from whom I bought the ship and will do what I can; even if I have to loose on it myself as regards $600 duty is too much. Very likely they charge duty according the insurance; by showing my letters to the customs they will see that the high insurance was taken out owing to the war and, they may refund you a few hundred dollars and take it out of the Customs as if you will see it entirely out of the case, you will see that it is a model! And very much finer that the one sold for $900 at Muller, which that man, from whom I bought this sold for nearly double, the price he paid for it. This one has a carved back, which is of a much earlier period and which the one from Muller did not have!

However I am very sorry that I got this in such a hurry, but if I had not been proven, that there was someone else after it, which was absolutely the truth! I would not have bought it so quickly. To correspond with the dealer is not any good. I shall try to see him personally, will see what I can arrange and when I have seen him will let you know on my return from Amsterdam. I have received a letter from Van Gelder saying that he will try to write to you himself, probably you have heard from him by now.

---

503   Letter in VHFF (7/13).

Van Slochem, still not at all happy, wrote Van Horne again on October 30:[504]

> I hereby enclose a copy of a letter from the dealer from whom I purchased the ship. He wrote in Dutch and I have translated same: I am very sorry that it cannot be given back in short. I am upset about so many different things beside this that I have been ordered by the doctor to go to the seaside and am leaving therefore from here and going to Brighton for a few weeks. My address will be 12a Waterloo Street Hove Brighton. I have had a visit here from W. Decock with his wife. They came from Brussels yesterday. He told me that Van Gelder and his family are all right. He brought me a letter from Van Gelder in which he said he would try to write to you soon himself. DeCock asked about the Aart van Gelder, which is in the Montreal Museum. But I am not in a position to say anything to him about it, as I have written twice to Mr. Abbott but I have had no reply from him. I did not go to Holland as I anticipated, my family objects to me crossing the channel owing to the mines but if I feel better after a little while, I will go there and then to Antwerp. I have had reports that the house has suffered on the roof but not entirely gone, perhaps the worry about this has some effect upon me.

The letter from the dealer, who sold the ship model (translated into English by Van Slochem) reads as follows:

> I received yours of Oct. 24 and was most unpleasant to learn that the ship I forwarded for you to your client did not please and in which you also ask me if I would take the

---

504   Letter in VHFF (7/13).

ship back. Even if you would loose some money on same but this I can not very well do. In ordinary times I would have done so but just now business in Holland is very bad and nothing to be sold. If it was not in wartime I would let you return same to me without hesitating, as you will no doubt remember that I offered you 300 guilders profit on behalf of another dealer but you refused saying you bought it for a client and you would not like to miss it. You also say that your client writes the ship to be a model of the late XVIIIth century.

I have to contradict this, as it is early seventeenth century and a unique ship of which is no duplicate.

I regret very much not being in a position to take it back. Will you lease [at least] let your client know that the ship I sold you is not to be compared with the one sold at Frederick Muller and that I sold again for a much higher price that you said me for the one you bought.

On November 4 Van Horne wrote to Eilers in Amsterdam:[505]

The financial situation is very bad with us yet but I have been doing my best to save up some money for you and I now enclose London exchange for £600. We have no markets for securities as yet but even if we had, the prices would be ruinous and so we have to wait for "Windfalls."

PS. I am not sure that I wrote you after the receipt of the Corot that is was not the one that interests me. Art is dead here at present and I can't get anybody to look at the picture. What shall I do with it; shall I ship it back?

505   Letter in VHFF (3/27).

Did Van Horne mean that he could not get anyone to authenticate the Corot?

Anyhow, Van Horne's secretary must have been surprised when he opened the following letter of November 18.[506] It was from Lany Nardus in reply to a long letter Van Horne had written to say he was worried about the Nardus family.

> I received with great pleasure your long and distinct letter. Your kind words are always such a comfort, and, especially in these difficult days, they are so precious. On our way here, we had to stay a fortnight in Bordeaux as the children fell ill there with high fever. I was very much afraid of some kind of illness but fortunately they recovered quickly, but anyhow, I was feeling so tired that I had to wire to Nardus to come and fetch us! After 3 weeks being away we were extremely happy to meet again in good health and we all arrived here in better conditions then I expected.
>
> Nardus had been very busy to find us a little house and to furnish it although there is but just the necessary! We have a wonderful view over the town and the mountains. The air, here, is delicious and the climate most agreeable. We would really feel most happy if our thoughts were not so often with our poor, suffering country. Nardus has a quite nice little studio and enjoys painting some awfully strange types of gitanes. If, for a long time, we shall have to remind some of the miserable scene of the war, here, the beauty and quietness of nature and souls will help us to take patina. We have not the least idea how long this awful war shall last. Some people talk of months, some others of years. What do you think! We have some good friends here, doing their best to distract us. Today, I cannot find at all my words in English; I expect it is because we are

---

506   Letter in VHFF (5/4).

learning Spanish! Well, dear Sir William, let us hear soon again from you and don't forget to give our kindest regards to all. We are happy to know that you are in good health and that you have not too much trouble from our troubles. Everyone has now but one wish, we hope, it is to have peace. One of my sisters, who I am so pleased to have with me, was very sad of hearing the sudden death of Mr. Conrad Porthens, which you much surely have known? She heard also that one of his brothers has come over for the war. Really, Canada is taking a glorious part in our great effort. Here, in Spain, their sympathies are all for the allies and no one doubt of our final victory! Hoping to hear very soon again from you, believe me your always most affectionate and grateful friend Lany Nardus.

Gorre Gobernador. Avenida Tibidabo. Barcelona.

On November 30, Eilers wrote to thank Van Horne for his letter and the London exchange £600, "which we have got in your credit." He went on:[507]

We were very glad to get your letter as in these horrible times we don't see many of such kind, even no mail of importance comes in. Nobody shows any interest for pictures; all we hear is war and nothing else. I presume however, that will be nearly everywhere, we will have to wait until the last combatant of Europe and the interested countries is killed or taken prisoner and that will take still some time. It is my intention to go next year – about February – to San Francisco, before leaving I will try to get some information to know if it is not foolish to go.

---

507   Letter in VHFF (3/27).

You wrote me already about that little Corot and I was waiting too long before answering you, for which, please excuse me.

I didn't answer because I was so very busy, but because I had nothing to do at all! If you have a job for me, please remember me!

About the Corot, if you do not object, I should like to see that you could keep it for us until I come next year to America. There is still a little picture by Dijsselhof at yours, so I could get them both together.[508]

There was not much more art-related correspondence during the rest of 1914. Van Horne's art collecting came to a halt.

Back in Europe, Dutch painter Willem Witsen (1860-1923) and his second wife Maria Schorr (1875-1943) had embarked on the *New Amsterdam* on December 30. Witsen was to become the representative of the Dutch government at the 1915 World Fair in San Francisco. This fair was organized because of the occasion of the opening of the Panama Canal. Witsen's trip would end up in an extended stay at Covenhoven, where he would paint Edith van Horne-Molson, Billy's wife and Van Horne's daughter-in-law, which portrait would be the last addition to the Van Horne collection.

The year 1915 started with an upbeat note in *American Art News* of January 9, reporting that Bourgeois, who was apparently free to go wherever he wanted to go despite his German ancestry, had arrived the previous month from Rotterdam and, in August, had travelled to Germany, where he spent some time in Cologne. He had brought a number of important

---

508   The Wickenden catalogue lists neither a Corot, nor a Dijsselhof. Cat. 1933 lists four Corots: no. 125 "Les Gaulois;" no. 126 (encircled by Lugt) "Landscape – Sand Dunes;" no. 127 "Peasant Girl by a Wall" and no. 128 (encircled by Lugt) "Mother and Child."

and interesting pictures and art objects, and would "later in the season hold some important exhibitions in his galleries."

A few days later, on January 13, 1915 Bourgeois, New York, wrote Van Horne:[509]

I am sending you enclosed a paper cut which appeared in this morning's paper, telling that Cottier & Co have failed.[510] I am extremely sorry about Fearon and you will feel the same as he is a good friend of you as well as of myself. I did not know anything about this matter that he was in such a bad position.

I hope to have the pleasure of seeing you in New York soon and that you will have the time to see some exhibitions, especially the Goya and Greco exhibition at the Knoedler Galleries and the display of the Altman collection which would be the two most interesting ones.

I think your two Goya's made excellent impression between the paintings shown now at Knoedler's. There is nothing so fine as your Lady Portrait. I saw there for the first time Frick's large Greco representing a nobleman, short trousers, his helmet standing on the floor near him; it is certainly the most wonderful Greco I have ever seen and marvellous harmony in color. There [are] also two painting belong to Mrs. Havemeyer: "Le Grand

---

509 Letter in VHFF (2/1).
510 Cottier & Co. was a New York gallery from 1873 to 1914. Cottier designed and created furniture and sold these items as fine art as well, next to American art and European Old Masters (Goldstein 2000: 53). Dekkers (1996: 62) attributes the introduction of the The Hague School to Daniel Cottier, a Scottish art dealer, designer of glass, furniture and interiors. E. J. van Wisselingh started his career, after his training with Goupil in Paris, with Cottier. In 1873 Cottier branched out to New York. On May 25, 1913, the *New York Times* wrote the following: "At the Cottier Galleries Mr. Fearon has placed on view a series of panels in English painted glass of nineteenth century workmanship. Most of the designs are by Daniel Cottier, the founder of the firm, whose early work was in this field, and who drew at one time under Ruskin's guidance."

Inquisitor", and "View of Toledo" two paintings of the greatest distinction and power.[511] Please call me up when you come next time to New York because it would give me a great pleasure to see those things with you together.

On January 14, 1915, Van Horne told "My Dear Bourgeois" that he had received his letter of the 13th and that he was exceedingly sorry to hear of Mr. Fearon's financial difficulties:[512]

for I have always had a high regard for him and felt much interest in his success. I wish I were in a position to help him but just now that is impossible because I have my hands very full taking care of the different enterprises I am interested in and that is all or a little more than I can do until the skies begin to clear. I should like very much to see the exhibition at Knoedler's, but I may not be able to get down for nearly two weeks. I hope then to see the Altman collection with you and some other things at the Metropolitan Museum. I am very well, but very busy.

On January 20 Bourgeois thanked Van Horne for his letter of January 14th, and said that he would be very glad to meet him in New York.[513] The letter reads as if Van Horne had suggested that Bourgeois should go into banking:

You will remember that we talked last summer in London about Mr. S. Peters Chinese pottery collection and that

---

511   Mrs. Louisine Havemeyer (1855-1929) had bought El Greco's *Grand Inquisiteur* around 1904 and *View of Toledo* in 1909 shortly after the death of her sugar baron husband Henry O. (Harry) Havemeyer (Saltzman 2008: chapter IV).
512   Letter in VHFF (2/1).
513   Letter in VHFF (2/1).

you would like to see his things. Mr. Peters came in yesterday; I had a nice talk with him, and shall see his collection next Sunday.[514]

We talked about your things and he told me he would be delighted to show you his collection, the next time you will be in town.

I think you will be astonished to see his things. His collection ranks surely as the finest of that kind.

Things are picking up slowly here, and I hope to have soon some success to tell you. Of course it is very hard now to sell anything – less for financial reasons but because people imagine that [...] to the war, fine arts can be bought for nothing. I am of a different opinion and for lots of reasons. In my case nobody is now taking advantage of the situation to buy for reasonable prices. And its affects very bitterly our affairs. Poor Fearon had to close his business and this account especially, and I myself, I am struggling terribly since seven months. As you will recall, Nardus left me the whole business last November in order that I might direct it in my own ideas, leaving to me a stack of about $220 000 but not sufficient funds to reorganize things, as I intend to do them. He was himself very hard up and when the war broke out, he was personally terribly hit in his affairs. He could not help me in any way, in the contrary; he wants that I send him money from here.

Since months we tried hard to sell any of the fine paintings we have, which would give us a chance to settle immediately with all our creditors and to reorganize affairs, as I intend to do it All my efforts were in vain.

---

514 In 1914 the Knoedler Galleries held a loan exhibition of several selections of pottery, the one of Samuel L. Peters among them. Cf.: http://www.worthpoint. com/worthopedia/1914-exhibition-of-japanese-korean-chinese (last accessed in February 2014).

The debts we [illeg.] not large, $15 000, in all. I could make an arrangement with B. Altmann & Co.[515] They were very/so kind to me, leasing it entirely to me to settle my account with them. I owe Dinacen Brothers $3 000, which I have to pay back end of February.

A three-month note, which amounts to $1 000 was discounted by my bank, [illeg.] and $750 which Nardus lent me, permitted me to handle the affairs till now, but I am now really at the end of my knowledge & as to meet the current expenses as rent, insurance and sellings.

Since last spring I cut, of course, all expenses down, and of all the art dealers in this city I have the lowest amount of expenses.

What my affair needs is reorganization – in that way, that I can buy for reasonable prices and sell quickly. A rapid sale permits me to use the same [illeg.] different times in the same year, and by selling quickly and for reasonable prices I make a clientele.

But in the way, as I do it today, I shall always struggle and not succeed. I need the necessary money in the bank in order [to keep?] the art I have [and] not to fight for the daily existence.

The business needs enthusiasm to make people love art and especially to make them penetrate the inner value of every masterpiece. For to make money is a very bad policy and has only as result that the client get suspicious, believing that we are going to take advantage of him.

I write you all this because I know that you regarded always my affairs and aspirations with warm interest. I

---

515   Altman's obituary in *The New York Times* of October 11, 1913, mentions: "A big wreath of orchids from Henry Duveen of London was under the pulpit [...] Mr. Altman's art collection, which is variously estimated to be $15 000 000 may become a public collection in the Altman private gallery in Fiftieth Street or it may have place in the Metropolitan Museum." It is now in this museum.

need a friend's advice and that is the only reason why I explain you all this. I know how to buy and to sell paintings but business in general and especially banking business is a thing entirely unknown to me.

You advised me in many things, please think this over for me. Perhaps you see a solution. I do not invite you to trouble you since our affairs, knowing that you are hard up yourself in this moment. It is only for an advice, and when you come to NY you can perhaps tell me what I might do.

In mid January, Van Horne had told Bourgeois he was "very well, but very busy." However, perhaps he was not as well as he liked people to believe. He was still suffering the effects of the type 2 diabetes that had plagued him for a number of years, as well as Bright's (kidney) disease. Both conditions were made worse by his over indulgence in rich food and alcohol. Also, perhaps the stress of dealing with his many businesses worries, as well as with the woes of his art dealers, was beginning to tell on him. Taking all this into consideration, it is not surprising that, on the 26th of January, Van Horne had his will drawn up.

By this time, the letters to and from his dealers were becoming few and far between. However, judging by a letter Bourgeois wrote from New York on February 15, 1915, Van Horne was still helping his dealers/friends:[516]

Thank you so much for your kind letter of Febr. 2nd and excuse, please, that I did not express you sooner my gratefulness for your efforts to help me out of France. I was the last weeks very busy, to keep things going and succeeded to have a few weeks quiet. And then I followed your good

516   Letter in VHFF (2/1).

advice, and that helps splendidly. Have four very good businesses in view and if I succeed one it will be easy to start a new line, as I conceive it. The people are yet hesitating but, when general business will be for some weeks as it is now, I shall extinct here my share.

Let me thank you sincerely for your kind interest in my affairs and believe me very faithfully yours.

I have written over to Spain to find out the exact name of the persons representing your two Goyas. As far as I know the name is Castrofuente and that is too [also] the opinion given by Dr. Mayer. Castro comes from the Latin word Castrum which means fortified camp. Names of old families go mostly back and certain cities, villages or mountains, and not impersonal particularities that makes one believe that the name is not Castrofuente.

On March 26 Van Slochem, wrote from the RMS Lusitania, that he would arrive in New York shortly and hoped to hear whether Van Horne would be in Montreal in April.[517] Apparently there was not much to keep him in New York, so, on March 30th Van Slochem announced that he would be in Montreal the next day. On the 31st Van Horne cabled back "shall be here all week. Come directly house." [518]

A few days later, on April 4, Van Horne cabled Eilers in Amsterdam that he had enclosed: "London Exchange for £410.19.2.[519] It is very hard to squeeze any money now, but I am saving up all I can for you. I shall be glad if when you acknowledge the receipt of this you will send me a memorandum of my account so that I may make sure of my figures."

517   Letter in VHFF (7/14).
518   Letter in VHFF (7/14).
519   Letter in VHFF (3/27).

Van Slochem, still in New York on April 16, gave Van Horne his new address in London. He had closed his business, and asked – again – for help:[520]

This is to inform you that I am going to sail next Wednesday on the Adriatic. I suppose you are not coming to New York before I sail. The business is closed and everything is here in storage, and I hope to come back in September or October, perhaps the war is over by this time, and the chances of selling some fine pictures may be better but for the present I consider myself out of business!

Now Sir William, I wonder if you can put me on the track, of recurring any orders, from the French or English or Russian Government. I can devote my time to it while over there, if I only could find out, or be introduced to someone in Europe, who is in position to help me to get the order.

Perhaps you could introduce me to some in New York, or in Canada whom I could represent on the other side, and if I should succeed in getting the order, that I could cable such a party first, if such an order could be filled. If I am asking you too much, I hope you will excuse me, but I would like to have something in the way of business on my mind, and perhaps you may hear of an opportunity, it is not very easy to get in touch with any such diplomat without being properly introduced. I have heard that various foreign gentlemen are over here, trying to get orders filled. I feel confident that I would make a good representative for some on the other side, but the trouble is to meet the right man whom I could represent.

Should you hear of such an opportunity for me, I shall only be too glad to jump at it and put all my time and

---

520   Letter in VHFF (7/14).

energy to it. I hope you will be in New York before I sail or else I should like to hear from you. I enclose a card with my address in Brighton and conclude with my best regards to yourself and family.

H. Van Slochem. 139 Western Road. Brighton. England.

On April 18 Adaline Van Horne informed Van Slochem, who was still staying at the Hotel Manhattan in New York, that she and "Sir William" had just returned from St. Andrews and that Van Slochem could expect him in New York on Tuesday morning.[521]

For Van Horne New York was just a stop on his way to Cuba. Knowles (2004: 423) writes that Van Horne, heading to Cuba in order to escape the cold, had taken his seven-year old grandson Billy along to show him New York. He had shown the little boy the wonders of the big city: the Bronx Park, the high-speed elevator of the Woolworth Building, the Hippodrome. From Adaline's letter we know Van Horne also sneaked in a meeting with Van Slochem before embarking on the SS Havana for Cuba.

On May 10 back in Montreal, Van Horne's secretary wrote to Van Gelder at 64 Willem de Zwijgerlaan, The Hague, that Van Horne would leave that same night for Cuba.[522] Van Gelder apparently had asked about a letter that Van Horne had not answered. The secretary noted that Van Horne was: "uneasy about a letter, which he wrote you recently, and which he thinks was among the mails in the "S. S. Lusitania" which was sunk. Will you kindly advise if you received his letter. However, he will write you again on his return to Montreal."

---

521 Letter in VHFF (7/14).
522 Letter in VHFF (32/14).

Whether Van Horne did write again as he promised, or whether his letter to Van Gelder had ended up at the bottom of the ocean is not known. However, there is no trace of further correspondence from him to Van Gelder.

We do know that Van Horne's interest in collecting fine art waned as he began to give more time to the war efforts, such as the training of sea lions to detect submarines (Knowles 2004: 425, 26). Back in St. Andrews, on June 28, he accepted an invitation by Prime Minister Borden to join a commission that would examine "agriculture, immigration, transportation, the borrowing of capital and the marketing of food products." But, because of his declining health, Van Horne had to withdraw from active participation. However, he said he was willing to make changes.

Willem Witsen

Willem Witsen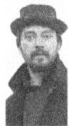

Meanwhile, the 1915 Panama–Pacific International Exposition (PPIE), held in San Francisco, had come to an end and the visitors had gone. One of them was the Dutch painter Willem Witsen (1870-1923). His painting of Van Horne's daughter-in-law, Edith, would be the last addition to Van Horne's collection. On July 9 Witsen wrote from The Queens, Toronto, to his sister Cobi, J. H. E. Arntzenius-Witsen, that he and his wife just had arrived in Toronto after a journey of three days and nights from San Francisco. [523] He described their

---

523   Letter in Koninklijke Bibliotheek (KB) (79E 42). All Witsen letters are from "Jansen et al.," written in Dutch and accessible on: http://www.dbnl.org/tekst/

trip through the Rocky Mountains: climbing until 5 000 ft, a thunderstorm in Lake Louise, then fields, wheat and meadows [prairies], and past Winnipeg, hills, rocks, birches, a big lake with red rocks, [Lake Superior] firs, more lakes, more trees and burned birches.

Witsen and his (second) wife traveled by train, a fitting mode of transport for someone on his way to the Van Horne's.[524] The train compartment was very cozy, "you are absolutely private and when you call, a negro is right away at hand and takes very good care of you and then a few cars to the front you may have breakfast, three meals daily." Witsen continued: "I have an introduction to Sir Edmund Walker from Van Wisselingh & Co. whom we will visit this afternoon, and in Montreal one from Boissevain to Sir William Van Horne. I am curious whether we will find these gentlemen at home." [525]

On July 20 the Witsens had made it to Hotel Albert in New York. Witsen wrote another letter to his sister to say

wits009brie01_01/wits009brie01_01_1656.php (last accessed in October 2014).

524 Witsen's first wife was Betsy Witsen-van Vloten. His second Augusta Maria Witsen-Schorr.

525 Sir Byron Edmund Walker (1848-1924), president of the Canadian Bank of Commerce (1907-24) "was a well-known art connoisseur, and had much to do with establishing the National Art Gallery in Ottawa, of the board of which he became chairman," in *The Encyclopedia of Canada VI*: 251-252.

Van Uuden & Stokvis (2007: 175) write that Witsen sometimes experienced his relationship with Van Wisselingh & Co. as "knellend (oppressed)." Perhaps that was of his own doing. According to Heijbroek and Wouthuysen (1999: 115) Witsen had proposed to Groesbeek, partner in Van Wisselingh & Co., that he should be paid *f*300 per month. In return, Witsen would give Groesbeek whatever he had produced during that period. But he soon fell ill. Heijbroek and Wouthuysen conceded (1999: 93) that he stood every year in the red. However, on page 113 they note that his relationship with Eilers and Groesbeek "from the start on was good."

See: http://faculty.marianopolis.edu/c.belanger/quebechistory/encyclopedia/ SirByronEdmundWalker-CanadianHistory.htm (last accessed in February 2014).

Adolphe Boissevain is mentioned in footnote 2 of this book. Knowles (2004: 267) describes him as "Van Horne's friend Adolphe Boissevain, the Dutch financier whose Amsterdam firm floated CPR shares in European financial markets."

that he had found a letter from Sir William Van Horne at the consulate:[526]

> He invited us to stay at his estate in New Brunswick in Canada and because he is here one of the great men who also has a big influence in art affairs but also, and in particular, because he is such an especially cordial man (and wrote so cordially and nice) we both would regret not to take the opportunity. So, by the end of the week, we go, through Boston. From there it is still 15 hours by train [...] I love to go New Brunswick, and I just fear to make a fool of myself at Sir William's through all the shortness of spirit, education and character. Fortunately Marie is with me and can I hide my failures behind her skirts.

The letter sounds as if Witsen had heard good stories about Van Horne from Eilers. Biographer Vaughan wrote, that at the age of seventy Van Horne "was freed from his correspondence and the entertainment of his guests." Obviously, this was not the case. On August 2 Witsen reported to his sister:[527]

> In two days we are here already one week and I did not have opportunity so far to write, dear Cobi and even now I have only little time. If it would not rain so much it would not even happen.
>
> This morning we drove to town to shop and it reminds so much of Groningen while it is so much different at the same time. But, it started to rain and so heavy, that I had to change upon coming home. We were in a cabriolet, a kind of carriage with two horses and six seats and I

---

526 Letter in KB (79 E 42).
527 Letter in KB (79 E 42)

was seated just in the drips of the umbrellas. It is here a marvellous place, on an isle, and upon arrival Miss. Van Horne picked us up with a small motorboat. But with the carriage one has to wade on a shallow place through water, but, depending on the tides the difference is very big. This morning it was nearly dry and last week, when we went along, the horses walked until their knees through water. When it is high tide, it is of course impossible. The width is about three times the Amstel River. Upon arrival at Minister's Isle it is still some distance before you reach the house through a yard with the most beautiful flowers in all kind of colors. At the end of the yard is a tower at the beach, in which are rooms for those who want to bath. The beach is rocky and overgrown, very beautiful. The house is very roomy, cozy and of course comfortable. Our room is on the main floor with windows overgrown with a vine. Indoors it ends up in a hall, which is more like a drawing room with a grand piano, many paintings, rugs and an enormous hearth in which big logs are crackling. Sir William is a most lovable man, full of jokes and friendliness.

Covenhoven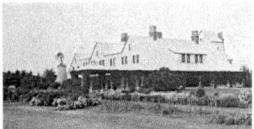

Lady Van Horne is an old lady, very simple and cordial. Mr. van H., the son, is a goodhearted giant, but he thinks he is a pope. His wife is very nice, fine and a bit melancholic, while she does not show it. I painted her portrait, but it is not yet finished and today she left for a few days. Their son, William, the grandson is the idol of the entire family and is being spoiled very much. He is nearly always with the nurse and does not come to the table. Further there is Mrs. Bennett and her son Fred, a Japanese with two daughters, a Miss Vipond, a good person but not much fun and Miss. Van Horne, a giant just like her brother but with the same good heartedness and much nicer. She is so fat as I have never ever seen a woman with a big round face that reminds of Roman emperors. Further more there is Mr. Stanley, Sir W's secretary, a young, very modest man. While the people are all very simple, one dresses for the dinner, but not in evening dress. The meals are enormous, of quality as much as of quantity, because breakfast already starts with fruit, cereal, meat, fish, eggs and bacon, toast, muffins & coffee.

About the melancholic Edith van Horne-Molson and her son, idol Billie, Molson (2001: 323) remarks that there was, unfortunately a great deal of conflict in little Billy's environment, much that he felt, but could not articulate at the age of seven. Billy may have been aware, at some level, of his mother's unhappiness. Mrs. Van Horne had noticed her daughter-in-law looked "worn and sad." Yet public decorum prevailed.

Because this study of the establishment of the Van Horne collection started with Caroline Pierson's description of the Van Horne collection in the mansion in Montreal, it seems fitting to finish with a description of the Covenhoven estate by Witsen, who also added the last piece to the Van Horne collection.

On August 4, Witsen again wrote to his sister from Covenhoven, New Brunswick:[528]

I still have three quarters of an hour before breakfast that is usually at 10 a.m. Yesterday we toured to the farm and the forest. The farm is not picturesque as the Dutch farms (besides the beautiful white cows in the barn!) but

528   Letter in KB (79 E 42)

very modern and practically organized. I only counted 24 cows, but there are certainly more since outside there were more. The building looks more like a castle than a farmhouse, with two huge round towers in which pigeon cages. And, the chicken coop is a palace! With different rooms for the species and races, with corridors and behind it an enormous meadow.

Sir W. told us that he has a farm of 61 miles sq. in Winnipeg and two more of 5. This one is only small, but the entire isle is 8 miles in circumference and 3 long and the most part is wooded. That is so beautiful, that wild forest and lanes or better natural roads like the one on Buys' hill on Ew. [Ewijk], but high and low and with very different kind of trees.

At the north of the isle were splendid red rocks with grotto's where the beach does not continue and where you would be locked in during high tide. I hope to have an opportunity to work there and in the forest. Too bad that Tholen is not here.[529] He would make here such beautiful things. I keep thinking this because I can't do it.

I played three games of chess with Van Horne 2-2 and one with Sir W which I won. I find it not pleasant to see how people take it badly when they lose! With pool I had 28 with Mr. van H. 600. But it is a giant pool table, which I am not familiar with at all and with pockets. He plays very strong; I have never seen it this way. I suffer much from my deafness, especially in a large company, so mainly at the table. And when I have to eat I cannot hear one word of the conversation. I already suffer from it at your table when people speak Dutch, so you will understand how it is when they speak English with a Canadian accent. Mr.

---

529   William Bastiaan Tholen (1860-1931) was a Dutch artist with a deep love for the Zuiderzee (now called IJsselmeer).

Van Horne speaks so inarticulate, that I have great trouble with it and Lady Van H. has a very weak voice. Enfin, I already wrote you that I was certain of a fiasco and would make a fool of myself. That is how it is! But with Marie it is different. She speaks very easily, hears everything and is always nice and pleasant. I do my best, but it is a big effort and hopeless. The only good thing is that I don't eat much because of the attention and because these meals three times daily are enormous, it benefits me.

Yesterday I made drawings at the beach and today I planned to paint there, but the weather is so cold and bad. Yesterday it was so nice! We also played croquet, but I was badly beaten by Fred. Mrs. Y, the Japanese, was my partner, but did not play as well as Miss. Vipond, Fred's partner. I forgot how to do it.

Well, I will finish. People are showing up and soon the bell will be heard. Later more [news]. Hope that every-thing is ok!

Best wishes to all, also from Marie and see you soon,

Shortly after Witsen wrote this letter, Van Horne must have left for Montreal to see a doctor. In the August 8 letter published in Sullivan (2007: 107), Van Horne wrote his wife, who was still at Covenhoven, that he had been under Dr. Hamilton's observation "for that fever which hasn't all gone yet." He added that the doctor would consent "to my going down to St. Andrews Tuesday evening, but wants me to have a nurse to continue his observations and look after my diet." Van Horne continued:

I may not be able to comply with his wishes in that regard for I don't know where Miss Caldwell is and I wouldn't give a rap for any of the rest. She is at Arn prior or somewhere up in the Ottawa area visiting her mother. I don't need anybody here for Leonard does everything required and does it very well. The doctor wants me to be X-rayed before going down – to help him guess I suppose. However, I am feeling very well, save that I don't like the diet.

In this letter Van Horne mentions Witsen, Mr. Yada, (probably the husband of Witsen's croquet partner), a Mr. and Mrs. Whigham, and Mr. Craig. He added that Onslow [sic] would not come and that he had not heard from Edith yet.

On August 15 Witsen wrote, this time in English, about his stay in Covenhoven:[530]

On our way back we had a very interesting and comfortable journey by Canada, where, at our stay in Montreal we were invited by Sir William Van Horne to spend some time at his place in New Brunswick. I had much pleasure in painting the portrait of young Mrs. Van Horne to the satisfaction of Sir William who advised me, just in the same way as you did in San Francisco, to come back to America. If the German submarines do not interfere, I think I will do it, and if so I certainly will let you know.

Vaughan (1920: 367) reports that Van Horne made several visits to Covenhoven in 1915, "while there he prepared, with the vice-president of the Cuba Company, the annual report of their corporation."

From Witsen's letters we know that many more people were hosted at Covenhoven during Van Horne's last sojourn. About this period Vaughan writes that Van Horne "could still give thought to every detail of his affairs, but his apparent weakness and effort in his work caused much anxiety to his family

---

530   Letter in KB (75 C 51)

and his guests. They were more disturbed than he." Witsen's letter doesn't show much anxiety; he must have tried to focus on painting young Mrs. Van Horne.

Knowles (2004: 426) writes about this portrait as follows: "The affectionate father-in-law also arranged for a portrait to be painted of his daughter-in-law, Edith. This was only accomplished with increasing difficulty, however, as he was becoming progressively weaker and weaker."

Perhaps Van Horne needed to coax his daughter-in-law to 'sit' for the painter and, yes, he was becoming weaker and weaker. Around the 15th of August Van Horne was taken to Montreal again "for observation and tests." Apparently Witsen and his wife left that same day. On August 19, Witsen wrote from New York to Lady Van Horne. He must have known that Sir William had had to leave for Montreal that same day as he thanked Mrs. Van Horne for her kind hospitality and the very pleasant time: [531]

It has been most gracious of you to keep us such a long time especially as I am perfectly aware to be a very poor society man indeed. I think it must have been for the sake of my wife who is always trying her best to make much good where I am failing. Of course it is to me an enormous handicap on account of my deafness not to be able to follow the conversation, but I have to accept my fate, seeming to be a tedious and dull fellow, and I quite agree with everybody who is of that opinion.

I have, in fact, to apologize for going in society at all, but the invitation of Sir William was so very kind and we both like him so much; that in accepting I hoped you might excuse me. Besides I had the wish to be of some use and that is why I painted the portrait of your charming

---

531 Letter in KB (75 C 51)

daughter-in-law, and feel so grateful and awfully glad Sir William likes it, though I am sure the praises I heard are very much exaggerated.

I should be exceedingly sorry if circumstances would not allow me to come back and see you again. We are sailing Saturday next but as soon as we arrive in Amsterdam I will write to Sir William.

But that letter to Sir William was never to be written. On August 22 Van Horne was rushed from his Montreal home to the royal Victoria Hospital were he underwent surgery the next day. On the 26th of August the *Beacon* reported:

Sir William Van Horne

A bulletin issued at the Royal Victoria Hospital at ten o'clock this morning stated that Sir William Van Horne, who was operated on in that institution [that was on the 23rd] early this morning, had "recovered from the anesthetic, is resting and free from pain. Sir William, who is former president of the Canadian Pacific Railway, had been in indifferent health for the past few days and was removed early this morning from his residence on Sherbrooke street west, to the Royal Victoria Hospital. It was decided that an immediate operation was necessary, and this was performed by Dr. George E. Armstrong and Dr. W. F. Hamilton. The operation revealed the fact that the patient was suffering from an abdominal abscess."

Van Horne appeared to be recovering well. He was kept in hospital while recuperating and entertained visitors with his plans for a new type of hospital (Knowles 210: 195). But then things took a turn for the worse; he died three days later, on September 11, 1915.

Collard (1991: 46) writes that "death had not been welcome," for Van Horne. "When I think of all I could do," he is supposed to have said, "I should like to live for 500 years."

Witsen did not find out about the death of his prospective patron until after he returned to Holland. On September 13 he wrote to Dutch painter and author Jacobus van Looy (1855-1930) that the journey back to Vancouver and through the Rockies had been very interesting, and that he had seen the gorgeous Van Horne collection of paintings in Montreal.[532] He enthused about his visit to Van Horne in New Brunswick:

> where we spent fourteen days and where I had the occasion to paint the portrait of his daughter-in-law. He was so pleased with it that he counseled me to return to America to paint portraits and then I had to start with his and he would take care that I got to paint much. You may understand I was glad. After we were home one week we got notice of his death. Being born in the shadow!

Looking for the whereabouts of the last addition to the Van Horne collection, Witsen's portrait of Edith Van Horne-Molson, I approached Karin Molson, author of the *Molsons, Their Lives and their Times, 1780-2004*. She referred me to Edith's niece, Maggie Oliphant-Molson (daughter of Hobart Molson, Edith's brother).[533]

Asked about the painting in spring 2010, Maggie said she had not found it among her aunt's possessions. She told me that after her aunt Edith's death, she was summoned to the Van Horne mansion by Margaret Van Horne (the widow of William Van Horne's grandson). Margaret, who was "a tough

---

532   Letter in Frans Halsmuseum Haarlem, VanLooyarchief iv. no. 1246.
533   Maggie Oliphant-Molson died in 2014.

cookie," in Maggie's estimation, had shown her the rooms on the top floor where Edith had lived her last years – Edith had married the Honorable Randolph Bruce in 1932, one year after the death of her first husband, Bennie Van Horne. She returned to her former home after the death of Bruce.[534] In these rooms on the top floor, Maggie was shown a few trunks containing her aunt Edith's clothes and a few strings of pearls. Witsen's portrait of her aunt was not around.

But something else came up: another painting. Maggie told me about a landscape by Sir William in her possession. It was painted in 1911 and dedicated to Edith's mother, Esther Molson-Shepherd (1854-1912).[535]

But where is Edith Molson's portrait? Perhaps it is the painting listed as "V. H. 417, Witsen, Wm. 'Lady' 20×16 f5" in Carter (1932), see Appendix I. If so, Witsen's "Lady" had to content herself with a place in the storage closet, of the NE Guest room. Rather an ignoble resting place for the last addition to the Van Horne collection.   ✕

---

534   Honorable Randolph Bruce; see: http://www.freemasonry.bcy.ca/biography/lieutenant-governors/bruce_r.html (last accessed March 2014).

535   The other Witsen in this list is "V.H. 436 Witzen W., [sic] Amsterdam-winter" – etching 19×27 $15."

SUMMARY

THIS BOOK WAS triggered by penciled scribbles such as "can be a Rdt" and "not a Maes" on the 1933 catalogue of Van Horne's collection of fine paintings by Frits Lugt, a Dutch art connoisseur. These scribbles raised the question, did Caroline Pierson, who mentioned four Rembrandts in her 1926 description of Van Horne's collection, really see four Rembrandts? By the end of her description she notes young William moving through the hallway, and hears a "boom" from the pontifical front door being slammed and thought: *"youth had passed through this now very quiet and dignified house."* And so it was with the fine art that had moved through the house – it might have caused Van Horne to also slam some doors.

According to Dr. Frits van de Wetering, director of the Rembrandt Research Project, *Old Man with Slashed Black Cap* and *Head of an Old Man* were deemed not to be Rembrandts but *Portrait of a Young Rabbi* was found to be genuine. *The Landscape*, was stolen in 1972, one day before it could be assessed.

Still, Rembrandts or not, my next question was: Which dealers supplied these paintings to Van Horne? Looking into the establishment of the Van Horne's collection, along a paper route of correspondence, brought to light that more paintings – a Maes, a Rosa, a Reynolds, a Holbeijn, a Cranach and a Benson – were not deemed what they were said to be. The dealers of the questionable works were Nardus and Van Gelder. Their involvement in the build-up of Van Horne's collection also led to understanding why, after 1908, engaging art connoisseurs became so popular in North America.

Answers to other questions such as about why and how Van
Horne had collected comes from the Van Horne biographies by
Vaughan (1920) and Pierson (1926/1929), contemporaries who
knew him, and by Knowles (2004/2010). Vaughan character-
ized Van Horne and his collection:

> A lover of beauty and perfection in every guise, he added
> examples of every school to his collections, but he had
> come to admire most the Dutch and Spanish masters.
> Canvases by Rembrandt, Hals, Velasquez, Cuyp, Terburg,
> Ruysdael, Goya, El Greco, Mauve, Renoir, Reynolds,
> Gainsborough, Turner, Constable, Hogart, Holbein,
> Guardi, Tiepolo, Géricault, Millet, Courtbet and [...] works
> by famous Japanese and Chinese artists.

Vaughan mentions that Van Horne periodically weeded out
pictures that had ceased to please him, and quotes Van Horne
as saying: "Never buy a picture that you do not fall in love with,
or it will always be an incubus and a source of dissatisfaction.
The purchase of a picture, like the selection of a wife, can
hardly be done by proxy."

We know that Van Horne's second biographer Pierson
(1926/1929: 46) was familiar with Vaughan's biography
because he refers to it twice. Pierson writes that Van Horne
gradually collected the same Masters as Vaughan did. The only
additional purchase listed in Pierson's biography is the 1909
purchase of Rembrandt's *Rabby* and the *Cavalier* by Murillo.

Knowles (2004: chapter 11) describes Van Horne's way of
collecting not as "gradually," but in terms of amassing, sweep-
ing through exhibitions, galleries, museums and private collections, seeing "oceans of pictures" (Van Horne's own words)
at his friends houses in Paris, going on buying sprees, and so
on. Knowles writes that Van Horne purchased in person and
not "by proxy," as Vaughan said he would not have done.

Van Horne's correspondence with his art dealers reveals a different picture about the ways he acquired paintings. On numerous occasions Van Horn bought whatever his dealers suggested. Later, the connoisseurs he engaged also urged him to buy certain pieces.

Van Horne, like many other North American collectors, started with the Barbizon School. When this source seemed to have been exhausted around 1884, like his fellow-collectors, Van Horne turned to the "The Hague School." The dealers Nardus and Van Gelder encouraged Van Horne to buy these paintings and happily supplied him with them.

After a break in his collecting, roughly from 1900 to 1904, he started to buy again. By this time he had established personal relationships with Nardus and Van Gelder; they became his friends and they also invested in a few of Van Horne's his side-businesses. Van Horne, an astute businessman, must have soon become aware of the notoriety of these two dealers, but he supported them unfailingly. Did he continue to support them out of loyalty as friends, or was it just plain good business sense to stay on good terms with his dealers/investors? These questions linger.

In 1908 the art world of the superrich was riddled with scandals. This prompted Van Horne to engage connoisseurs, while at the same time embarking on a period of almost frenzied acquisition.

From October 1912 on Van Horne's collecting fever cooled. He had become disappointed, and perhaps disillusioned. Doubts with regard to the authenticity of Rembrandt's *Old Man with Black Cap* led to Van Horne's denial of the possibility that beautiful things could be "wrong." Art historians argue that most collectors follow the taste of their dealers. By comparing the lists of paintings and pieces of art Van Horne was offered and the lists of what he subsequently bought, it seems this statement rings true of Van Horne's collection.

In 1913 a global economic decline set in. Bourgeois, a respected dealer, felt that things might be better in Europe than in North America, but Van Gelder wrote from Europe that money was scarce and business bad there also. It was so bad that he was no longer able to buy more shares in Van Horne's Sardine business.

During 1913, Van Horne enjoyed visits from Bredius and Kronig, two respected connoisseurs, and he became interested and involved in Bredius' battle about the Elizabeth Bas painting. But his interest in collecting continued to wane.

At the start of 1914 Van Horne's activities were severely curtailed by his failing health. In July the Great War broke out. Still, by mid 1914 Van Horne seemed to have recovered his health and again taken up collecting and corresponding. But it would not last long.

Although the 1915 letters from Dutch painter Willem Witsen describe Van Horne's Covenhoven household in full swing of summer entertaining, Witsen also mentions that Van Horne's body could no longer could keep up with his mind.

We know that Witsen's portrait of Van Horne's daughter-in-law was the last painting added to the Van Horne collection. Unfortunately, nobody knows where that portrait is. Nor do we know the whereabouts of the stolen Rembrandt.

THE WHO'S OR WOES

Setting out to find out how the Van Horne collection became established, and how it may have contained questionable paintings, I soon came across Leo Nardus and Michel Van Gelder. Nardus is well-known in art history circles. After the 1908 Widener affair, he withdrew from the North-American art world and had himself represented by VG and Bourgeois.

Nardus continued to collect and deal in art, while spending his leisure time paintings, fencing and playing chess. Neslis (2010) paints an intimate view of Nardus' latter years, disturbed as he was by the loss of his art collection. He had handed it over to his Jewish friend Arnold van Buuren in Amsterdam. In 1940 Nazi Germans confiscated it. Nardus died in 1955, impoverished, in a pink castle in Tunisia, facing evacuation.[536]

Van Gelder was an artist turned dealer turned self-labeled gentleman turned collector. Art-historians knew about him, but not exactly who he was. His name is said to have been written in invisible ink. But, he was well-known in the world of fancy-fowl breeders with his Uccle Booted Bantam. Van Gelder, as well as his partner Nardus, often found himself in hot water, but he did not get scalded as badly as Nardus did.

My research into the questioned Rembrandts also led me to Van Slochem and Bourgeois, two art experts who associated with Nardus and Van Gelder. It can be said that Van Slochem, Nardus' supposed brother-in-law, that his personal feelings about his association with Nardus and Van Gelder are not known, but it is clear that he kept an assiduous eye on the art business and did not shy from selling Van Horne all kinds of artifacts that could embellish his households. Van Slochem, more modest than Nardus and Van Gelder, lived comfortably, but not in a chateau. He would die in 1923, but his wife Ester died in 1943 in Auschwitz.[537]

As I have mentioned, Van Horne's long-lasting friendship with these four dealers/investors/friends, despite all the problems they caused him, remains a puzzle.

Perhaps the friendships survived because Van Horne was impressed by their European life style, or perhaps it was simply because they were also shareholders in some of his businesses so he could not afford to break with them, despite the scandals.

Van Horne's public display of ongoing trust in these dealers may have caused people to wonder about his role in, and

---

536   See also Neslias (2010) on Nardus' final period in Tunisia, and http://www.babelio.com/livres/Neslias-Butin-Nazi/449789
537   Information in e-mail from Ester Quadbach, November 2014.

knowledge of, the deals that led to the Johnson unease, the Widener affair, and the Borden matter. It is not known for sure whether Nardus or Van Gelder knowingly sold fakes or forgeries to these collectors; however, it is possible that the scandals were caused by the dealers' poor business acumen, inexperience, and over-enthusiasm (for their money-consuming lifestyle), rather than a conscious decision to cheat their clients.

In business affairs, Van Horne was not perfect himself. America-born, he did not like to pay taxes – who does? – and had his secretaries instruct his dealers to declare a much lower value in order to avoid custom taxes. This could have made him vulnerable, but there seems to have been mutual trust and some genuine fondness between him and his dealers (and his secretaries).

Van Horne's dealings with Eilers and Van Wisselingh are quite a contrast to this dealings with the cumbersome group-of-four. While Eilers and Van Wisselingh were on friendly terms with Van Horne, but they did not become investors, they didn't bother him with their personal affairs, and did not sell him any wrongly attributed works of art.

Looking into the build-up of the collection also led to Van Horne's acquaintance with connoisseurs such as Hofstede de Groot, Bredius, and Kronig and others, which began after the Widener affair of 1908.

That Van Horne had not always followed the advice of the connoisseurs did not escape one of Van Horne's biographers. Vaughan (1920: 268) reported that Van Horne followed his own judgment "in the selection of the canvases he bought," and, he writes, "The authenticity of some of his purchases was subsequently questioned by experts, he had much amusement in argument and contention over them and he placed little faith in the infallibility of expert opinions." Vaughan adds that Van Horne had admitted "the unpleasantness of paying a Rembrandt price for a Ferdinand Bols [sic]."

Pierson (1929: 46) quoted Vaughan, noting that Van Horne "loved to sit before them [paintings] and let them sink into his soul," adding that he once observed Van Horne looking at Rembrandt's "Six portraits" in Amsterdam: "He stood in front of them, seemed to would have liked to look through them in order to discover the secret of this art." After reading the Van Horne correspondence, one wonders whether he rather tried to guess the authenticity of the pictures in the gallery in Amsterdam, as well as those he had purchased.

With regard to authenticity, Knowles (2004: 293, 94) reports, just as Vaughan did, that Van Horne had little faith in the infallibility of judgments delivered by most of the so-called experts, but that he went "so far as to admit that he regretted having paid a Rembrandt price for a Ferdinand Bols [sic]."

A look at the correspondence presented in this book shows that Van Horne was very much aware that some of the paintings he bought might not have been what they were reputed to be. Bredius and Hofstede de Groot made much money with their expertise business, thanks to the reputations of dealers such as Nardus and Van Gelder. Bredius left his estate to the Municipality of The Hague, which now proudly boasts the Bredius Museum. Hofstede de Groot left his estate to the state, now known as the Rijksbureau voor Kunsthistorische Documentatie, also at The Hague. He quietly engaged connoisseurs to expertise pieces in his collection, sometimes under the guise of having a catalogue drawn up. Van Horne is quoted as saying (Vaughan 1920: 269 and Knowles 2004: 294 referring to Vaughan): "It doesn't matter a damn whether a great man painted the poor one or an unknown man painted the fine one." This quote does not seem to come from the same man who engaged connoisseurs, but perhaps Van Horne simply wanted to hide what was going on from Vaughan, his contemporary.

As quietly as Van Horne did, dealers also started to engage and even to instruct connoisseurs, as can be seen in the Van Gelder/Hofstede de Groot correspondence. A next shift in professionalism occurs when we see connoisseurs acting as dealers.

The long, drawn-out 1914-15 correspondence illustrates the impact of the Great War on the art world, and to the dealers' cozy existence in particular.

All in all, the history of the establishment of Van Horne's collection exemplifies the good, the bad, and the ugly that is the art trade. ✕

THANKS AND

ACKNOWLEDGEMENTS

A NUMBER OF people helped me to find my way in what was for me a new area, art dealing, which Van Horne called "an extraordinarily dirty art." First, I would like to thank my husband, Jos Eggermont, for his never-failing support that goes far beyond financial borders. Many people helped out in one way or another; I list them here and extend my thanks to them.

In the Netherlands

Amsterdam:
Paula Kruseman, Gerard Greidanus, Hermine Voûte, Wilco Jiskoot, Margreet Oomen, Ernst van de Wetering, Baldy Tjia, Erik-Jan Zürcher, Ester Wouthuysen, Freek Heijbroek of the Rijksmuseum, and Ariane Swiers of the Nieuw Israelitisch Weekblad

Hulst: Tiny and Eugène Fassaert.

The Hague: Albert Blankert, Ad Leerintveld of the Koninklijke Bibliotheek, and Elly Klück and Suzanne Laemers of The Netherlands Institute for Art History

Beek-Ubbergen: Paul Nève

Winterle: Piet van der Veen

In Belgium

Brussels: Wim Vandenbussche

Pittem: Paul Callens

Ukkel: Jan Vissers of the the Municipal Library

In France

Paris: Floortje Damming of the Institut Néerlandais, and Rhea Sylvia Blok of the Fondation Custodia

In Canada

Toronto: Dawn Logan, Karen Molson, and staff of the Art Gallery of Ontario

Calgary: Harry van den Elzen, Colin McDonald, Pat Kozak, Nora Aukes

Montreal: Peter Lowensteyn, Danielle Blanchette of the Montreal Museum of Fine Arts, and the staff of the McCord Museum

St. Andrews: David Sullivan

Victoria: Maggie Oliphant-Molson and Charles Muhldorpfer

Ottawa: Staff of the National Gallery of Canada

In the United States

New York: Esmée Quodbach of the Frick Collection

Philadelphia: Jennifer Vanim of the Philadelphia Museum of Art ⊠

LIST OF

ILLUSTRATIONS

John G. Johnson 100

Cornelis Hofstede de Groot (1863-1930) 100, 114, 209

Abraham Bredius 100, 208, 286

P.A.B. Widener 101

RKD archives 101, 209

Museum Bredius 101, 208

M.C.D. Borden 159

Cogels-Osylei 7, Antwerp 159, 166

Berend Berenson 159, 173

Willem Witsen 305, 363

REFERENCES AND

BIBLIOGRAPHY

Art Association of Montreal. *The Sir William van Horne Collection. Exhibition: a Selection from the Collection of Paintings of the late Sir William van Horne, K.C.M.G. 1843-1915.*

Baedeker, Karl. 1910. *Belgium and Holland, including the Grand-Duchy of Luxembourg.* With 19 Maps and 45 Plans. Fifteenth edition. Leipzig: Karl Baedeker. (Online: Boston Public Library).

Barnouw-de Ranitz, Louise. 1978/80/90. "Abraham Bredius, een biografie" in: Albert Blankert. *Museum Bredius: Catalogus van de schilderijen en tekeningen.* Zwolle: Waanders. The Hague: Museum Bredius.

Berenson, Bernard. 1948. *Aestehtics and History in the Visual Arts.* New York: Pantheon Books Inc.

Berton, Pierre. 1971. *The Last Spike: The Great Railway, 1881-1885.* Toronto: McClelland and Stewart Limited.

Bertuca, David J., Donald K. Harman and Susan M. Neumeister. 1996. T*he World's Columbian Exposition. A Centennial Bibliographic Guide.* Westport CT: Greenwood Press.

Blankert, Albert. 1978/80/90. *Museum Bredius: Catalogus van de schilderijen en tekeningen.* Zwolle: Waanders. The Hague: Museum Bredius.

————. 2006. "The Case of Han van Meegeren's False Vermeer Supper at Emmaus Reconsidered" in *In His Milieu: Essays on Netherlandish Art in Memory of John Michael Montias*. Ed. A. Golahny, M. M. Mochziuki and L. Vergara. Amsterdam: Amsterdam University Press.

Boser, Ulrich. 2008. *The Gardner Heist: The True Story of the World's Largest Unsolved Art Theft*. New York: Collins, Smithsonian Books.

Bredius, Abraham. 1969. *Rembrandt: The Complete Edition of His Paintings*. Revised by Horst Gerson. London: Phaidon.

Broos, Ben. 1991. "Bredius, Rembrandt en het Mauritshuis!!!" in: *Bredius, Rembrandt en het Mauritshuis!!!* Den Haag: Mauritshuis. Zwolle: Waanders.

Boulet, Roger. 2009. *Vistas: Artists on the Canadian Pacific Railway, With an essay by Terry Fenton*. Calgary: Glenbow Museum.

Carter, Sydney. 1932. *List of Paintings in Oil, and Watercolours, Pastels, Draqings, Etchings, etc. in the Collection of the late Sir William Cornelius van Horne, K.C.M.G. of Montreal in order of Rooms at the Residence, Sherbrooke Street West. Montreal*. Montreal: Montreal Museum of Fine Arts, Archives, file Van Horne.

Collard, E. A. 1991. *Montreal: 350 Years in Vignettes*. Montreal: *The Gazette*.

Conway, Martin. 1905. "Sir William van Horne" Collection at Montreal" in *The Connoisseur, an Illustrated Magazine for Collectors*. Vol. XII, no. 47 (p. 135-143). London: Otto Limited.

Dekker, Dieuwertje. 1996. "Where are the Dutchmen? Promoting The Hague School in America, 1875-1900" in *Simiolus: Netherlands Quarterly for the History of Art*. Vol. 24, no. 1 (pp. 54-73).

Eggermont-Molenaar, Mary. 2010. "De Van Horne kunstcollectie: 1926, 1933, 1972" in *CAANS/ACAEN Newsletter* (pp. 16-26).

Ekkart, R. E. O. 1999. "Cornelis Hofstede de Groot, een Groninger in Den Haag" in *Jaarverslag 1998 of the Netherlands Institute for Art History* (pp. 72-96). Den Haag: Geschiedkundige Vereniging Die Haghe.

Friedländer, Max J. 1929. *Echt und Unecht: Aus den Erfahrung des Kunstkenners*. Berlin: Bruno Cassirer.

Furness, Amy Aarchall and Gary Fitzgibbon. 2008. *Description & Finding Aid: Van Horne family fonds. CA OTAG SC065*. Montreal: Art Galley of Ontario. E. P. Taylor Research Library and Archives.

Goldstein, Malcolm. 2000. *Landscape with Figures: A History of Art Dealing in the United States*. Oxford: Oxford University Press

Grijpma, Dieuwke. 1999. *Kleren voor de elite. Nederlandse couturiers en hun klanten 1882-2000*. Amsterdam: Balans.

Gross, Michael. 2009. *Rogues' Gallery – The Secret History of the Moguls and the Money That Made the Metropolitan Museum*. New York: Broadway Books.

Hadley, Rollin Van N. ed. 1987. *The Letters of Bernard Berenson and Isabella Stewart Gardner 1887-1924 with Correspondence by Mary Berenson.* Boston: Northeastern Univerity Press.

Heijbroek, J. F. 2008. "Nieuwe Inzichten over Toorops Oude Tuin der Weeën (New Views on Toorop's Old Garden of Tears)" in *Bulletin van het Rijksmuseum* 56 (2008), nr. 1-2, (p. 102-107.)

—————— . 2010. *Frits Lugt 1884-1970. Leven voor de kunst.* Parijs: Fondation Custodia/Rotterdam: Toth.

Heijbroek J. F. and E. L. Wouthuysen. 1999. *Portret van een kunsthandel. De firma Van Wisselingh en zijn compagnons.* Zwolle: Waanders. Amsterdam: Rijksmuseum.

Hofstede de Groot, Cornelis. 1907. *A Catalogue Raisonne of the works of the Most Eminent Dutch Painters of the Seventeenth Century Based on the Work of John Smith.* London: Hawke, Edward G.

—————— . 1909. "Nieuw-Ontdekte Rembrands (Lately Discovered Rembrandts)" in *Onze Kunst,* Deel XVI (pp. 172, 73).

—————— . 1911. "Twee Nieuw aan het licht gekomen portretten van Frans Hals. In *Onze Kunst.* Deel XX (pp. 172-73).

—————— . 1912. "Deux portraits nouvellement attribués à Frans Hals" in *L'Art Flamand & Hollandais, Revue Mensuelle Illustrée,* vol 17 (pp. 1-2).

—————— . 1912. "Nieuw-Ontdekte Rembrandts II (Lately Discovered Rembrandts II)" in *Onze Kunst.* Deel XXII (pp. 173-88).

Houpt, Simon. 2006. Foreword by Julian Radcliffe. *Museum of the Missing: The High Stakes of Art Crime*. Toronto: Black Walnut / Madison Press Books.

Hündgens, C. E. 1999. *Inventaris van de archieven van Cornelis Hofstede de Groot. (1853) 1880-1930 (1942)*. The Hague: Rijksbureau voor Kunsthistorische Documentatie.

Jansen, Leo, Odilia Vermeulen, Irene de Groot and Ester Wouthuysen (Ed.) *Willem Witsen, Volledige briefwisseling*. Online at http://www.dbnl.org/tekst/wits009brie01_01/wits-009brie01_01_1656.php.

Kipling, R. 1937. *Something of Myself: For my Friends Known and Unknown*. New York. Doubleday, Doran & Company, Inc.

————— . 1990. "Letter to James M. Conland, 25-9 March 1897 (vol. 2, 1890-99)" in *The Letters of Rudyard Kipling*. Ed. Thomas Pinney. Iowa City: University of Iowa Press (p. 292).

————— . 1995. "Letter to John and Elsie Kipling, 29 September 1907(vol. 3, 1900-10)" in *The Letters of Rudyard Kipling*. Ed. by Thomas Pinney. Iowa City: University of Iowa Press (p. 268).

Knowles, Valerie. 2004. *William C. van Horne: From Telegrapher to Titan*. Toronto: The Dundurn Group.

————— . 2010. *William C. van Horne: Railway Titan*. Toronto: The Dundurn Group.

Laemers, Suzanne. 2009. "Der Kenner im Museum – Max J. Friedländers letzte Jahre in Berlin und sein Leben in den Niederlanden (1867-1958)" in *Jahrbuch der Berliner Museen*. Berlin: Staatliche Museen zu Berlin. Stiftung Preußischer Kulturbesitz.

Lopez, Jonathan. 2007. "Gross false pretenses: the misdeeds of art dealer Leo Nardus," in *Apollo: The International Magazine for Collectors*. Vol. 166, Issue 549 (p.76). Online at http://www.jonathanlopez.net/Nardus.html

————. 2008. *The Man Who Made Vermeers*. Orlando: Harcourt Inc..

Lowies, Jean. 1997. "Le barbu d'Uccle" in *Ucclensia*: no.'s 157, 158 and 165.

Manuth, Volker. 2005. 53-64. "Een levenslange passie voor Rembrandt" in *Van Cuyp tot Rembrandt*. Luuk Pijl Ed. Groningen: Groninger Museum.

Mayles, Stephen. 1976. *William van Horne*. Tr. 1978 by Gabrielle et François Raymond. Ed. Bernard-Pierre Paquet. Ontario: Fitzhenry & Whiteside Limited. Longueil, Québec: Les Editions Julienne Inc.

Molson, Karen. 2001. *The Molsons: Their Lives & Times. 1780-2000*. Willowdale: Firefly Books.

Narriman El Kateb-Ben Romdhane. 1997. *Léo Nardus, Un peintre hollandaise en Tunisie*. Quoted in Lopez (2007).

Neslias, Patrick. 2010. *Butin Nazi* (Nazi Loot). Confolens en Charente: Geste editions.

Overmars, Herman and Henk van Veen. 2005. "Hoeveel originaliteit bezit gij? Cornelis Hofstede de Groot en zijn plaats in de Nederlanse kunstgeschiedenis (How original are you? Cornelius Hofstede de Groot and his place in Dutch Art History)" in *Van Cuyp tot Rembrandt: De verzameling Cornelis Hofstede de Groot*. Luuk Pijl, Ed. Groningen: Groninger Museum/Ermelo: Snoek.

Pierson, J. L. 1929. *Sir William van Horne en de Canadian Pacific spoorweg. Met een brief van Mevrouw C. Pierson over haar bezoek aan het huis van Van Horne in Montreal.* Amersfoort: S. W. Melchior.

Pijl, L. Ed. 2005. With contributions of: Kees van Twist, Herman Overmars and Henk van Veen, Rudi Ekkart, Volker Manuth, Esmee Quodbach and Diewertje Dekkers. *Van Cuyp tot Rembrandt. De Verzameling Cornelis Hofstede de Groot.* Groningen: Groninger Museum/Ermelo: Snoek.

Quodbach, Esmée. 2002. "The Last of the American Versailles" in *Simiolus: Netherlands Quarterly for the History of Art.* Vol. 29, No 1/2 (pp. 42-96).

——— . 2005. "American Collections Rich in Dutch Art. De eerste Amerikaanse reis van Cornelis Hofstede de Groot in 1908 (The first American journey by Cornelis Hofstede de Groot in 1908)" in Pijl, L. Ed. 2005. *Van Cuyp tot Rembrandt. De Verzameling Cornelis Hofstede de Groot.* Groningen: Groninger Museum/Ermelo: Snoek.

——— . 2009 "I want this collection to be my monument: Henry Clay Frick and the formation of The Frick Collection" in *Journal of the History of Collections* (21(2): 229-240), first published online on April 7, 2009.

Ranger, H. W., 189? "Notes on Private Picture Collections in Montreal" in *The Art Amateur* (p. 67).

Regehr, T. D. 1988. "Ames, Sir Herbert Brown" in *The Canadian Encyclopedia*. Edmonton: Hurtig Publishers.

Saarinen, Aline. 1958/65. *The Proud Possessors: the lives, times and tastes of some adventurous American arte collectors*. New York: Random House.

Saltzman, Cynthia. 2009. *Old Masters, New World: America's Raid on Europe's Great Pictures*. New York: Penguin Books.

Scallen, Catherine B. 2004. *Rembrandt, Reputation, and the Practice of Connoisseurship*. Amsterdam: Amsterdam University Press.

Samuels, Ernest. 1979/87. *Bernard Berenson: The Making of a Connoisseur*. Cambridge, Massachusetts, and London, England: The Belknap Press of Harvard University Press.

Secrest, Meryle. 1979. *Being Bernard Berenson: A Biography*. New York: Holt, Rinehart and Winston.

——— . 2004. *Duveen: a Life in Art*. New York: Knopf.

Shiff, Richard. 2007. "Risible Cézanne," in: *The Repeating Image: Multiples in French Painting from David to Matisse*. New Haven: Yale University Press/Walters Museum (pp. 127-72).

Stechow, Wolfgang. 1975. *Salomon van Ruysdael. Eine Einführung in seine Kunst*. Berlin: Gebr. Mann Verlag.

St. John, Gerard J. 2007. "John G. Johnson: Giant of the Philadelphia Bar" (Vol 69. no. 4). Online at *http://www.philadelphiabar.org/page/TPLWinter07Johnson?appNum=2*

Strachey, Barbara & Jayne Samuels. Ed. 1983. *Mary Berenson: a Self-Portrait from her Letters & Diaries.* London: Victor Gollancz Ltd.

Sullivan, David. 2007. *Minister's Island. Sir William Van Horne's Summer Home in St. Andrews.* St. Andrews: Pendlebury Press Ltd.

Van Uuden, Cornelie & Pieter Stokvis. 2007. *De Gezusters Van Vloten. De vrouwen achter Frederik van Eeden, Willem Witsen en Albert Verwey (The Van Vloten Sisters. The women behind Frederik van Eeden, Willem Witsen and Albert Verwey).* Amsterdam: Bert Bakker.

Vaughan, Walter. 1920. *The Life and Work of Sir William Van Horne.* New York: The Century.

Von Boden, Wilhelm. 1930. *Mein Leben.* Herausgegeben von Thomas W. Gaehtgens und Barbara Paul. Berlin: Reckendorf/ Nicolai.

Wallis, Hugh M. 1960. Preface. *Canada Collects: European Paintings, 1860-1960 (Le Canada collectionne: Peintures Européenne, 1860-1960).* Montreal: Montreal Museum of Fine Arts.

Winter, Edward. 2009. *Léonardus Nardus.* Online at http://www.chesshistory.com/winter/extra/nardus.html

✕

APPENDIX 1

1932 LIST OF PAINTINGS AT MONTREAL & 1959 LIST OF PAINTINGS AT COVENHOVEN

☞ 1932 LIST OF PAINTINGS AT MONTREAL

List of Paintings in Oil, and Water-colours, Pastels, Drawings, Etchings, etc. in the Collection of the late Sir William Cornelius van Horne, K.C.M.G. of Montreal in order of Rooms at the Residence, Sherbrooke Street West. Montreal (Carter 1932).[538]

The Van Horne Mansion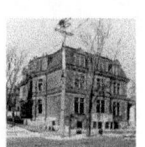

Main hall - ground floor

....

VH129   Welgemut, Michael   *Altar Triptych*

---

538   The 1932 current values have been omitted from this list.

Main hall - ground floor

VH95	Leonardo, Jose	*Dragoons Waiting*
VH90	Mazo, Juan Baptista Martinez del	*Portrait of three girls with a dog*
VH92	Zurbaran, Francisco de	*A Franciscan Monk*
VH89	Mazo, del, J.B.M.	*Port. of an Ecclesiastic*
VH 99	Velasquez, Don Diego de Silva	*Portrait of young nobleman*
VH 88	De la Cruz, Juan Pantoja	*Bernardo de Sassonia, Duke of Weimar*
VH104	Goya, y Lucientes Francisco	*Portrait of Marquez del Castrofuerte*
"		*Portrait of Marquese de Castrofuerte*
VH108	"	*Peasants fighting soldiers*
VH118	Magnasco, Allesandro	*Capuchin Monks around a Refectory Fireplace*
VH91	Orrente, Pedro	*Belated Mountebanks*
VH119	Magnasco	*Franciscan Monks in their Refectory*
VH98	Velasquez	*Philip IV*
VH109	Goya	*Horrors of War*

Main hall - ground floor

VH96	Velasquez	*Christ on the Cross*
VH100	Murillo, Bartholeme-Esteban	*A Spanish Gentleman*
VH94	Velasquez	*Philips V*
VH 103	Theotocopuli (El Greco)	*El Senor de la Casa de Leiva*
VH 301	Van Horne, Sir William C.	*Canadian Village in Winter*
VH117	Labrador, Juan	*Still Life Fruit*
	"	*Still Life Fish*
VH302	Van Horne	*A lowering Sunset*
VH115	Ribera, Jusepe	*Diogenes*
VH 106	Goya	*The Actress Rita Molinos*
VH101	El Greco	*Head of St. Maurice*
VH93	Zurbaran	*St. Elisabeth of Hungary*
VH107	Goya	*Portrait of sculptor Cameron*
VH233	Corot, J.B.C.	*Summer Landscape Study*
VH256	Corot	*Study of Sheep*
VH296	Mathews, R. C.	*Rudyard Kipling, crayon*

Main hall - ground floor

VH278	Newman, Robert L.	*2 drawings in charcoal*
VH296	Van Gelder, M.	*A Sea Sketch*
VH303	Van Horne	*View from Minister's Island*
VH149	Tieplo, Giovanni Battista	*Submission of Henry IV to Pope Gregory VII at Canessa*
VH114	Luca, Eugenio the Younger	*Monk Montifex inciting populace*
VH280	Newman	*Little Red Riding Hood*
VH289	La Farge, John	*Old Newport house in Winter*
VH102	El Greco	*Holy Family*
VH288	Hart, William	*Ben Lomond*
VH112	Goya	*Sketch of an Orator of Madrid*
VH265	Renoir, Firmin-Auguste	*The Sisters*
VH304	Van Horne	*Japanese Fete-Nocturne*

Reception room

VH56	Rembrandt, Van Rijn	*An old Man with slashed black Cap*

Reception room

VH55	"	Head of an old Man
VH54	"	A Landscape Study
VH53	"	Portrait of a Young Rabbi or Young Man with Skull-cap
VH62	Backer, Jacob Adriaense	Young Girl in Riding Habit
VH57	Fabritius, Karel	Head of a Young Man in Fur Cap
VH66	Hals, Franz	Portrait of a Dutch Gentleman
VH67	"	Portrait of a Dutch Lady
VH68	"	The Jolly Trooper
VH69	"	Samuel Ampzing
VH253	Hervier, Adolphe	Landscape
VH59	Studio of Rembrandt/Ferdinand Bol	Young Man holding Medallion
VH79	Mieris, Frans Van	Portrait of a Gentleman

Library

VH165	Corneille, Claude, 16th Century	A French Ecclesiastic in his Study

Library

VH150	David, Gerard	*Mary Magdalen in Prayer*
VH151	Master of the female half length figures, XVI C.	*The Descent from the Cross*
VH134	Fourbus, Pieter Janez	*Portrait of a Noble Man*
VH154	Moroni, Giambattisa	*Portrait of a Young Italian Nobleman*
VH127	Holbein, Hans, the Younger	*Portrait of Philip Melanchthon*
VH157	Leonardo da Vinci	*Study of a Woman's Head*
VH158	Cima da Conagliano, C. B.	*Virgin and Child*
VH	Hellenic or Greco-Egyptian, 2nd C	*Lady's Portrait*
VH170	"	*Young Girl's Portrait*
VH155	Lotto, Lorenzo, (attributed to)	*Praying Figures fragment*
VH153	Koffermans, Marcellus	*Christ on the Cross*
VH140	Huysmans, Cornelius	*Classical Landscape with Figures*
VH141	"	*A Mountainous Landscape*
VH159	Titian	*The Mystic Marriage of St. Catherine*

Library

VH148	Canaletto, Giovanni Antonio	*Interior of St. Marks, Venice*
VH126	Elsheimer, Adam	*Leto with Apollo and Artemis*
VH152	Robusti, Jacopo (Tintoretto)	*A Venetian Counselor*
VH97	Velasquez	*Miniature of Infanta Margarita*
VH135	Ysenbrandt, Adrien	*Lady reading her Breviary*
VH138	Van de Vaken	*Modern Lady*
VH110	Goya	*Miniature of Washington after Stuart*
VH128	Cranach	*Martin Luther with a Beard*
VH111	Goya	*A Slave Market*
VH156	Ansuino da Forli	*Young Nobleman in red Cap*
VH132	Master of the female half l. figures	*A Lady Writing*
VH139	Benson, Ambroisius	*Portrait of a Gentleman*
VH136	Rubens, P. P.	*Adoration of the Shepherds*

Drawing room

VH164	Greuze, J. B.	*Madame Mercier*
VH294	Morrice, James W.	*Café Terrace*
VH35	Ruisdael, Jacob Van	*Fishing Boats*
VH210	Diaz, de la Pena	*Le Plains de Barbazon*
VH9	Hoppner, John	*Elizabeth, Countess Waldegrave*
VH244	Monticelli, Adolphe	*The Kitchen*
VH5	Reynolds, Sur Joshua	*Master Gawler*
VH245	Monticelli	*The Decameron*
VH178	Bosboom, J.	*The Chamber of the Council*
VH241	Monticelli	*Walled Lane*
VH242	"	*The Adoration of the Magi*
VH137	Rubens	*The Feast of Herod*
VH240	Monticelli	*Gateway to an old Fort*
VH245	"	*Fete Champetre*
VH300	Van Horne	*Shadow of Covenhoven*
VH31	Lawrence, Sir T.	*Georgiana, Lady Dover*

Drawing room

VH216	Bargue, Ch.	*Moslems at Prayer*
VH247	Monticelli	*Mountainous Landscape*
VH248	"	*The Fountain*
VH174	Maris, Jacob H.	*Girl Knitting*
VH264	Mettling	*A Cup of Tea*
VH249	Monticelli	*Festival of Baccus*
VH238	"	*The Concert*
VH150	Tiepolo	*Lady in Page's Costume*
VH243	Monticelli	*Conversion of St. Paul*
VH147	Guardi	*Storm at Sea*
VH6	Reynolds, Sir Joshua	*The Lady Talbot*
VH151	Tiepolo	*Apelles painting portrait*
VH25	Landseer, Sir E. H.	*Fox Hounds*

Dining room

VH17	Constable, John	*Niedpath Castle*

Dining room

VH7	Reynolds, Sir Joshua	*Countess of Carnarvon*
VH17	Constable	*Jack Straw's Castle*
VH8	Raeburn, Sir Henry	*Mrs. Glengowen and daughter*
VH2	Hogarth, Wm.	*Portrait of a little Girl*
VH17	Constable	*Landscape with Cottages*
VH17	"	*Vale of Dedham*
VH19	Turner, J.M.W.	*Shakespere's Cliff*
VH10	Constable	*The Villa*
VH14	Romney	*June, Duchess of Gordon and Son*
VH4	Constable	*The Glebe Farm*
VH13	"	*View on the Stour*
VH275	Newman, R. F.	*The Wandering Mind*
VH175	Maris, Matthew	*A Service to Isis (four pan. screen)*
VH30	Morland, George	*The Fisherman's Dog*
VH277	Newman, R. F.	*Magdalene*

Dining room

VH254	Roybet, Ferdinand	*The Intercepted Letter*
VH214	Rousseau, Theodore	*Landscape with Poplars*
VH290	Ryder, A. P.	*Autumn Landscape*
VH255	Michel, Georges	*Windmills at Montmartre*
VH213	Rousseau T.	*Thatched Cottage*
VH221	Daubigny, C. P.	*In Brittany – evening*
VH263	Mettling	*Paring Apples*
VH3	Romney	*Portrait of Miss Morland*
VH18	Crome, John	*Sunset Effect – Norwich*

Billiard room

VH 25	Helst, B. van der	*Cornelius Tromp*
VH73	Witte, Emmanuel de	*Skating Scene*
VH80	Goyen, Jan van	*Spinoza*
VH70	Vermeer, Jan	*Young Girl Reading*
VH43	Cuyp A.	*River View with Cattle*

Billiard room

VH74	Molenaer, Jan	*The Singer*
VH65	Borch, Gerhard ter	*An Ecclesiastic*
VH71	Koninck, Philip	*The Dunes*
VH75	Ochtervelt, Jacob	*Mistress & Maid*
VH39	Brouwer, Adrien	*Peasants near a Village Inn*
VH77	Steen, Jan	*Children playing with a Cat*
VH51	Ruysdael, Salomon van	*Marine View*
VH64	Roghman, R.	*Wooded Landscape*
VH44	Beyeren, A. H. Van	*Graves and Walnuts*
VH46	Ruysdael	*Landscape with Waterfall and Church*
VH172	Chinese Painting, Ming	*Lady and Vase of Flowers*
VH61	Maes, Nicolas	*Old Woman with Bible*
VH81	Goyen, Jan Van	*Winter Sports*
VH60	Cuyp, (attributed)	*Woman with a Ruff*
VH169	Chines WU Dyn	*The Three Sages*
VH52	Ruisdael	*Landscape near Arnheim*

Billiard room

VH50	"	*Marien-Kirche at Utrecht*
Vh63	Bramer, Leonard	*Rembrandts's Studio*
VH42	Cuyp	*Stable Interior*
VH41	"	*A Girl's Head*
VH58	De Heem	*Vanitas-Still life-globe etc.*
VH173	Chinese, attr. to Han en T'ang Dynasty	*Tartar Huntsman*
VH76	Brekelenkam, Q. C.	*The Doctor's Family*
VH72	Witte, Emmanuel de	*Interior of a Church*
VH47	Ruysdael	*Bleaching grounds at Haarlem*

Sitting room

VH217	Decames, A. G.	*Saul pursuing David*
VH207	Diaz N. V.	*Venus disarming Cupid*
VH216	Decames	*Horsemen on a Mountain Road*
VH236	Ribot	*A little girl seated*

Sitting room

VH262	Mettling	*A Child's Portrait*
VH268	Bonvin, François	*The Cook*
VH 205	Millet, J. F.	*A Smithy in Normandy*
VH215	Troyon, Constant	*George Sand (la Guitariste)*
VH269	Bonvin	*Maid drawing Water*
VH206	Courbet, Gustave	*Still-life of Fruit*
VH236	Corot	*Sand Dunes at Dunkirk*
VH227	Ribot, T. A.	*The Artists' Daughters*
VH219	Daubigny	*Building the Stack*
VH229	Daumier, H.	*The Attractive Window*
VH201	Delacroix, E.	*Christ on the lake of Galilee*
VH234	Corot	*Mother and Child*
VH211	Rousseau, T.	*Great Oaks, Fontainebleau*
VH231	Daumier, H.	*Bathing the Baby*
VH232	,,	*The Fugitives*
VH270	Bonvin	*Studio Still Life*

Sitting room

VH202	Delacroix, E	*Lioness and Lion in a Cavern*
VH235	Corot	*Peasant Girl by a Wall*
VH237	"	*Gallic Horseman*
VH212	Rousseau, T.	*The Brook*
VH271	Bonvin, F.	*The Studio Table*
VH208	Diaz	*Forest Interior with Shepherdess*
VH28	Miles, Frank	*Study of a Child's Head*
VH209	Diaz	*The Tryst*
VH199	Dagnan-Bouveret, P.A.J.	*Mdme D.-B. as Fish Wife*
VH257	Michel, Georges	*Peasant Woman & Child*
VH228	Daumier	*A Musical Party*
VH182	Cezanne	*Portrait of the Artists' Wife*
VH176	Maris, M.	*A View of Freiburg (sepia)*
VH297	Mathews, R. G.	*A Covenhoven Study*
VH298	Roussoff, A.N.	*San Gregoria (W.C.)*

Breakfast room

....

VH506	Van Horne	*Moonlight at St. Andrews, N.B.*
VH514	"	*Before Sunrise*
VH515	"	*The Equinocials*
VH516	"	*Forest Fire at Night*
VH510	"	*Across the Inlet*
VH561	"	*View from Driveway*
VH517	"	*Path through the Woods*
VH518	"	*Late Autumn Impression*
VH519	"	*Canadian Farm*
VH496	"	*Autumn Pastures*
VH511	"	*Harvest Scene*
VH521	"	*Golden Autumn*
VH522	"	*A Glimpse of the Sea*
VH512	"	*Woodland Pasture*
VH513	"	*Forest Giants*
VH509	"	*Winter Sunshine*

Breakfast room

VH520	"	*Steel Hills at Sydney, C.B.*
VH525	"	*After Sunset*
VH499	"	*Fields and Farm Houses*
VH523	"	*The Gorge*
VH525?	"	*Woods and Fields*

Stairways, first and second floors

VH225	Ribot	*Sill Life, Apples and Pot*
VH224	"	*Balzac in his Study*
VH223	"	*Children of the Artist*
VH222	"	*A Young Vendean*
VH258	Michel	*Hillside Landscape*
VH291	Ryder, A.P.	*Constance*
VH292	Ryder	*Siegfried and the Rhine Maidens*
VH142	Huysmans, Cornelius	*A Valley Farm*

Stairways, first and second floors

VH293	Ryder	*Moonlight on Sea*
VH253	Michel	*Old Quarry at Montmartre*
VH287	Hammond, John	*Windmills*
VH335	Monticelli	*A Southern Garden*
VH231	Newman, R.L.	*Hagar and Yshmael*
VH198	Fortuny, M	*Cosmopolitan Sketch*
VH208	Delacroix, E	*Samson & Delilah*
VH305	Van Horne	*Autumn Woods*
VH82	Du Jardin, H.	*Crossing the Stream*
VH 197	Brown, John Lewis	*34 ½ x 45 ¼*
VH275	Baker W.B.	*Fel en Monarchs [*
VH299	Dankmeyer	*Market Place in Amsterdam*

Second floor hall

VH 273	Wyant, A. H.	*Adirondack Landscape*
VH273	Immes, George	*Sunrise in the Woods*

Second floor hall

VH 286	Weir, P.A.	*Vermont Farmer*
VH306	Van Horne	*Sunrise, Dominio Square*
VH307	"	*Evening in the Clearing*
VH220	Daubigny, C. F.	*Sheep Fold at Lawn*
VH230	Daumier, H.	*Nymphs pursued by Satyrs*
VH308	Van Horne	*Birches*
VH26	Morland, George	*Light in the Sty*
VH166	Rosa, Salvatore	*Mountainous Seashore*
VH196	Bauer, M.A.J.	*A Castle in Spain*
VH29	Gainsborough, Thomas	*Landscape with Cattle*
VH28	Constable	*Four Riverside Sketches*
VH252	Gericault, T.	*Horses in the Stable*
VH260	Michel	*Open Fields and Windmill*
VH27	Dadd, Richard	*The Corsican*
VH350	Morrice, J. W.	*Landscape*
VH351	French School XIXC (attr. to Monet)	*Winter day in a French Village*

Second floor hall

VH134	Monet, Claude	*Normandy Coast*
VH187	Toulouse-Lautrec	*At the Café*
VH189	Cassat, Mary	*Mother and Child*
VH282	Newman, R.L.	*The Woodland Spring*
VH352	Roullet, Gaston	*Blackfoot Indian Camp*
VH190	Pissaro, C.	*Old Chelsea Bridge*
VH353	French School, c 1830	*Athens and the Acropolis*
VH266	Renoir, P. A.	*La Toilette*
VH186	Sisley, Alfred	*Autumn, Banks of the Oise*
VH267	Renoir, P. A.	*Neapolitan Girl's Head*
VH283	Newman, R. L.	*Brother and Sister*
VH354	Ribot, T. A.	*Peasant Woman Sitting*
VH78	Wouwerman, P.	*Landscape with Horseman*
VH355	French School	*Squally day of the French Coast*
VH183	Cezanne, P.	*Holiday in Provence*
VH356	Rossi	*A Woodland Hillside*

Second floor hall

VH185	Monet	*The Seine at Bougival*
VH251	Monticelli	*Returning from the Chase*
VH188	Toulouse-Lautrec	*In the Garden*
VH319	Van Horne	*Evening, Old Chester*
VH310	"	*Nocturne at St. Andrews*
VH311	"	*Autumn Woods*
VH203	Gericault, T.	*Study of a Negro's Head*
Vh191	Boudin	*A Corner of Louvain*
VH192	Lapostolet, Charles	*Harbour Scene*
VH23	Newton, G. S.	*Portrait of Wm. Collins*
VH312	Van Horne	*The French Frigate*
VH313	"	*Woodland Sunshine*
VH313a	"	*The Ancient Birch*
VH24	Reynolds, Sir Joshua	*Two Studies after Rubens and Snyders*
VH250	Monticelli	*Dancers in a Wood*

Studio, second floor

VH193	Daubigny	*Sunset on the Oise*
VH160	Tempesta, A.	*Three Biblical Subjects*
VH357	Hartz, Louis	*The Red Wagon, crayon*
VH36	Sully, Thomas	*Portrait of an old Lady*
VH272	Ribot	*Jews Disputing*
VH358	Benjamin-Constant, J. J.	*Montreal from Mountain*
VH314	Van Horne	*Railroad Station at Nigh*
VH315	"	*Autumn Fields*
VH316	"	*The Edge of the Wood*
VH317	"	*Monochrome study of Woods*
VH318	"	*The Elbow of the Saskatchewan*
VH319	"	*Autumn Fields*
VH320	"	*L'Argent*
VH321	"	*Look-out Tower*
VH322	"	*A Winter Morning*
VH323 a&b	"	*Tow pastel Studies*

Studio, second floor

....

VH234	"	A Woodland Glimpse
VH325	"	Sunset in the Woods
VH359	Newman	Hagar and Ishmael (unframed)
VH284	"	The Sibyl
VH285	"	The Bather
VH360	"	Eight drawings – in lower drawer
VH361/ 362/363	Sterne, M.	Balinese Woman
VH364	Asabey, e.	French Fishing Boat
VH365	Nardus, Leo	Self Portrait
VH366	"	Still Life
VH367	"	Still Life
Vh368	" (attributed)	Peasant
VH369	Perrigard, H. R.	Pastime
VH370	Okamuru, T.	Lake scene
VH371	Hiroshige	Landscape and coast scent

Studio, second floor

VH372	Hammond, J.	*Dutch Cottages*
VH373	American school, unsigned	*In a Country Hotel*
VH374	Coloured Engraving	*Place d'Armes*
VH375	Japanese Sumi Painting	*Thousand Carps*
VH376	Unsigned canvas	*Red Marshmallows*

In gilded cabinet – studio

VH564	Ming Painting	*Bird on Branch*
VH565	Late Ming	*Villas among Mountains*
VH566	Honnama Koyetsu	*Makemono*
VH567	So-Sen	*Monkey holding spray of leaves*
	"	*Chinese and Japanese Kakemonos*
VH568	Okinobu, AD 1700	*Herons*
VH569	Ki Ku-Chi Yoasai	*Carp*
VH570	Okio, A. Y.	*Stork*

In gilded cabinet – studio

VH573	Yei-Sen	*Hen with two Chicks*
VH574	"	*Lady on Bamboo Branch*
VH576	Modern Japanese	*Portrait Group*
VH577	"	*Portrait of Mr. R. B. Van Horn*
VH563	Van Horne	*Sun Rise*
VH578	Gio Ku Ko	*Mountain Valley*
VH204	Hokusai	*Fan Paining, River with Islands*
VH579	Japanese	*Three Mushrooms*
VH575	"	*Six Figures, Bridge and water*
VH580a	Indo-Persian	*Rival Warriors*
VH581a	"	*An Oriental Assembly*
VH582	"	*An Oriental Procession*
VH580	"	*Rival Kings*
VH581b	"	*A Royal Banquet*
VH794	Whistler	*Venus, etching*
VH795	Washburn, C., etching	*Head of Jap*

Sir William, Lady and Miss Van Horne's Rooms

Lady van horne's room

VH467	Brown, N. A.	*Thinking it over*
VH452	Saunier, O.	*French Farm Yard*
VH466	Mettling	*Low Tide*
VH467	Baker, W. B.	*Spring Landscape*
VH468	Woodcock, B.	*Two Portraits*
VH469	Mathews, R. G.	*Lady van Horne, pastel*
VH471	O'Brien, L. R.	*Niagara Falls*
VH470	"	*Summer in Canadian Rockies*
VH473	"	*Spirit in a Rose*
VH475	Morrice, J. W.	*Canadian River Side*
VH121	Breton, Jules	*The End of the Day*
VH389	Wickenden, R. J.	*A Glimpse from Covenhoven*
VH389	Dabo, Leon	*Snapdragons*
VH346	Van Horne	*A Picnic in the Woods*

Sir William's room

VH456	Eaton, Wyatt	*Lady Van Horne*
VH457	"	*Miss Van Horne*
VH458	Lund, H.	*Sir William Van Horne*
VH462	Schildt, M.	*Threading a Needle*
VH461	"	*Making Soup*
VH464	Nardus, Leo	*A Sketch in the Park*
VH274	Innes, Geo.	*The Old Mill*
VH459	Brymner, Wm.	*Sketch of Sir William, Pastel*
VH345	Van Horne	*Minister's Island*
VH344	"	*A Patriarchal Birch*
VH343	"	*Old Birch Tree*
VH463	Greaves, W.	*Boating Pond*
VH180	Bosboom, J.	*Farm Cottage Interior*
VH 450	Phelan, C. J.	*Sheep Pasture*

Miss Van Horne's room

VH488	Wolter, H. J.	*Lady Crocheting, Tempera*
VH33	Inskipp, J.	*Lady with Black Hat*
VH167	Michel, C.	*A Mountain Road*
VH449	Edson, A	*Gleaners Resting*
VH447	Seymour, M.	*Landscape with thatched cottage*
VH446	Woodcock, F.	*Winter Twilight*
VH450	Hartz, L.	*Old Amsterdam*
VH451	Saunier, O.	*Norman Farm Yard*
VH458	E.S.	*Old World town*
VH431	Bauer, M. A.J.	*Funeral of a Pharaoh, etching*
VH455	Seymour, Haden	*Sawley Abbey, etching*
VH331	Van Horne	*Autumn*
VH332	"	*Canadian Landscape*
VH333	"	*Miniature Landscape*
VH340	"	*Building the Stacks*
VH341	"	*Across the Meadow*

Miss Van Horne's room

VH342	"	Autumn Study
VH498	"	The Gateway
VH337	"	Early Spring
VH338	"	Springtime
VH339	"	Maples and Birches
VH334	"	Castle near a Lake
VH335	"	Rainy Day
VH336	"	Rocks and Trees

North east guest room and storage room

VH1	Bonington, R. F.	Landscape with Windmill
VH146	Guardi, F., (attributed)	Santa Maria della Salute
VH11	Constable, (attributed)	East Bergholt
VH177	Maris, M and Lesore J.	An English Village
VH377	Boulard, A.	Thatched Cottage
VH46	Van den Tempel, A.	Lady with Dog

North east guest room and storage room

VH195	Michel, C.	*Landscape with Windmill and River*
VH392	Sterne, T.	*Sleep*
VH208	Hoxusai	*Jap. fan decoration*
VH393	Rosetsu	*Landscape, in on silk*
VH394	Tosa Missunaca	*Two fold (c. 1240), Warriors*
VH161	Florentine, W.	*Century St. Louis*
VH379	Lawson, E.	*Spring*
VH391	Laurensen	*Child's Portrait*
VH380	Sterne, M.	*Dawn*
VH381	Burroughs, B.	*Wash Day*
VH194	Ribet	*Head of a Young Woman*
VH383	Dabo, L.	*The Garden Party*
VH378	Boulard, A.	*The Artist's Daughter*
VH34	Brookings, C.	*A Gale at Sea*
VH120	Palazzi, F.	*Donkey and Sheep in a Stable*
VH83	Craesbeecke J. Van	*A Game of Cards*

North east guest room and storage room

VH327	Van Horne	*Sunshine after Rain*
VH328	"	*A Stormy Day*
VH329	"	*Moon and Mountain*
VH330	"	*A Stormy Evening*
VH396	Wickenden	*Oldest house on Long Island*
VH397	"	*Old Fire Place*
VH395	"	*Van Horne Homestead*
VH398	..	*Van Horne Homestead*
VH399	Hammond, J.	*Sheep and Figures in Wood*
VH400	Filley, G.	*Yachts at Anchor*
VH401	Nardus, L.	*Seaside Portrait*
VH402	De Belle, C.	*Winter Landscape*
VH403	Rougeron, M.	*Master E. C. Van Horne*

Storage closet – north east guest room

VH382	Burroughs, B.	*Valley of the Ladies*

Storage closet – north east guest room

VH404	Bauer, M.	*Joseph's Brethren*
VH405	"	*Jacob*
VH406	Corot	*Study of an Oak*
VH408	Ravier, A.	*Sunrise at Champrofind, w.c.*
VH409	"	*Corner of the Lake, w.c.*
VH410	"	*Twilight*
VH411	Jongers, A.	*Lady's Head*
VH412	Watrous, H. W.	*An Old Score*
VH413	Washburn, C.	*Negro*
VH414	Nardus, L.	*Man in a Black Hat*
VH415	"	*Young Woman*
VH416	"	*Girls' Head*
VH417	Witsen, Wm.	*Lady*
VH418	Mathews, R. G.	*Sketch of Sir William, crayon*
VH419	Pinhey, J. C.	*Sunset*
VH420	Aitken, J. A.	*Winter Sunset*

Storage closet – north east guest room

VH422	Hiroshige,	*Winter Scene, print*
VH421	De Belle	*Summer Joy*

North west guest room and centre room

VH429	Neuhuys, A.	*Lady before a mirror*
VH179	Bosboom, J.	*Farm near Woods*
VH427	Kamerlingh, O.	*Still Life of Fruit*
VH428	"	*Still Life of Flowers VH21*
VH21	Turner, J.M.W.	*A launch at Chatham w.c.*
VH388	Dabo, L.	*The Jersey Coast*
VH384	"	*Autumn Birches*
VH387	"	*After Rain*
VH430	Ede, F.E.V.	*On the River's Bank*
VH432	"	*Woman Pasturing Cows*
VH431	Hammond, J.	*Port of Saint John N.B.*
VH385	Dabo, Leon	*New Milford*

North west guest room and centre room

VH386	"	*Spring Morning*
VH423	Hartz, L.	*A Corner of Amsterdam*
VH426	Nardus, L.	*Roses*
VH168	Wiertz, A.J.	*Insurrection in Greece*
VH153	Veronese (school of)	*St. Catherine*
VH424	Barnsley, J. M.	*Misty Moonrise*
VH425	Pokitanow, J.	*Winter in Little Russia*

Middle guest room

VH433	Kamerling	*Peonies*
VH434	Kimber, H. S.	*Cape Breton*
VH435	Conraets, F.	*Port of Antwerp*
VH22	Cotman, J. S.	*Riverside Landscape*
VH443	Hammond	*Low Tide*
VH84	Kuypers, J.	*Dressmaker's Shop*
VH22	Cotman, J. S.	*Riverside Landscape*

Middle guest room

VH443	Hammond, J.	*Low Tide*
VH444	"	*Sunset on Dutch River*
VH445	"	*Canadian Rockies*
VH438	Jacomin, M.	*Woodland Pastures*
VH439	Georget, Ch.	*Summer Morning*
VH440	"	*Evening*
VH441	Colona, E.	*Sunset*
VH85	Siekierz, S.	*Roadside Meeting*
VH442	Wolter, H. J.	*Old Trees and Houses*
VH436	Witsen, W.	*Amsterdam-winter, etching*
VH437	Moran, T. (etching)	*After Chase, Dutch Fishing boats*

Third floor hand and storage room

VH181	Bosboom, J.	*Church interior (tiles)*
VH125	Fry, Roger	*The Hunt*

Third floor hand and storage room

VH488	Daubigny, F. F. (early)	*Riverside Study*
VH143	Decamps, A. G. (attributed)	*Elijah*
VH144	Cabat, L.	*Valley of the Tiber*
VH11	Diaz	*Before the Storm*
VH38	Corot	*Forest of Ramboillet*
VH49	Rembrandt (school of)	*Head of man with Brooch in hat*
VH477	Cullen, M.	*St. Lawrence Market*
VH261	Mettling	*Testing Wine*
VH486	Wickenden	*Sir William Van Horne*
VH87	Diaz	*Study of Rocks*
VH37	Michel	*A Stormy Sunset*
VH481	Unknown	*Head of a man in Cocked hat*
VH480	Eaton, W.	*Girl with Chicken*
VH86	Dore, C. P.	*Les Fins Sauvages*
VH479	Bierstadt, A.	*Rocky Mountains*
VH407	Corot	*Study of a French Church*

Third floor hand and storage room

VH122	Bauer	*The Alhambra*
VH145	Canaletto, C. A. (attributed)	*Santa Maria della Salute*
VH32	Barker, T.	*Italian Courtyard*
VH124	"	*Near an Italian Lake*
VH476	Cullen, M.	*Ox in Snow*
VH123	Bauer	*A Turkish Armoury*
VH162	XVI Century	*Head of a Man with a Ruff*
VH482	Colonna, E.	*Winter Landscape*
VH483	"	*The Last Rays*
VH484	"	*Twilight*
VH489	Nardus, L.	*Winter Landscape,*
VH490	"	*Seashore*
VH491	"	*A Masquerader*
VH494	Washburn, C.	*Oriental Bazar*
VH493	Jackson, A. Y.	*Old Street in France*
VH497	Seymour, M.	*Lachine Rapids*

Third floor hand and storage room

VH485	Spoor	*View in Holland*
VH492	Unknown	*Old world village*
VH487	Glazed tile	*Old Man*
VH478	Carlisle, M. H.	*Pekinese Spaniel*
VH390	Dabo, L.	*Teddy Bears*
VH532	Japanese	*Tigress and Young*
VH503	Van Horne	*Stormy moonrise*
VH504	"	*Dawn*
VH505	"	*Souvenir of Holland*
VH500	"	*Roadway through the Woods*
VH501	"	*Riverside sketch*
VH502	"	*Rider in the wood*
VH347	"	*Winter Landscape*
VH348	"	*Moonlight on a Canadian River*
VH495	Watson, Homer	*The Lumber Mill*

In storage cupboard, third floor

VH526		*H.M. Queen Victoria of England and (illeg) Albert, 26 etchings*
VH527	Whistler	*Fumette, etching*
VH528	"	*Annie, etching*
VH529	"	*Rotherbithe*
VH530	"	*Fulham*
VH531	"	*Marked Place, Bruges*
VH534	Ribot, t.	*A Scullery maid, oil*
VH543	Maris, M.	*The Sower, etching after Millet*
VH544	Ribot, T.	*Cooks Consulting, etching*
VH533	Pinhey, J. C.	*Woodman's head*
VH535	Wickenden	*Study of Woods*
VH549	Smith, F. P.	*Beach in Autumn*
VH550	Inglis, T.	*After Harvest*
VH551	De Belle	*Winter Snow*
VH555	Fraser, J. A.	*Landscape*
VH556	Unknown	*Mountain stream, w.c.*

In storage cupboard, third floor

VH538	Barnes, W. F.	*Lady's Portrait, crayon*
VH537	B[o]urgeois, A.	*Head of a Lady*
VH547	Aitkan, J. A.	*Canadian Rockies*
VH548	Kelly, J. D.	*Among the timer booms*
VH548		*Autograph[ed] letter and engraved portrait of George Washington*
VH545	Nardus, L.	*Evening*
VH558	"	*Portrait of Sir William*
VH560	"	*Portrait of a Man*
VH540	"	*Portrait of Mrs. R. B. van H. (pastel)*
VH552	Julien, Henri	*Girls Head, ink*
VH553	Mathews, R. G.	*Quidi Vidi, ink*
VH554	"	*Sketch of Lady, crayon*
VH539	"	*Margaret Clark, crayon*
VH507	Van Horne	*A Showery day*
VH506	"	*The Old Plainsman*

In storage cupboard, third floor

VH536	Spoor	*Holland Landscape*
VH541	Laguillermie, after Vibert	*Gulliver, engraving*
VH542 a+b	Washburn, C.	*Venice and Japan, etchings*

Rooms of miss Van Horne, Mr. And Mrs. R. B. Van Horne and Mr. W. Van Horne

VH720	Van Horne	*Champlain's Island*
VH721	Bonvin	*A Roadside Study*
VH722	Fraser, J. A.	*A Glimpse of the Sea*
VH723	Kilpin	*Portrait of Master Mm. van H.*
VH724	Russell, G. H.	*Calves*
VH725	Stacquet, B.	*A Village Street in Winter, w.c.*
VH726	Bosboom, J.	*Church Interior, tiles*
VH727	Slocombe, F.	*Country Road, etching*
VH728	Spohler, J. F.	*View of Amsterdam*
VH729	Kilpin	*Portrait of Lady Van Horne*

Rooms of miss Van Horne, Mr. And Mrs. R. B. Van Horne and Mr. W. Van Horne

VH730	Farrer, Hy.	*Windmills*
VH731	Van Horne	*Moonlight in the Sea*
VH732	Wickenden, R.J.	*10 x 14*
VH735	Hammond, J.	*Low Tide*
VH734	Phelan, C. t.	*Two sheep and a lamb*
VH735	Van Horne	*Sunset*
VH736	Van Anrooy, J. A.	*Dutch City – winter, w.c.*
VH737	Barnsley, J. A.	*Wintry Sunset*
VH738	Van Horne	*French Canadian Village, w.c.*
VH739	"	*Quebec in Winter*
VH740	Parsons, B.	*The Rectory Garden, w.c.*
VH741	Whistler, (after)	*Miss Alexander, facsimile*

William's room

VH742	Van Horne	*Teddy Bears*

William's room

VH743	Fles, E.	*Winter, w.c.*
VH744	"	*Winter Twilight*
VH745	Smithson, H.	*Winter Evening*
VH747	Van Horne, Miss Mary after Edson	*Winter*
VH748	"	*Autumn*
VH749	"	*Road through Woods*
VH750	" Miss Mary, after Phelan	*2 sheep and lamb*
VH751	Moran, T.	*Return of Lifeboat, etching*
VH752	Barnsley, J. (attributed)	*Woodland Trees*
VH753	Hammond, J.	*Holland Landscape*

Mrs. R. B. Van Horne's sitting room

VH754	Des Clayes	*Reverie*
VH755	Ter Meulen, F. P.	*Sheep leaving Stable*
VH756	Woodcock, P.	*The Cornfield*
VH757	Fraser, W. A.	*Portrait of Sir William*

Mrs. R. B. Van Horne's sitting room

VH758	Ravier, A.	*Near Thuile*
VH759	"	*Environs of Cremieux*
VH760	Hartz, L.	*By the Sea*
VH761	Weissenbruch, J. H.	*Canal*
VH762	Constable, J.	*Early Morning*
VH763	Van Gogh, V.	*Purple Fleur de Lys*
VH764	Van Horne	*Autumn Landscape*
VH765	"	*Camp Fire in Woods*
VH766	"	*Gale on Lake Superior*
VH768	"	*Study of the Rocks*
VH767	"	*Santa Maria della Salute*
VH769	"	*Misty Sunrise*
BH770	"	*Windmills*
VH771	"	*Railroad yard at Night*
VH771a	"	*Roadway from the Lake*

Mrs. R. B. Van Horne's room

VH772	Van Horne	*Autumn*
VH773	"	*Homeward Bound*
VH774	"	*Sunset Impression*
VH775	"	*The Sand Pit*
VH776	"	*Rocky Banks*
VH777	"	*An Opening in the Woods*
VH778	Hammond, J.	*Grey day on the Oise*
VH779	Jacobi, O. R.	*Thunder Cape, w.c.*
VH780	French School, IXI Century	*On a French River*
VH871	O'Brien, L. R.	*Low Tide, w.c.*
VH782	Gassies, C.	*The Early sportsman*
VH783	Eaton, W.	*Portrait of Sir William*
VH784	Melrose, A.	*Riverside Sunset*
VH785	Dabo, L.	*Moonrise*
VH786	"	*Misty Morning*
VH787	Vrolijk, Jan,	*Landscape with Cattle, w.c.*

Mrs. R. B. Van Horne's room

VH788	Mathews, r. C.	*Portrait sketch*
VH789	Parsons, B.	*A Riot of roses*

Dressing- and spare-rooms

VH790	Adam, F.	*Kittens*
VH791	Reynolds (after)	*(illeg.) by Mollyer*
VH792	Jongers, A.	*Portrait of Sir William*
VH793	Unknown	*Head of a Man*

☞ 1959 LIST OF PAINTINGS AT COVENHOVEN.

December 1959 (Sullivan 2007: 171-73).

Covenhoven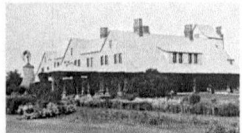

Dining room

....

663	*Foothills in the Rockies*	Van Horne
655	*The Derelict*	Munsey Seymour
656	*Autumn Woods and Fields*	Van Horne
657	*Passamaquoddy Bay-Yacht Race*	Van Horne
658	*Covenhoven Birches*	Van Horne
659	*The Path around the Cliff*	Van Horne
661	*Fishing Boats, Bay of Fundy*	John Hammond
651	*Thor's Anvils*	Van Horne
652	*Moonlight on the Sea/Ocean (NBr.) – At Minister's Island*	Van Horne

....

Hall between dining room and drawing room

Sunburst Over Minister's Island	Van Horne

Drawing room

640	*Watching her Chickens*	Helen S. McNicholl
641	*Dutch Fishwife, knitting*	Louis Hartz
642	*Stormy Day off York Beach, Maine*	Wm. Hope
643	*The St. Lawrence in Winter, from Port Levis*	Maurice Cullen
644	*The Tyorolese Alps near Botzen*	C. F. Daubigny
645	*Evening near Valmondois, Seine and Oise*	C. F. Daubigny
646	*The Old Road to the River*	H. Bolton Jones
647	*A Summer morning Sketch*	John Hammond
648	*A Misty Sunrise, Bay of Fundy*	John Hammond
649	*Evening near a Lake*	B. R. Fitz

South-West blue room ground floor

627 *A visit to the Nursery*   Otto (C.)

Sir William's south-east room, ground floor

2   *Covenhoven Woods*   Van Horne

Music hall, ground floor

612 *Pyreneen Peasant and Wife*   G. Pangorst

614 *Moonrise*   Van Horne

615 *Madonna and Child*   R. L. Newman

616 *Still Life – Azalea and other Flowers*   Georget-Faure

617 *The Sandpit*   Van Horne

618 *In a French Garden*   H. S. McNicholl

619 *Autumn Groves and Meadows*   Van Horne

620 *April Washday*   C. Washburn

621 *Montreal Docks in Winter*   Maurice Cullen

Music hall, ground floor

622	*Noon-Tide in the Hayfield*	R. J. Wickenden
623	*Laurentian Landscape*	S. Dryonnet
624	*Autumn Landscape*	Munsey Seymour
625	*Old Windmill near Lower Lachine Road*	Munsey Seymour
3	*Castle near a Stormy Sea*	(Unsigned)
613	*The Watering Place, Sunset*	G. Innes
605	*The Watering Place, Sunset*	Laurs Muntz-Lyall
606	*Girl Acrobats*	Isaac Israels
607	*Still Life with Flowers*	Jean Marchand
608	*Rocks and Sea*	Jean Marchand
609	*Girl Riding Donkey on Seashore*	Isaac Israels
610	*Cap Rouge River*	H. I. Neilson
611	*Swawinigan falls, PQ*	James S. Aitken

Studio, ground floor

597	*Primeval Dance*	Phelan Gibb

Studio, ground floor

598	*The Lily Pond*	Van Horne
599	*Still Life, Onions and Pot*	Leo Nardus
600	*Still Life, Peaches on Plate*	Leo Nardus
601	*Summer Pastures*	Van Horne
603	*Moorland Landscapes*	John Hammond
604	*A Moroccan Chief*	Leo Nardus
5	*Sir William van Horne*	(no author)

Billiard room, ground floor

583	*Work Horses at Montmartre*	G. H. Breiner
584	*Peasant Drinking Wine*	G. Pangorst
585	*Cattle near a French River*	F.E.V. Ede
	Two small Landscapes	
587	*1. Brown Trees in Glazed Tones*	E. Colonna
588	*2. Autumn Landscape*	[Colonna]
589	*Mount Cheops, Canadian Rockies*	Van Horne (Enroh Nav)

Billiard room, ground floor

590	*Holland Fishwives Awaiting Boats*	Louis Hartz
591	*The Brook at Valmondois*	C. P. Daubigny
592	*Seashore near Scheveningen, Holland*	Louis Hartz

Three Impressionist Studies, Unsigned

593	*1. Red Sails*
594	*2. Hillsides near a Port*
595	*3. Fishing Boats in Port*

Upper hall and staircase

274	*Dutch Types, Kalverstraat, Amsterdam*	Izaac Israels
275	*The Top of Montmartre in Winter*	H. Chennard
276	*Woman's Head and Shoulders*	Leo Nardus
674	*Dutch Girls conversing, Amsterdam*	Izaak Israels

North-West guest room, second floor

6	*Sunset, Port of St. John, NB*	John Hammond
679	*Summer Afternoon, Montigny, France*	Albert Gihon

Front middle guest room, second floor

5	*A Mountain Homestead, Yale, BC*	Wm. Hope

Miss Van Horne's room, second floor

664	*Portrait of Sir Wm. Van Horne*	Wyatt Easton

Mrs. H. R. Bruce's [Edith Van Horne-Molson] room, second floor

233	*Among the Poppies*	S. Des Clayes
713	*A Canal in Holland*	Louis Hartz

Lady Van Horne's room, second floor

....

Pastel   R. G. Mathews

_____

Sir Wm. Van Horne Painting

....

✕

APPENDIX 2

DISPOSITION

DISPOSITION OF THE Van Horne family collection, based on overviews in the Van Horne Family Fonds (2008).

1915: Van Horne's art collection passed to the joint ownership of Lady Van Horne and her children Adaline and Richard Benedict.

1928: Grandson Billy marries Audrey Fraser.

1929: Lady Van Horne dies Montreal, part of the art collection went to the Montreal Museum of Fine Arts.

1931: Son Richard Van Horne dies St. Andrews at Covenhoven from hepatitis of his liver, cirrhosis-hepatic contributing.

1932: Billy and Audry's daughter, Beverley Ann Van Horne, born.

1932: Edith Van Horne-Molson marries Randolph Bruce (1861-1942) at Covenhoven.[539]

1934: Audrey Fraser killed in car accident at Oak Bay.

1935: Billy marries Margareth Hannon.

1939: Adaline bequeaths Minister's Island to Billy's daughter, Beverly Ann.

1941: Adaline van Horne dies Montreal. *Ownership of the Van Horne estate went to Richard Benedict, his son Billy and*

---

539   See: http://www.columbiavalleyarts.com/pynelogs.html (last accessed February 2014).

Margaret. Her part of her father's collection was bequeathed to the Montreal Art Association in 1941.

1942: Randolph Bruce, husband of Edith Molson, dies.

1945: Adaline's part, bequeathed in 1941, obtained by the Montreal Museum of Fine Arts.

1946: Grandson Billy Van Horne dies in his 40th year.

1946: Adaline's heirs, the Hannon family, auctioned off the remainder of the collection.[540] Sale on January 24 at Sotheby's (Parke-Bernet), New York.

1947: Another version about the estate's dispersion is the following provenance that accompanies one of the Washington National Gallery of Art paintings[541]

1949: Beverley Ann Van Horne runs away from home to Vancouver, where she lives in a rooming house and supports herself as a dishwasher.

1959: Minister's Island sold to the American Van Horne Island Club.

1972: Sale at Sotheby's, London on December 6, nos. 10-22 and on December 13, nos. 132-133. Two months after the visit of members of the Rembrandt Research Project the remainder of the Van Horne collection is sold at Sotheby's.

1972: Minister's Island becomes Harbour Farm, an American company.

---

540 Ibid.

541 She [Margaret van Horne, widow of grandson Billy] wrote to James Lane at the National Gallery of Art (letter of 11 December 1947, in NGA curatorial files) the following explanation of the disposition of the Van Horne collection: "When Sir William died in 1915, the Art Collection was left to his widow, his son and his daughter.... The Collection was not divided until February 1945. Until then, the entire Collection was in "The Estate of the late Sir William Van Horne".... 'Siegfried and the Rhine Maidens' fell into my share at the time of the division." See: http://www.nga.gov/collection/gallery/gg68/gg68-32624-prov.html (last accessed in February 2014)

1973 After many local protests the Van Horne mansion met with a vicious wrecking ball.[542]1977: Minister's Island a provincially protected site

1978: Minister's Island a National Historic Site

1987: Margaret Van Horne died; ownership went to her brother Matthew Hannon.

1988: Ownership went to Matthew Hannon's heir, to Janet Hannon.

---

542 "Ray Murphy," a McGill graduate student, who lived nearby the mansion in 1973, wrote the following about the demolition: The questionable legitimacy of this demolition is evidenced by the fact that it took place quite unexpectedly one day starting at 3:00 AM. No preparations like street closures had been put into effect. A couple of cranes drove up and started swinging wrecking balls at the structure; by daylight there was not much standing. Letter of December 12, 2009 in: http://www.trainorders.com/discussion/read.php?15,2088545 (last accessed February 2014).

OVERVIEW OF SALES OF OR GIFTS FROM THE VAN HORNE COLLECTION

Abbreviations:
Montreal Museum of Fine Arts Association – MMFAA
Van Horne Family Fonds – VHFF

Title	Artist	Gifted to, by	Year
Birch Trees	Van Horne	R. MacKay, since 1978 in St. Andrews public library.	1906
Saint Jérôme dans sa cellule	Reymerswaele	MMFAA. Sir W.	1913
The Landscape	Rembrandt	MMFAA. Adaline	1945
Paysans a l'auberge	Brouwer	MMFAA. Adaline	1945
Intérieur de Saint-March, Venise	Canaletto	MMFAA. Adaline	1945
La route tournante en Provence	Cézanne	MMFAA. Adaline	1945
Cottages at Bearsted, Kent	Constable	MMFAA. Adaline	1945
The Glebe Farm	Constable	MMFAA. Adaline	1945
Les Gaulois	Corot	MMFAA. Adaline	1945
Portrait de femme (Girl's head)	Cuyp	MMFAA. Adaline	1945

Title	Artist	Gifted to, by	Year
La mise en meule (sheepfold?)	Daubigny	MMFAA. Adaline	1945
Femmes poursuivies par des satyres	Daumier	MMFAA. Adaline	1945
Saül poursuivant David	Decamps	MMFAA. Adaline	1945
Portrait d'homme de la maison de Leiva	El Greco	MMFAA. Adaline	1945
Un village français	Ecole française XIXe	MMFAA. Adaline	1945
Portrait de Juan Camaron	De Salvadore	MMFAA. Adaline	1945
Portrait d'une jeune fille	Hogarth	MMFAA. Adaline	1945
Philippe IV d'Espagne	Velasquez	MMFAA. Adaline	1945
Moine franciscain	Zurbaran	MMFAA. Adaline	1945
Aciérie a Sydney, Cap Breton	Van Horne	MMFAA. Adaline	1945
Portrait du marquis de Castrofuerte	Goya	MMFAA. Adaline	1945
Portrait de la marquise de Castrofuerte	Goya	MMFAA. Adaline	1945

Title	Artist	Gifted to, by	Year
Tempête en mer	Guardi	MMFAA. Adaline	1945
Girls Singing (or) The Sisters	Renoir	MMFAA. VHFF(43/10)	1945
Moslems at Prayer	C. Bargue (Time, Can. ed)	MMFAA. VHFF(43/10)	1945
The Dunes, Valley of the Rhine	Dekoninck	Speelman NY VHFF(48/6)	1961
Autumn Landscape	Ryder	VHFF(45/12)	1964 /65
Portrait of Samuel Ampzing	Hals	VHFF(45/12-48/3)	1964 /65
Launch at Chatham	Turner	VHFF(45/12)	1964 /65
Autumn Landscape	Ryder	VHFF(45/12)	1964 /65
Portrait of Samuel Ampzing	Hals	VHFF(45/12-48/3)	1964 /65
Launch at Chatham	Turner	VHFF(45/12)	1964 /65
Peasant Girl by a Wall	Corot	Wildenstein NY 47/17	1965
La Dune de Dunkerque	Corot	Wildenstein NY 47/17	1965

Title	Artist	Gifted to, by	Year
Landscape with Popular Trees	Rousseau	Wildenstein NY 47/17	1965
Horses in their Stable	Géricault	Wildenstein & Co. NY	1965
Normandy Coast near Villarville	Monet	Wildenstein & Co. NY	1965
Mistress and Maid	Ochterfelt	Wildenstein & Co. NY	1965
Capuchin (Franciscan) Monks Round a Refectory Fireplace	Magnasco	Mortimer Brandt NY	1967
Jack Straw's Castle (Niedpath?)	Constable	Mortimer Brandt NY	1967

Twenty Important Modern Paintings from the Collection of the Late Sir William Van Horne, K.C.M.G. Montreal.

Sold by Order of his Heirs. Public Auction Sale, January 24, 1946 at 8 p.m. At Parke-Bernet Galleries Inc. 30 East 57 Street. New York 22.

Catalogue no. + title	Artist	From VH collection	Price ($ US)
1	*Moonlight at Sea*	Albert P. Ryder	Coll. J. Popham	6 200
2	*The Concert*	Monticelli		450
3	*Early Spring*	Ernest Lawson	Daniel Gallery, NY	900
4	*Dawn*	Maurice Sterne		600
5	*Femme au Chapeau Bleu et Noir*	Marie Laurencin		900
6	*Gueule de Bois or La Buveuse*	Toulouse-Lautrec	Bourgeois, NY	30 000
7	*La Toilette*	Renoir	Durand-Ruel, NY	12 000
8	*Le Premier Bain*	Daumier	Durand-Ruel, Paris	15 250
9	*Christ on the Sea of Galilee*	Delacroix	Boussod Valadon & Co., Paris	12 500
10	*Nourrie Allaitant (Fond de Paysage)*	Corot	1909: Knoedler & Co., NY	18 000

Catalogue no. + title	Artist	From VH collection	Price ($ US)
11 *L'Etalage*	Daumier	Durand-Ruel, NY	11 500
12 *Portrait of the Artist's Wife*	Cezanne	1913: St. Bourgeois, NY	24 500
13 *Les Soeurs*	Renoir	Durand-Ruel, NY	10 500
14 *Femme Rousse Assise dans le Jardin de M. Forest*	Toulouse-Lautrec	1911: Paul Rosenberg, Paris	27 500
15 *Old Chelsea Bridge, London*	Pissarro	Durand-Ruel, NY	7 000
16 *The Seine at Bougival*	Monet	1911: Bernheim-jeune, Paris	11 000
17 *Mother and Child*	Mary Cassatt	Durand-Ruel, NY	7 500
18 *Siegfried and the Rhine Maidens*	Albert P. Ryder	Purchased from artist.	23 500
19 *Festival of Bacchus*	Monticelli	Th. Lawrie & Co., Glasgow	1 000
20 *Moslems at Prayer*	Charles Bargue		700

New York Times of January 1946:

Twenty Paintings Sell for $221 500. Modern Items From Van Horne Collection Bring Spirited Bidding at Auction.

A sale of modern paintings brought record prices last night at the Parke-Bernet Galleries, 30 East Fifty-seventh Street. The crowd overflowed the auction rooms, with enthusiastic bidders competing for the canvases.

Twenty important modern painting from the collection of the late Sir William Van Horne, K.C.M.G., of Montreal, went under the hammer and brought $2 212 500, nearly double the figure expected by the galleries

----

DONATIONS BY THE VAN HORNE FAMILY

Tatar Huntsman	Ms. Alice Boney	VHFF 40-10	1954?

Landscape	Dekoninck	VHFF 43/11	1956

Sotheby & Co. 34 & 35 New Bond St., London WI. Catalogue of Important Old Master Painting including Paintings formerly in the Collection of the late Sir William Van Horne, K.C.M.G.. Day of Sale Wednesday, 6 December 1972, at Eleven O'clock precisely

----

Catalogue no. + title	Artist	VH provenance	Price (£)
10	*A girl in sixteenth-century page's costume*	Tiepolo		
11	*The actress Rita Molinos*	Goya y Lucientes	Solomon, London, Van Gelder Uccle, 1913: Van Horne	
12	*Portrait of a lady as the magdalen*	Ysenbrandt	1911. Acq. from Van Slochem	
13	*Portrait of the lady as the Magdalen*	Master of the female half-lenghts	From Van Gelder coll. Uccle	
14	*The adoration of the shepherds*	Rubens	Roo van Westmaas Holland, L. Nardus, M. van Gelder, 1912: Van Horne	

Catalogue no. + title	Artist	VH provenance	Price (£)
15 *Landscape with stream*	Ruysdael	Comte de Narbonne 1851	
16 *The interior of a Dutch house*	Van Brekelenkam	Coll. Capt. R. Langton Douglas, London.	
17 *Latona and the Peasant*	Johan König	Coll. Capt. R. Langton Douglas, London	9 000
18 *Portrait of Madame Mercier*	Jean-Baptiste Greuze	1905: Van Horne	22 000
19 *Portrait of a preacher*	Lucas Cranach the elder	Voordauw, Holland, L. Nardus. M. van Gelder, Uccle 1900: Van Horne	6 500
20 *Portrait of a gentleman*	School of Augsburg, 16th cent	Canvas transferred from panel	24 000
	A. Coorte	On panel	1600
132 *Portrait of Jane, Duchess of Gordon and her son George, 1st. Marquis of Huntly.*	George Romney	1910: from Blakeslee, NY	70 000
133 *Portrait of Mrs. Glengowen and her daughter.*	Sir Henry Raeburn. P.R.S.A.	Blakeslee (W) From coll. Sir Th. Andros de la Rue	4 500

Sullivan (2007: 170): In 1975 fifteen of Sir William's own paintings were sold to A. N. Dennigar (Belfast), in 1976 Robert

Manuge, art dealer in Halifax, bought it for 18 000, Imperial Oil bought twenty-one for 180 000.

During an auction in 1977 the whole island was up for sale, for $2.5 million, a newspaper advertisement stated:

> You will find many items from Sir William's private collection as well as furnishings depicting a Dutch heritage. Sir William, a painter himself, made close friends with artists around the work. Two examples of seascapes by William Hope, RCA and John Hammond, RCA will be among the varied works of art to be auctioned. There are oils, water colours, engravings, etchings and prints by other Canadian Artist as well as a modern mural "The last Spike" oil on canvas ... (cited in Sullivan 2007: 164-65)."[543]

---

543   Sullivan adds that the WILLIAM HOPE went for $4 200 and the John Hammond for $4 500.

VAN HORNE'S IN THE NATIONAL GALLERY IN OTTAWA

23849	*A Scene from the Rockies*	Van Horne (painting) (1893) ("99 on list New Br. Museum)	Purchased	1980
36115	*Treeline with Swirling Sky*	Van Horne (drawing)	Anonymous donor	1991
36116	*French Frigate at St. John's NFl.*	Van Horne (water-color) 1892	Anonymous donor	1991
36117	*Sunrise Dominion Square*	Van Horne (oil on c.)	Anonymous donor	1991
36118	*Moonlight, St. Andrews New Brunswick*	Van Horne (oil on ac. board) 1906	Anonymous donor	1991
36119	*Sunset, Montreal from the St. Laurence*	Van Horne (painting)	Anonymous donor	1991
[]	Portrait d'Elisabeth, comtesse de Waldegrave	Hoppner	AGO/Adaline	2008

INDEX

A painter's name may also stand for one or more of his or her works.

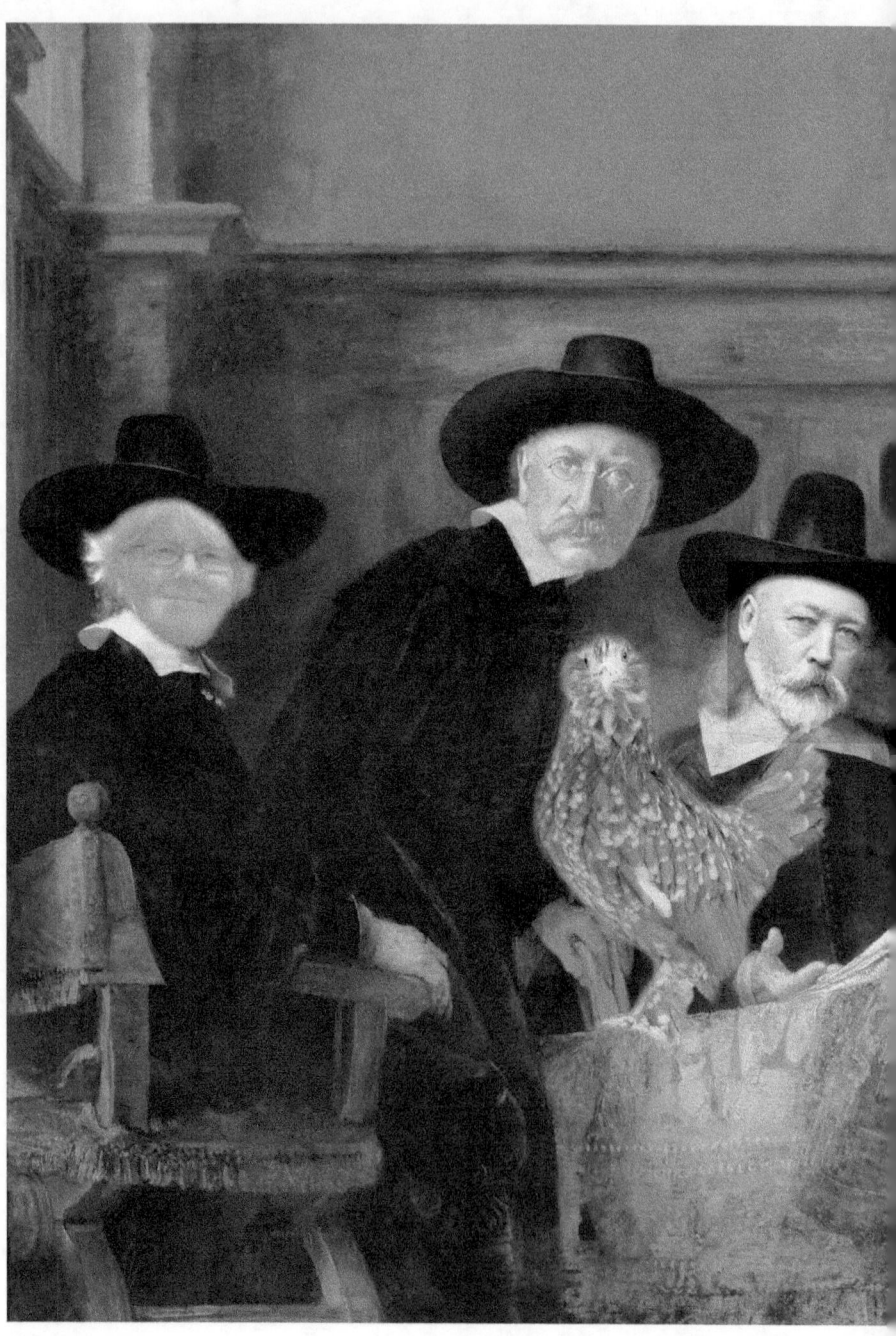

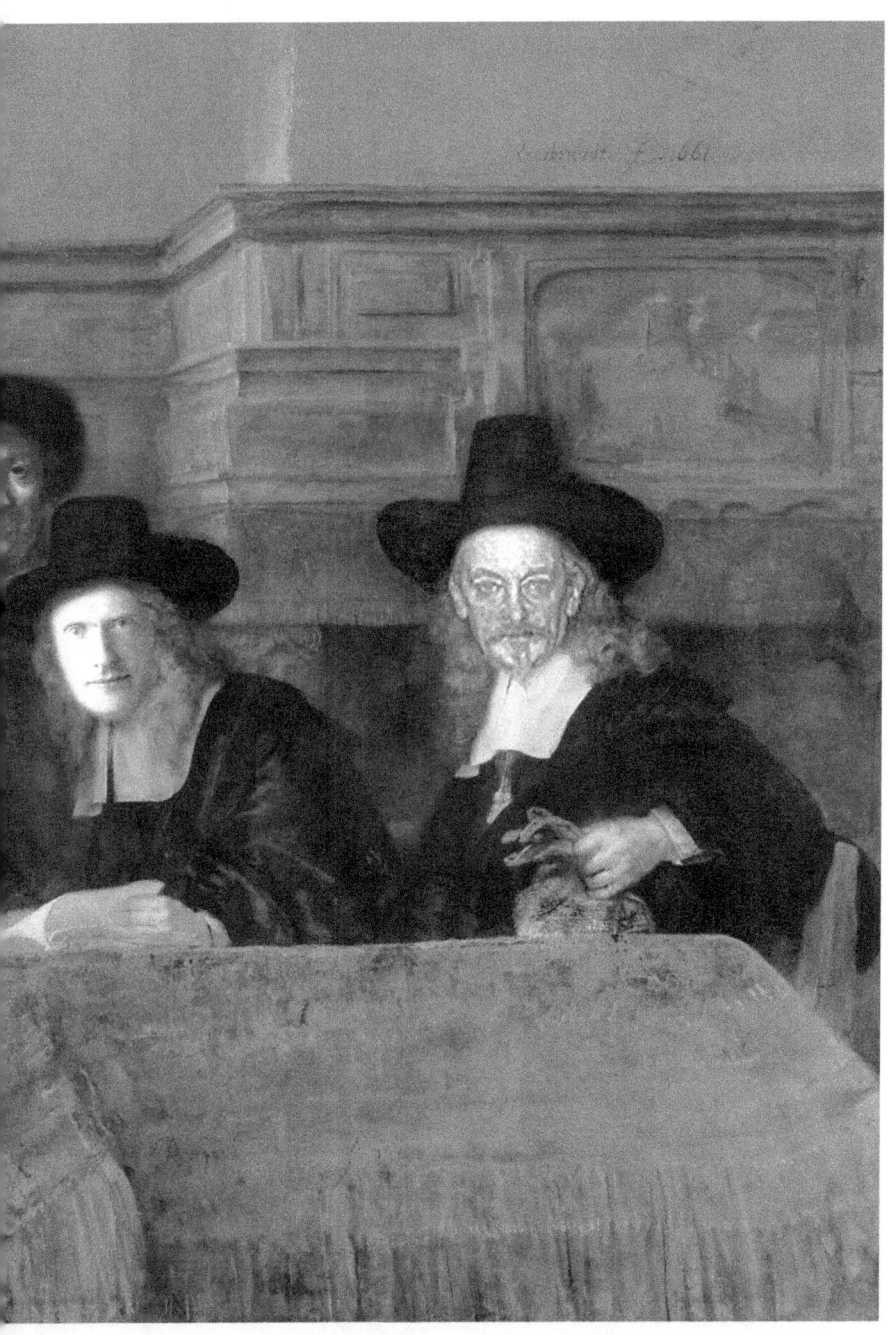

www.ingramcontent.com/pod-product-compliance
Lightning Source LLC
Chambersburg PA
CBHW072128170526
45158CB00004BA/1296